The Economy of Ireland

TWELFTH EDITION

National and Sectoral Policy Issues

The Economy of Ireland

TWELFTH EDITION

National and Sectoral

Policy Issues

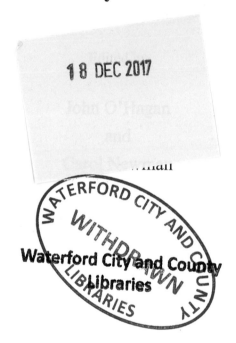

Edited by

John O'Hagan

and

Carol Newman

GILL & MACMILLAN

Gill & Macmillan
Hume Avenue
Park West
Dublin 12
www.gillmacmillan.ie

© Individual editors and contributors 2014

978 07171 5975 8

Print origination by Carole Lynch
Printed by GraphyCems, Spain
Indexed by Cliff Murphy

The paper used in this book comes from the wood pulp of managed forests. For every tree felled, at least one tree is planted, thereby renewing natural resources.

A CIP catalogue record is available for this book
from the British Library.

For updates and more information go to
www.gillmacmillan.ie/economyofireland

Contents

Section II
POLICY IMPLEMENTATION

Section III
POLICY ISSUES AT A NATIONAL LEVEL

Section V
POLICY ISSUES IN THE NON-MARKET SECTOR

Contributors

Chapters 1 and 7
Jonathan Haughton has a BA(Mod) from Trinity College Dublin and a PhD from Harvard University. He is currently Professor of Economics at Suffolk University, Boston, and Senior Economist at the Beacon Hill Institute for Public Policy.

Chapter 2
Dermot McAleese has a BComm and an MEconSc from the National University of Ireland (University College Dublin), and an MA and PhD from Johns Hopkins University. He is Emeritus Whately Professor of Political Economy, Trinity College Dublin.

Chapter 3
Philip R. Lane is Whately Professor of Political Economy at Trinity College Dublin. He has a BA(Mod) from Trinity College Dublin and a PhD from Harvard University.

Chapter 4
Micheál Collins has a BA and an MA from the National University of Ireland (University College Galway and University College Cork) and a PhD from Trinity College Dublin. His current position is Senior Research Officer at the Nevin Economics Research Institute (NERI).

Chapter 5
Francis O'Toole has a BA(Mod) and an MMangSc from the National University of Ireland (University College Dublin) and a PhD from Georgetown University. He is currently Associate Professor of Economics, Trinity College Dublin.

Chapter 6
John O'Hagan has a BE and an MA from the National University of Ireland (University College Dublin), and a PhD from Trinity College Dublin. His current position is Professor of Economics, Trinity College Dublin.

Tara McIndoe-Calder has a BA(Mod) and a PhD from Trinity College Dublin and an MPhil from Oxford University (Hertford College). She is currently working as an economist at the Central Bank of Ireland.

Chapter 8
Michael King has a BA(Mod) and a PhD from Trinity College Dublin and an MPA in International Development from Harvard University. His current position is Assistant Professor at the Department of Economics, Trinity College Dublin.

Chapters 9 and 13
Carol Newman has a BA(Mod) and a PhD from Trinity College Dublin. Her current position is Assistant Professor at the Department of Economics, Trinity College Dublin.

Chapter 10
Eleanor Denny has a BA, an MBS and a PhD from National University of Ireland (University College Dublin). She is currently Assistant Professor at the Department of Economics, Trinity College Dublin.

Chapter 11
Alan Matthews has a BA(Mod) from Trinity College Dublin and an MSc from Cornell University. His current position is Professor Emeritus of European Agricultural Policy, Trinity College Dublin.

Chapter 12
Anne Nolan has a BA(Mod) and a PhD from Trinity College Dublin. She is currently on secondment from the Economic and Social Research Institute (ESRI) to Trinity College Dublin, where she is Research Director of the Irish Longitudinal Study on Ageing (TILDA).

Preface

When the last edition of this book was going to print in April 2011 the economy of Ireland was still reeling from a tumultuous three years of economic setback. Output had declined on a scale almost never seen in peacetime anywhere, unemployment had trebled, employment had declined by almost 300,000 and large-scale net emigration had resumed for the first time in almost 25 years.

The country had been hit by a property crash of unprecedented scale with house prices falling by over 50 per cent and some commercial property by much more. Huge private and public sector debt problems ensued and the banking system almost collapsed. Part of these problems could be linked without question to the international banking collapse and the subsequent large and sustained recession in the developed world. The fact that the institutional structures of the euro zone were ill equipped to cope with this financial crisis greatly exacerbated the problems.

But Ireland's difficulties were at the acute end of the range and at times it seemed that the political system could not survive intact in the face of widespread anger and with huge numbers facing large-scale financial problems arising from negative equity, lost jobs and a fear that the euro zone might implode.

Three years on, things look a lot brighter. As some populist commentators fuelled the flames of discontent, most of the Irish population got on with dealing with a crisis that was largely of our own making. There is only so long one can lament events and attempt to blame others, be it at a personal or societal level, but ultimately we must move on, try to make good the damage and plan for a better future.

Many of those most affected in fact complained least; the newly unemployed, the people trapped in negative equity and the young who took the brunt of the pain. Very often it was those least affected who complained the most; those in secure, pensionable jobs and many of the elderly who were largely protected from the effects of the recession.

ANOTHER REMARKABLE TURNAROUND

The year 2013 now appears to have seen a major turning point. The economy, after flatlining in 2011 and 2012, expanded in GNP terms (see Chapter 7 for a discussion of this) by over three per cent and employment increased by 60,000+. Predictions from independent sources suggest a further increase of 50,000+ jobs in 2014 with possibly a similar increase in 2015. If this turns out to be the case, then a remarkable recovery in employment will have taken place in just three years, again, as in 2007, with no agency predicting this major turning point.

Property prices, in particular in Dublin, have risen again, in some cases quite significantly; not to the unsustainable levels of 2007, of course, but back to long-term norms. The loss in competitiveness that had taken place between 2002 and 2007 has been largely reversed. The euro crisis has abated, at least in terms of bond yields and the value of the euro. Few are betting on its break-up now, at least not in the foreseeable future.

As argued throughout this book, though, one should not be deflected from the medium- to long-term focus, by short-term gyrations of financial markets or predictions of imminent doom or boom. The world is a much more complex place. Things come in cycles; and how easily people forget the past, even the immediate past. That is the real danger that confronts Ireland in the years ahead.

WHERE NOW? THE WIDER CONTEXT

This book is not and never was concerned primarily with shorter-term economic issues. It generally takes a much longer-term historical perspective, a perspective that is salutary in reminding us that booms come to an end and, in the recent context, that the 'bad times' do not last for ever. Indeed, in some cases they can end much more rapidly than expected, as in the mid 1970s or early 2000s, or last much longer than is necessary, as was the case in the 1950s and 1980s (see Chapter 1).

This book is also much more about general policy issues, thereby providing the context for debate, be it in the short, medium or long term.

There is no reason why Ireland cannot prosper in years to come and remain one of the high-income countries of the world (see Chapters 1, 6, 7 and 9). The country has a healthy, stable democracy and a well-established rule of law. Its people and its level of human capital are the same as they were prior to 2008 (see Chapter 13). There is an openness to competition and entrepreneurship that simply did not exist in the 1980s. Ireland has the security of membership of the euro zone and a strong commitment to the EU and thus to free trade, international competition, a cleaner environment, and all that the EU stands for on the world stage (see Chapter 3).

All democracies are flawed to some extent and economic debates are often fraught and misinformed, Ireland over the last four years being no exception.

Predictions of economic decline or success can be altered within months. And it is also worth remembering that economic policy is exercised in the political marketplace. Economists may have forgotten their history up to recent times but they also often forget that economic policy and politics are inseparable. Having a good solution to an economic problem is of little benefit if the political system cannot be assured of delivering on it.

The euro crisis is proof positive of this: too often the political difficulties of responding to the crisis were overlooked by many economists. Very often the same people who were criticising policymakers for not responding firmly and quickly enough to the crisis were at the same time castigating them for lack of democratic accountability.

The equity issues of the crisis of the last six years, though, will be played out for some years to come (see Chapter 8). The most important antidote to inequity is to create employment; as mentioned, this is happening now in Ireland on a large scale. But there are still very high unemployment levels, almost three times those in the mid 2000s.

There is also a strong intergenerational inequity resulting from the crisis. It is the younger age groups who almost certainly bought houses at the top of the boom, with most of the older generation having long paid in full for their properties, purchased at times of much lower real prices. Besides, to pay for the debt the burden will again continue to fall mostly on the younger generation, through reduced incomes for those starting out at work, fewer promotional opportunities, particularly in the public sector, and longer working lives. A disturbing reflection of this is the exercise of 'grey power' in recent years, as a result of which payments to the over-65s, regardless of their circumstances, have been largely protected while those to other, younger groups have been cut (see Chapter 8).

There are potential disasters that should continue to concern us, such as the threat of a major terrorist attack, especially if it involved the use of biological or nuclear weapons, or indeed a war initiated by the aggression of a nation state. Events in Ukraine in recent months have been a stark reminder of this. The possibility of a major military confrontation in some part of the world, but particularly in Europe, would have quite catastrophic consequences for the economy of Europe upon which Ireland depends so heavily.

There is also the possibility of a major environmental disaster leading to the loss of hundreds of millions of lives and the danger of major water shortages for tens of millions of others: events in Japan in 2011 reminded the world starkly of this (see Chapter 10). There is also the possibility of severe energy shortages, either because the world runs short of the exploitable natural resources required or because of the actions of some states in cutting off supply. Again events in Ukraine have brought home a timely reminder of this threat. On all of these issues Irish interests and concerns are best voiced at an EU level and through the EU on the global 'stage' (see below).

As urgent and pressing as some of the economic decisions of the next few years are, they must be seen in this context. These global problems are outside the control of Irish policymakers acting on their own and yet could have catastrophic consequences for Ireland. The problems we face in the years ahead – resolution of the remaining problems of the banking sector, continued restoration of balance to the public finances and maintaining competitiveness – are all largely within our own remit and can be resolved, given the political will and an informed and realistic public debate. In relation to the former, the vociferous objections of special interest groups (and often those who suffered least in the recession) must be resisted, and in relation to the latter, alternatives must be presented, especially by those whose job it is to sift and present information/arguments in a balanced way, so that informed decisions can be made.

LONGER-TERM ECONOMIC POLICY FRAMEWORK

Ireland is now a region of the euro zone, with the euro having replaced Irish notes and coins in January 2002. As such, there are no chapters in this book on monetary policy or on balance of payments and exchange rate policy in Ireland.

The policy emphasis now at an Irish level, though, is almost exclusively on the competitiveness of the EU region, 'Ireland Inc.', and this is reflected in many chapters throughout the book (see in particular Chapters 2, 6, 7 and 9). Even in relation to this Ireland must operate within an agreed competition and regulatory environment determined, with Ireland as a voting member, at EU level (see Chapter 5). Competitiveness is a key determinant of our attractiveness to foreign direct investment: the scale of US investment has been such that Ireland might be viewed in an industrial sense as a region of the American economy (see Chapter 9), despite the fact that in a monetary sense the country is an integral part of the euro zone (see Chapter 3). International benchmarking in terms of competitiveness is now commonplace and the *Annual Competitiveness Reports* produced by the National Competitiveness Council each year since 1997 are some of the most talked-about reports published.

Despite the industrial connection with the USA and the economic, monetary and political links with the EU, the euro zone in particular, Ireland's relationship with the UK is still very important, for a variety of reasons (see Chapter 1). While the nature of this relationship may have altered significantly, its substance has remained the same.

In terms of simple geography, Ireland is a tiny country, an island to the west of Britain, which in turn is a somewhat larger but much more densely populated island to the west of mainland Europe: its population is over 15 times that of Ireland. Ireland and the UK have a common labour market, a common language, and huge trade and tourism flows in both directions; by and large people in both jurisdictions watch the same TV programmes and follow similar key sports and cultural events. These are inescapable facts, which, as shall be seen throughout the book, are important for an understanding of the Irish economy, past and present.

Ireland's relationship with its closest neighbour is crucial not just to its economic success but also to continued peace on the island. This is because the island of Ireland consists of two political units, the larger portion of which forms the Republic of Ireland and the smaller portion Northern Ireland, which is part of the UK. This too has had an impact on economic, social and political life in the Republic.

This book is about the economy of the Republic of Ireland, and henceforth the terms 'economy of Ireland' and 'Irish economy' refer to this economy, unless otherwise stated. Some reference is made to the Northern Ireland economy, but since Northern Ireland's economic policy is largely determined in London, it is difficult to devote much attention to policy there without also reviewing British economic policy in general. There has been, though, as Chapter 3 points out, greatly increased cross-border co-operation on the economic front since the Good Friday Agreement of sixteen years ago.

The links, economic and cultural, to continental Europe are strengthening, something that low-cost air travel and the use of the euro has facilitated. Irish people are now much more familiar than they were even 25 years ago with political developments in Europe, and with European sporting and cultural events. Indeed as a result of the previous boom in incomes many own second homes there.

But Ireland and the EU have also to look at the wider world, as issues and problems that are truly global in nature must be addressed. Top of the list is the environment and the danger of serious global warming (see Chapter 10). Not far behind are a secure energy supply, terrorism, free trade, sharply increased world food prices resulting from new demands for food and land use (see Chapter 11), increased migration, legal and illegal, and international crime.

As Chapters 2 and 10 point out, concerns about environmental degradation must qualify any endorsement of economic growth as a policy objective. Chapter 3, though, highlights the governance difficulties faced when dealing with environmental issues that extend beyond national boundaries. This, as seen already, also applies to many financial issues. Later chapters discuss various policy measures being adopted to address such issues, both within Ireland and internationally.

The rise of China and India in particular is an economic reality that has affected not just small countries like Ireland but also the two largest trading blocs in the world, namely the EU and the USA. It has led to a huge increase in competition, for both goods and investment flows. It has also of course led to a huge increase in trade and investment opportunities.

China hosted the Olympic Games in 2008, its military prowess is growing, and Mandarin is the mother tongue for by far the largest number of people in the world. As such, its influence will soon extend well beyond the economic to the cultural and military spheres. Ireland, as part of the larger EU, will have to learn to adapt to such seismic geopolitical changes in the global economy.

STRUCTURE OF BOOK AND ACKNOWLEDGEMENTS

This book has grown out of an earlier book, first published 39 years ago. The Irish Management Institute published the first six editions, Macmillan what in effect was the seventh edition and Gill & Macmillan the eighth and subsequent editions. The broad structure and purpose of the book have remained the same over the years, but in terms of content there have been sweeping changes, even since the last edition. Apart from updating, major changes have also been made to all chapters, including Chapter 1 on the historical background, to reflect the rapidly changing circumstances and policy issues facing the Irish economy.

As mentioned, the overall structure of the book has been unchanging over the years. Section I provides the key policy background, namely the historical evolution of the economy up to 2012 (Chapter 1) and a discussion of what are the key policy objectives and issues for a regional economy such as that of Ireland (Chapter 2). It is important to know what we want from the Irish economy before asking how to achieve these aims and how well we have done in so doing.

These are the questions looked at in Sections II and III. Chapter 3 sets out the role of the state, in terms of rationale, levels of government and size of the state sector. It also addresses in some detail the recent fiscal crisis in Ireland and the euro zone. Chapter 4 examines how state involvement is funded and the issues to which taxes give rise, including the use of borrowing to defer taxation decisions. Chapter 5 examines the issues of competition and regulation, drawing on recent findings from behavioural economics in this regard. State regulation permeates our lives to an extraordinary extent, for various valid reasons.

Section III comprises three quite lengthy discussions of Ireland's success or otherwise in meeting the three objectives outlined in Chapter 2, and the policy issues to which this give rise, namely employment (Chapter 6), growth in living standards and output (Chapter 7) and equity and social justice (Chapter 8). Some of the key statistical material in the book is presented in these chapters.

Section IV contains a detailed discussion of policy issues and performance in the market sector and builds on much of the book's earlier material. Chapter 9 examines the market sectors perhaps of most importance to the success of the future economy, namely manufacturing and internationally traded services. Chapter 10 looks at the vitally important energy sector, with its huge dependence on sources abroad and its major environmental impact. The latter is considered in the context of some wider environmental issues. Chapter 11 looks not only at the agricultural sector but also at the issues of food distribution and consumption and the rising concern over security of supply and food safety.

Section V concludes the book with an examination of two key areas of the public sector, namely health (Chapter 12) and education (Chapter 13). Both of these sectors are not only crucial to the well-being of the population at large but also to the future success of the economy. Both are also sectors of major economic significance in their own right, although assessing performance in either is fraught with difficulty. Both areas are also faced with the reality of possible sweeping technological change impacting significantly on the delivery of outputs.

There are many people we would like to thank who have facilitated the publication of the twelfth edition of this title. We would like to thank staff at Gill & Macmillan for their central role in bringing this book to publication. We would also especially like to thank our copy-editor Jane Rogers; she was a pleasure to work with.

The book would not of course exist without the contributed chapters. As always, it was most enjoyable work liaising with each of the contributors at each step of the process. In particular, it was rewarding seeing chapters take shape and mesh into the overall structure of the book following comments and suggestions. We very much appreciate the input and co-operation of each and every contributor.

We would also like to thank the many lecturers and students who have used this book over the years. This has made the book both financially viable, despite the small size of the potential market, and a very satisfying experience for us. The book is also read widely outside academia and, indeed, beyond these shores, and we hope that this will continue to be the case. This is the type of book, and related courses, which students seem to enjoy immensely and we are sure lecturers in other colleges have also found this to be the case. It does after all deal with the political economy of one of the most interesting case studies in world economics of recent decades!

John O'Hagan and Carol Newman
Trinity College Dublin
June 2014

SECTION I

POLICY CONTEXT

CHAPTER 1

Historical Background

Jonathan Haughton

1 WHY ECONOMIC HISTORY?

Why take the trouble to study history, and particularly the economic history of a minor European island? Six good reasons spring to mind.

History tests theory. The propositions of economics are often best tested by exposing them to historical evidence. Was Malthus right when he argued that population growth would inevitably outstrip food supply? Irish experience, even during the Great Famine, suggests not. Do farmers respond to changes in the prices they face? Evidence from late nineteenth-century Ireland confirms that they do. Does emigration serve to equalise wages between Ireland and Britain? Data for this century indicate that, broadly speaking, it does. Cicero took this view of history, writing that 'the causes of events are even more interesting than the events themselves' – surely a view espoused by most academic economists!

History gives perspective. Standard economics textbooks typically provide a short-run and partial approach to economic problems. While this may be appropriate for tracing the immediate effects of a shift in demand, or a monetary expansion, it provides fewer insights into the fundamental determinants of economic growth or of income distribution, since these may only be observed over long periods of time. The historian Joe Lee has made the point forcibly, writing that 'while contemporary Irish economics can be impressive in accounting for short-term movements, it has contributed relatively little to understanding the long-term development of the Irish economy'. He argues that most economists are 'blind to either long-term perspective or lateral linkage' and that 'with the exception of a handful of superior intelligences, Irish economists are far more impressive as technicians than as thinkers'.

An important lesson from economic history is that it provides a sense of the fragility of economic growth, and of its intermittent nature. For instance, many look back to the 1960s as a golden era of Irish economic growth. Yet Kennedy, Giblin and McHugh, in their interesting study of Irish economic development in the twentieth century, argue that 'a sense of historical perspective would have encouraged greater modesty about the achievements of the 1960s by recognising that they depended heavily on a combination of uniquely favourable external and internal circumstances'. Yet not everyone is convinced that history is good at giving perspective: in the view of Aristotle, 'poetry tends to express the universal, history the particular.'

History fascinates. While the study of any subject may be justified on the grounds of its intrinsic worth, economic history is particularly interesting. The visible remains of the past are everywhere – ports, houses, crooked streets, abandoned fields and ruined cottages. It is natural to wonder about their origins. Less visibly, our view of history informs our view of who we are, and what our culture stands for. These roots merit exploration. History also has its share of intellectual puzzles: Why was economic growth in the 1950s so anaemic? How did per capita incomes rise faster in Ireland between 1850 and 1920 than anywhere else in Europe? Was the tariff regime of the 1930s a failure?

History debunks. Ideologues of all stripes invoke history to bolster their claims. When John Mitchel argued that 'The Almighty, indeed, sent the potato blight, but the English created the famine' he was revisiting history to support his nationalist position. Marxists turn to the land question as evidence of class conflict. An appreciation of history is essential if one is to make an informed judgement about the solidity of such ideas. Once again, Lee states it well, arguing that 'the modern Irish, contrary to popular impression, have little sense of history. What they have is a sense of grievance, which they choose to dignify by christening it history.' He concludes, 'it is central to my argument that the Irish of the late twentieth century have still to learn how to learn from their recent history.' Although written only a few years ago, this view may already be outdated, prey to what F.S.L. Lyons refers to as the dilemma of the contemporary historian – recent events may still be too close in time to allow for enough historical perspective. On the other hand, there is no such thing as a single correct historical perspective, which is surely the idea behind Oscar Wilde's quip that 'the one duty we owe to history is to rewrite it.'

History instructs policy. Ireland has tried laissez faire (1815–45); import substitution (1930–58); export promotion with foreign direct investment (1958–80). It has had budgetary discipline and chronic deficits, fixed exchange rates and floating, price controls, incomes policies, free trade zones, and public and private enterprise. Out of this varied experience there are lessons. While, in Santayana's famous words, 'those who ignore history are condemned to repeat it', the study of history is not merely to avoid making mistakes, but also to learn what works well and merits copying.

An interesting example of the relevance of history for policy is the 2011 book by Reinhart and Rogoff entitled *This Time is Different: Eight Centuries of Financial Folly*. Their exhaustive review of financial collapses in scores of countries over many decades shows that time and again governments, bankers and others simply ignored the lessons of the past, rationalising their actions with the thought that no two situations are the same, things had changed, and this time was different. The Irish housing bubble that began in 2000 and collapsed in 2008, bringing down the country's entire banking system, is a case in point.

The Irish case has served as a positive role model too. Ireland's torrid economic growth in the late 1990s interested many in less developed countries, which too are typically small open economies with a colonial past. Ireland in the twentieth century was a tardy bloomer, and a major theme of this chapter, indeed of this book, is to try to understand why.

History can be misused. Interpretations of history can have real consequences, for good or for bad, because they help form the world view of subsequent generations. George Orwell famously wrote, 'who controls the past controls the future: who controls the present controls the past.' The different versions of history taught in Protestant and Catholic schools in Northern Ireland, for instance, have contributed to an enduring communitarian divide. Nazi teachings on racial purity contributed to the horrors of the Holocaust, but Hitler wrote, 'the victor will never be asked if he told the truth.' The antidote to the misuse of history is to inform oneself, to apply an enquiring mind even to received wisdom, in short to develop some knowledge of history.

The main focus of this chapter is on how Ireland has developed economically. Crotty defines such development as 'a situation where (a) more people are better off than formerly and (b) fewer people are as badly off'. By this yardstick it is necessary to look at population growth, since an economy whose development is accompanied by massive emigration has in some sense failed. This parallels the suggestion of the 1948 Emigration Commission, which proposed that 'a steadily increasing population should occupy a high place among the criteria by which the success of national policy should be judged.'

Economic development also requires that incomes rise (growth), including, or especially, those of the least well off (equality), and this is presumably facilitated by an efficient use of resources (notably full employment).

The starting point, arbitrarily chosen, is 1690, with the consolidation of the Protestant ascendancy. The subsequent years are divided into sub-periods: growth and early industrialisation during 1690 and 1815; rural crisis between 1815 and 1850; the population decline that accompanied increasing prosperity from 1850 to 1921; and the intermittent economic development between independence and about 1960, when the story of modern Irish economic growth begins – as discussed in more detail in Chapter 6.

2 FROM THE BATTLE OF THE BOYNE TO 1815

The Eighteenth Century

At the time of the Battle of the Boyne the Irish economy was predominantly rural, although it was no longer a woodland society. Population stood at a little under two million, roughly double the level of a century before, and was growing at an historically high rate of at least half a per cent per year. With the spread of population the forest cover was rapidly disappearing, giving way to both grazing and tillage. The largest town, Dublin, had about 60,000 inhabitants.

The country was an important exporter, especially of grain, beef, butter, wool and, to a lesser extent, linen. Presaging the situation of three centuries later, almost half of all exports went to continental Europe, notably to France. Earnings from these exports were spent on items such as coal and tobacco, and a surplus on current account amounting to perhaps 10 per cent of exports allowed for the remittance of rents to absentee landlords. Petty, visiting the country in 1672, commented on the large number of people who rode horses, and the high standard of clothing relative to France and most of Europe. He also noted the shabbiness of the houses, of which he reckoned only a fifth had chimneys. The implication was that Ireland was not significantly poorer, and was possibly better off, than most of continental Europe at that time, although less affluent than most of England.

Income was distributed unevenly. Land was owned by perhaps 10,000 landlords, and six-sevenths of the land was held by Protestants. Much of this was let out to farmers, who in turn frequently sublet small plots to cottiers, or hired casual labour. By one estimate, a little over half of the population constituted a rural proletariat, with minimal access to land and close to the margin of subsistence. The potato had been introduced early in the seventeenth century, but was only an important part of the diet of the poor, although its spread allowed for rapid population growth throughout the eighteenth century.

Growth and Structural Change
The essential features of economic growth during the period 1690 to 1815 were: a rapid recovery from the war; a period of relative stagnation (1700–20); 25 years of crisis that included two famines (1720–45); and a long wave of sustained and relatively rapid economic growth (1745–1815). The evidence for these is indirect, since few economic statistics were collected at the time, but trade data show a steady increase in exports, with relatively rapid growth between 1740 (£1.2 million) and 1816 (£7.08 million). The structure of exports changed, as shipments of cattle and sheep gave way to beef, butter, grain and linen.

These changes were driven in part by policy. In 1667 the Cattle Act excluded Irish cattle, sheep, beef and pork from England. The country responded by exporting wool rather than sheep, and by searching for new markets for meat, notably the important provision trade serving transatlantic ships and the West Indies, and the extensive French market. It also shifted resources from dry cattle to dairying, and butter exports grew rapidly. This process was speeded by the Woollen Acts, passed in 1699, which prohibited the export of wool from Ireland or England to other countries, and imposed a stiff duty on Irish wool entering England. More positively, the granting of duty-free access to England for linen helped that industry.

The significance of English laws for Irish economic growth is a matter of controversy. Writers in the nationalist vein have stressed the ways in which English law handicapped Irish growth, for instance by hampering the development of the woollen industry. However, Cullen has argued that the negative effects were minimal, as producers shifted rapidly and effectively into new lines of production.

The changes in the structure of production during the eighteenth century also occurred in response to an increase in the relative price of agricultural commodities, especially grain. Increasing urbanisation in Britain raised the demand for food, and Ireland was favoured as a source of supply during the Napoleonic wars. The most important effect of this improvement in Ireland's terms of trade (price of exports relative to imports) was to raise the incomes of farmers. Ireland continued to export grain until the late 1860s, when the falling costs of shipping, coupled with the opening up of the American midwest, brought cheaper grain to Europe.

Agricultural structure was also influenced by the diffusion of the potato. An acre of potatoes could support twice as many people as an acre of grain. Moreover, potato cultivation does not reduce soil fertility, and potatoes contain substantial amounts of protein and essential minerals. Cullen argues that as the eighteenth century progressed, cottiers increasingly ate potatoes instead of butter or oats, and sold these instead, using their earnings to buy other goods; thus the shift towards the potato is seen as 'related to commercialisation and the urge to increase cash incomes ... for luxuries'.

The expansion of potato cultivation contributed to the dramatic expansion of Ireland's population, from a little more than a million people in 1600 to over eight million by 1841. It was checked briefly by a severe famine in 1740–1, which was caused by a cold summer and led to as many as a quarter of a million deaths. But population growth accelerated after 1750: better nutrition reduced the death rate, and the availability of conacre may have contributed to a reduction in the marriage age. The population rose despite substantial emigration from the northeast, which began early in the eighteenth century and became self-sustaining, and may have been as high as 12,000 annually in the difficult years of the 1770s.

Industry

Industrial change was dominated by the rise of the linen industry, which Cullen calls 'perhaps the most remarkable instance in Europe of an export-based advance in the eighteenth century'. From a low base in the 1690s linen exports rose rapidly, accounting for a quarter of all exports by 1731. The first linen weavers were mainly skilled immigrants, especially Huguenots who had fled France after 1685. Duty-free access to the English market helped, and in 1711 the Irish Parliament set up the Linen Board to regulate the industry, spread information and subsidise projects. Based solidly in the rural areas, an elaborate network of merchants bought the raw linen and undertook the more capital-intensive activities of bleaching and finishing. By the early nineteenth century linen was increasingly spun and woven under the 'putting-out' system; cottiers would be provided with raw materials, and paid in cash for the amount they spun or wove.

Even as late as 1841 an astonishing one person in five stated their occupation as being in textiles, and most of these lived in rural areas. Fully a third of all counties reported in 1821 that more individuals were occupied in 'manufacture, trade and handicrafts' than in agriculture. It has been argued that this type of 'proto-industrialisation' is usually a prelude to full (i.e. factory-based) industrialisation, fostering as it does entrepreneurial skills, monetisation of the economy, and commercial links. In the Irish case no such evolution occurred, although it is not clear why.

Other industries also expanded and modernised, notably those based on the processing of agricultural products, such as brewing, flour milling, and distilling. After 1800 the cotton industry flourished, albeit relatively briefly.

It is important to realise that the Industrial Revolution did in fact come to Ireland, initially. The organisation of many industries was radically changed, with the establishment of breweries, textile factories and glass works large enough to reap economies of scale. At first these factories were located where water power was available, but steam power was introduced early too. In the eighteenth century the road network was greatly improved and expanded, at first by private turnpikes and later by local government (the 'Grand Juries'). The first canals were built.

By 1785 Pitt and others saw Ireland as a viable competitor to English industry. But by 1800 this was not the view in Ireland, and it is ironic that the areas that most favoured union were Cork and the south, with their strong agricultural base; opposition was strongest in Dublin and the north.

Distribution of Income and Wealth
The benefits of economic growth in the late eighteenth century were not spread equally. The most evident rift was that between landowners and the large rural proletariat. Rents of a third of the gross output were probably normal. In 1687 Petty estimated rent payments at £1.2 million, of which £0.1 million was remitted to absentee landlords abroad. Rents thus came to approximately double the level of exports, or almost as much as a quarter of national income. It was this surplus, and tithes paid to the Church of Ireland, that financed the magnificent country houses, churches, Dublin squares, university buildings, paintings and follies that stand as monuments to the eighteenth century.

Most farmers were tenants of large landlords, and in turn rented out land to cottiers. Frequently such plots were confined to conacre (potato land), whose quality improved as they were planted in potatoes. Cottiers also performed work for the farmers to which they were attached. Labourers did not have even the security implied by access to a plot of land. The position of these groups did not improve in the 50 years prior to 1745. There then appears to have been a period of rising real wages, which probably ended in the 1770s, and may never have resumed.

A second divide was between Catholic and Protestant. The Penal Laws placed restrictions on the right of Catholics to purchase land, to worship, to run schools, to vote, to take public office, to enter the professions, to take long leases, and to bequeath property. Barred from the professions and politics, able Catholics often turned their energies towards commerce, and the expansion of trade helped create a significant Catholic middle class. By 1800 the wealthiest Dubliner was Edward Byrne, a Catholic businessman. Presbyterians and Quakers, faced with similar restrictions, also turned to commerce and industry, with some success. Over time most of the restrictions were removed or fell into disuse, and by 1793 Catholics could vote and attend Trinity College, but could not stand for office or fill certain government positions. At times friction boiled over, as reflected in the strong sectarian component of the insurrection of 1798.

The third divide was between town and country. Dublin grew to be the second town of the UK by 1800, with a population of about 200,000. Cork, basing its role on the profitable provision trade, had 80,000 inhabitants, or approximately the same population as a century later. Third came Limerick, with a population of 20,000; Belfast was still a minor town. That the country was able to support such a significant urban population, and to export increasing quantities of food, reflected a growing agricultural surplus and rising agricultural productivity.

3 FROM 1815 TO INDEPENDENCE

1815 to 1850

The period 1815 to 1850 was one of rural crisis, culminating in the disaster of the Famine. The crisis was reflected in rising emigration. This was also the period when Ireland most clearly failed to participate in the Industrial Revolution that was then in full spate in Britain.

The census of 1841 enumerated 8.2 million people in Ireland, a higher level than any measured before or since, and over half the level of Britain. Since 1750 the population had risen at an average rate of 1.3 per cent per year, which was well above the annual rates recorded in England (+1 per cent) or France (+0.4 per cent).

Yet by the 1830s the growth rate had fallen to 0.6 per cent, due almost entirely to massive emigration, mainly to North America; this accounted for a third of the free transatlantic migration of the period. Without emigration, the pre-Famine population would have grown at a rapid 1.7 per cent per annum, due in part to a very high rate of marital fertility. Life expectancy at birth was 37–38 years, lower than in Britain or Scandinavia, but higher than in most of the rest of Europe.

Living Standards
On the eve of the Famine, Ireland was one of the poorest countries in Europe, as the comparative figures in Table 1.1 show. Per capita income was about 40 per cent of the British level, and contemporary visitors were particularly struck by the shabbiness of clothing and the poor state of rural houses.

Yet if the country was poor, it was also well fed, on grain, potatoes and dairy products. Peter Solar estimates that in the early 1840s potatoes and grain alone provided a substantial 2,500 calories per person for direct consumption, two-thirds of it from potatoes. Observers at the time generally thought that the Irish were healthy and strong; they grew taller than the typical Englishman or Belgian. Also compensating for low incomes was the wide availability of cheap fuel, in the form of peat.

Table 1.1 Real Product per Capita (UK=100)

	(1) 1830	(2) 1913	(3) 1950	(4) 1992	Population growth (%) 1919–92
UK	100	100	100	100	31[1]
Ireland (South)	40[2]	53[3]	51	73	13
Ireland (North)	–	58	68	–	27[5]
USA	65	119	170	142	–
Denmark	61	80	99	112	57
Finland	51	47	66	96	60
Greece	39[4]	26	27	52	109
Italy	65	49	53	102	60
Portugal	68	22	23	61	54
EU-15	–	–	69	102	–

Sources: Adapted by the author from K. Kennedy, T. Giblin and D. McHugh, *The Economic Development of Ireland in the Twentieth Century,* Routledge, London 1988, pp. 14–15; J. Lee, *Ireland 1912–1985,* Cambridge University Press, Cambridge 1989; and R. Summers and A. Heston, *Penn World Tables Version 5.1,* National Bureau of Economic Research, Cambridge MA 1995.
[1] GB only [2] 1841, all Ireland [3] 1926 [4] 1841 [5] 1984

Industry and Agriculture

It has become common to consider the 1815 to 1850 period as one of 'deindustrialisation', during which the importance of industry in the economy fell. This is only partly correct. For the island as a whole industrial output appears to have increased. Large-scale and more efficient production methods were applied to milling, brewing, shipbuilding, rope making and the manufacture of linen, iron, paper and glass; the road system was improved and reached a good standard; banks were organised along joint-stock lines. But rural industry declined. Thus, for instance, while Bandon boasted over 1,500 handloom weavers in 1829, the number had shrunk to 150 by 1839.

The first cause of rural deindustrialisation was that the woollen and cotton industries wilted in the face of competition from Britain. This prompted Karl Marx to write that, 'what the Irish need is ... protective tariffs against England.' On the other hand, Ireland was not denuded of purchasing power or exports, for otherwise it could not have afforded to buy British textiles.

A second blow to rural industry was the invention of a method for mechanically spinning flax, which made hand-spinning redundant. It also led to a concentration of the linen industry in the northeast. The weaving of linen was still done by hand, and was boosted by the development. In 1841 Armagh was the most densely populated county in Ireland, testimony to the importance of cottage-based textiles as a source of income.

Despite the rapid fall in prices after 1815, agricultural exports continued to rise, notably livestock and butter and, most dramatically, grain and flour. By the

9

1830s Ireland exported enough grain to feed about two million people annually, testimony to the dynamism of the agricultural sector, which increasingly used new technologies such as improved seeds, crop rotations, better ploughs, and carts.

The Famine

The most traumatic event of the period was the Famine. After a wet summer, blight arrived in September 1845 and spread over almost half the country, especially the east. Famine was largely avoided at first, mainly thanks to adequate government relief. But the potato crop failed completely in 1846, and by December about half a million people were working on relief works, at which stage they were ended. The winter was harsh. By August 1847 an estimated three million people were being supported by soup kitchens, including almost three-quarters of the population of some western counties. The 1847 harvest was not severely harmed, but it was small because of a lack of seed. The blight returned in 1848, and in 1849 over 900,000 people were in workhouses at some time or another. After 1847 the responsibility for supporting the poor had increasingly been shifted from the government to the local landowners who, by and large, did not have sufficient resources to cope. Noting that a few years later Britain spent £69 million on the (futile) Crimean war, Mokyr argues that for half this sum 'there is no doubt that Britain could have saved Ireland.' It is also unlikely that an independent Ireland, with a gross national product (GNP) of £85 million, could have done so without outside support.

As a direct result of the Famine about one million people died, representing an excess mortality of about 3 per cent per annum during the Famine years (and 4 per cent in the north-western counties). Ireland was not the only country hit by the potato blight – excess mortality was comparable in the Scottish Highlands, and the excess mortality rates were 2 per cent in the Netherlands and 1 per cent in Belgium – but given its high dependence on the potato, Ireland was especially vulnerable, particularly its poorer and remoter districts. Three-fifths of those who died were young (under 10) or old (over 60), and labourers and small farmers were hit most severely. These unequal effects have led Cullen to argue, controversially, that 'the Famine was less a national disaster than a social and regional one.'

In the course of the Famine, the output of potatoes fell by about three-quarters, the use of potatoes for animal fodder ceased, and food imports rose very rapidly. As a result the amount of calories available for direct consumption barely fell, on a per capita basis. This gives credence to Amartya Sen's contention that famines are rarely caused by an absolute lack of food, but rather by a change in the food entitlements of major groups in society. So, for instance, labourers were unable to find employment when blight reduced the need for harvesting and planting potatoes; without income they could not buy food, and so became destitute.

Distribution

Pre-Famine Ireland probably had a 'very unequal distribution of income by West European standards'. According to the 1841 census, 63 per cent of the population had access to less than five acres of land, or were 'without capital, in either money, land or acquired knowledge'. Just 3 per cent were professionals and rentiers, and this included the approximately 10,000 proprietors, or 0.12 per cent of the population, who owned at least 100 acres.

Rent, including payments in kind, accounted for about £15 million, or almost a fifth of the national income of £80 million. Presumably the bulk of this rent accrued to the wealthiest 3 per cent or so of the population, implying a very great degree of income inequality. Rough calculations suggest that this group probably had per capita incomes averaging over £100 per annum, compared to a national average of £10, and an estimated £4 for poor households.

By 1845 a rudimentary welfare structure was in place, with the completion of 130 workhouses having a total capacity of 100,000. In practice the numbers living in the workhouses rarely exceeded 40,000, except during the Famine.

There is no shortage of hypotheses as to why Ireland remained poor, and hence uniquely vulnerable by European standards to the chance failure of the potato crop. Thomas Malthus, writing in 1817, considered that population growth was running ahead of food production; however, the more densely settled countries were not necessarily the poorest ones. Other writers blamed the insecurity of tenancy for low agricultural investment, although it is not clear how insecure tenancies really were. Some have pointed to agrarian violence, or the lack of coal deposits, or inadequate financial capital, or insufficient human resources (especially entrepreneurs) as barriers to economic development. None of these explanations is waterproof, and Ó Gráda wrote recently that 'exactly why comparative advantage dictated industrial decline for Ireland is still unclear.'

Fewer but Richer: 1850 to 1921
The 70 years following the famine witnessed enormous changes in Irish society and saw the emergence of the modern economy. Over this period per capita incomes more than doubled, and came closer to the British level, while the population fell by a third. A rural middle class emerged, replacing the landlords and squeezing out the rural labourers. In agriculture tillage declined, and the production of dry cattle increased. The northeast became industrialised.

The dominant demographic fact of the period is that population declined, from 6.6 million in 1851 to 4.2 million by 1926. Without emigration the population would have risen, by about 1 per cent annually in the 1860s, and by 0.5 per cent annually at the turn of the century, a decline largely explained by a falling marriage rate. Almost 2 per cent of the population left annually in the 1850s; the pace slowed markedly to less than 1 per cent after 1900. The early emigrants were drawn from all areas of the country, but in later years the bulk of the emigrants came from the poorer, mainly western, districts. Over the period 1820 to 1945 an estimated 4.5 million Irish emigrated to the USA, comparable in magnitude to the flows from Italy, Austria and Britain.

Living Standards

Astonishingly, between 1840 and 1913 per capita incomes in Ireland rose at 1.6 per cent per year, faster than any other country in Europe. Where Irish incomes averaged 40 per cent of the British level in 1840, this proportion had risen to 60 per cent by 1913. During this period Irish incomes came from behind, and then easily surpassed, those of Finland, Italy and Portugal.

Part of the explanation is statistical. The Famine, and subsequent high levels of emigration, removed a disproportionate number of the very poor; even if those who remained experienced no increase in their incomes, average income would have been higher than before. The poor were more likely to leave because the gap between Irish and foreign wages was greatest for unskilled labour. In 1844 the wages paid to a skilled builder in Dublin were 14 per cent *higher* than in London, but the wages paid to an unskilled building labourer were 36 per cent lower. A comparable gap persisted until at least World War I.

Incomes also rose because of dramatic increases in output per worker. The northeast became highly industrialised; in the rest of the country agricultural productivity rose rapidly. Almost all of the expansion of the modern industrial sector was in the northeast. While linen output increased slowly, it was increasingly concentrated in factories in Belfast and the Lagan valley: between 1850 and 1875 employment in linen mills and factories rose from 21,000 to 60,000 as power weaving replaced the cottage industry.

The manufacture of boilers and textile equipment needed in the mills helped diversify the industrial base, and provided the skills and infrastructure that were important for the growth of shipbuilding. Harland and Wolff, the celebrated firm that built the *Titanic*, grew from 500 workers in 1861 to 9,000 by 1900. The shipbuilding industry also provided an impetus for other upstream activities, including rope making, paint, and engineering.

Benefiting from 'external economies of foreign trade' – regular trade links with markets and suppliers, and a financial system geared towards supporting such links – Belfast rivalled Dublin in size by 1901, when it had about 400,000 inhabitants. Londonderry became the centre of an important shirt-making industry, employing 18,000 full-time workers and a further 80,000 cottage workers at its height in 1902.

By 1907, industrial activity in Ireland as a whole employed a fifth of the work force, making the country at least as industrialised as Italy, Spain or Portugal. Half of all industrial output was exported, Ireland had a worldwide reputation in linen, shipbuilding, distilling, brewing and biscuits, and the volume of trade per capita was higher than for Britain.

It is sometimes wondered why Ireland did not become even more industrialised, more like Clydeside than East Anglia. And related to this question, why did the northeast industrialise while by and large the rest of the country did not? Put another way, why did Irish labour emigrate, rather than capital immigrate?

There was no lack of capital, and indeed from the 1880s on, Irish residents were net lenders of capital to the rest of the world, investing in British government stock, railways and other ventures overseas. The banks may have been cautious about lending, but in this they were no different from their counterparts in England, where industrial development was rapid. Nor is there evidence that skills were lacking. The primary school system expanded rapidly, enrolling 282,000 pupils in state-subsidised schools in 1841, and 1,072,000 by 1887. Whereas 53 per cent of the population was illiterate in 1841, this fraction had fallen to 25 per cent by 1881 and 16 per cent by 1901. Enterprise may have been lacking, although clearly not in the Lagan valley. The absence of coal probably had some effect, not because this raised costs of production unduly, but because coal itself was a big business; in 1914 a quarter of the British labour force was directly employed in coal or iron and steel. Ireland was next door to, and had free access to, the world's most affluent market.

Perhaps the explanation rests largely on chance, the idea that once Belfast grew as an industrial centre, accumulating skills, capital and infrastructure, it became an increasingly attractive location for further investment – an argument that might also be made about the unanticipated growth spurt of the 1990s.

Agriculture

Between 1861 and 1909 gross agricultural output rose by a quarter; since the rural population fell sharply, output per capita in agriculture more than doubled, a solid performance, but less impressive than that of Denmark, where output per male agricultural worker almost quadrupled over the same period.

This growth masks an important change in the structure of agriculture, which shifted from crops to cattle in response to a fall in the price of grain relative to cattle. Tillage, including potatoes, shrank by two-thirds between 1845 and 1913. Farmers were not, as is sometimes supposed, slow to change or innovate. For instance, when circumstances demanded it they rapidly adopted the creamery system. Faced with changing prices and technology, wrote Hans Stahl, 'the response of the Irish agriculturalist ... was rational and normal.'

Distribution

Between 1870 and 1925 the landed proprietors 'surrendered their power and property' to an increasingly 'comfortable, educated, self-confident rural bourgeoisie', thereby effecting one of the most extensive land reforms in history, although it should be noted that a similar land transfer occurred a century earlier in Denmark, and half a century later in Finland, so the Irish case was by no means unique.

As late as 1870, 97 per cent of all land was owned by landlords who rented it out to others to farm. Just 750 families owned 50 per cent of the land in the country. About one landlord in seven lived outside Ireland, and another third lived outside their estates; the remaining half were not absentees. Two-fifths of all landlords were Catholic.

The agricultural crisis of the late 1870s meant lower agricultural prices and this, coupled with fixed rents, squeezed tenant farmers. By now they felt confident enough to agitate for the 'three Fs' – fair rent, fixity of tenure, and free sale of 'tenant right'. Michael Davitt's Land League forged a link with Parnell and the Irish Party in parliament. Their efforts resulted in the Land Act of 1881, which established land courts to hear rent appeals. The courts reduced rents by an average of about 20 per cent, and later courts reduced rents by about another 20 per cent after 1887. In a formal sense this diluted the power of the landlord – Moody refers to it as 'dual ownership' – although it is noteworthy that during the same period real rents fell by comparable amounts in England.

Further efforts prompted legislation that provided tenants with government loans with which to purchase their land, including the Ashbourne Act of 1885, and the Wyndham Act of 1903, and paid 12 per cent bonuses to landlords who sold their entire estates. The result was that 'by 1917 almost two-thirds of the tenants had acquired their holdings.'

With rural depopulation, land holdings increased in size. The number of cottiers working less than five acres fell from 300,000 in 1845 to 62,000 by 1910. The same period saw the 'virtual disappearance of the hired labourer from Irish agriculture', as the number of 'farm servants and labourers' fell from 1.3 million in 1841 to 0.3 million in 1911.

The distribution of income can be considered in other dimensions too. Thus, for instance, Protestants maintained their share of national income. This largely reflected the growth of the industrial northeast, which was dominated by Protestant interests, and the fact that Catholics were more likely to emigrate (and more died in the Famine). Catholics did come to fill an increasing proportion of government and professional jobs, although not in proportion to their number. The Catholic Church itself grew rapidly, with a spate of church building between 1860 and 1900, and church-going became much more common. The number of Catholic priests, nuns and other religious rose from almost 5,000 in 1850 to over 14,000 by 1900, making it one of the fastest-growing professions during this period.

The small towns stagnated, and so did Dublin until late in the century. Kevin O'Rourke contrasts the dynamism of Danish agriculture after 1880 with the slow development of Irish agricultural production, particularly dairying, and suggests that the violence associated with Irish land reform, the diversion of talent from the business of farming to the politics of redistribution, and a deficit of community trust in Catholic parts of Ireland help explain the difference. In contrast to the rest of the country, Belfast grew rapidly. The zenith of its prosperity came during and immediately after World War I, with a boom in shipbuilding and engineering; as David Johnson put it, 'in economic terms the last years of the Union were the best ones'.

4 FROM INDEPENDENCE TO 1960

When it finally achieved independence, the Irish Free State could count some important assets. It had an extensive system of communications, a developed banking system, a vigorous wholesale and retail network, an efficient and honest administration, universal literacy, a large stock of houses, schools and hospitals, 3.1 million people, and enormous external assets. By the standards of most of the world's countries Ireland was well off indeed.

On the other hand the new state faced some serious problems. It had to establish a new government; the civil war had been destructive and had helped prompt 88,000 people to emigrate in 1921–22; the dependency ratio was high – Catholics marrying before 1916 had an average of 6.0 children per family; and the post-war boom had run its course. We now document its subsequent achievements, and evaluate its performance as an independent country.

1921 to 1932: Agriculture First
The growth model pursued by the Cumann na nGaedheal government was based on the premise that what was good for agriculture was good for the country. Patrick Hogan, the Minister for Agriculture, saw the policy as one of 'helping the farmer who helped himself and letting the rest go to the devil'. This emphasis on agriculture was not surprising. In 1926 agriculture generated 32 per cent of gross domestic product (GDP) and provided 54 per cent of all employment. The government relied heavily on the support of the larger farmers. The expectation was that not only would agricultural growth raise the demand for goods and services from the rest of the economy, but would also provide more inputs on which to base a more substantial processing sector. The three major industrial exporting sectors at the time – brewing, distilling and biscuit making – were all closely linked with agriculture.

The essential elements of the policy, which has come to be known as the 'treasury view', were free trade; low taxes and government spending; modest direct state intervention in industry and agriculture; and parity with sterling. Free trade was seen as essential if the cost of farm inputs was to be kept low.

The support for free trade was perhaps surprising given that Griffith had argued that one of the main benefits of independence would be that the country could grant protection to infant industries. On the other hand, the government was cautious about making such changes, perhaps for fear of upsetting the financial community, whose opposition to protection was well known, or perhaps because they were, in the words of Kevin O'Higgins, 'the most conservative revolutionaries in history'. The government sought to deflect pressure for stiffer protection by establishing the Tariff Commission in 1926, and appointing members who were, in the main, in favour of free trade. The onus of proof was on any industry wishing to be protected, and the Commission moved slowly on requests, granting few tariffs other than for rosary beads and margarine.

Government spending was kept low, the budget was essentially balanced, and revenues came to just 15 per cent of GNP in 1931. This was a remarkable achievement, given that military spending had trebled during the civil war. One serious consequence was that welfare spending remained low, and in the absence of major government assistance, housing for the less well off remained scarce.

Ideologically the government did not favour taking a very active role in promoting economic development. Despite this, it intervened pragmatically in several ways. The Department of Agriculture was greatly expanded, although the impact of this on agricultural output has been questioned. The Congested Districts Board was replaced by the Land Commission, which transferred 3.6 million acres, involving 117,000 holdings, to annuity-paying freeholders during the period 1923 to 1937. Laws were passed to improve the quality of agricultural output, by regulating the marketing of dairy produce (1924) and improving the quality of livestock breeding by registering bulls (1925). The Agricultural Credit Corporation (ACC) was set up to provide credit to farmers. The government subsidised a Belgian company to establish a sugar factory in Carlow, and provided incentives to grow sugar beet.

A major innovation was the establishment of the Electricity Supply Board (ESB) in 1927. This, along with the ACC, represented the first of the state-sponsored bodies (SSBs) that were established during the ensuing years. The ESB successfully undertook the Ardnacrusha hydroelectric scheme: when it came on line in 1927 it was the largest hydroelectric plant in the world, and by 1935 it provided 80 per cent of the country's electricity. The completion of the project boosted the country's prestige, and was the most visible accomplishment of the first decade of independence.

In due course state-sponsored bodies were set up in many fields, including air, train and bus transport, industrial credit, insurance, peat development, trade promotion and industrial development. By the early 1960s, when the most important of these bodies had been established, they employed about 50,000 people, representing about 7 per cent of the total labour force. The SSBs were not the outgrowth of any particular ideology, but were rather 'individual responses to specific situations'. This, along with their ability to attract good managers, may help explain why they are generally considered to have been successful agents of economic development, especially in the first few decades after independence, when the private sector did not appear to be very enterprising.

Parity with sterling was the final ingredient in the development model pursued. Few countries at the time had floating exchange rates, and since 97 per cent of exports went to, and 76 per cent of imports came from, Britain, it seemed logical to peg the pound to sterling. The Currency Act of 1927 established an Irish currency, fully backed by British sterling securities; until 1961 Irish banknotes were inscribed 'payable in London'. By linking the currency with sterling the Free State gave up the possibility of any independent monetary policy, in return for greater predictability in trade with Britain, and lower transaction costs.

The economic policy of the Free State in the 1920s was similar to the typical prescription given by the World Bank to less developed countries in the 1980s: get the prices right, using world prices as a guide, reduce budget deficits, keep government 'interference' to a minimum, and follow a conservative monetary policy. Did it work?

The simple answer is 'in the circumstances, yes in most respects, eventually'. The young nation got off to a rocky start. Between 1920 and 1924 agricultural prices fell 44 per cent; the civil war, which only ended in 1923, arrested investment; after independence, a significant proportion of the skilled labour force left; and the recession in the UK after sterling's return to the gold standard in 1925 reduced the demand for Irish exports. However, between 1926 and 1931 real per capita GNP rose about 3 per cent per annum; exports rose 20 per cent, reaching a peak of 35 per cent of GNP in 1929, and a volume that was not exceeded until 1960. Industrial employment rose by 8 per cent.

1932 to 1939: Self-sufficiency, Economic War and Depression

Fianna Fáil came to power in early 1932, with an economic policy that differed in two fundamental ways from its predecessor; it was ideologically committed to a policy of greater economic self-sufficiency, and it reneged on paying land annuities to Britain. It also came to power during the darkest hour of the Depression, a time when most countries were erecting tariff barriers.

Why self-sufficiency? The case for limiting economic interactions with the rest of the world is more cultural than economic, but it attracted some intellectual support. John Maynard Keynes, lecturing at UCD in April 1933, said, 'I sympathize with those who would minimize ... economic entanglement between nations. ... But let goods be homespun whenever it is reasonable and conveniently possible.' Perhaps these oft-quoted remarks are out of context, for he went on to argue that only 'a very modest measure of self-sufficiency' would be feasible without 'a disastrous reduction in a standard of life which is already none too high'.

How self-sufficiency? The main instrument used was more and higher tariffs, which rose to a maximum of 45 per cent in 1936, dipping to 35 per cent by 1938. In Europe only Germany and Spain had higher levels by then; Irish tariffs were twice as high as in the USA, and 50 per cent higher than in the UK. They were introduced piecemeal and so formed an untidy pattern that, in FitzGerald's view, had 'no rational basis'; Meenan considers that they fell more heavily on finished goods, and so provided an incentive for domestic assembly using imported raw materials. The pursuit of self-sufficiency would justify indefinite tariff protection; in this it differs from the views of Griffith, who saw a role for temporary protection to encourage infant industries to take root.

Self-sufficiency was also pursued by introducing price supports for wheat, which was instrumental in raising the acreage planted to wheat from 8,000 hectares in 1931 to 103,000 by 1936. Somewhat inconsistently, bounties were paid for exports of cattle, butter, bacon and other agricultural products in order to expand the volume of exports, and this resulted in a significant rise in the share of government spending in national income. To foster Irish involvement in industry the Control of Manufactures Act (1932) required majority Irish ownership, although in practice exceptions were usually granted upon request. The Industrial Credit Corporation was set up to lend to industry, and issued £6.5 million in its first four years of operation.

It is difficult to assess the effect of the policy of self-sufficiency because it became inextricably tangled with the effects of the economic war. Previous Irish governments had recognised an obligation to pay land annuities to Britain to cover the cost of money lent under the various pre-independence Land Acts. These came to about £5 million annually, or about one-fifth of government spending and almost 4 per cent of GNP.

On coming to office in March 1932, de Valera refused to continue the annuities. In July Britain retaliated by imposing special duties, initially at 20 per cent and later at 40 per cent, on imports of livestock, dairy products and meat, and also imposed quotas, including halving the number of cattle permitted to enter the UK. The Free State countered with tariffs on British goods, including cement and coal – surprising choices for a country bent on industrialisation. After these escalations tempers cooled.

Under the Cattle–Coal pacts Irish cattle had easier access to Britain, and Ireland agreed to buy British coal. Initially agreed for 1935, the pact was extended and renewed in 1936 and 1937, and the Anglo-Irish Trade Agreement ended the 'war', with Ireland agreeing to pay a lump sum of £10 million and Britain ceding control of the 'treaty ports'. Given that the capitalised value of the annuities was close to £100 million, this was considered to be a major diplomatic and economic victory for de Valera.

The combined effects of protection and the economic war were initially dramatic. Industrial output rose 40 per cent between 1931 and 1936. Population stabilised, standing at 2.93 million in 1931 and 2.94 million in 1938 – the first period since the Famine when there had not been a substantial decline – but the amount of unemployment soared, almost quintupling between 1931 and 1934 to about 14 per cent of the labour force by 1935. In large part this reflected reduced opportunities to emigrate to the USA. Despite rapid industrial growth, agriculture stagnated, as exports fell sharply. Where exports and imports together amounted to 75 per cent of GNP in 1926, they constituted 54 per cent in 1938, although this decline pales beside the two-thirds reduction in trade that the USA faced in the early 1930s. The existing manufacturing export industries also suffered some decline. By 1936 import-substituting industrialisation had run its course, and industrial output only rose a further 4.5 per cent between 1936 and 1938. It is widely accepted that the slow growth of the economy in the 1950s was largely because of the inefficiency of the industrial sector that developed during the 1930s.

One other event of this period merits a brief discussion. With the onset of the Depression, Britain erected tariffs on a wide range of items, including beer. This prompted Guinness to establish a brewery at Park Lane near London. Beer had been Ireland's single most important industrial export, and brewing had accounted for 30 per cent of manufacturing value added in 1926. Once the Park Lane brewery was established, there was little incentive to return to the earlier pattern of concentrating Guinness's production in Dublin. In this case British tariffs led to the establishment of an efficient new factory in England, at the expense of Ireland. It is possible that some Irish tariffs did the same in the other direction, although with a smaller internal market it is less likely to have been common. Using tariffs to promote investment and industry in this way has come under increasing scrutiny by economists in recent years, under the rubric of strategic trade policy.

Historical Debate: Was the Drive for Self-sufficiency a Mistake?
Joseph Johnston, writing in 1951, argued that but for the economic war 'our real National Income might well have been 25 per cent more in 1939 than it actually was and 25 per cent more today that it actually is. ... The process of cutting off one's nose to spite one's face is sometimes good politics, but always bad economics.' He might have noted that between 1931 and 1938 Irish GNP rose about 10 per cent, compared to 18 per cent in less protectionist Britain. He might also have questioned how many industrial jobs were really created, noting that while the 1936 census enumerated 199,000 individuals 'involved in industrial occupations', this was only 11,000 higher than the number enumerated in 1926.

Johnston's estimate of a 25 per cent decline has been sharply questioned. Recent research, which tries to recreate what might plausibly have happened in the absence of tariffs by constructing a computable general equilibrium counterfactual, suggests that the total cost of protection might have been 5 per cent of GNP per year, or £7–8 million annually during the late 1930s, of which perhaps two-thirds is attributable to the economic war. Against this, Ireland gained the treaty ports and received a £90 million write-off on its foreign debt. The expansion of the industrial sector may have provided experience in business management, which was valuable in later years.

Having built high tariff barriers, Ireland was slow to reduce them later, and the average rate of effective protection of manufacturing was still an exceptionally high 80 per cent in 1966. If some of the economic sluggishness of the 1950s was the result, the protection of the 1930s may appear more damaging; had Johnston been writing in 1960 he would perhaps have been closer to the truth. One might also wonder whether a policy of more selective protection, perhaps along the lines favoured by Taiwan or South Korea, could have proved more valuable.

1939 to 1950: The War and Rebound
The most important economic result of World War II was that it opened a wide gap between Northern Ireland and the Republic. Between 1938 and 1947 national income grew just 14 per cent, compared to 47 per cent in the UK and 84 per cent in Northern Ireland. Where incomes, north and south, were broadly comparable before the war, by 1947 incomes per head in the Republic had fallen to about 40 per cent of the British level, while in the north they had risen to close to 70 per cent. Why did the south perform so poorly?

Between 1938 and 1943 the volume of exports fell by a half, and imports fell even more. During this period industrial output fell 27 per cent, and industrial employment dropped from 167,000 to 144,000. The main reason was the scarcity of raw material inputs for industry, and the shortage of shipping capacity. Completely reliant on outside shippers until 1941, the government founded Irish Shipping, and moved rapidly to purchase ships, which soon proved their worth. Because of the difficulty of obtaining imports, the country built up significant foreign reserves, and by 1946 residents had external assets totalling £260 million, approximately equivalent to GNP in that year.

The total value of agricultural output fell during the war period, but net agricultural output (i.e. total output less the cost of non-labour inputs) rose, by 17 per cent between 1938–39 and 1945. This reflected the drastic fall in the use of fertiliser and other inputs, and is generally acknowledged to have exhausted the soil significantly. The structure of agriculture changed, as the area planted in grain and potatoes almost doubled, due in part to the introduction of compulsory tillage.

During the war real GNP fell, especially initially. Living standards fell further as households, unable to find the goods they wanted, were obliged to save more. The stock of capital in industry became run down. With emigration to the USA blocked, the population rose, by 18,000 between 1938 and 1946. The unemployment rate stood at over 15 per cent in 1939 and 1940, but declined thereafter to a little over 10 per cent in 1945. The decrease was due to a sharp rise in migration to Britain, reaching near record levels in 1942, as people left to work in factories and enrol in the armed forces.

The war was followed by a rebound, and per capita real GDP rose by 4.1 per cent per annum between 1944 and 1950. This occurred despite the fact that agricultural output stagnated, with gross volume falling between 1945 and 1950, and net output shrinking by 5 per cent. Not surprisingly, 70,000 people left agriculture between 1946 and 1951; yet during this period the unemployment rate fell and population increased. Much of this is attributable to the expansion of industrial production, which more than doubled during the same period.

Government spending rose rapidly in the early war years as the army was increased from 7,500 to 38,000 men. After the war, government spending grew far faster than national income, increasing its share of GNP from 23 per cent in 1945 to 39 per cent by 1951. In large measure this increase occurred as Ireland sought to emulate the 'social investment' of the Labour Party in Britain by expanding welfare spending.

1950 to 1958: Decline or Rebirth?

It had become standard to consider the 1950s as a period of stagnation and failure. This is a half truth. Between 1951 and 1958 GDP rose by less than 1 per cent per year. Employment fell by 12 per cent, and the unemployment rate rose. Irish GDP per capita fell from 75 per cent to 60 per cent of the EU average. Half a million people emigrated. Yet between 1950 and 1960 real product per capita grew at 2.2 per cent per year, possibly the fastest rate recorded up to then, and industrial output expanded at 2.8 per cent per annum. Output per farmer grew at a respectable 3.4 per cent per year. Rural electrification spread, and the housing stock improved appreciably. Was the glass half full or half empty?

The key to understanding the 1950s is to note that this was the decade when Europe rebounded; Ireland's performance looks disappointing only by the standards of neighbouring countries, not by historical standards. Much of the emigration reflected the lure of improving wages elsewhere, notably in Britain.

Why did output not grow faster in the 1950s? FitzGerald believes that the key problem was a 'failure to reorientate industry to export markets', considering that 'the naïveté of the philosophy that underlay the whole protection policy was not exposed until the process of introducing protection had come to an end.' By the 1950s Irish industry was supplying as much of the domestic market as it reasonably could, and in order to expand had no option but to seek markets overseas. But since much of the industrial sector could only survive because of protection, it was too inefficient to export successfully, although it was certainly strong enough to lobby against any liberalisation.

To help provide incentives to industries to switch to exporting, export profits tax relief was provided in 1956, and in 1958 the Industrial Development Authority (IDA), which had been set up in 1949, was granted more powers to provide tax holidays for export-oriented companies. The Shannon Free Airport Development Company was set up in 1959.

One might better view the 1950s as a period of transition rather than one of failure, much as it was in Taiwan and South Korea. It has been argued that the economy was in fact in the process of reorienting itself towards export markets, and that any such change was bound to be slow. As J.J. McElligott put it in the 1920s, when warning of the dangers of protection, 'to revert to free trade from a protectionist regime is almost an economic impossibility.' Exports of manufactured goods rose quite rapidly, accounting for 6 per cent of all exports in 1950 but 17 per cent by 1960. Dramatic as this change was, the increase was from a very low base, and the export sector simply was not large enough to be a potent engine of growth.

An entirely different explanation comes from Kennedy and Dowling, who state baldly that 'the chief factor seems to us to be the failure to secure a satisfactory rate of expansion in aggregate demand', most notably unduly restrictive (in their view) fiscal policy in response to the balance of payment crises of 1951 and 1955. This argument provides an intellectual underpinning for the highly expansionary, and ultimately disastrous, fiscal policy experiment of the late 1970s and early 1980s.

Whatever the causes, the poor overall economic performance created a feeling of pessimism, and this in turn probably deterred investors. As T.K. Whitaker, then secretary of the Department of Finance, put it, 'the mood of despondency was palpable.' In 1958, at the request of the government, he wrote the report *Economic Development*, best remembered now for the optimistic note that it struck in pessimistic times. The report proposed that tariffs should be dismantled unless a clear infant industry case existed, favoured incentives to stimulate private industrial investment, and proposed expanded spending on agriculture. On the other hand it warned against the dampening effects of high taxes. With such measures, it suggested, GNP could grow 2 per cent annually, although it stressed that this was not a firm target. These measures were incorporated in the First Programme for Economic Expansion, which appeared in November 1958, but generally not implemented.

Economic growth during the period of the first plan exceeded anyone's wildest expectations, reaching 4 per cent per annum instead of the anticipated 2 per cent. At the time much of this increase was attributed directly to the impact of the First Programme, and support for such indicative planning increased. The Second Programme, introduced in 1963 and designed to run to 1970, was far more detailed and ambitious, forecasting an annual increase in GNP of 4 per cent per annum; industry was to expand 50 per cent and exports 75 per cent during the plan period. When it appeared that these targets would not quite be met, the Second Programme was allowed to lapse. A Third Programme was produced, but quickly sank into oblivion, along with most of the enthusiasm for indicative planning.

5 FROM 1960 TO 2012

1960 to 1973: From Protection to Free Trade

Between 1960 and 1973 real output increased at 4.4 per cent per annum, the highest rate sustained until then. Immigration began. Per capita incomes rose by three-fifths, kept up with income growth elsewhere in Europe, and significantly outpaced growth in both Britain and Northern Ireland.

This first wave of substantial economic growth has been largely attributed to the strategy of export-led growth that the government, heeding the recommendations of *Economic Development*, pursued; less publicised, but important nonetheless, were a notable improvement in the terms of trade (39 per cent better in 1973 than in 1957), expansionary fiscal policy, the boom in the nearby European economy, and the fact that solid institutional foundations had been laid in the 1950s.

The policy of export-led growth stood on two legs – trade liberalisation, and the attraction of foreign direct investment (see Chapter 9). Trade liberalisation called for reducing tariffs; these, by making inputs dearer and by drawing resources away from other sectors of the economy, had worked to inhibit exports. Foreign investment, it was hoped, would bring new skills to the country and help raise the overall investment, and hence growth, rate.

Trade liberalisation was begun in the 1960s as Ireland unilaterally cut tariffs in 1963 and 1964, negotiated the Anglo-Irish Free Trade Area Agreement in 1965 and subscribed to the General Agreement on Tariffs and Trade (GATT) in 1967. These moves also prepared for eventual membership of the European Economic Community (EEC), as it was called then.

With a panoply of tax breaks and subsidies, Ireland successfully, although at considerable expense, induced foreign companies to set up branches in Ireland, and by 1974 new industry accounted for over 60 per cent of industrial output. The

10 per cent tax on profits in manufacturing also made the country something of a tax haven, although it did require at least a fig leaf of manufacturing presence.

The final thrust of government policy was wage restraint, viewed as necessary, especially with a fixed exchange rate, to help keep industrial costs at a competitive level. In the 1960s government efforts amounted to exhortation. In the 1970s wage bargaining was centralised under the National Wage Agreements. Given the option of emigration, the scope for manoeuvre here was small. If real wages were pushed below the British level they would simply stimulate faster emigration, and so could not be sustained.

Into Europe: Trade, Investment, and Subsidies

In 1973 Ireland, along with the UK and Denmark, joined the EEC (referred to here as EU).

Membership immediately led to a reduction in trade barriers. The EU was founded as a customs union, with low internal barriers to trade and a common set of external barriers. By joining, Ireland was committed to trading freely with the other member countries, and by 1977 all tariff barriers had been removed. Many of the remaining, less obvious, restraints on trade within the EU were dismantled as part of the effort to create a Single European Market. Officially these changes came into effect in 1992, although the full elimination of barriers remains a work in progress.

With lower trade barriers, it was recognised that some of Ireland's industry would wither under the competition, but it was also expected that Ireland would become a good platform from which companies from outside the European Community could serve the European market.

These expectations were met. While Irish exports amounted to 34 per cent of GDP in 1963, and 38 per cent in 1973, the proportion had risen to 94 per cent by 2002, one of the highest in the world (see Chapter 9). This burst of exports paralleled a similar increase in intra-EU trade that took place in the 1960s, and shows how even small reductions in the cost of trading can have a large impact on the volume of trade.

Membership of the EU also led to a net inflow under the Common Agricultural Policy (CAP), which subsidises farm prices. Higher farm prices help farmers at the expense of consumers, but as a net exporter of farm produce, Ireland was a net beneficiary (see Chapter 11).

Although about two-thirds of EU transfers to Ireland are farm-related, the remaining third consists mainly of transfers from the 'structural funds,' including the Regional Development, Social, and Cohesion funds. In principle these funds might have added to investment and thereby boosted economic growth, but in practice they mainly appeared to have substituted for projects that the government would otherwise have had to finance; they thus made a more important contribution to living standards than to growth. Net receipts from the EU peaked at 6.5 per cent of GDP in 1991, and had fallen to 0.3 per cent of GDP by 2011.

✸ 1979 to 1986: Growth Interrupted

Between 1979 and 1986, per capita consumption in Ireland actually fell slightly and GDP rose very slowly (see Table 7.4). What went wrong?

Membership of the EU coincided with a fourfold increase in the price of oil (from $3 to $12 per barrel) that resulted from the first oil shock in late 1973; a sharp worldwide recession followed.

The government's response was thoroughly Keynesian. The higher price of oil meant that spending was diverted towards imports, thereby depressing aggregate demand for Irish goods and services. The solution adopted was to boost government current spending, and as a consequence the current budget deficit rose from 0.4 per cent of GDP in 1973 to 6.8 per cent by 1975. For a while the policy worked: despite a difficult international situation, GDP growth during the first six years of EU membership was robust.

Then came the mistake, the source of the failure of the fiscal experiment: successive governments were unwilling to reduce the budget deficit, and continued to borrow heavily, so the ratio of government debt to GDP rose from 52 per cent in 1973 to 129 per cent by 1987, by then easily the highest in the EU. By 1986 the cost of servicing this debt took up 94 per cent of all revenue from the personal income tax (see Chapter 4). Although efforts were made to solve the problem by raising tax rates, especially in 1981 and 1983, these changes hardly increased tax revenue, suggesting that the country was close to its revenue-maximising tax rates. Much of the additional spending went to buy imports, and the current account deficit widened to an untenable 15 per cent by 1981. Partly as a result, the Irish pound was devalued four times within the European Monetary System (EMS) in the early 1980s. In 1986 an estimated IR£1,000 million of private capital left the country, anticipating a devaluation; the smart money was right, and the Irish pound was devalued by 8 per cent in August.

In 1987 the Fianna Fáil government introduced a very tight budget, cutting the current budget deficit to 1.7 per cent of GDP through reductions in real government spending that made Margaret Thatcher's efforts look gentle. Capital spending was also sharply cut, especially on housing, and by 1992 the ratio of debt to GDP had fallen below 100 per cent.

The 1987 reform worked. Economic growth resumed, as confidence (and investors) returned, and exports boomed, thanks in part to the devaluation of 1986 and to continued wage restraint. But the lessons of the failed fiscal experiment are important and have been largely internalised: fiscal rectitude is important for long-term growth, and taxes cannot be pushed too high.

1979 to 1999: From Sterling to EMS to Euro

In 1979, in a move that was hailed at the time as far-sighted, Ireland broke the link with sterling (which dated back to 1826) and joined the EMS. The reasoning was straightforward: Ireland had experienced inflation averaging 15 per cent between 1973 and 1979, necessarily the same rate as in Britain, and it was believed that the key to reducing the inflation rate was to uncouple the Irish pound from high-inflation sterling and attach it to the low-inflation EMS, which was dominated by the deutschmark. Some also argued – correctly as it turned out – that sterling would appreciate with the development of North Sea oil, and that this would hurt Irish exports. Although over 40 per cent of exports still went to the UK in 1979, about a quarter went to the other EU countries, and so a change in exchange regime was considered feasible.

The adjustment to the EMS was slow and rocky. In the early 1980s inflation actually fell faster in the UK, which stayed out of the EMS, than in Ireland. The slow reduction in Irish inflation towards German levels meant that the Irish pound became overvalued, and had to be devalued within the EMS. The standard explanation is that wage demands – which often respond to recent inflation – were slow to change, so wage increases continued to be too large to be consistent with very low inflation. The lesson here was clear: economic growth and macroeconomic stability can all too easily be undermined if wage increases get out of line.

By about 1990 Ireland could boast of low inflation, a tight budget, and a falling ratio of government debt to GDP, and it looked as if, after a decade of relative economic stagnation, the decision to join the EMS was finally paying off. Then in late 1992 the EMS fell apart. High interest rates in Germany, resulting from that country's need to finance reunification, caused the deutschmark to appreciate. Sterling devalued, and the Irish pound ultimately followed, because 32 per cent of Irish exports still went to the UK, and in the absence of a devaluation, Irish competitiveness in the important British market would be too severely compromised.

After the collapse of the EMS, it became clear that a regime of 'fixed but flexible' exchange rates is an oxymoron. Without a viable middle way between floating exchange rates and a single currency, the EU opted for the latter. The schedule was set out in the Treaty of Maastricht, signed in 1992 and ratified the following year. As the decade progressed, it became increasingly clear that Ireland would qualify to join the euro. At the same time, the Single European Act came into effect in 1992, breaking down many of the remaining barriers to the movement of goods and people among the countries of the EU.

The more open common market, and the prospect of a single currency, made Ireland a viable, even attractive, destination for US investors aiming to serve the EU as a whole. By then, Ireland's public finances were under control, there was a substantial pool of available, well-educated, English-speaking workers, and a regime of low corporate taxation and industrial subsidies firmly in place. The inflow of highly productive export-oriented labour-using investment, particularly in pharmaceuticals and information technology, had surprisingly large knock-on effects, boosting the large services sector, and raising employment substantially for the first time in a generation. The nature and causes of the first boom, which ran from about 1994 to 2000, are discussed in more detail in Chapter 7. By 2000, Ireland had caught up economically with its peers in the EU, and the country became the poster child for the benefits of economic integration.

1999 to 2012: Life in the Euro Zone

Ireland easily met the criteria for graduating to the euro, and the exchange rate was locked at €0.787564 per Irish pound on 1 January 1999. Ireland, like the states of the USA, no longer has the option of an independent monetary policy. This is not a radical break from the past; an independent monetary policy was not possible when the Irish pound was linked with sterling (1826–1979), and was severely circumscribed during the period of the EMS. The main advantage of a common currency is lower transaction costs, and perhaps a steadier hand at the tiller; the cost is a reduced ability to respond when faced by an external shock or domestic rigidity – for instance, if export prices fall or wages fail to adjust.

By 2000 the unemployment rate had fallen to 4 per cent, the wave of American foreign direct investment had subsided, and one might have expected the boom to end – but it did not! The explanation follows from Ireland's accession to the euro. Prior to the single currency, credit was more expensive in Ireland than in Germany or France, in part because of currency risk; with the advent of the euro, interest rates were essentially equalised across the euro zone, as money flowed from (low-interest) Germany to (high-interest) Ireland. Irish banks, flush with funds, lent freely; households, increasingly accustomed to higher wages and lower unemployment, took on more loans; the government expanded tax incentives for housing; and inexperienced Irish regulators believed that this time was different. The result was a housing boom, sustained by a large inflow of workers from Eastern Europe (mainly Poland and Lithuania).

As early as 2000 the IMF warned that property prices in Ireland were too high and that a housing bubble was in the making; the growing chorus of warnings went unheeded, and house prices doubled between 2000 and 2006 before stabilising in 2007. The bubble burst in 2008, and by 2010 prices in Dublin were less than half of their peak level; by the end of 2012 a fifth of commercial loans and more than a quarter of all mortgages were in arrears. By 2009 the major banks were insolvent, and only survived because of a government guarantee to creditors, which in turn required the government to borrow heavily to pay the bill.

The collapse of the housing bubble coincided with a serious recession – world GDP fell by 0.6 per cent in 2009, the first decline since the end of World War II – and this ended any prospects of a rapid recovery for the Irish economy. By late 2010 the government was obliged to accept a €85 billion rescue package from the IMF and EU, with its accompanying strictures on taxation and spending. With little or no economic growth (see Chapter 7 for details), unemployment rose sharply, as did emigration. The process of recovery was slow, in part because fiscal transfers among the states of the euro zone are unresponsive to economic shocks – in contrast with the states of the USA, where a recession in a single state is substantially offset by lower tax payments to, and more receipts from, the federal government.

A mixture of fiscal restraint, falling house prices and wage reductions have helped restore Ireland's competitiveness, the US economy has largely recovered, exports have rebounded, and job creation was strong enough in 2013 to reduce the unemployment rate markedly and prompt substantial immigration. The banking system is no longer in intensive care, but the government has acquired a large debt, which will constrain its actions for some time to come.

6 CONCLUDING OBSERVATIONS

The significant events of Irish economic history have been marshalled to support a number of different interpretations.

Nationalists emphasise the ways in which the links between the Irish economy and Britain have worked to Ireland's detriment. Writers in this vein have stressed the damage caused by the plantations, the Navigation, Cattle and Woollen Acts, the solid growth during the years of Grattan's Parliament, the lowering of tariffs in the years after the Act of Union, the ineffectiveness of relief efforts during later years of the Famine, and the costs of Ireland's inability to protect its industry from British goods during the second half of the nineteenth century. This approach has typically been used to lead to the conclusion that Ireland would be better off economically with independence.

Support for the nationalist interpretation waxes and wanes with the performance of the economy of the Republic. When independence did not bring a dramatic improvement in growth, and when the import substitution policy of the 1930s created an inefficient industrial base which stagnated in the 1950s, the advantages of independence came to be seen as less obvious, especially as Northern Ireland appeared to be prospering at the time. However, from 1960 to 1980, when growth in the Republic was faster, and dependence on the British market reduced, the nationalist view became respectable again, despite, or perhaps because of, the dismantling of tariff protection.

Outside the Irish context, this view is comparable to the approach of *dependency theorists*, who emphasise the harmful results of links between peripheral areas and the major industrial powers. The main weaknesses of this approach are that it has tended to neglect the potentially beneficial effects of links with the metropolitan area, and has overestimated the ability of independent states to make wise decisions, as exemplified for instance by Ireland's disastrous fiscal experiment in the late 1970s.

Membership of the EU has not made the nationalist view completely obsolete, but it has been stripped of its anglophobic character. There remains space for a nationalism, or perhaps localism would be a better term, to counteract the tendencies of the EU to regulate from the centre what would be better done at a much lower level of government.

Marxists stress the role of the conflict between different classes within the country. Thus, for instance, the Famine and subsequent emigration swept away the greater part of the rural proletariat, paving the way for the emergence of a rural bourgeoisie, which in due course wrested control over land from the aristocracy and provided the leaders of a conservative independent state. In this view the labouring class, whether agricultural or industrial, never achieved enough strength to effect significant social or economic change, and the indigenous capitalist class failed in its mission of creating a dynamic industrial base, thereby forfeiting its right to the perquisites that it continues to enjoy. The conclusion most commonly drawn is that the state needs to take a more active role in filling this entrepreneurial function. Foreign investment by footloose companies is seen as conveying few benefits.

The Marxist view fails to explain why largely nonclass conflicts, such as that in Northern Ireland, can persist. It typically overstates the ability of the state and public enterprises to create sustainable jobs; once this prop falls, it is not clear what prescription for economic growth remains.

In reaction against the weaknesses of the nationalist and Marxist interpretations, most recent writers have tended to view economic events as having a significant life of their own, being 'substantially independent of political and constitutional issues'. Hence the roles of the Cattle Acts, or the Act of Union, or the replacement of tenant farmers by smallholders, are seen as minor. Economic actors are believed to redirect their energies fairly quickly, and seize the available opportunities. This perspective, epitomised in the large body of revisionist writings of Cullen, could be labelled the *classical economics approach*. In the hands of a new generation of economists this approach to history has become increasingly quantitative.

This view too has its faults, in that it can go too far in neglecting political events and institutional arrangements. In the words of Douglass North, 'institutional change shapes the way societies evolve through time and hence is the key to understanding historical change.' North originally believed that inefficient institutions would be weeded out over time, but in his more recent writings he is less sanguine about this prospect. The *institutional approach* complements rather than supplants the classical economics view, and we have drawn on these two perspectives in writing this chapter.

In the mid nineteenth century Denmark was substantially better off than Ireland, despite facing a similar external environment – both depended on the British market, and both were open to free trade. O'Rourke suggests that Denmark maintained its lead, and (unlike Ireland) expanded its population because it had successfully introduced land reform a century before Ireland, and, perhaps more important, achieved universal literacy much sooner.

The most interesting lessons from Irish economic history are about growth strategies. Economic growth comes from a multitude of sources such as new technology, capital investment, education and training, land reclamation, enterprise, shifting prices, higher aggregate demand and chance. However, these are only the raw ingredients, and must be combined to sustain growth. It is easy to see these ingredients at work. The new technologies of the potato, railways, power weaving and computers have all been influential. Capital spending is essential at all times, although rarely needs to be above a fifth of GDP. Higher levels of education and improved training have boosted labour productivity. Chance brought the potato blight and two world wars. Land reclamation helped fend off famine in the early nineteenth century. Enterprise was at the heart of the introduction of shipbuilding in Belfast. A secular increase in wheat prices radically changed agriculture in the eighteenth century. Low aggregate demand reined in growth in the 1950s.

Recognising the role of these elements is important, but holds few lessons. The study of growth *strategies* is more illuminating. The policy of laissez faire need not guarantee growth, as experience from 1815 to 1850 demonstrates. Nor does a strategy of import substitution necessarily fare better, for while it may have been helpful in the short run in the 1930s, protection left a legacy of inefficient industry in the 1950s. An approach which favours agriculture-led development, such as that followed by the Free State in the 1920s, may succeed in raising real incomes, but given the small size of the agricultural sector (2 per cent of GDP in 2012) it is no longer a realistic option. An industrialisation strategy based on attracting foreign capital also has some advantages, but is expensive to implement, and risks leaving a country more vulnerable to decisions outside its control.

As a practical matter Ireland has limited room for pursuing independent economic policies. Fiscal restraint is needed because persistent expansionary fiscal policy does not work well in a small open economy, as the experiment of 1978 to 1987 shows. With the euro in place, monetary policy is not an option. Industrial policy is increasingly circumscribed by the rules that have applied since 1993 to the Single European Market. Recognising the need for greater efficiency, the country has privatised or closed down several state-owned enterprises. Ireland now has only a little more autonomy than a typical state of the United States.

That leaves a narrower and more difficult field for local economic policy. The focus has shifted to the factors needed to maintain 'competitiveness' – what Michael Porter calls the 'microeconomic foundations of prosperity'. This includes bending to such tasks as gearing society to produce entrepreneurs, vitalising indigenous enterprise, providing adequate and appropriate education and training, evaluating public investment more thoroughly, introducing flexibility into the labour market, reducing the disincentives to do unskilled jobs, and fostering competition among firms. Affluence requires efficiency in the public arena – in the provision of services and the formulation and targeting of policy – in addition to efficiency by businesses.

Since wages in Ireland are closely linked with those in Britain and the EU, once individuals have been equipped with education, economic policy has limited influence on the standard of living they will enjoy in Ireland. What it can still influence, perhaps more thoroughly than was commonly believed just a few years ago, is the number who enjoy that standard of living in Ireland rather than elsewhere.

Suggestions for Further Reading

The literature on Irish economic history is already enormous. A few suggestions for further reading are given here, and much of the information in this chapter comes from these sources.

General History:
R. Foster, *Modern Ireland 1600–1972*, Allen Lane, London 1988.
J. Lee, *Ireland 1912–1985*, Cambridge University Press, Cambridge 1989.
F. Lyons, *Ireland Since the Famine*, Weidenfeld and Nicolson, London 1971.

Economic and Social History:
R. Crotty, *Irish Agricultural Production*, Cork University Press, Cork 1966.
L. Cullen, *An Economic History of Ireland Since 1660*, Batsford, London 1972.
M. Daly, *Social and Economic History of Ireland Since 1800*, Educational Company, Dublin 1981.
K. Kennedy, T. Giblin and D. McHugh, *The Economic Development of Ireland in the Twentieth Century*, Routledge, London 1988.
J. Mokyr, *Why Ireland Starved*, Allen and Unwin, London 1983.
C. Ó Gráda, *The Great Irish Famine*, Macmillan, London 1989.
C. Ó Gráda, *Ireland: A New Economic History 1780-1939*, Oxford University Press, Oxford 1995.
C. Ó Gráda, *A Rocky Road: The Irish Economy Since the 1920s*, Manchester University Press, Manchester 1997.
K. O'Rourke, *Late 19th Century Denmark in an Irish Mirror: Land Tenure, Homogeneity and the Roots of Danish Success*, Working Paper, Department of Economics, Trinity College Dublin 2005.

CHAPTER 2

Policy Objectives and Competitiveness for a Regional Economy

*Dermot McAleese**

1 INTRODUCTION

The policy objectives of a regional economy and a national economy are very similar. Both are concerned with achieving higher living standards, full employment, a fair distribution of income, and economic stability. Both worry about competitiveness. And the balance of payments has implications for both the region and the nation state, though as we shall see these implications are far more transparent in the case of a nation.

The main difference between a region and a nation is the *policy context*. A region has no independent currency and no control over its monetary policy. Its trade policy is determined by outside forces and balance of payments issues have to be radically reinterpreted. It has limited discretion in the use of fiscal policy. Seen in this context, a region's approach to policy has a dual dimension. First, it has to consider how to use its limited influence on policy developments where the key policy decisions are being made. In the case of the Republic of Ireland, this might be Brussels, Frankfurt or Strasbourg, depending on the issue being decided; in Northern Ireland, London would figure prominently. Second, in areas where they do possess policy autonomy, regions must ensure that this degree of policy discretion is used effectively.

As Ireland becomes increasingly integrated into the European economy, the Republic is losing many of the trappings of a national economy. The completion of the single market and the establishment of economic and monetary union constitute important turning points in this respect. Hence, the focus in this chapter is on the policy objectives from the perspective of a regional economy. This perspective is of special interest at present because the Irish Republic is a comparative newcomer to regional status, unlike, say, Northern Ireland or Scotland, and it has had to acclimatise itself rapidly to the economic limitations of regional dependence. At the same time, as a nation state, the Republic could, if it managed its economic affairs well, exert more influence at the centre of European policymaking than many European regions of much larger size.

The plan of this chapter is as follows. In Section 2 we explain why output growth is regarded as the primary objective of economic policy and how it is related to employment. In Section 3 the limitations of this objective are analysed by taking account of the complex linkages between advances in material living standards and human welfare in the broad sense. Section 4 examines the goal of equity and the relationship between economic growth and happiness. In Section 5 we discuss various dimensions of economic stability, including price stability, as objectives of policy. Competitiveness is discussed in Section 6; the search for ways of restoring competitiveness has become the *leitmotif* of economic policy in recent years. Section 7 concludes the chapter.

2 GROWTH AND EMPLOYMENT

Introduction

Rapid, sustained growth is a primary objective of economic policy. Fast economic growth means higher living standards, and is associated with an expanding and dynamic business environment. Slow or zero growth is perceived as stagnation. Confronted with the record of a slow-growing economy, we instinctively ask what has gone wrong. Policymakers are always on the lookout for advice about ways of promoting economic growth. An advance in living standards is something that most people want, enjoy and expect to be delivered.

Economic growth is desired for many different reasons. Affluent countries see growth as an essential contributor to ever-higher living standards, full employment and healthy government finances. They also perceive faster growth as a way of maintaining their economic and military position relative to other countries. Not long ago, Americans worried about being overtaken by the Japanese; and the Japanese in turn worry about their economic standing relative to China. By contrast, governments of developing countries see faster economic growth as a means of escaping from poverty and material want, and in particular from the vulnerability and sense of inferiority that, rightly or wrongly, attaches to low economic development. For them, 'catching up' on the living standards of the affluent countries is a key policy imperative. All countries appear to view growth as an indicator that resources are being employed efficiently, and faster-growing economies are often taken as models for slower-growing economies to copy and learn from.

Growth and Efficiency

Economics generally endorses the idea that efficiency and growth are related. Most fast-growing economies are efficient, and most efficient economies tend to grow faster than economies of similar size and scale that are inefficient. The meaning of efficiency and growth in an economic sense is illustrated in Figure 2.1.

Imagine an economy that produces only two goods, X and Y. We set up a list of combinations of X and Y that the economy could produce if its resources were utilised in the most efficient way. In other words, for any given level of X, we find out the maximum amount of Y that can be produced in the economy. The various combinations of X and Y derived in this way are known as the *production frontier*. The production frontier is TT in Figure 2.1.

Figure 2.1 The Production Frontier

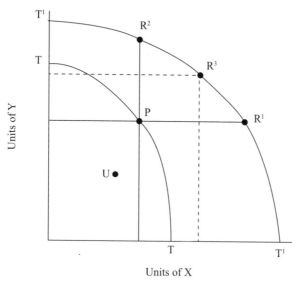

Units of X

Provided production takes place on the production frontier, where resources are fully employed, more of good X implies less of good Y. In other words, in order to produce more of X, scarce resources have to be transferred from industry Y to industry X. One can go further and define the cost of X as the amount of Y that has to be sacrificed in order to produce one extra unit of X. This is called *the opportunity cost of X*. The opportunity cost concept has many practical applications and serves as a reminder of the obvious point that 'free' education, 'free' transport and other 'free' goods and services offered by the state are not costless. The resources used to supply these goods and services could have been used to produce cars or holidays instead. Hence the well-known maxim that in economics there is no such thing as a free lunch.

An *efficient* economy is one that operates on its production frontier (i.e. at a point such as P in Figure 2.1). At any point below the production frontier, society could have more of X and Y simply by moving to the frontier. Thus, by definition, a point such as U is not an efficient outcome. At that point, some productive resources are either being used inefficiently or, worse, not being used at all. At a point such as P it is not possible to make one person better off without leaving the other worse off. This condition applies to all such points on the production frontier and hence all are efficient. The choice between these points then is a question of distributional justice (see later).

Why Growth is Important

Over time, growth, or pushing out the production frontier, will be the main force in determining living standards. A GNP growth rate of 4 per cent maintained for 17 years will result in a doubling of the original GNP level. Even a more modest 2 per cent growth rate will translate into a doubling of living standards every 33 years. Figures such as these indicate the potential gains from raising the growth rate. In terms of Figure 2.1, outward shifts in the production frontier will over time dominate the effects of movement to a given frontier from off-frontier points such as U. However, since countries that are efficient normally grow faster than those that are inefficient, the objectives of efficiency and growth are in practice complementary.

To illustrate the benefits of growth, we can depict it as a series of outward shifts in the production frontier, such as that represented by the move from TT to T^1T^1. The T^1T^1 frontier shows the expanded range of options growth provides to society. Economic growth is a 'good thing', in so far as it enables the consumers in the economy to enjoy:

- more of X and the same amount of Y – at a point such as R^1;
- more of Y and the same amount of X – at a point such as R^2;
- more of both X and Y – at a point like R^3;
- any other desired combination of X and Y – at any point on the expanded frontier.

Growth extends the range of consumption possibilities, and people choose between these different possibilities through the market system, supplemented by government intervention.

The production frontier can be shifted outwards by two forces: first, increases in the *quantity* of productive factors and, second, improvements in the *productivity* of these factors. Since we are primarily concerned with growth per person rather than total growth, it is common to abstract from the increase in growth that is attributable solely to the increase in the population. Growth in living standards, or GNP per person, depends on (see also Chapter 7):

- the *amount* of productive factors at each person's disposal (the more machinery and the more hectares of land at the disposal of a worker the more will be produced per worker);
- the *productivity* of these factors of production (better machinery, better seeds and fertilisers, better technology);
- the knowledge, skills and motivation of the workforce (see Chapters 6 and 13).

Growth and Employment

Full employment means that there is work available for everyone willing to seek it at prevailing pay levels. This is obviously a desirable objective of economic policy. There is a strong empirical association between full employment and economic growth and this explains why one of the major perceived benefits of faster growth is that it provides more job opportunities and reduces the unemployment rate.

Yet in strict logic there is no reason why growth should be a necessary condition for full employment. To see this, go back to Figure 2.1. Assume a situation where TT is fixed (i.e. zero long-run growth). At point U, there is unemployment. As noted above, this is an inefficient point, indicating waste of resources. The solution is to implement policies that address the unemployment problem. As more people are employed, we move towards a point like P on the production frontier TT.

The necessary policies might take any of the forms outlined in Chapter 6. Hence full employment can be regarded as an indicator of efficiency. In moving from U to P, there will be an increase in output and therefore some faster economic growth will be recorded. But once attained, there is no reason why full employment should not be maintained at P. Faster growth at that stage makes no difference one way or another. Hence the 'classical' conclusion: *full employment is always attainable irrespective of the level of output or of the growth rate of output.*

Intuition and empirical fact, however, suggest that full employment is easier to attain when an economy is growing. Also, when growth declines, unemployment rises. For example, South Korea, long used to near zero unemployment rates, found itself facing unemployment of an unprecedented 7 per cent following the 1997–98 currency crisis. In a similar manner, Ireland's unemployment rate rose from 4 per cent to over 14 per cent following the post-2008 property crash and the collapse in its GDP. The amount of unemployment associated with the fall in output between 2008 and 2013 has varied across EU countries, with Greece (8 to 27 per cent), Spain (11 to 27 per cent) and Cyprus (4 to 16 per cent) being the most markedly affected. In Ireland's case, the collapse in the construction industry, an exceptionally labour-intensive activity, was a key factor in generating job losses. Thus, growth is desired not just for its own sake but for the indirect benefits it provides, such as helping to keep unemployment low.

Growth of GNP per Person as a Policy Objective

The focus on income per person rather than total income (GNP) as the policy objective has profoundly important implications.[1] Suppose one had to choose between three growth profiles as indicated in Table 2.1.

Total GNP is increasing fastest in situation A. If total GNP were the policy objective, A would be the preferred situation. If GNP per person were the policy objective, situation C would be chosen. Ranking A and B would be more difficult. The only difference between them is that there are more people around in A to share a given GNP per person growth rate. Suppose these additional people happened to be immigrants from Africa. The economy's faster growth means that they can be accommodated without impairing the average living standards of the existing population, while at the same time the immigrants' living standards are much higher in the host country than they were at home. Also if the host country had a large national debt, this debt could be shared among a larger population. This would suggest a preference for A over B. But there may be other effects to consider, relating to the broader social impact of immigration and effects on income distribution. An influx of unskilled immigrants, for instance, would tend to reduce earnings of native unskilled workers, but would tend to benefit the middle and upper class generally by reducing the cost of unskilled labour that these more affluent people employ (such as domestic help, catering staff, construction workers). Clearly personal values and one's position in the income distribution ranking influence preferences between the various growth and population combinations.

Table 2.1 Growth: Illustrative Example

Growth Profile	Total GNP (% p.a.)	Population (% p.a.)	GNP per person (% p.a.)
A	5	3	2
B	4	2	2
C	3	0	3

In the above example, population growth is treated as if it were independent of GNP growth. A crucial question is whether and how population growth interacts with GNP and the consequential effect on living standards per person. Take, for example, a country such as Uganda with an annual population growth of 3.2 per cent. Its population has grown from 19m in 1990 to 36m in 2012 and it is estimated that it will reach 60m in 2030. Output growth of over 3 per cent will be needed simply to prevent living standards from falling.

Many argue that population growth at that rate has a negative effect on total GNP growth and hence can depress income per person. An expanding population of young people and large family size reduces national savings and consequently limits the volume of investment. Simultaneously, a burgeoning population puts pressure on a country's natural resources. If the rate of population growth interacts negatively with GNP per person, a vicious circle of economic decline can be generated. At the other end of the spectrum, excessively low population growth can be equally problematic. The 'greying' of Europe's population has led to concerns about the financial viability of pension schemes, escalating medical costs, ability to finance public debt and an erosion of social dynamism and innovation. Considerations such as these reinforce the case for using GNP per person, not total GNP, as the relevant policy objective.

Affluent households tend to have smaller families than poor households. Likewise, developed countries have lower population growth than poor countries.

Thus, since 1980, population has grown in higher-income countries by only 0.6 per cent per annum, compared with 2 per cent in low-income countries. Ireland too has experienced the same phenomenon. As Chapter 6 will show, with increasing prosperity its birth rate has declined. But have we become better off because of a low birth rate, or is the birth rate low because we are more affluent? There is no definitive answer to this question, but many governments in less developed countries now believe that lower population growth would help to raise living standards and have introduced strong family planning programmes to encourage smaller family size. Irish governments have never gone as far in this direction as governments in developing countries such as India and China. One reason for this is that Irish people, unlike many in the present developing world, had the option of emigration.

Migration and Growth
The impact of emigration on living standards has long been a controversial topic. Some argued that a larger population would have raised living standards in Ireland. Patrick Pearse believed that the country could support a population of 30 million. With a bigger population would come larger domestic markets, greater economies of scale, higher productivity and, eventually, more growth. Higher living standards and a more dynamic local community would in turn induce skilled and talented Irish people to stay at home, thus reinforcing faster growth. This is a rather rosy view of what might have happened to living standards in the absence of emigration. Demographers, however, agree that if there had been no emigration since 1841, the population in the Republic would be in the region of 20 million instead of 4 million. Some argued that a growing population was a good thing in itself, irrespective of its effects on material welfare.

An opposite viewpoint was that emigration acted as a welcome safety valve, enabling the amount of land and capital per person remaining in Ireland to be increased, with beneficial effects on Irish productivity. At the same time Irish emigrants were able to find more productive employment and acquire valuable work experience and skills abroad. A win–win outcome for all parties, just as predicted in John Kenneth Galbraith's famous dictum that 'emigration helps those who leave, the country they go to, and the people they leave behind'.[2]

Underlying this approach was the idea that the primary focus of economic policy should be the living standards of Irish people wherever they happened to live, not just of those residing in the Irish state. Thus the policy objective should be to encourage Irish people to go to where their productivity would be highest and their material rewards greatest. According to this logic, Ireland's access to the comparatively prosperous labour markets of the USA, the UK, Australia and Canada has been a tremendous boon and the Irish government's main responsibility is to provide education to its citizens and equip them to make maximum use of the opportunities open to them at home *and* abroad.

During Ireland's boom the focus of interest changed to the effects of immigration rather than emigration. For the first time in centuries foreigners came each year to work in Ireland. At a broad level, this change in demographic pattern was benign. Higher output growth involved both significant net immigration *and* an improvement in living standards. Now the pendulum has swung back and Ireland has reverted to being a country of net emigration. At a broader societal level migration, inward and outward, brings its own set of problems and opportunities that the policymaker must not overlook. Paul Collier, in a recent major study of global migration, concluded that the question is not really whether migration per se is good or bad, but rather how much migration there should be and who benefits from it. In his view, 'moderate' migration is mostly advantageous, but 'runaway', or what used to be called 'catastrophic', migration can result in severe economic losses due to the breakdown of social solidarity and trust in the host countries.[3]

3 GNP GROWTH AND HUMAN WELFARE

Optimal Growth, not Maximum Growth

While growth is a primary policy objective, it does not follow that the aim is simply to *maximise* growth. One reason for this is that growth involves a degree of intergenerational distribution. By cutting down on its consumption and investing more, any present generation can raise economic growth rates. Japan's average investment/GNP ratio during the period 1960–95 exceeded the investment ratio in the EU and the USA by more than 10 percentage points (31 per cent as against 22 per cent and 18 per cent respectively). Not surprisingly, Japan's growth rate of 6 per cent per year was twice the rate of most industrial countries. China and some other fast-growing emerging economies put aside as much as 50 per cent of their GDP for investment. By investing so much, the present generation sacrifices its material welfare in the interests of future generations. But for how long can, and should, this process be maintained? Clearly different societies place a different premium on the future relative to present living standards. Authoritarian societies are often able to achieve extraordinarily rapid growth, but at serious cost to the people who had to produce the necessary saving.

Another reason for not choosing maximum growth as a policy objective relates to its potential undesirable spillover effects. These became apparent in the early 2000s in Ireland. Traffic congestion worsened markedly; water quality declined; hospital resources were overstretched. Another spillover effect was the inflow of job seekers from abroad. Initially the decline in emigration was widely welcomed. No less welcome was the inflow of former emigrants returning to a buoyant domestic market. These immigrants helped to sustain the boom by moderating pay growth and plugging vital gaps in labour supply.

Generally there is no problem with immigrants of similar nationality and background to the host country. Difficulties arose, however, when unskilled immigrants of more diverse background entered the picture. Also there were income distribution effects to consider. Middle- and upper-income groups gained from the entry of the unskilled into the Irish labour market, but those at the lower end of the income profile tended to lose out. Finally, excessively rapid growth can often lead to inflation and to escalating property prices. Inflation can cause many problems, as we shall see below.

One important, intangible benefit of growth is the influence and power that it brings with it. We can learn from the dominance of the USA in the world economy how economic success and political and military power are closely linked. Also faster growth facilitates adjustment in a country's productive structure (from import-competing to export activities, for example) and enables desirable social change. A further advantage is that economic growth tends to boost a country's international reputation. Successful countries are listened to with respect. Economic success engenders a virtuous circle and a palpable air of self-confidence, as Ireland's experience during the Celtic Tiger boom demonstrated. Economic decline since 2008 has led to the opposite: a severe reputational loss, and exposure to criticism and mockery; all deeply discouraging to a country that had become used to taking praise and admiration for economic achievements as a matter of course.

These advantages and disadvantages must be weighed in determining a country's optimum growth rate. Choosing an optimum growth path requires careful consideration of the broader socio-political factors mentioned above, as well as of the limitations of GNP as an indicator of welfare, a subject to which we turn next.

Three Standard Limitations of Using GNP
So far we have discussed economic growth as if growth, as measured by GNP in the numerator, were the main objective of economic policy. But it is well known that GNP is an inadequate indicator of human welfare. As one critic expressed it:

> The Gross National Product does not allow for the health of our children, the quality of their education or the joy of their play. It does not include the beauty of our poetry or the strength of our marriages; the intelligence of our public debate or the integrity of our public officials. It measures neither our wisdom nor our learning, neither our compassion nor our devotion to our country; it measures everything, in short, except that which makes life worthwhile.[4]

GNP does not account for many of the things that make for the good life and some items are included in GNP that may worsen rather than improve human welfare. Three specific criticisms of GNP have been made on this account. First, that it puts no value on leisure and the household economy. Second, that it takes inadequate account of environmental issues such as pollution and resource depletion. Third, some items are recorded as outputs although in reality they are inputs or costs. Also some outputs that add to quality of life – such as access to a good public infrastructure – are difficult to value properly in money terms. In Section 4, we consider two further factors that bear on the relationship between material growth and welfare: income distribution; and the elusive question of the relationship between growth and happiness.

Leisure and the Household Economy

Leisure is a good like any other, so theoretically it should be included alongside other goods and services when choosing growth as a policy objective. The difficulty arises because of the way growth is measured. For various reasons, changes in leisure hours are not taken account of in the GNP statistics. Hence if GNP growth is rising but everyone is working harder and longer hours, the net improvement in human welfare may well be much lower than appears. In 2009, the average American worked 1,768 hours per year; the average German 1,390 hours per year. Americans have more goods and more GNP per head, but they have miserably short vacations. Irish employees work 1,549 hours per year (see Chapter 6).

A feature of rich societies is that employees are well paid. They are well paid because they are productive and that in turn means that the opportunity cost of leisure increases as economies become more prosperous. Hence the widely observed phenomenon that people in affluent societies tend to be more harried and harassed, and have less time for talk and a chat, than their counterparts in poorer countries. The process of economic growth inherently tends to accentuate this problem.

To take another example, suppose that a person takes a second job. This makes large inroads into leisure time. The GNP measure includes all the output generated but ignores the welfare cost of the loss of leisure. Human welfare has presumably increased as a result of this decision – otherwise the second job would not have been taken – but the net increase in welfare will be much less than the increase in GNP indicates. The individual is likely to be more stressed and to have less time for enjoying domestic life.

GNP includes only transactions that involve a monetary exchange. Hence leisure is excluded. But this is not the only excluded output. Housework done by members of a household, being unpaid, is not recorded in GNP. As members of the household enter the workforce and household tasks such as repair, maintenance, care of children and the elderly, are passed over to paid professionals, GNP rises. Yet all that is happening is that these functions have been shifted from the traditional realm of the household and the community to the monetised economy. Welfare has presumably increased, since the decision to work outside the home was taken voluntarily. But the increase in GNP will grossly exaggerate the increase in welfare. These examples help to explain why economic growth will bring fewer real benefits than appears.

Growth and the Environment

Conventional GNP measures do not deal satisfactorily with environmental and ecological factors. Higher GNP has implications for the environment on several levels that fail to be recorded in the statistics. Three aspects, in particular, merit attention: (a) higher levels of pollution; (b) depletion of natural resources; and (c) global warming.

First, no deduction is made in GNP statistics for the higher levels of pollution and chemical waste that often accompany economic growth. Attempts have been made to compute 'green' national accounts that allow for these negative effects, but there is as yet no consensus on how the pollution effects should be computed.

Second, depletion of a nation's stock of non-renewable resources such as oil and coal is not accounted for in GNP calculations. Even in the case of renewable resources, problems can arise if economic growth leads to their being exploited in excess of the replacement rate. For example, the serious decline in the water table caused by increased economic activity in the countries bordering the Aral Sea, in Northern China and in Israel-occupied Palestine is ignored in the national accounts.

Third, economic growth is associated with deforestation, change in land use and most notable of all with burning fossil fuels. As a result the concentration of greenhouse gases has risen alarmingly – the current level is higher than at any time in the last 650,000 years and there has been an accompanying rise in world temperatures. Already, an increase of 0.6°C has been recorded since the mid 1970s. A change of this magnitude may appear small, but its effects over time could be enormous (see Chapter 10). Long time lags between today's greenhouse gas emissions and future damage to climate and the environment mean that the adverse effects will not be reflected in GNP for many years. Although Ireland might not be as badly affected by global warming as other countries, we are expected in the interests of EU solidarity to pay carbon taxes (see Chapter 4), to restrain energy consumption and, in short, to become much more 'green' than before (see Chapter 10).

Inputs Recorded as Outputs

By a perverse quirk, the cost of moderating the adverse effects of pollution is sometimes included in GNP as an output (service provided) instead of as an input (a production cost to society). For example, the medical attention given to a victim of air pollution will be recorded in the national accounts as an addition to GNP instead of as a deduction from it. This is part of a more general criticism of GNP relating to inputs misclassified as outputs. For example, military spending is included as a positive contributor to GNP, even if that spending is undertaken at the behest of reckless political leaders and with disregard of the needs of the people. Likewise, the inclusion of expenditure on crime prevention as an output in GNP has been criticised. To be sure, such spending could represent improved living standards in so far as the community obtains greater security and more orderly traffic; but it could equally be a sign of diminished quality of the social environment and hence a cost of securing higher GNP (e.g. if more police were needed to maintain the same level of security and traffic movement).

A final example relates to spending on information systems and some types of research and development (R&D) in the private sector. In the EU this is treated as an input, whereas the US Bureau of Economic Analysis considers this spending as investment, hence part of output. In 2013, a new investment class called 'intellectual property products' was created, spending on which is classified as investment. The effects on GDP are far from trivial. In the USA GDP was revised upwards by $560 billion, or 3.6 per cent of GDP as a result of these classification changes.

GNP and Human Development Indicators

Making growth in GNP per capita a primary objective is really shorthand for something much more complex. In evaluating a country's economic performance, account must be taken of the quality of the lifestyle enjoyed by the population as well as the quantity of goods and services consumed. Imagine two countries. One has a lower GNP per person than the other, but it happens to have a healthier, more literate and less crime-ridden society. In this instance, GNP is an inaccurate measure of the relative welfare of the two countries, and making GNP growth a primary policy objective may not be an appropriate response. Instead of economic growth, can we find a way of measuring human development and making it the primary policy objective?

In an effort to develop a more comprehensive socioeconomic measure than GNP, the United Nations has developed the Human Development Index (HDI). The HDI is a composite index and consists of a weighted average of data on GDP/GNP per person, life expectancy and educational attainment of the population (see also Chapter 7). An adjusted HDI is also computed that takes account of income distribution.

As one would expect, such exercises lead to some changes in ranking. The 2013 *Human Development Report* reveals an HDI ranking higher than the GDP per person ranking for New Zealand, Australia, Germany and Ireland; the opposite is the case for Singapore, China and South Africa.[5] Ireland was placed seventh of 186 countries in the HDI league; a position that flatters and is unlikely to last. By adding to the list of indicators, and measuring them in different ways, more radical alterations in ranking can be computed. Experimentation and analysis along these lines is continuing.

Yet the limitations of GNP as a measure of welfare must not be exaggerated. For all its defects, a higher output per person gives society the *capacity* to achieve a better quality of life. This explains the close positive correlation between the HDI and total output per person. There is also a strong positive correlation between GNP per capita growth and some important empirical measures of the quality of life. Countries with higher GNP per capita tend to be healthier and better educated than those with lower GNP per capita. They also tend to be better policed and more secure in a financial and physical sense.

London is safer than Lagos, Manila or São Paolo. Affluent Tokyo is one of the safest cities in the world. While many forms of recorded crime have increased since 1945, prosperity has tended to result in a reduction in crime and disorder. During the nineteenth century, industrial nations became less crime-ridden as they became more industrialised. Indeed, as pointed out in Chapter 1, these two factors are interrelated: the rule of law and good governance are essential prerequisites of a prosperous market economy.

Faster growth makes it easier to reduce unemployment, to lessen poverty, to improve education and health services and to provide all the other good things that constitute prosperity. There are, of course, negative aspects of growth, such as damage to the environment, erosion of community life and destruction of rural values. Since the birth of the Industrial Revolution in the late eighteenth century, economic growth has had its critics, some of the most trenchant of whom have been economists. The tradition of scepticism, verging on hostility, towards growth remains active to this day. Despite these downsides, governments and those who elect them evidently believe that the positive effects of growth outweigh its negative effects, and both continue to accord it a high priority.

4 EQUITY, INCOME DISTRIBUTION AND HAPPINESS

What is a Fair Distribution of Income?

GNP per person, being an arithmetic average of total output divided by total population, reveals no information about the distribution of resources within a society. It could rise, even though the majority of the population may be getting worse off. For example, if the income of the most affluent one-third of a population rose by €50 billion, and the income of the poorest two-thirds fell by €30 billion, GNP would increase. But does it follow that society as a whole is better off?

Some argue that the long-run sustainability of growth depends on income being shared on an equitable basis. Successful policymaking requires change, and such change can only be achieved if the majority of people believe that they have a stake in the economy and will benefit from its continued growth. But this still leaves open the question of what is meant by sharing income on an equitable basis? Since Chapter 8 is devoted to this topic, a brief outline of the main parameters of this debate will suffice at this stage.

The value judgements underlying modern economics are derived from a philosophy of individualism and liberalism. *Individualism* means that what ultimately counts is the utility every individual attains and that the utility of each individual should be given an equal weight. *Liberalism* signifies that individuals should be free to decide what provides the greatest utility. Individual preferences are taken as given. The task of the economist, in this view, is to devise market structures that will enable individuals to satisfy their preferences, not to pass judgement on them.

Diminishing Marginal Utility Argument

Utility and income must be distinguished in this analysis. The standard assumption underlying economic reasoning is that the marginal utility of income is positive but decreases as income rises. Individuals always prefer a higher income to a lower one, but the intensity of this preference diminishes as income rises. A systematic relationship thus links utility to income. On the face of it, the individualist principle of treating the utility of every person equally, coupled with the assumption of declining marginal utility for all individuals, would imply that the total utility in society is maximised when income is distributed perfectly evenly. But there are two reasons why even committed utilitarians do not push the argument to the extreme of total income equalisation.

First, different people derive different amounts of satisfaction from the same income levels. Material wealth does not matter equally to all. However, utility is difficult (some would say impossible) to measure and compare among individuals. Hence it is simply not practicable to redistribute income on the basis of differences in capacity to enjoy income.

Second, the adverse effect on incentives to work and enterprise of policies to achieve greater equality may, up to a point, lead to a fall in total income. The more we try to increase equity by the redistribution of income, the more we reduce efficiency. In transferring income from the high-income group to the low-income group of society, the authorities levy taxes on income from employment and capital holdings. There can be unwelcome consequences of these taxes. Thus a rise in income tax can discourage work while capital taxes discourage investment and savings. In theory, both effects lead to a reduction in the amount of income available for redistribution. (The empirical importance of these effects varies and is much disputed.) The less well-off in society may well lose rather than benefit from such policies in the long run.

Rawlsian Perspectives

The assumption of decreasing marginal utility implies that when we take a given amount from the rich to give to the poor, the rich will suffer less of a utility loss than the utility gain enjoyed by the poor. If asked to choose between a perfectly equal distribution of income and an unequal distribution *of exactly the same total income*, a utilitarian would favour the equal distribution. Egalitarian predispositions also emerge from other philosophies and schools of thought. Some argue that society should give the utility of the poor greater weight than the utility of the rich on grounds of need, regardless of fine points about diminishing utility. Others, such as the philosopher John Rawls, have pushed this line of judgement to the extreme, arguing that any economic change that increases inequality would be acceptable only if it also makes the poorest better off. This implies that the utility of the worst-off individual takes precedence over all others and that a fair distribution of income is one that makes the poorest person as well off as possible after taking all costs of income transfers into account.[6]

Irish policy objectives have a Rawlsian flavour. Thus governments have tended to prioritise social inclusion as a strategic objective in its own right, the primary objective being to ensure that the benefits of economic growth and related social improvements are shared by all sections of the Irish population. Social inclusion has been a major theme of successive agreements with the social partners (see Chapters 3 and 8). Does the same principle apply in the case of economic decline? Should the losses in income be shared by all sections of the population? Not much explicit consideration has been given to how the losses of economic decline should be shared – until 2008, this type of problem seemed almost inconceivable.

Equality of Opportunity

In opposition to the egalitarian presumption, Robert Nozick argued that the idea of fairness as an outcome cannot be justified. Fairness must be based on rules, not outcomes.[7] Two rules are crucial: (a) the state must enforce laws that establish and protect private property; and (b) private property may be transferred from one person to another *only* by voluntary exchange. Provided markets are open to competition and there are no major market 'failures' (a hugely unrealistic assumption), the resulting distribution of income is, by Nozick's definition, fair. It does not matter how unequally this income is shared provided it is generated by people each of whom voluntarily provided services in exchange for market-determined compensation. The entrepreneur who accepts business risks and has succeeded deserves to be rewarded. Redistribution of these earnings is unjustified. By the same token, in times of recession, business losses are solely the responsibility of the entrepreneur and no government bailouts are justified. From this perspective the key issue is equality of opportunity, not equality of outcome. Indeed, given an uneven distribution of skills, motivation and willingness to work, equal opportunities will inevitably entail unequal outcomes.

Horizontal Equity

So far the discussion has focused on *vertical equity*. This refers to the proposition that differently situated individuals should be treated differently. The well off, in other words, should be taxed in favour of the poor because they can afford to pay these taxes with less pain. *Horizontal equity* is also important. The underlying principle is that people with the same incomes and same circumstances should be treated in a similar fashion. For example, families with the same number of dependants and the same income should pay the same rate of tax (see Chapter 4). Horizontal equity requires that property developers, farmers and PAYE employees should be subject to the same tax unless there is a clear demonstration of different circumstances.

Perceived breaches of this equity principle can be a source of major grievance. By extension, people in different circumstances should not be asked to pay the same taxes. This principle is the motivating force of many income distribution policies (see Chapters 4 and 8). The case for regional grants and incentives, for example, is based on the idea that people in less developed regions do not enjoy the same access to infrastructure as those living in richer regions.

The relationship between equity and growth depends ultimately on individual attitudes and culture. Income inequalities are more acceptable and financial work incentives valued more in some societies than in others (see Chapter 8). The combinations of growth and equity attainable in a competitive market economy full of individualistic materialists will be different from those attainable in a co-operative economy run by and for ascetic altruists! In practice, people have voted with their feet on this question. Comparison of income distribution before and after tax and state benefits shows that major transfers take place from richer to poorer income groups in all industrial economies (see Chapter 8).

Economic Growth and Happiness

In recent years, the research agenda has been widened even further by tackling the much broader question of how GNP per capita is related to happiness. Do higher standards of living, whether defined on broad or narrow definitions of the term, translate into greater happiness? Economists have had a long-abiding interest in this correlation. In the light of our discussion of GNP per capita as a measure of welfare and of the importance of income distribution, the reader will not be surprised that economic research has come up with some complex findings.

A first step is how to measure happiness. The main source of information comes from large-scale citizen surveys that ask individuals to report on how happy they feel, how satisfied they are with their lives and/or with their jobs. Sometimes this is supplemented by data on suicide rates and health status as proxies for (un)happiness. Defined this way, happiness is clearly dependent on many variables other than the level of income – contrary to the much-quoted adage that 'anyone who says money can't buy happiness doesn't know where to shop.' The key methodological challenge is to identify the specific contribution of increases in GNP per capita, and by extension individual income levels, to the happiness index.

Research over the past decade enables us to draw several broad conclusions.[8] First, for any one individual, more income leads to more life satisfaction, everything else being equal. Within a single country, at a given moment in time, those in the highest income groups are happier than those in the lowest income groups. Second, citizens of very poor countries tend to be happier as living standards increase. Studies of former Soviet Union countries, for instance, show a clear positive correlation between income per capita and reported happiness. Third, beyond a certain level of income, the average person does *not* become significantly happier as income increases. At an aggregate level there has been no increase in reported happiness over the past 30 years in Japan and Europe, with, if anything, a decline in the USA. This is called *the Paradox of Happiness*. Fourth, *relative* income matters as much, if not more, to most people than *absolute* income levels. People's definition of what constitutes an 'adequate' level of income seems to depend as much on the level of income enjoyed by their neighbour as on the absolute value of their own income (see Chapter 8). Fifth, virtually all studies show that being unemployed has a strongly negative effect on happiness. Joblessness depresses well-being more than any other single characteristic including divorce and separation. Not only those who are made redundant suffer, but the spread of job insecurity lowers welfare among those still in employment. For this reason, those working in the private sector tend to be affected more strongly by economic downturns than those working in the public sector.

In Ireland, too, the relationship between happiness (measured as percentage of the population who described themselves as 'very satisfied with their life') and material welfare is decidedly weak. The annual *Eurobarometer* survey showed that 40 per cent of Irish people fell into the very satisfied 'happy' category in 1980. There is no evidence of the proportion of happy people rising since then, notwithstanding the huge increase in material income. Curiously, even after the trials and tribulations of the economy and society post 2007, Irish people were still ranked eighth in the EU-27 in terms of life satisfaction, according to the 2011 *Eurobarometer* survey. A surprising 88 per cent of those surveyed described themselves as 'very satisfied' or 'fairly satisfied' with life. That state of satisfaction went hand in hand with a grim assessment of the situation of the national economy – 84 per cent (compared with an EU average of 26 per cent) described the national economic situation as 'very bad', and 72 per cent considered that the impact of the crisis on the job market was likely to get worse.

One element on the happiness spectrum *did*, however, change. The number of people who were acutely *dis*satisfied with their life declined consistently since 1990. The fall in Ireland's unemployment since that time was most likely a key factor in this development. Hence, to the extent that fast economic growth has helped to reduce unemployment, we can conclude that economic growth in Ireland may not have added much to the happiness of already happy people, but it made those at the bottom of the happiness league feel less dissatisfied. A recent study shows that, as unemployment has risen, dissatisfaction has increased, though to a less pronounced degree than we might expect.[9]

Archbishop Whately, who established the Chair of Political Economy in Trinity College in 1832, took an interest in a related question of whether economic growth has an impact on moral behaviour. Unlike a modern social scientist, he had to rely on deductive reasoning instead of mass opinion surveys. As a general rule, he concluded, 'advancement in National Prosperity, which mankind is by the Governor of the universe adapted and impelled to promote, must be favourable to moral improvement.'[10] Whately championed the cause of teaching and research in economics because he believed that economic growth would lead to moral improvement, and moral improvement would in turn bring as much 'happiness' as we can reasonably expect in this life. This is an alternative perspective on the GNP/happiness correlation that would no doubt prove controversial in modern Ireland.

The literature on happiness continues to grow. It is a subject that requires cross-disciplinary research involving economics, statistics, psychology and philosophy. As yet conclusions are tentative, but the general thrust of the findings suggests two conclusions. One is that it would be a mistake for economists in the twenty-first century to focus excessively on ways to increase the level of GNP per capita, or to accept too readily that slow economic growth necessarily indicates 'failure'. A second conclusion is that, as prosperity increases, more emphasis should be placed on the provision of public goods than on facilitating the output of more private goods and services. The 'well-being' of an individual includes much more than income: access to decent public amenities, pollution-free air, good education, secure employment, a fair distribution of income and a crimeless environment contribute more to happiness than any monetary measure can adequately convey.

5 ECONOMIC STABILITY

So far we have outlined the advantages and limitations of using the level of GNP per person as an indicator of well-being and as a policy objective. But the level of GNP is not the only factor that matters. The stability of that level also impacts on society's welfare. In a market economy, a boom that gets out of hand (as nearly all do sooner or later) leads to a bust and with it a steep downturn that can have a devastating impact on people's lives. A well-run economy, therefore, must have regard to the objective of stability.

Economic stability has three dimensions: first, macro-stability, which refers to the avoidance of boom and bust cycles; second, financial stability, which is concerned with the viability of the banking and financial system; and third, price stability. The first two types of stability are examined in other parts of this book. In this chapter we focus on price stability. Note, however, that the three types of stability are interlinked. Maintaining price stability, for example, can be one of the most effective ways of avoiding macro fluctuations; and ensuring macroeconomic stability lessens the risk of instability in the financial sector. As we shall see, for a regional economy like Ireland, price stability is a particularly important objective.

A region will experience price stability only if the centre provides it. In the Republic's case the centre is Frankfurt, the headquarters of the European Central Bank (ECB), while for Northern Ireland the relevant policy centre is the Bank of England. Policymakers in the regional economy must therefore support the establishment of strong financial institutions at the centre.

What is Price Stability?
In the past, inflation was so rampant and endemic that price stability was largely understood as the absence of inflation. In recent times, deflation (declining prices) has become the more pressing threat to price stability.[11] While deflation means that the purchasing power of the currency is increasing – good news for those with cash balances – it has serious damaging side-effects, especially on countries with large government debts and a heavily indebted private sector. Hence price stability is the objective; inflation and deflation must both be avoided.

Price stability is defined as the absence of any persistent and pronounced rise or fall in the general level of money prices. The general level of prices is measured by the Consumer Price Index (CPI). This index is defined by reference to the price of a fixed 'basket' of consumer goods. In the Republic, the selection of items for the basket is made using results of the national household budget survey. Every five years new weights and new items are introduced into the index.

The ECB defines price stability as year-on-year increases in the CPI of the euro zone *below but close to* 2 per cent, maintained over the medium term; the Bank of England adopted a similar definition in December 2003. The US Federal Reserve's target is also 2 per cent, but in September 2013 it announced its readiness to condone inflation of up to 2.5 per cent as long as the level of unemployment was above 6.5 per cent. The central banks of Sweden, Norway, New Zealand and Canada have opted for a target inflation rate in the wider 1–3 per cent range.

Asset Prices, Price Stability and Central Bank Targets

The issue of whether *asset prices*, and in particular house prices, should be included in the CPI has been much debated in recent times. The issue arose because in many countries (Ireland, the UK and Spain, for example) house prices were rising well above the CPI rate for several years. While housing costs are included in the CPI (they have a weight of 7 per cent in the Irish CPI), the authorities in Ireland, and also in the UK, USA and Spain, took too little account of the implications of booming property prices on long-run disposable income.

An important matter, then, is whether a central bank should monitor asset prices as well as the CPI in assessing how well it is doing its job. It is clear, with the benefit of hindsight, that the answer is yes. Prior to the 2008 financial crisis, CPI prices were stable in the industrial world, clustering around an average of 2 per cent. Central banks grew complacent, ignoring the fact that asset prices were escalating at extremely high levels. As we have learned, the ensuing collapse in asset prices inflicted terrible harm on the economy – as much as any deviation from price stability narrowly defined. Leaving asset prices to market forces and ignoring the damage they might cause was a grave mistake made by central banks. Asset prices are highly relevant both to price stability and to economic and financial stability.

It is now accepted that central banks should have acted pre-emptively, raising interest rates and/or curbing property loans when asset markets were in the grip of 'irrational exuberance' and boom-time psychology. Furthermore, they should have been more vigilant in ensuring that banks remained liquid and solvent and did not lend too much in the good times.

In practice, this policy prescription is not always easy to implement. Asset bubbles are obvious in retrospect but not in prospect. Often they begin as rises in asset prices that are founded on fundamentals. The correct value of an asset depends on projections of future income flows from that asset that are difficult to evaluate objectively. Taking action to head off an asset boom requires clear lines of responsibility.

Thus, in Ireland's case the Central Bank saw its role as limited to giving advice. It claims that it issued repeated warnings of the dangers of excessive property lending; and this is indeed correct. From its perspective the problem was that its advice was ignored by the banks and other relevant parties (such as the Financial Regulator and the Department of Finance). But giving advice and issuing warnings is relatively easy. The difficult part lies in deciding who should do something about it, when they should intervene, and what form of intervention is likely to be most effective (see Chapters 3 and 5).

In assessing the immediate danger of a price collapse, one problem familiar to all those who have studied economic cycles is that of premature warnings. This applied in the Irish case, where early warnings of an asset bubble as far back as 2003 did not materialise and hence undermined the credibility of future warnings. The key point is that it is very difficult to identify, and to anticipate the consequences, of an asset price collapse, even with the support of a strong economics research team. In retrospect, we see that Ireland suffered a near-perfect example of what Nassim Taleb defines as a Black Swan: an event or combination of events that (1) lies outside the realm of regular expectations, (2) carries an extreme impact and (3) can be explained retrospectively but not prospectively.[12] Banks are particularly prone to Black Swans. They can hide explosive risks in their portfolios and in just one day can lose the profits of decades.

As a result of post-2008 reforms, the financial authorities have been given more explicit responsibility for dealing with asset price volatility and have been provided with stronger policy instruments and controls to ensure that this responsibility can be effectively discharged (see Chapters 3 and 5 for further discussion of this issue).

Why Consumer Price Stability is Important

Although asset prices have attracted much attention in recent years, it is useful to consider the arguments for price stability in the narrower context of the CPI.

Failure to achieve price stability impacts adversely on both economic growth and income distribution. As we have seen, deviations from price stability can take the form of inflation or deflation. Of the two, inflation has presented the more prevalent and persistent danger over time.

Deflation, defined as a persistent decline in the general price level, has been a rare phenomenon. The most traumatic case of deflation was the 25 per cent decline in US prices during the Great Depression of 1929 to 1933. Another case has been the deflation in Japan after the mid 1990s. Japanese consumer prices fell in every year (save 2008) between 1999 and 2012.

Anticipated Inflation
Suppose we focus on inflation, or upward deviations from price stability. Theories of inflation distinguish between anticipated inflation and unanticipated or 'surprise' inflation. The principal welfare costs arise only when inflation is not fully anticipated. If inflation were to proceed at a steady (or otherwise predictable) rate that the public would learn to anticipate, and if institutions adapted fully to

this anticipation, people could adjust their economic behaviour accordingly. In such an economy, the welfare cost of inflation involves only two types of cost: 'shoe leather' costs and 'menu' costs.

Cash balances yield an implicit social return by virtue of the convenience they afford in making transactions. Inflation can be regarded as a tax on cash balances: the negative yield on cash balances is equal to the rate of inflation. The higher the rate of inflation, the larger is the negative yield and the opportunity cost of holding cash. Anticipated inflation also imposes the so-called menu cost of actually changing prices in what have been called 'customer markets' (i.e. those markets in which prices are set and, in the normal course of events, kept unchanged for some time, such as labour markets, retail and wholesale trade, pay telephones, ticket machines and parking meters). Both shoe leather and menu costs increase rapidly with the magnitude of the inflation rate.

Unanticipated Inflation

The costs of anticipated inflation may appear rather theoretical, but they are empirically significant, even at relatively low rates of inflation. Far more important, however, are the costs arising from unanticipated inflation.

First, uncertainty about the inflation rate undermines the role played by money in economising on transaction costs. Fixed-price orders, leases and other explicit long-term contracts, fixed-time schedules for price changes and the broad general commitment to continuity of offers by suppliers are important ways of assisting forward planning. Uncertainty about the future price level shortens the time horizon of such agreements, thus imposing a welfare loss on society.

Second, uncertainty about future price levels results in an arbitrary redistribution of income and wealth. A faster than expected inflation rate, for instance, will tend to discriminate against creditors in favour of debtors. It will also harm those whose incomes are fixed in nominal money terms or which are indexed only after a lapse of time (pensioners), in contrast with those whose incomes are more easily adjustable to inflation, such as unionised wage earners and owners of capital. Another effect is the redistribution of real wealth from the old (who have accumulated assets) to the young, who are, in general, net borrowers.

The haphazard nature of the income distribution effects can lead to social unrest and general discontent as people find it increasingly difficult to estimate the growth in their real incomes and to predict what their real earnings will be in the future. In a period of 1 per cent inflation, people who receive pay increases of 4 per cent recognise clearly that they have gained in real terms. In a world of 15 per cent inflation, those receiving pay increases of 19 per cent are likely to be much less confident about how they are faring.

Third, inflation can have adverse consequences for economic growth. Efficiency losses, though small in any one year, can accumulate over time into a significant aggregate loss. In addition, inflation has a tendency to shorten investment horizons. It attracts capital to 'inflation hedges' such as property at the expense of long-term investment in industry.

Empirical evidence indicates that high inflation (in excess of 40 per cent per annum) is bad for growth. No surprise there. But the evidence is less compelling when it comes to identifying the consequences of one low level of inflation relative to another. Does it matter that much if inflation is 4 per cent rather than 2 per cent? Provided inflation remained constant it probably does not. But inflation has a nasty way of feeding on itself – an *inflationary spiral* is generated whereby today's rise in prices is used to justify tomorrow's pay rises, which increases costs and prices thereafter. This explains why central banks tend to be cautious in diverting from the objective of stable prices.

Deflation and Stability

The above analysis has focused on inflation. Deflation brings similar welfare costs in its train, but for subtly different reasons. Thus, the menu costs apply in the case of anticipated deflation, with the added problem that nominal interest rates cannot be negative (the zero interest rate constraint), an inflexibility that can lead to excessively high real interest rates. At a macroeconomic level, anticipated deflation can prolong a recession by giving consumers and investors an incentive to postpone spending. It benefits lenders at the expense of borrowers and, because downward adjustments in nominal pay are often problematic, it can lead to real wage inflexibility. Thus, the deflationary environment in the euro area has added to the adjustment problems of the heavily indebted countries of the EU by increasing their real debt burden. Like inflation, deflation tends to be self-perpetuating and deflationary spirals are difficult and costly to reverse.

Opinion surveys suggest that the public values price stability for its own sake, apart from the economic costs outlined in this section. Also it should be kept in mind that stability in general, and not just price stability, must be given high priority among a region's policy objectives. Prior to 2008, the stability of banks and credit institutions was taken for granted and threats to that stability were unfortunately ignored. As already mentioned, a major shake-up of regulation is under way in the EU with the aim of protecting the integrity of the financial system and preventing a recurrence of another crash.

6 COMPETITIVENESS

Small regional economies are largely 'importers' of price trends abroad. Thus if the CPI is rising at around 2 per cent in continental Europe and the UK, inflation in both parts of Ireland will also approximate 2 per cent. This is a valid generalisation over the long run. But it is not universally the case and significant short-run deviations between a region's inflation rate and the national/area average do occur. During the period 1999–2008 Irish prices rose twice as fast as average euro area prices. As a result, Ireland became one of the most expensive countries in the euro zone. The excess has been only partially reversed by price restraint (and an actual decline of 6 per cent in the Irish price level up to 2010). Theory indicates that there will be *mean reversion* (i.e. sooner or later price levels in Ireland will revert to the euro area average), but serious damage to the economy will have been done in the interim.

Why do cost divergences occur between a country such as Ireland and the euro zone average and what can or should be done about them?

Price and Cost Divergences

One reason for the divergence in price trends stems from Ireland's rapid growth relative to the euro zone. Faster growth translates into higher pay. This is non-inflationary where productivity rises in line with pay. Thus a 5 per cent pay rise matched by a 5 per cent productivity increase leaves unit cost, and hence prices, unaffected. However, in those parts of the economy where productivity growth is relatively modest, employers will have to increase wages in line with other sectors (or else their workers will leave for better pay elsewhere). Hence unit costs and prices will tend to rise.

Second, changes in the euro exchange rate have had a strong effect on domestic prices. A 20 per cent decline in the value of the euro has been estimated to lead to only a 1 per cent rise in the average euro zone price level. However, because of the Republic's higher trade dependence and the higher proportion of trade with countries outside the euro zone, the impact of such a depreciation of the euro on the Irish CPI is far higher. The weakness of the euro for several years after 1999 imparted a strong 'imported inflation' push on Irish prices which the subsequent strengthening of the euro has been unable to reverse.

Implications of a Loss of Cost Competitiveness

When a region's prices/costs rise relative to other regions, this is termed a loss of cost competitiveness. One immediate impact of such deterioration is a decline in exports as they become more expensive to foreigners. For the same reason, domestic goods become more expensive relative to imports and the import bill rises.

For a country with an independent national currency the next question is the effect of the deficit on the exchange rate. If the exchange rate devalues, this offers a short-run solution to the loss of competitiveness. But the resultant rise in domestic prices could set in motion an inflationary spiral, with devaluation causing domestic price increases, which lead to compensatory pay claims. This is the classic downside of devaluation as a policy response to deficits induced by cost-competitiveness problems.

In the case of a small regional economy, the exchange rate is fixed and it will not change in response to the region's loss of competitiveness. If Northern Ireland loses cost competitiveness and runs a deficit, this will not materially affect the value of sterling. Likewise the Republic's competitiveness will have no impact on the fortunes of the euro. In each case the region is too small to affect the bigger picture.

The region may thus be left with a situation where imports rise and exports lose momentum. This means that the region is spending more on foreign goods and services than it is earning from exports. In this sense, a deficit signifies that a country is 'living beyond its means'. The deficit will have to be matched by foreign borrowing, and the corresponding capital inflow will eventually have to be financed and repaid.

An adverse movement in a region's cost competitiveness cannot be indefinitely sustained. As regional prices increase, the region's cost structure becomes more and more out of line with its competitors. It will begin to lose export markets and will become less attractive as a location for investment. Borrowing abroad will become more expensive or even dry up entirely. Eventually growth will slow, labour demand will decline, and pay pressures will ease.

The speed of this process was a much debated issue in Ireland prior to the crisis. Ireland's price level had risen by 40 per cent above the euro zone average. In a situation like this booming regions hope for a 'soft' landing, whereby rising costs will gradually be restrained to more sustainable levels over time. Unfortunately, the historical experience provides many examples of 'hard' landings where adjustment takes place abruptly, property markets collapse and unemployment rises. Ireland was to prove no exception to this rule. We have suffered an exceptionally hard landing and the slow painful process of restoring competitiveness has had to begin in earnest after 2008.

This suggests that the major concern of any region must be to safeguard its competitiveness, achieving its economic potential while moderating booms and avoiding busts along the way. The importance of avoiding deviations from competitiveness in a common currency union has long been accepted. In 2011, the German chancellor Angela Merkel floated the idea of a Competitiveness Pact among euro area members whereby price deviations from the euro area average on the part of a member state would be monitored and would trigger a collective response to correct it. The aim would be to ensure much closer economic and fiscal co-ordination in the euro zone.

Thus for a region lacking an independent exchange rate and with largely downward-inflexible labour costs, domestic competitiveness policy is an instrument of major importance.

Broad Definition of Competitiveness

Competitiveness has become something of a global preoccupation since the 1990s. Every region worries about it and governments everywhere feel compelled to do something to improve it. Practically every country in Europe has set up competitiveness councils. The *World Competitiveness Report* and its rival, the *Global Competitiveness Report*, are published annually and attract worldwide publicity. Their findings are scrutinised with a fine-tooth comb by development agencies and government commissions.

Competitiveness has been a well-established theme in economic debate in Ireland. In the Republic, the National Competitiveness Council was set up in

1997. Its *Annual Competitiveness Report* is a rich source of information on competitiveness indicators (see Chapters 9 and 10, for example). The council's remit is to examine key competitiveness issues and to make recommendations on policy actions required to improve Ireland's competitive position.

Competitiveness can be defined in a narrow sense or in a broad sense. The narrow definition focuses on trends in pay, productivity and unit costs. These components are aggregated into a cost competitiveness index and movements in the index are tracked over time and compared with trends in competing countries. For many years, emphasis was placed on this narrow definition, partly because of data limitations (information on the components of the broader definition has only recently become available) and partly because Ireland's performance on the cost competitiveness definition was exceptionally poor.

The broader definition includes price and non-price factors such as product quality, reliability of supply, back-up marketing services and taxation, and extends to consideration of human resource development, business services, infrastructure and public finance and administration. A country's long-run competitive position can also be profoundly influenced by its R&D policy, and by its success in product innovation and technology. Innovation and R&D are the key ingredients of a region's infrastructure (see Chapters 7 and 9). Competitiveness authorities in both parts of Ireland currently use the broader definition of competitiveness.[13]

Competitiveness is a relative concept. Success in the competitiveness league depends on how well an economy is progressing relative to others. It is possible for all countries to grow faster, to generate more employment, to export more; but by definition only some countries can become more competitive. In other words, the process of striving to be more competitive, in so far as it improves economic growth and efficiency, is a positive-sum game. But in terms of ranking in competitiveness leagues it is a zero-sum game: one region advances in the ranking order only if some other region declines. Failure to recognise this point can lead to competitiveness becoming what has been called a 'dangerous obsession' instead of a stimulus to improved performance.

Strategy to Improve Competitiveness
Policies to improve competitiveness constitute the theme of many chapters of this book. These policies change over time and according to circumstances will differ across region and nation. To date the policy objective has focused on creating an environment that would encourage (see Chapter 9 in particular):

- the growth of export-oriented firms, especially Irish-owned firms;
- the retention and attraction of foreign direct investment in knowledge-based sectors and activities such as electronics, pharmaceuticals, bio-technology and software;
- the development of linkages between existing and new green-field firms;
- a balanced location of economic activity within the island.

This ambitious programme has involved several policy dimensions and instruments, which will be analysed throughout this book.

Policy measures taken at the centre (Brussels/Frankfurt/London) are becoming increasingly important. Monetary and exchange rate policy is the obvious example. The centre also exerts major influence over fiscal, competition, transport and agriculture policy as well as state aids and taxation. The European Commission is concerned about competitiveness at the EU-wide level, and action taken to improve it will have important implications for Ireland.

The scope for regional policy initiatives, though declining, remains of crucial importance. A key fiscal incentive in the Republic is the 12.5 per cent tax rate for all corporate income from 2003. In addition, domestic authorities have some degree of discretion in the payment of capital grants, training grants, R&D support and so on. The extension of these fiscal and financial concessions to internationally traded service industries has proved to be a significant incentive to the development of the Irish Financial Services Centre and the attraction of major multinationals to Ireland (see Chapter 9). Provision of a good physical environment and human capital structure (education) is also an intrinsic part of a strategy for improving competitiveness (see Chapters 9, 10 and 13).

7 CONCLUSION

The first priority of economic policy is to ensure high and rising standards of living. In practical terms, this means that economic performance is judged mostly by reference to changes in GNP per person. People want economic growth because of what it can do for them in terms of higher purchasing power and also because of the other good things that often accompany growth such as more employment, generous safety nets for the poor and greater security.

Growth is a primary objective, but there are limits to what it can deliver. Growth at any price is not a sensible objective, nor is the attainment of maximum growth, particularly when this would involve environmental damage, an excessively large increase in immigration, and other undesirable spillover effects. In setting medium-term targets, rather than targeting the maximum growth an economy can reach and then working out the implications of this for policy, we should instead be asking what growth we wish to obtain and work backwards from there.

GNP per capita has many limitations as an indicator of output and human welfare. It leaves out of account leisure, the environment and global warming, and misclassifies many inputs as outputs. Another limitation is that GNP per capita neglects important indicators of human welfare such as education and health. Despite its many failings, however, the GNP per capita statistic serves as a remarkably good proxy for more sophisticated measures of human welfare, as comparisons between rankings based on GNP per head and the United Nations Human Development Index demonstrate.

Equity in the sense of a fair distribution of income and an adequate level of income for all individuals is an important policy objective. The issue of equity is indeed a central aspect of most economic problems. In the Irish political domain concerns with equity and income distribution often outweigh concerns with economic efficiency in discussion of policy alternatives. Policymakers seek to reduce social exclusion and long-term unemployment by widening opportunities for education and work. Care should be taken, however, when deciding on the degree of redistribution to avoid penalising the achievers and stifling economic growth. Protecting the vulnerable is good, but encouraging those who will restore the Irish economy to health must, for the next decade at least, be paramount.

It is also important to consider the 'well-being' or happiness of the community in the broadest sense when formulating economic policy. The weak association between GNP per person and happiness gives pause for reflection. There is some evidence that this relationship also applies when income is falling. With good management perhaps the painful effects of the loss of income can be moderated. This reinforces the need for policies that will seek to maximise societal welfare and that will deliver a full-employment, pollution-free, low-crime and safe society.

Economic stability is a policy objective that is desired both for its own sake and as a means to the end of attaining growth. There is now more conviction among politicians of the electoral advantages of running an economy in a way that maintains macroeconomic, financial and price stability. As a population ages, it is likely that the constituency in favour of stability will grow. Politicians seem increasingly content to leave monetary policy to independent central banks. Some elements of sovereignty in relation to fiscal policy have also been voluntarily relinquished. This new approach is helpful for price stability and good for the overall economy, since price stability and output growth complement one another in the long run.

Has the adoption of price stability as a policy target been associated with a demonstrable improvement in economic efficiency and social stability? Many argue that it has. They would agree with Keynes that deviations from price stability, whether in the form of inflation or deflation, have inflicted great injuries; 'both evils are to be shunned.'[14] Hence the importance of ensuring that price stability, once restored, is thereafter maintained.

Experience over the past few years has, however, taught a further important lesson. Price stability (in terms of consumer prices) is not enough. The authorities also need to pay careful attention to the evolution of asset prices. Stability of the financial system is an even more important objective that, we see in retrospect, was given all too little attention in the lead-up to the banking crisis. The remit of central banks and the financial authorities will need to be expanded and refined and the process of finding an agreed formula for doing this at a European level has become the subject of continuing intensive consideration.

As we advance into the twenty-first century, we can expect competitiveness to occupy the high ground as a major secondary policy objective for the economy. Competitiveness covers a wider spectrum of economic variables. Irish policymakers used to focus on standard comparisons between cost and price indicators here and those in competitor countries. These indexes continue to be relevant. Within the space of a few years, the Republic became a comparatively expensive location for visiting or doing business, and prices and pay rates converged towards the higher end of the European spectrum. The detrimental effects of this loss in competitiveness became apparent as the post-2008 crisis evolved. In the longer run, it clearly will be necessary to justify these higher earnings by higher productivity. It is here that the broader definition of competitiveness comes into play. Competitiveness in this broader sense includes R&D, education, quality improvement, marketing and physical infrastructure – the intangible and often difficult to measure aspects that impact crucially on an economy's ability to perform well.

Notes

* The author wishes to thank the editors for their percipient and helpful comments. He has drawn on Chapters 2 and 12 of D. McAleese, *Economics for Business*, Financial Times Prentice Hall, London 2004.

1 See Chapter 7 for a discussion of the difference between GNP and GDP, an issue of particular importance in Ireland. In most countries they give the same numbers but in the case of Ireland GNP (income) is around 20 per cent less than GDP (output) and hence we will use GNP for the remainder of this chapter.

2 J. Galbraith, *The Nature of Mass Poverty*, Harvard University Press, Cambridge MA 1979.

3 P. Collier, *Exodus: Immigration and Multiculturalism in the Twentieth Century*, Allen Lane, London 2013.

4 R. Kennedy, quoted in *Finance and Development*, Washington, December 1993, p.20.

5 United Nations Development Programme, *Human Development Report 2013* (http://hdr.undp.org).

6 J. Rawls, *A Theory of Justice*, Harvard University Press, Cambridge MA 1971.

7 R. Nozick, *Anarchy, State and Utopia*, Basic Books, New York 1974.

8 A readable and enlightening overview of the literature is provided in R. Layard, *Happiness: Lessons from a New Science*, Penguin Books, New York and London 2005.

9 B. Walsh, 'Adjusting to the crisis: well-being and economic conditions in Ireland', *International Journal of Happiness and Development*, Vol. 1, No. 1, 2012.

10 R. Whately, *Introductory Lectures on Political Economy*, London 1831.

11 The title of the lead article in *The Economist* of 9 November 2013 – 'The perils of falling inflation' – said it all.

12 N. Taleb, *The Black Swan: The Impact of the Highly Improbable*, Penguin Books, London 2007.

13 See D. O'Brien, 'Measuring Ireland's price and labour cost competitiveness', *Central Bank Quarterly Bulletin*, No. 1, 2010; and A. Gray, G. Swinand and W. Batt, *Economic Analysis of Ireland's Competitive Advantages for Foreign Investment*, Indecon, Dublin 2010.

14 J.M. Keynes, *The Economic Consequences of the Peace*, in *Collected Economic Writings*, Macmillan, London 1971, p. 149.

SECTION II

POLICY IMPLEMENTATION

CHAPTER 3

Role of Government: Rationale and Issues

Philip R. Lane

1 INTRODUCTION

Chapter 2 established economic policy objectives for Ireland. The government, on the premise that it indeed cares about national welfare, is responsible for the attainment of these goals, either directly or in tandem with its international counterparts. The government's ability to achieve its policy goals is facilitated by the special powers assigned to the state, most notably its powers of compulsion. In this chapter, the role of government in pursuing these policy objectives is addressed.

The rest of the chapter is organised as follows. Section 2 reviews the theoretical basis for government intervention in the economy. The allocation of responsibilities across different levels of government is described in Section 3. In Section 4, the central role played by public expenditure and taxation policies is analysed. Section 5 addresses other policy instruments available to the government, while Section 6 discusses the economic and political factors determining the size of the government sector. Section 7 concludes the chapter.

2 RATIONALE FOR GOVERNMENT INTERVENTION

There are a number of classic arguments that provide a rationale for government intervention in the economy. The starting point is to recognise the absurdity of a no-government economy. A central authority and a *legal system* are necessary to permit the (implicit or explicit) contracts that govern all economic activity, for example through the design and enforcement of corporate and labour laws. Cross-country evidence and historical examples show that anarchy and the absence of a 'rule of law' result in very poor economic performance (and the emergence of private contract enforcement systems, such as Mafia-style organisations): the evidence from 'failed states' lends considerable support to these concerns.[1]

Put another way, we can interpret economic activity as an elaborate game: as with any other game, a set of rules and a referee are required. The state is responsible for designing and enforcing the rules that determine permissible behaviour on the parts of firms and consumers: the anarchic alternative would be unstable and highly deleterious for economic performance. Some rules of the game relate to ensuring that the level and mix of economic activity is not unnecessarily hampered by a lack of enforceable agreements (that is, contracts that can be protected through the legal system); other rules are intended to ensure that the game meets some minimum degree of fairness (for example by ensuring that people can obtain some level of education and healthcare, irrespective of household income levels).

A second function relates to the efficient allocation of resources. A laissez-faire economy will not efficiently provide *pure public goods* (e.g. national defence). A public good is non-rival (it can be collectively consumed) and non-excludable (its benefits cannot be easily withheld from individuals): examples include the provision of national security and basic scientific research (a new mathematical formula can be used by everyone and, once published, is non-excludable). Non-excludability prevents market provision, since no one has an incentive to pay for a good if it can be freely consumed. The state must step in to provide such public goods and raise the resources required by levying taxation.

Similarly, market prices do not reflect *external effects*, with the result that activities generating positive externalities are underproduced and those gener-ating negative externalities are overproduced. A good that produces a positive externality is similar to a public good, in that some of its benefits are non-excludable and accrue to others than just the direct consumer. However, such goods may be rivalrous and may be partially excludable, so that some private provision occurs even if the level of production is inadequate.

The road network is a good illustration of a positive externality: the gain to building an extra kilometre of motorway increases the productivity of other parts of the road network that become more accessible. One obvious example of a negative externality is environmental pollution. A second example is provided by commonly held resources such as fisheries, whereby individuals are not responsible for the maintenance of a sustainable stock. To promote goods that generate positive externalities, the state may engage in direct provision or offer subsidies. In contrast, it may impose quotas or taxes on goods that generate negative external effects.

. Other sources of market failure include *monopoly power* and *imperfect information*. The former means that prices will be too high and output too low relative to the competitive outcome (see Chapter 5). The latter means that many credit and insurance markets are missing or incomplete, since it is impossible for private firms to adequately evaluate projects, accurately calculate default risks and monitor the behaviour of individual agents. Such market failures provide a *prima facie* case for some kind of government intervention, either by direct provision or through subsidisation.

However, the desirability of actual intervention is tempered by 'government failure': it is not clear that, in many cases, governments can deliver a more efficient outcome than that generated by even imperfect markets. Electoral pressures; interest group lobbying; perverse incentives in administration; corruption; restrictive practices and inflexible procedures in the public sector; and inadequate management skills may all lead to welfare-decreasing interventions in the economy. Accordingly, the optimal degree of government intervention must balance the prospective gains against potential implementation problems.

Even if free markets delivered a perfectly efficient outcome, *distributional considerations* would still justify government intervention (see also Chapter 8). The income distribution attained by a market economy is conditional on the initial distribution of endowments (both monetary and individual characteristics such as intelligence, good health and family background). Being lucky in one's choice of parents is an important determinant of success in a market economy: for example, in Ireland and elsewhere, educational attainment levels are highly correlated with family income levels and social background (see also Chapter 13). Moreover, economic outcomes have a random element. The weather influences the success or failure of many agricultural projects and many entrepreneurs recognise the role played by fortune in creating viable new businesses.

Accordingly, voters typically demand that the government redistributes income in order to protect the poorly endowed and the unlucky. However, the ability of the government to redistribute income is constrained along two dimensions. First, excessively high taxation depresses incentives, reducing the level of income and growth rates. Second, mobile factors (capital, highly skilled workers) may leave jurisdictions that impose harsh tax burdens.

Finally, it should be clear that government performance is an important determinant of international competitiveness. An efficient government enhances the ability of domestic firms to compete in international markets, by reducing the taxation and other costs of attaining policy objectives; in international empirical studies, an efficient government is highly correlated with strong growth performance.[2]

3 LEVELS OF GOVERNMENT

Different levels of government can intervene in the economy. While the traditional focus has been on national governments, global, European and local levels of government are also increasingly important.

Global Governance

For some issues, global levels of government are best placed to deal with a given issue. Ireland participates in the World Trade Organisation (WTO), is a member of the International Monetary Fund (IMF) and the World Bank, and subscribes to various international policy agreements, such as on climate change.

The driving force behind global levels of governance is that the globalisation of many economic activities enhances efficiency and is facilitated by a common set of international rules. For instance, it would be an extremely tedious procedure for each country to negotiate bilateral agreements with all its potential trading partners: the WTO and the various regional trade agreements greatly reduce the transaction costs in ensuring trade liberalisation.

Similarly, in tackling problems that are fundamentally global in character, non-co-ordinated national policy responses make little sense.[3] The most obvious example is the climate change problem: carbon emissions in each country symmetrically affect the global climate. However, similar considerations apply in the domain of public health: high levels of air travel mean that a virus that emerges in one area can quickly be transmitted around the world. To the extent that some security threats are global in nature (for example the control of nuclear weapons and the risks posed by dissident groups that seek to disrupt global economic and social systems), there is also a global level to defence policies. Finally, large international income inequalities, especially the extreme poverty of the 'bottom billion' of the global population (primarily in sub-Saharan Africa) constitutes a global problem across many dimensions.[4] In addition to ethical issues, it is in the self-interest of advanced economies to promote international development, in view of the interconnections between extreme poverty, political instability, mass migrations and public health.

Moreover, the globalisation of economic activity also makes national or regional policy actions less effective: for example, high tax rates or excessive regulation may prompt mobile factors to relocate to more business-friendly regimes. Conversely, national subsidies or tax breaks distort international location decisions, since a firm may opt to produce even in an inefficient location if it receives sufficiently high compensation from the host government. For these reasons, co-ordinating international policies can potentially restore the ability of governments to tax mobile factors and avoid undesirable 'subsidy auctions' in competing for footloose firms.

That said, the difficulty with international policy co-ordination is that there is not always consensus on the correct policy. Preferences may legitimately differ across countries on important issues such as: the appropriate level of taxation; the ideal level of social protection; and the optimal degree of risk aversion in food regulation. Accordingly, global governance arrangements are more easily achieved on technocratic issues such as elements of the world trade and financial systems, with less progress on social issues. For this reason, it is sometimes argued that the development of global governance has been unbalanced: much progress has been made on co-operation in economic policy but with less effective co-ordination of labour or environmental regulations. However, in the absence of a directly elected 'world government', it is unlikely that much progress can be made on controversial issues that are the subject of much disagreement both within and across countries.[5]

Moreover, cross-country distributional issues also limit the scope for global co-operation. While there is a strong intellectual consensus (reinforced by the 2007–8 global financial crisis) that the largest global financial institutions require a common global regulatory approach, progress in designing a common set of rules has been relatively weak, with each country seeking rules that suit its own financial institutions.

These factors mean that global levels of governance are likely to remain quite circumscribed in the absence of sufficient consensus on various issues across sovereign nations. In relation to new initiatives, a primary area where global action may occur is in relation to climate change, in view of the emerging consensus on the nature and urgency of the problem. Even in that domain, the capacity to forge a global agreement that tackles global warming in an efficient yet equitable manner is open to question.

One basic problem is that a fair global solution plausibly involves a significant transfer of funds from the advanced economies to the developing world, to compensate for the fact that the accumulated stock of carbon emissions has been primarily generated by high-income countries over many decades of industrial activity: achieving agreement on the scale of such redistribution will be difficult. A second problem is that it is difficult and costly to impose sanctions on non-compliant nations, so that any global initiative must rely on softer methods of promoting compliance – for example peer pressure across member governments, plus monitoring by national and international 'civic society' groups such as Saving the Earth, Greenpeace and other activist organisations.

EU Governance
EU membership is the most important international commitment of the Irish government. Although the scale of inter-governmental co-operation at the EU level faces many of the difficulties encountered at global levels of governance, the scope for establishing common policies is much greater at the EU level. This reflects the very close economic and social ties across the member countries, plus the elaborate institutional structure that has been developed (European Commission, Council of Ministers, European Parliament, inter-governmental treaties) to promote and sustain policymaking at the EU level.

Moreover, since member states bargain over many issues, decision making is facilitated by the multi-dimensional nature of political relations among the member states: for instance, some undesirable regulation in one area may be accepted in exchange for a concession on another issue. In other cases, the level of disagreement may be so strong that co-ordination is not possible, with countries retaining independent national policies. Although a national veto still remains on some policy issues (e.g. taxation), majority voting now applies in many areas.

The 'Four Freedoms'
In order to create a single market, EU law guarantees the 'four freedoms': the free movement of goods and services; freedom of establishment; the free movement of persons (and citizenship), including free movement of workers; and the free movement of capital. In addition, EU competition law also now sharply restricts national autonomy in industrial and competition policies, with EU-level monitoring of state interventions in domestic markets. In addition, large public

contracts must be advertised at an EU-wide level, rather than directly allocated to domestic firms. In these ways, the EU can be interpreted as an international 'agency of restraint' that promotes more efficient allocations and depoliticises many economic decisions.

That said, the difficulty with international policy co-ordination is that there is not always consensus on the correct policy. Preferences may legitimately differ across countries on important issues such as: the appropriate level of taxation; the ideal level of social protection; and the optimal degree of risk aversion in food regulation. Since member nations bargain over many issues, some undesirable regulations may be accepted in exchange for concessions on other issues. In other cases, the level of disagreement may be so strong that co-ordination is not possible, with countries retaining independent national policies.

Democratic Accountability

A common criticism of international policy co-ordination is that it leads to a 'democratic deficit', with decisions made at a level that is too far removed from ordinary voters. Although the 2008 Treaty of Lisbon introduced some reforms to improve democratic accountability, it remains an ongoing concern that EU institutions are perceived as too remote by the general European population. Since 2008, the policy response to the European financial crisis has underlined the lack of trust in EU-level institutions that are not directly controlled by national governments.

As a result, there is a tension in the operation of the EU between taking decisions through the official EU institutions versus inter-governmental negotiations. While the former may be more efficient, the latter ensures that national governments have a greater say in EU policymaking. For instance, the allocation of official loans is now controlled by the European Stability Mechanism (ESM), which makes decisions on the basis of unanimity among the member governments. Given the large sums controlled by the ESM, the inter-governmental nature of its governance underlines the limited autonomy acceded to EU institutions by the member states, with the main exception in the economic sphere being the exceptional independence accorded to the ECB.

Taxation

As indicated, many decisions concerning government spending and taxation remain at the national level, providing scope for significant variation in the level and nature of government intervention across member countries. Following the earlier discussion, harmonisation of tax rates on mobile capital is advocated by some member countries. However, there is little agreement on the appropriate tax rate: a high capital tax rate may be progressive and reduce pressure on other parts of the tax base but at the cost of a negative effect on growth performance, with countries having different preferences as to the optimal trade-off across these dimensions.

Ireland has opted for a low-tax strategy and currently resists pressure to harmonise rates at a higher level. However, there is also a current proposal to design a common consolidated tax base, such that a multinational firm need only produce a single set of European financial accounts, with capital income taxed according to a formula that reflects its economic activities (such as sales revenues) in each country (for detailed discussions of this see Chapters 4 and 9). To the extent that this is a voluntary code, the impact on Ireland may be relatively minor, but widespread adoption of a common tax base would limit the level of corporate income that is taxable in Ireland, in view of the export orientation of most multinational firms operating in Ireland.

Single Currency

In 1999, a subset of eleven EU members adopted the euro as a single currency. By 2014, eighteen EU members had joined the euro area, with further members expected to join over the next decade. A monetary union offers microeconomic efficiency gains and facilitates the development of a deep, liquid capital market. Moreover, a large bloc is plausibly insulated from destabilising speculative attacks on its currency, permitting lower average interest rates.

A core feature of European monetary union is that the member governments have delegated the operation of monetary policy to an independent agency – the ECB. Perhaps the most important advantage is that a supranational central bank may be more effectively insulated from political pressures than are national monetary authorities.

The delegation of technocratic forms of government intervention, such as the conduct of monetary policy, to semi-autonomous institutions can be interpreted as a useful agency of restraint that ties the hands of political leaders who face enormous short-term pressures to adopt populist policies that may damage the economy in the long term. Democratic accountability is ensured through several mechanisms: the mandate of the ECB is fixed by treaty; the President of the ECB testifies before the European Parliament on a regular basis; and the ECB is in regular dialogue with the European Commission and the Euro Group of finance ministers.

However, a 'one size fits all' monetary policy may itself be a source of instability for member countries with business cycles that are not highly correlated with the core of the euro zone. In the early years of the Economic and Monetary Union (EMU), Ireland fell into this category: in view of our high growth rates, interest rates were inappropriately low and excessive inflation was the result. In the other direction, countries such as Germany, Portugal, and Italy may have preferred a looser monetary policy at various times, in view of poor domestic performance in these economies.

Financial Crisis

Since the onset of the financial crisis in 2007, EMU has been subject to a severe test. In one direction, a common currency provided a lot of insulation during the initial stages of the crisis. The ECB cut interest rates sharply in late 2008 and early 2009 from 3.75 per cent to 1.00 per cent. This cut in interest rates provided substantial relief for indebted households and firms throughout the crisis. In addition, the ECB provided general liquidity to the European banking system, substituting for the breakdown of the inter-bank wholesale market in 2008. The liquidity operations of the ECB have provided extraordinary support to the troubled banking systems in the euro periphery, with an outflow of private capital from these countries partly replaced by an inflow of official funding from the ECB.

However, the European periphery had accumulated a lot of debt during the pre-crisis years, with the global credit boom between 2003 and 2007 allowing the private and public sectors in these countries to borrow large amounts (with the relative contributions of the private and public sector differing across the individual countries). In early 2010, debt markets became sceptical about the capacity of the new Greek government to meet its debt obligations (which had been partly concealed by the previous government), with the EU and IMF eventually combining to provide a bailout package for Greece in May 2010. Ireland also received a bailout at the end of 2010, with Portugal following in 2011 and Cyprus in 2013. (Spain also received a limited type of bank-related bailout in 2012.)

These bailouts were intended to provide bridge financing for a temporary period during which the recipient countries reduce their dependence on external debt, by cutting fiscal deficits and deleveraging banking systems. Such fiscal austerity is more costly under a monetary union, since the negative output effects of a fiscal contraction cannot be offset by a monetary expansion or currency devaluation.[6] At the end of 2013, Ireland was able to exit the bailout programme, while it is currently expected that Portugal will also return to market funding in 2014. (It is likely that further official assistance will be required for Greece.)

Another form of adjustment is to conduct a debt restructuring, by which part of the debt is written off, inflicting losses on bond holders. In the initial phases of the crisis, there was considerable resistance to this option, with the fear that it might trigger contagion across the global financial system and damage a fragile European banking system (banks are major holders of government bonds). However, it was eventually recognised that the scale of the Greek debt problem was just too large, so a large sovereign debt restructuring took place in 2012.

Between 2011 and 2012, market fears that adjustment pressures might prompt some countries to leave the euro led to a further broadening of the crisis, with speculators requiring extra risk premia to hold the debt of larger member countries such as Spain and Italy. However, the Outright Monetary Transactions (OMT) programme that was announced by the ECB in September 2012 successfully calmed the markets by providing reassurance that the ECB would intervene if the existence of the euro were threatened by speculative pressures.

Financial and Fiscal Reform
At a deeper level, the crisis has underlined that a common currency area will be more robust if there is a common financial regulatory system (and a shared approach to resolving banking crises) and if common oversight of fiscal policy not only avoids excessive deficits but also ensures that sufficiently large surpluses

are accumulated during good years in order to reduce fiscal vulnerability during bad years.

Accordingly, an extensive reform programme has been rolled out in order to avoid such a crisis in the future. To this end, the Single Supervisory Mechanism (SSM) will begin operations in late 2014, providing central control of European banking regulation under the auspices of the ECB. In addition, other components of a European banking union are gradually being put in place, with the harmonisation of policies to deal with failing banks and the progressive adoption of a limited type of common resolution fund (so that the costs of a bank bailout will ultimately be shared across the member countries).

Similarly, fiscal policy has to be more prudent in order to avoid vulnerability to a sovereign debt crisis. Under the 2012 Fiscal Stability Treaty, governments must now adhere to new fiscal rules and accept EU-level oversight of the budget process – we return to this topic later in the chapter. Only countries that adhere to this fiscal framework will be eligible in the future for assistance from the ESM.

A wider perspective on macro-financial risks is also provided by the new Macroeconomic Imbalance Procedure (MIP) by which the European Commission monitors a wide range of risk factors (housing prices, credit growth, current account deficits, wage dynamics), with countries required to show adjustment plans to mitigate excessive risk signals.

Local Government

At the other end, some policy issues are being devolved from national to local and regional levels of government. Local government plausibly has an information advantage in designing and implementing policies that better reflect the preferences and needs of local residents. A closer relationship with the electorate may also improve the responsiveness and accountability of government. However, decentralisation also brings risks, especially if fiscal and functional responsibilities are not clearly allocated between the centre and the periphery.

In Ireland, local government has traditionally played a very limited role. However, with the switch towards greater local financing and autonomy in the provision of services (e.g. waste collection, water services), the trend is for greater diversity in local government in Ireland. In principle, this can be supported by the new property tax, which provides a new source of locally controlled funding (see Chapter 4).

The application of the subsidiarity principle is also more evident at the EU level: there is greater recognition that the EU should focus its energies on those policy areas where co-operation is most effective, with the return of some policy issues to national governments. For instance, with the move to direct payments in subsidising the agricultural sector, it is predicted that responsibility for the agricultural sector will be shifted from Brussels to national levels of government (see Chapter 11).

Finally, in light of the improved political climate since the 1998 Good Friday Agreement, progress has been made in improved policy co-operation between the

Republic of Ireland and Northern Ireland, with considerable scope for yet further integration. Significant scale economies can be achieved in areas such as tourism (e.g. with the creation of the all-island Tourism Ireland marketing organisation) and network externalities can be better exploited by more efficiently integrating the transport and energy networks between the two jurisdictions. Moreover, the economic success of the Republic of Ireland has led to some reorientation of activity in Northern Ireland, with a greater focus on pursuing cross-border business opportunities. Under the Good Friday Agreement, a number of inter-governmental agencies have been established to facilitate enhanced policy co-operation in areas such as environment, agriculture, education, health, tourism, and transport.

National Governments
In this section, we have shown that global, EU and local levels of government play important roles. However, by default, the primary level of government remains at the national level, since national boundaries define the most advanced current levels of democratic political systems.

Over the last thirty years, it has been recognised that globalisation and international (global and EU) levels of government make it more viable for smaller nations to operate independently.[7] In the European context, the security provided by the dense level of EU integration means that smaller nations need not be part of a large multinational political unit for national defence purposes, while international and EU trade liberalisation means that smaller nations need not be too worried about the economic costs of a small domestic market. Since the 1990s, Europe has seen the break-up of the former Yugoslavia into its constituent nation states and the Velvet Divorce, by which the former Czechoslovakia broke up into the Czech Republic and the Slovak Republic. In September 2014, Scotland will vote on whether to become independent, while there are also strong independence movements in Catalonia and other semi-autonomous regions in Spain and persistent strains between the Flemish and French parts of Belgium.

4 PUBLIC EXPENDITURE AND TAXATION

There are three types of government spending: public consumption; transfers; and public investment. The first category incorporates the provision of government services such as the civil service, education, health, the justice system and defence. The second includes social welfare payments, payments to the EU central budget and debt interest payments. The third refers to spending on infrastructure (e.g. the road network) and on the buildings and equipment associated with the provision of government services.

Public Consumption

Education and healthcare are the major items of public consumption. We only briefly review these sectors, since they are covered in more detail in Chapters 12 and 13. Spending on education and healthcare is in part motivated by redistributive considerations, to ensure access for all to at least a minimal level of services. At an efficiency level, private financing of education is plagued by credit problems and the healthcare sector suffers from myriad asymmetric information problems. Finally, promoting education arguably confers positive externalities and is necessary to a healthy democracy, since political participation is positively related to education levels. Although these arguments justify public financing of the education and healthcare sectors, this need not involve monopoly public provision of these services: for instance, the state could provide vouchers to parents that could be used to pay fees at private schools or to pay insurance premia to private healthcare companies.

Transfers

The welfare budget is the largest component of transfer spending. Some transfers can be justified by imperfections in insurance markets. For example, private insurance schemes are unlikely to provide fairly priced protection against the risk of unemployment. However, the stronger motivation behind transfers is redistribution: voters are unwilling to allow the incomes of unemployed people, the sick or the old to fall below a minimum level (see Chapter 8 for a full discussion of this issue). In designing a welfare system, there is a clear trade-off between the level of benefits and the need to provide incentives to seek employment (in the case of unemployment benefit) or to save privately for retirement (in the case of pensions).

Producer subsidies are another kind of transfer. Although these have been declining in recent years, subsidies are still used to attract multinational corporations and support local start-ups. One problem with producer subsidies is that behaviour is distorted: rather than focusing on innovation and maximising profitability, entrepreneurs may divert resources to lobbying the government for subsidies. However, the worst excesses of this kind of behaviour have been sharply circumscribed by stricter EU regulations on the allocation of state aids to industry. Most notably, the European airline industry has historically been a major recipient of state subsidies but the European Commission now regularly prohibits the protection of 'national champions'. A second problem with producer subsidies is that Ireland competes with other EU countries for footloose firms: this bidding war may result in the successful country suffering a 'winner's curse', having to offer a subsidy larger than any potential benefits.

Public Investment

Public investment has two economic functions: the provision of (1) public inputs that directly raise the productivity of the economy; and (2) public amenities that improve the quality of life and are valued by the community. Of course, the same project may contribute to both objectives. For example, an upgraded road network not only improves economic performance, but the elimination of traffic jams is to be welcomed for its own sake in terms of reducing stress levels. Conversely, cultural projects and sports facilities not only improve the quality of leisure time but may indirectly improve economic performance by making Ireland a more attractive location for internationally mobile workers.

The state plays a central role in ensuring the provision of infrastructure, such as the transport network or the planning framework for housing and urban development. Infrastructure is fundamentally characterised by external effects: the value of a network is greater than the sum of its parts. For this reason, the state plays a leading role in the planning and design of networks in transport, utilities, housing and urban development.

In addition to its planning role, the state also directly provides much infrastructure. For instance, although privately funded toll roads and bridges can make a contribution to the overall transport network, public good and equity considerations mean that much infrastructural investment is financed by the state. Direct provision also solves severe co-ordination problems: for instance, a laissez-faire system may see wasteful duplication in those areas likely to generate the highest toll revenues.

In the decade prior to the crisis, infrastructural investment was very high in Ireland, in a bid to redress the severe infrastructural deficit that emerged from a combination of low investment during the 1980s and early 1990s and rapid economic and population growth. During this period, there was a rapid expansion in the transport network (national highway system, Dublin Port Tunnel, Luas tram lines, Terminal 2 at Dublin airport), while there were also many capital projects in the health and education sectors. At a broader level, there was also a new focus on government investment in the 'knowledge' infrastructure (government investment in human capital and scientific research).

However, it may have been more effective to adopt a more gradual rate of increase in public investment. The pro-cyclical timing of the acceleration in public investment can lead to high inflation in the construction sector, especially if it is already under pressure due to rising private investment activity. The scale of the increase in public investment may also run into administrative, planning and legal bottlenecks that further reduce returns. Over the medium term, it is certainly the case that a stable level of public investment is far preferable to the 'stop-go' cycle that has historically characterised Irish public investment dynamics.

The flush state of the public finances up to 2007 meant that much of the investment was met by tax revenues. However, some of the investment took the form of public–private partnerships (PPPs), while tolls have partially financed some road and bridge projects. Although private sources of finance during normal times are typically more expensive (since a highly rated government can borrow at lower rates than private firms), it does enable the use of scarce private managerial talent to achieve social goals. Moreover, the PPP contract typically includes appropriate penalty clauses, such that the risk of cost overruns or time delays is potentially transferred to the private operator. There have been only a few PPP projects in Ireland, and the UK experience has been that the transfer of risk to the private operator has not always been successfully executed.

An important element in efficient provision of public infrastructure is that all projects are subjected to a comprehensive cost-benefit analysis. Economic analysis has a large part to play in such evaluations. However, especially with respect to the provision of public amenities, variation in individual preferences between private goods and public amenities means that evaluation of such projects also has to take into account social and political factors in addition to the economic dimension. In Ireland, full cost-benefit analyses have not been applied to all projects in a transparent manner, such that the rationale for some investment decisions is not always clear.

Furthermore, with the major downward shift in the projected growth of the Irish economy, the appropriate level of public capital is also smaller than previously estimated. Many projects that could be justified under optimistic growth scenarios are no longer sustainable, in view of the slower rate of population growth, lower activity levels and a higher level of public debt.

Taxation

Chapter 4 will focus on taxation and the public finances, so we will only briefly discuss the role of taxation as a policy instrument. At one level, the main impetus for taxation is to finance public expenditure and the design of the taxation system is accordingly targeted at collecting revenues in a manner that least distorts economic decisions. However, there is a secondary role for tax policies in order to correct market distortions – such tax interventions can be 'revenue neutral' by rebating the revenues collected through a reduction in other taxes.

In relation to environmental protection, the role of taxation as a method to alter behaviour is widely recognised. For instance, Ireland was a pioneer in reducing usage of plastic shopping bags, through the introduction of a small levy in 2002 that quickly converted most of the population to the use of reusable bags. Similarly, bin charges have induced households to recycle more and avoid unnecessary packaging. At a wider level, it is widely recognised that a carbon tax has a key role to play in reducing carbon emissions, both domestically and internationally (see Chapters 4 and 9).

Along another dimension, user charges may be required to ensure efficient use of congested networks. While there has been traditional resistance to charges for utilities in Ireland, the new water charge is an important step in providing incentives to limit over-consumption of water by households and firms. Moreover, it is likely that such charges will have to be extended over time to include even traffic taxes to relieve pressure on limited road networks, especially in the Dublin area. Designing a scheme that retains access for low-income households is a difficult challenge.

Another form of tax intervention is the deployment of tax breaks to encourage certain types of activity. Tax breaks are also termed 'tax expenditures' to capture the idea that a tax break is often a substitute for a direct subsidy payment. In

Ireland, tax breaks have been widely used to promote construction in certain areas and industries. In addition, tax breaks have also been used to promote the arts (income from artistic activity is tax free up to a generous threshold limit), the film industry and the bloodstock industry. In general, it is difficult to make the case for tax breaks – if an activity is evaluated as deserving of a subsidy it is more transparent to offer a direct subsidy rather than to provide indirect support through the tax system. Moreover, tax breaks are of most value to high-income households, such that the exploitation of tax breaks can lead to a regressive element in the tax system in relation to the highest earners. For such reasons, there is considerable political momentum to restrict the use of tax breaks.

5 OTHER POLICY INSTRUMENTS

State Financial Policies
In addition to direct public spending on goods, services and transfers, a government may acquire financial assets and financial liabilities.

National Pensions Reserve Fund
One motivation is to build a reserve fund that can help finance anticipated future increases in public spending. For instance, the National Pensions Reserve Fund (NPRF) was established in 2001 in order to finance future state pension liabilities. Rather than exclusively using budget surpluses to pay down the public debt, the plan was to allocate one per cent of GNP each year to the NPRF, which invests in a portfolio of financial assets. The dividend income and capital gains on these assets can then be employed to finance pension expenditures, as a partial alternative to raising future taxation.

However, the precise design of such a fund is critically important for its success and political acceptability. A major concern is the politicisation of investment decisions. At the extreme, this might involve discriminating between domestic projects on the basis of the political connections of entrepreneurs. Less obviously, it may induce the allocation of an excessive portfolio share to domestic over foreign assets, with lobby groups pressing the state fund to support domestic firms and workers.

This is a very difficult problem. On the one side, it is desirable to minimise political interference in the operation of the fund. On the other side, in a democratic society, the operators of a state fund must be politically accountable. Much of the international debate concerning the delegation of public tasks to independent agencies, such as central banks and industry regulators, is relevant here. An important principle is that the government defines the objectives of the agency but that the agency is given wide scope in the pursuit of these objectives, subject to the issuing of regular public reports justifying any deviations from targeted outcomes.

Under normal financial conditions, it should be clear that the correct investment approach for a state pension fund is to overwhelmingly hold overseas assets. First, this strategy minimises the politicisation problem. Second, it is a sensible hedge. Imagine if the state pension fund held domestic assets: in the event of a domestic downturn, the public finances would be hit not only by a decline in tax revenues but also by a contraction in investment income. By holding foreign assets, in contrast, 'tax base risk' is offset. Third, the state pension fund would be large relative to the domestic market but tiny in global terms such that investing overseas improves flexibility and liquidity in portfolio management.

The initial investment strategy of the NPRF largely respected these principles. Its equity and bond holdings were overwhelmingly international, with only modest holdings of domestic securities. However, it also had some involvement in funding domestic infrastructural projects, which increased the risk that the fund's strategy might be subject to political pressure.

However, a large proportion of the NPRF portfolio has been essentially converted into a bank rescue fund since late 2008. In order to relieve pressure on the government's direct balance sheet, the NPRF was directed to sell most of its assets in order to purchase equity claims in the main Irish banks. While these assets may provide a return to the NPRF in the coming years, such a crisis-related role was not in the original design of the fund. Rather, it became a 'rainy day' fund that could be rapidly deployed to assist in meeting the large fiscal costs of rescuing the banking system. In 2013, it was announced that the remaining part of the NPRF portfolio would be converted into a new Ireland Strategic Investment Fund (ISIF) that would focus on commercial investment opportunities in Ireland. While the switch from a foreign-focused portfolio to a domestically focused portfolio might not be advisable under normal financial conditions, it is arguable that the damaged state of the domestic banking system means that domestic economic performance can be significantly boosted by the greater availability of non-bank sources of finance. The same logic has justified the creation of state development banks in many countries: for example, the state-owned KfW development bank takes on this role in Germany.

NAMA and NTMA

The government also created a second major financial vehicle to help resolve the banking crisis. The National Asset Management Agency (NAMA) was created in 2009 in order to relieve the banking system of the development-related property loans that were the main source of bank losses. NAMA purchased these loans at steep discounts from the banks and now holds a huge portfolio of property loans. In cases where the debtor cannot repay the loan, NAMA can sell the underlying property assets in order to maximise recovery of funds.

The vast bulk of NAMA financing takes the form of government-guaranteed bonds. However, there is a minor role for private-sector financing, such that NAMA is not counted as part of the main public balance sheet. Accordingly, NAMA provides an important example by which the government can engage in 'financial engineering' to meet its policy goals. However, such measures are opaque and require extensive public monitoring in order to avoid the temptation to excessively use 'off balance sheet' devices to understate the true level of government intervention in the economy.

Finally, the management of the public debt is another important type of state financial policy. Ireland was an early leader in establishing an independent debt management agency that could provide specialist expertise in debt issuance: the National Treasury Management Agency (NTMA) was established in 1990. In recent years, the independent status of the NTMA (and its ability to recruit at market salary levels, unlike the rest of the public sector) has meant that it has become the home agency for the more recently established units such as NAMA and ISIF.

State-Owned Enterprises

State-owned enterprises, ranging from Aer Lingus to the ESB, have historically played a major role in the Irish economy. Government ownership in the commercial sector may be explained by a number of factors.

First, underdeveloped capital markets prevented private entrepreneurs from raising the finance required to build profitable firms in capital-intensive sectors such as transport. Second, rather than implement regulation of monopolies (as in the United States), European countries tended to favour government ownership of utilities such as electricity production and telecommunications. Third, state ownership was seen as facilitating the pursuit of social goals such as access to cheap services and regionalisation. Fourth, the investment policies of state-owned firms might be viewed as a substitute for official public investment, such that the investment programmes of these firms might be politically directed rather than determined on efficiency grounds. Finally, in many countries, state-owned enterprises have facilitated political patronage, with decisions concerning employment and investment being manipulated for electoral purposes.

In recent years, there has been a global shift towards the privatisation of such state-owned firms (see Chapters 5 and 10). The development of sophisticated capital markets now allows private entrepreneurs to finance efficiently even large-scale ventures. Market liberalisation, sometimes mandated by EU law, has reduced fears of monopoly power in many sectors. Moreover, as indicated earlier in the chapter, the EU prohibition on state aid to rescue non-viable firms means that such firms can no longer be protected for political reasons. Finally, technological innovations such as those in the telecommunications sector now make it more feasible to have multiple competitors even in 'network' industries (see Chapter 5).

Where monopoly power is likely to persist, governments typically now prefer to regulate private firms as an alternative to direct state ownership (see Chapters 5 and 10). Similarly, social goals (such as the provision of cheap postal services to remote areas) can be achieved by a combination of subsidies and regulation, without requiring actual government ownership. Finally, with accumulating evidence on the performance of privatised industries in other countries, ideological resistance to private ownership has weakened over time.

Another reason for the shift towards privatisation is that government ownership may actually be detrimental to performance. Managers and workers in a state-owned enterprise know that they need not seek to maximise profits, since there is no threat of loss of control to outside investors, and hence have a weak incentive to behave efficiently or control costs.

In addition, as indicated earlier, the government may direct state-owned enterprises to pursue non-commercial objectives, such as providing employment for supporters of the government or locating in disadvantaged or politically favoured areas.[8] A decline in clientelism and an improvement in the transparency of the political system have weakened the incentive of the government to manipulate the semi-state sector to achieve such non-economic goals. Even in the absence of privatisation, there are benefits to the de-politicisation of these enterprises. Commercialisation of many Irish state-owned enterprises occurred in the 1980s, with significant improvements in performance. More recently, the privatisation process gained pace, with the (full or partial) disposal of the government interest in firms such as Eircom, Aer Lingus and Bord Gáis. The privatisation process may also extend to health insurance (sale of VHI) and parts of the public transport system.

In designing a privatisation process, the government faces several conflicts. To maximise revenues, the government should seek the highest issue price or permit a concentration of ownership among large shareholders, but this may conflict with a social goal to broaden the shareholder base. To secure the co-operation of powerful unions, the government may feel compelled to offer sharply discounted shares to incumbent workers in the state-owned firms and insert worker protection clauses into the privatisation contract, even if this reduces the value of the firm. Of course, the privatisation process should be fully transparent, to prevent state assets being sold at artificially low prices to politically connected business interests.

Privatisation generates a one-time cash windfall for the government. However, it is important to understand that the net impact on the government's balance sheet is much smaller: by transferring ownership, the government no longer receives dividends from the firm, reducing future government revenues. That said, to the extent that the firm is worth more in private hands and the buyout of incumbent workers is not too costly, the net financial gain of privatisation to the government will be positive.

The 2011 report of the Review Group on State Assets and State Liabilities recognised that there are considerable gains to improved commercialisation of state-owned firms and that some level of privatisation proceeds might be helpful in reducing the high level of public debt, while recognising the limitations laid out in the above discussion.[9] In 2013, the government announced the establishment of NewERA (as part of the NTMA), which is intended to provide oversight of the group of state-owned enterprises and identify new investment opportunities in key economic infrastructure.

Regulation and Competition Policy

The privatisation of firms with considerable monopoly power (such as Eircom), together with the principle of operating the remaining state-owned firms (such as the ESB) on a commercial basis means that the role of regulatory agencies has taken on new prominence in recent years (see Chapter 5).

Ireland has a large number of sectoral regulators (such as the Commission on Energy Regulation, the Commission on Communications Regulation and the Commission on Aviation Regulation) that seek to prevent abuses of monopoly power by monitoring market conduct and retaining powers of approval over the prices charged by firms in these industries. While regulators rely heavily on economic theory to identify instances of market abuse or excessive price mark-ups, it is not always straightforward to establish the scope for greater competition in certain sectors or the best methods to encourage the entry of new firms. Moreover, especially in network industries, incumbent firms may frustrate efforts to reduce barriers to entry, especially by making it difficult for new entrants to obtain access to key distribution channels.

An important problem in the Irish context is that regulatory decisions are subject to judicial review, such that much regulatory energy is diverted to legal battles with regulated firms that seek to overturn decisions through submissions to the courts. The considerable resources of highly profitable firms are also deployed in public relations campaigns that may have the intent of placing pressure on regulators to favour the interests of producers over consumers.

Even in sectors with many suppliers, market inefficiencies may arise if mergers and acquisitions lead to a reduction in the number of firms or if incumbent firms collude (explicitly or implicitly) to raise prices or erect barriers to entry. Accordingly, the Competition Authority has an important role to play in ensuring that open competition is preserved. In recent years, the Competition Authority has received more powers to enforce competition and the rate and intensity of investigations into anti-competitive practices has increased. Moreover, the Competition Authority has been pro-active in researching and analysing the level of competition in many important services sectors (Ireland scores poorly in international comparisons in relation to the level of competition in sheltered services sectors).

Under the 2014 Competition and Consumer Protection Bill, the Competition Authority and the National Consumer Agency will be merged into a new Competition and Consumer Protection Commission (CCPC). The new legislation will further enhance the powers of the CCPC to investigate competition law offences, while also providing more effective protection of consumer rights.

In addition to preventing abuses of monopoly power, the government also regulates many spheres of economic activity in order to redress other perceived failures of a laissez-faire system (see Chapter 5). Informational asymmetries justify safety regulations, since individual consumers are ill equipped to evaluate products that potentially carry high risks (air travel, processed foods, machinery, to name just three examples); accordingly, the markets for such goods can only operate effectively under the assurance of government-approved safety regulations (see Chapter 5). Of course, the trade-off faced in such regulatory systems is ensuring that such standards are not distorted in order to discourage innovation, restrict entry by new firms or act as a barrier to international trade. Regulation is also employed in pursuit of social goals, to ensure that businesses do not operate in ways that are prohibited under the relevant social legislation.

Finally, regulation plays an important part in environmental policy. For asymmetric information reasons, a market system may not be able to ensure that all firms produce using environmentally responsible techniques – accordingly, firms are monitored to ensure that production does not violate environmental standards. In relation to managing climate change, the allocation of carbon quotas is widely used as an alternative or a complement to a carbon tax. The relative merits of 'quantity' regulation (quotas) versus 'price' regulation (taxes) depend on the precise scenario, but a hybrid system that employs both tools may be the prudent choice when faced with a very uncertain economic environment, which is surely the case in relation to the climate change phenomenon.

Social Partnership
The role played by the social partnership process in contributing to the success of the Irish economy has been widely debated (see Chapters 6 and 7). Social partnership refers to a consensus-based approach to policy making by which the government seeks to obtain agreement from the trade union movement, employer federations and other representative groups on key policy decisions and also to establish national benchmarks for important private-sector decisions (such as the appropriate level of wages).

There are several factors that point to a potential role for social partnership. First, a decentralised approach to wage agreements suffers from an externality problem: individual firms and unions do not take into account the national macroeconomic environment when setting enterprise-level or sector-level wages. Through a co-ordinating mechanism (national dialogue between the various representative groups), it is hoped that the feedback loops between wage dynamics, government fiscal policy and aggregate macroeconomic performance can be internalised. While this may not be feasible for very large economies, a social partnership approach might be achievable for smaller countries such as Ireland.

Second, it is arguable that social partnership can also make it easier to implement major reforms since significant changes are most likely to be successful if there is buy-in from all relevant stakeholders. This factor helped to justify the progressive expansion of the scope of social partnership agreements from the late 1990s onwards to cover a wider range of policy areas.

However, in the other direction, a social partnership framework runs the risk of promoting the interests of 'insiders' (those belonging to organised units such as large trade unions, especially in the public sector) over the interests of 'outsiders' (those working in non-represented sectors; those not participating in the organised labour market). In addition, a consensus-based approach to policy formation can be a barrier to tough decisions, especially to the extent that the government is unwilling to challenge the 'veto' threat posed by individual participants in the social partnership process.

Between 1987 and 2007, a succession of national agreements were negotiated between the government, trade unions, employer federations and a host of other representative groups. However, the scope of the social partnership approach narrowed quite substantially during the crisis. Widespread consensus across the social partners was not possible in view of the differing views as to the source of the crisis or the optimal path to resolve the crisis. Accordingly, the government opted to simply impose many fiscal measures, while the wide variation in conditions in the private sector meant that employers withdrew from a common approach to wage determination in favour of firm-by-firm settlements.

However, a core element of social partnership has survived in that there is a common approach to public sector reform that has been agreed between the government and the many different unions representing public sector workers. In return for limiting the scale of pay reductions and avoiding compulsory redundancies, the so-called Croke Park and Haddington Road agreements specify an extensive programme of reforms across the public sector. Such a reform programme may not have been feasible without the social partnership framework. As the economy recovers and momentum builds for pay increases across the economy, the potential value of a new wave of social partnership agreements may be recognised in addressing the risk that decentralised wage bargaining may lead to an excessive loss in international competitiveness.

6 SIZE OF GOVERNMENT: ECONOMIC AND POLITICAL FACTORS

In evaluating tax and expenditure policies, a fundamental question is the optimal size of government. If the size of government is too large, it makes sense to prune expenditure and cut taxation; conversely, increases in spending and taxation are required if the government is too small to achieve desired policy outcomes. Of course, determining the optimal size of government is a difficult challenge and involves both economic and political dimensions.

Trends and International Comparisons
Although the government can also exert much influence through legislation, regulation, social partnership, moral suasion and financial engineering, measures of public expenditure and taxation are most widely employed as imperfect proxies for the size of government. However, there has been much interest in recent years in measuring other dimensions of government intervention in the economy. For instance, the World Bank's *Doing Business* survey ranks countries on many dimensions of government regulation and bureaucracy, while the OECD maintains a comprehensive database on regulation in its member countries. As is

shown in Table 3.1, Ireland scores quite well along some dimensions of these indices but its rank is quite low in areas such as the ease of enforcing contracts.

Table 3.1 Business Environment[1]: Ranking of Selected Countries

	Doing business	Starting a business	Protecting investors	Enforcing contracts
Singapore	1	3	2	12
Hong Kong	2	5	3	9
New Zealand	3	1	1	18
UK	10	28	10	56
USA	4	20	6	11
Denmark	5	40	34	32
Korea	7	34	52	2
Norway	9	53	22	4
Ireland	*15*	*12*	*6*	*62*
Australia	11	4	68	14

Source: World Bank, *Doing Business Survey* 2013 (www.doingbusiness.org).
[1] In terms of government regulation and bureaucracy.

In relation to levels of public expenditure, Table 3.2 shows that the share of total government spending relative to GDP in Ireland declined dramatically between its peak in the mid 1980s and 2000. This initially reflected the fiscal austerity programme in the late 1980s. However, the rapid pace of output growth during the late 1990s meant that the relative size of the public sector declined.

In terms of the composition of public expenditure, a dramatic decline in debt interest payments as a share of GDP was a major driver of the shrinkage in government size. Other factors also contributed to a decline in the size of government spending. First, Ireland's relatively young population meant that public expenditure on pensions was naturally lower, which is reinforced by the relatively greater role played by the private sector in financing pensions in Ireland. Second, lower unemployment in Ireland meant that social benefit payments were a smaller burden. Third, Ireland has fewer defence commitments than the major countries, such that military expenditures are lower.

However, there was a significant increase in the ratio of public spending to GDP between 2000 and 2007, with public spending growing more quickly than output. In part, this reflected an ambitious public capital programme, to redress the infrastructural deficit that accumulated in the 1980s and 1990s. However, current spending also grew, with the employment and pay levels in the public sector both growing rapidly.

The 20 per cent decline in nominal GDP between 2007 and 2011, the increase in spending on unemployment benefits and debt interest payments and the relative stability of other types of public spending (relative to private sector output) meant that the ratio of public spending to GDP climbed during the crisis period (see Chapter 4). However, a decline in public investment, significant cuts in public sector pay, restrictions on public sector recruitment and declining unemployment have seen a partial reversal between 2011 and 2013.

Table 3.2 Composition of Public Expenditure[1] (as a proportion of GDP)

	Total	Consumption	Investment	Interest	Social benefits
1985	52.6	18.1	3.7	9.6	14.2
1990	42.3	16.2	2.1	7.7	12.4
1995	40.9	17.5	2.3	5.2	10.8
2000	31.1	14.7	3.5	2.0	7.7
2007	36.7	17.2	4.7	1.0	10.3
2011	47.1	18.4	2.4	3.2	15.2
2013	42.4	17.7	1.8	4.6	14.3

Source: European Commission, *AMECO Online* database.
[1] The category 'other' is not included in the table.

Causes of Variations in Size of Government

Wagner's Law

Many factors contribute to variation across countries and over time in government spending. First, across countries and over time, there is a clear positive correlation between the level of income per capita and the share of public expenditure in national income: this tendency is known as Wagner's Law. One reason is that public subsidies to healthcare, education and pensions may be interpreted as luxury items, with an income elasticity of demand greater than unity.

As incomes grow, voters demand more of these services, placing upward pressure on public spending. However, the damaging costs of excessive taxation place an upper bound on the sustainable level of spending on these items. The fiscal reforms attempted by many countries in recent years may in part be a result of having approached this upper bound. The increasing mobility of capital and skilled labour also places limits on the feasible size of government, by placing a cap on sustainable tax rates.

Baumol's Disease

Another driving force behind upward pressure on public spending is the so-called Baumol's disease, named after the American economist who proposed the hypothesis.[10] Baumol's hypothesis is that an economy can be divided into progressive and non-progressive sectors. Productivity gains in the progressive sector drive up wages, which must be matched by the non-progressive sector if it is to attract labour.

Provision of education and healthcare services plausibly falls into the non-progressive sector, on the basis that productivity growth in such labour-intensive sectors is limited. It follows that the implicit relative price of these services must rise, as wages increase without a compensating improvement in productivity. If the income elasticity of demand for these services exceeds the price elasticity of demand, the ratio of public spending to national income will increase, even if the volume of services provided is unchanged. For this reason, the rapid increase in education and healthcare spending in Ireland during the boom period was mainly absorbed by rising wages, with a much smaller improvement in the level of services (see Chapters 12 and 13).

It is wrong to assume, however, that productivity growth in publicly financed sectors is impossible, as another factor behind slow improvement is the lack of competitive pressure to produce efficiently. Improved management, stronger cost controls and the outsourcing of some services may help in forcing more rapid productivity growth in these sectors. Moreover, recent technological change may enable new productivity gains. For example, Internet-based courses and learning aids may be feasible in many education sectors, while the electronic transmission of X-rays and other medical information permits the remote provision of medical expertise. An important challenge for policymakers is to ensure that such new technologies are exploited, even in the face of resistance from traditional suppliers, such as public sector unions. In 2011, a new Department of Public Expenditure and Reform was established in Ireland, with a mandate to drive productivity growth in the public sector.

Demographic Factors
Demographic factors are also important in determining the level of public spending. In the 1970s and 1980s, Ireland had an unusually large cohort of children, placing pressure on the education budget. At the other end of the life cycle, many countries now face an increase in the proportion of old people in the population, with attendant growth in healthcare and pension expenditures. Currently, Ireland enjoys an unusually favourable demographic profile, with the vast bulk of the population in the working age bracket, which allows either a decline in government spending or an improvement in the quality of services and pension levels. However, the problems associated with the greying of the population will progressively place upward pressure on public expenditure levels in Ireland over the next fifteen years (see also Chapter 6).

Automatic Stabilisers
Welfare spending fluctuates over the economic cycle, as the number of unemployed falls during expansions and rises during recessions. Such 'automatic stabilisers' induce a natural counter-cyclical pattern in government spending: however, this may be attenuated by pro-cyclical shifts in the level of benefits: during booms, the level of benefits tends to improve.

Political Economy of Public Spending

The preceding analysis generally assumes that the government acts to maximise social welfare. While the bulk of public expenditure may be usefully interpreted in this way, a substantial component is influenced by a more overtly political process, in which public expenditure allocations are the outcome of a struggle between interest groups, public sector workers and politicians. This process may produce outcomes that are contrary to social welfare: government failure may be as important as market failure in deviating from optimal outcomes.

Public Choice Theory

One reason why social welfare is not maximised is voter ignorance of the true costs of public expenditure. The Downs paradox (individual votes have no influence over the result of an election) suggests that it is not individually worthwhile for the electorate to learn much about the costs of different public spending programmes. In contrast, some groups have vested interests in specific areas of public expenditure (e.g. farmers and agricultural subsidies) and will act collectively to promote these specific public expenditures. In a famous book, the late Mancur Olson pointed out that such interest groups are easier to organise in a rich society and hence this problem will increase over time.[11]

The characteristics of the civil service bureaucracy can also contribute to government failure. Civil servants act as agents for the government in evaluating and monitoring the effectiveness of public spending. An influential hypothesis is that bureaucrats like to maximise the size of their departmental budgets, as this is associated with power and status. With each department seeking to promote its own expenditure programmes, the net result is to place upward pressure on the level of public spending. Similarly, the political influence of a cabinet minister may increase in relation to the size of her departmental budget.

However, centralised oversight of spending by the Department of Public Expenditure and Reform (backed up by the Department of Finance) can provide a significant counterweight: arguably, its focus is on holding back the overall level of spending.

Design of the Political System

Much current research is devoted to analysing the impact of the structure of the political system on public expenditure decisions. For instance, it is suggested that governments that are coalitions of parties with significantly different political philosophies and short tenures in office are less able to control public expenditure. Each party in a coalition has a veto on reductions in its favoured areas so that a prisoners' dilemma results – it is in the collective interest to control spending but no single party has the incentive to accept unilateral spending reductions. Short tenures make it unfeasible to implement spending controls as it will not have the time to enjoy the benefits before the next election.

In such circumstances, it seems that fiscal control can only occur under 'crisis' conditions, with the public debt so high that there is no alternative to reform.

Once fiscal control is established, fear of a return to instability may restrain expenditure for a long period. However, memories eventually fade and the pressure for a relaxation on public spending may resume.

Another manifestation of politically driven fluctuations in public spending is the impact of the electoral cycle on public spending: in the run-up to elections, there is a tendency for public spending to increase (especially on visible projects) and taxes are reduced. The timing of these fluctuations suggests that such spending has little basis in terms of social welfare but rather is directed at winning favour for the incumbent government.

Formal Fiscal Framework
International evidence suggests that fiscal sustainability is facilitated by a formal fiscal framework that places a set of restrictions on the conduct of fiscal policy. A fiscal framework has several elements.

First, it may formalise the political process determining budgetary decisions, with fiscal control best achieved by a transparent system that places ultimate responsibility for fiscal policy on the finance minister rather than by a collegial and secretive system in which lines of responsibility are not clearly designated.[12] Second, it may provide a multi-year horizon for planning public spending, in order to avoid annual volatility in public spending levels. Third, it may specify a set of numerical fiscal rules to guide the medium-term behaviour of fiscal policy. The set of fiscal rules typically sets some medium-term budgetary objectives, such as keeping the level of public debt below a ceiling value and a target for the structural budget balance over the cycle. In turn, each annual budget must be set within the confines of these rules.

Finally, it may include a watchdog role for an independent fiscal council, with the remit to monitor the quality of budgetary decisions. Such a council can improve the public debate about fiscal policy by providing a non-governmental source of objective analysis of the public finances. This role can be especially important during boom periods, since it is politically difficult to run large surpluses in anticipation of future rainy days. Having an independent fiscal council may provide some support for politically-difficult but economically-desirable fiscal decisions.

The EU Growth and Stability Pact provided a limited type of fiscal framework (see also Chapter 4). It specified a debt ceiling of 60 per cent and a budget deficit ceiling of 3 per cent and also required governments to make an annual report regarding the state of the public finances. However, the Pact did not require governments to run sufficiently large surpluses during boom periods, nor was the level of external surveillance sufficiently robust to avoid the accumulation of fiscal vulnerabilities in some peripheral countries.

At an EU level, there has been a wave of reforms to strengthen the Pact. Under the new procedures, there is greater monitoring of budget setting across Europe under the 'European semester' fiscal process. In particular, budget plans must now be pre-approved at EU level, so that there is less risk of inappropriate budgets being implemented.

At a national level, the Fiscal Compact (and associated EU regulations) requires that each member country adopts a Fiscal Responsibility Law, so that numerical fiscal rules are embedded in the domestic legislative framework. In addition, each country must establish an independent fiscal council that can provide an objective opinion of the sustainability of the national budget plan and the macroeconomic forecasts that underpin budget plans.

In Ireland, the Irish Fiscal Advisory Council (IFAC) was established in 2011 and the Fiscal Responsibility Law was passed in 2012, following a constitutional referendum to transpose the European Fiscal Compact into the domestic legal framework. IFAC provides regular reports on Irish fiscal plans and also must endorse the official macroeconomic forecast.

7 CONCLUSION

The central theme of this chapter is that the state is a major economic actor. A well-functioning and effective government is necessary to achieve economic efficiency and redistributional objectives. The maximisation of social welfare requires that the government choose the optimal mix of policy instruments to attain its desired policy objectives.

The analysis in this chapter gives some clues as to the likely evolution of the government's role in the economy in the coming decades. One global trend is a shift from the government as provider to a greater use of private inputs to achieve social goals. Another trend is toward ever-greater internationalisation of the policymaking process, as trade and financial linkages bind countries closer together. In the opposite direction, further decentralisation of some government functions to local levels of government is also likely to occur.

Public expenditure policies remain the primary method by which the state intervenes in the economy. During the boom period, the decline in the public debt and an extremely favourable demographic structure meant that the government had considerable freedom in making spending decisions. However, the legacy of the crisis is a very high level of public debt that will limit the government's flexibility in terms of spending and taxation plans.

Accordingly, it has never been more important that rigorous evaluation procedures are employed to ensure that the state obtains value for money and delivers public services in an efficient and equitable manner. To this end, it is to be hoped that the new Irish Government Economic and Evaluation Service (IGEES) can provide the professional economic expertise to ensure that such evaluations are carried out to the highest possible standard.

Notes

1   See A. Shleifer and R. Vishny, *The Grabbing Hand: Government Pathologies and Their Cures*, MIT Press, Cambridge MA 1998.

2   See C. Jones and R. Hall, 'Why do some countries produce so much more output per worker than others?', *Quarterly Journal of Economics*, February 1999.

3   See J. Sachs, *Common Wealth: Economics for a Crowded Planet*, Penguin Press, New York 2008.

4   See P. Collier, *The Bottom Billion,* Oxford University Press, Oxford 2007.

5   See D. Rodrik, 'How far will international integration go?', *Journal of Economic Perspectives*, Winter 2000.

6   See P.R. Lane, 'The European sovereign debt crisis', *Journal of Economic Perspectives*, Summer 2012.

7   A. Alesina and E. Spoloare, 'On the number and size of nations', *Quarterly Journal of Economics*, November 1997.

8   See Shleifer and Vishny, *op. cit.*

9   See *Report of the Review Group on State Assets and Liabilities*, April 2011 <http://www.per.gov.ie>.

10 W. Baumol, 'Macroeconomics of unbalanced growth: the anatomy of urban crisis', *American Economic Review*, June 1967.

11 M. Olson, *The Logic of Collective Action: Public Goods and the Theory of Groups*, Harvard University Press, Cambridge MA 1965.

12 See P.R. Lane, 'A new fiscal framework for Ireland', *Journal of Statistical and Social Inquiry Society of Ireland*, XXXIX 2010.

CHAPTER 4

Taxation

Micheál Collins

1 INTRODUCTION

Taxation is a method for government to raise revenue by means of charges on persons or firms and it can be collected nationally or locally. Governments collect taxes for two broad reasons. First, taxes provide revenue to run the state, as outlined in Chapter 3, and pay for the provision of public services, infrastructure, and the funding of redistributive policies. Second, taxation is used by governments as a corrective device to alter the behaviour of individuals, firms or the economy as a whole. In such cases, governments can use taxation to, for example, discourage certain consumption choices, encourage investment in certain sectors, or reduce citizens' disposable income in an attempt to dampen the demand side of the economy.

In Ireland, the government alters its taxation policies annually via the Budget and Finance Act. However, the government's ability to choose these policies freely is limited by competitive forces, EU rules, rates in neighbouring jurisdictions and historical factors. In the case of the first of these, a small open economy such as Ireland cannot easily alter its company taxation structures without having consideration of the taxation regimes in competing economies. Similarly, the government is limited by EU rules which require it to adhere to certain fiscal targets and it is restricted by EU single market rules from altering many of its consumption taxes. Past economic policies funded through government borrowing also reduce taxation choices as this debt must be serviced and repaid from current taxation revenues.

The plan of this chapter is as follows. In Section 2 we consider the principles of a good taxation system. Section 3 considers the operation and features of the taxation system in Ireland and reviews that structure in both historical and international contexts. In Sections 4 and 5 we evaluate the Irish taxation system, first looking at taxes on income and then examining indirect taxation, corporation tax and property taxes. Section 6 discusses the issue of deferred taxation, namely borrowing, building on the discussion of this topic in Chapter 3. Section 7 concludes the chapter.

2 PRINCIPLES OF A GOOD TAXATION SYSTEM

In *An Inquiry into the Nature and Causes of the Wealth of Nations* Adam Smith set out a series of principles for the operation of a good taxation system.[1] Smith identified four maxims with regard to taxation in general, stating that:

(i) The subjects of every state ought to contribute towards the support of the government, as nearly as possible, in proportion to their respective abilities; that is in proportion to the revenue which they respectively enjoy under the protection of the state;

(ii) The tax which each individual is bound to pay ought to be certain and not arbitrary. The time of payment, the manner of payment, the quantity to be paid, ought all to be clear and plain to the contributor and to every other person;

(iii) Every tax ought to be levied at the time, or in the manner, in which it is most likely to be convenient for the contributor to pay it;

(iv) Every tax ought to be so contrived as both to take out and to keep out of the pockets of the people as little as possible, over and above that which it brings into the public treasury of the state.

Known as the *canons of taxation*, these principles are generally summarised under the headings of equity, efficiency and simplicity and they have changed little since 1776. We explore each of these principles in turn below.

In the context of taxation, *equity* can usefully be explained via the concept of *ability to pay*, which relates the quantum of taxes levied to an individual or household's economic resources. In general, an individual's economic resources are taken to be the flow of resources to them (their income) rather than their stock of resources (their wealth). What is known as *horizontal equity* implies that individuals with identical incomes should pay the same level of taxation, while *vertical equity* implies that individuals with different incomes should pay different amounts. In practice this produces a *progressive* taxation system where as income increases an individual pays a higher *proportion* of income in taxes. The precise nature of that progressivity will depend on government choices regarding the structure of a taxation system.

The opposite of a progressive taxation system is a *regressive* one, under which as income increases the average rate of tax paid by an individual decreases. When examining a taxation system over time we can also consider two other equity issues: *transitional equity* and *intergenerational equity*. The former reflects a challenge for tax policy reform, whereby adjustments from an undesirable structure to a more preferred outcome will in and of themselves produce inequitable outcomes in the short term. Such transitional outcomes may be an unavoidable feature of enhancing equity. Intergenerational equity implies that, ideally, each generation's taxes should cover its own expenses. Where a generation's expenditure exceeds spending, and unpaid public borrowing remains, one generation passes a burden of taxation on to another, violating the principle of intergenerational equity.

The issue of *efficiency* in a taxation system arises because, in general, the imposition of a tax distorts what would have been the market outcome. It does so by imposing a wedge between the price received by the seller and the price paid by the buyer. This *tax wedge* alters the behaviour of these participants in the market. For example, say a farmer is willing to sell 50 apples at a price of 50 cent each and consumers are willing to purchase all his output at this price. If a 10 per cent tax is imposed by government on all fruit sales, this creates a wedge between the consumer demand price and the producer supply price. Consequently, both the consumer and the producer find themselves away from the optimal levels of demand and supply they would have chosen without the existence of the tax. Examples in relation to labour and other taxes are provided later.

The flow of resources from consumers to government as a result of the imposition of a tax causes an *income effect* whereby the purchasing power of consumers is reduced. Simultaneously, a *substitution effect* occurs as a result of consumers' response to the change in relative prices caused by the tax. An efficient tax is one where this substitution effect, also known as the *deadweight burden* of the tax, is minimised subject to raising the revenue target required by government. While different taxes will give rise to different-sized substitution effects, in general efficient taxes are set with a negative relationship to goods' price elasticity – low taxes where elasticity is high and higher taxes where price elasticity is low. Such an approach minimises the deadweight loss.

A further alternative is *lump-sum taxes*, which are levied at the same amount on all taxpayers, thereby implying no substitution effect. Such taxes can be difficult to implement and tend to be accompanied by undesirable outcomes when judged from the perspective of equity. Of course, these complications and deadweight losses could be completely avoided if the tax was not imposed in the first place. However, governments need to source revenue from somewhere and the challenge, from an efficiency perspective, is to do so with minimal distortion.

A *simple* taxation system is one where the compliance and administrative costs of the taxpayer and tax authority are minimised given the requirement to raise sufficient revenue for the exchequer. Taxpayers face costs in understanding, completing and returning the appropriate tax payment, given their resources. Tax authorities face costs in administering and policing the system. In general, these costs are positively correlated with the complexity of the taxation system. Therefore, a simple and understandable taxation system is likely to reduce costs for both government and citizens. It should also minimise the incentives for taxpayers to pursue various routes to minimise their taxation bill either legally (*tax avoidance*) or illegally (*tax evasion*). Increasingly, tax authorities are recognising the relevance of behavioural economics concepts in monitoring and enhancing compliance. A simple system combined with a greater appreciation of social norms and the unacceptability of tax evasion has been found to boost compliance at limited additional administrative cost.[2]

For a policymaker, the design of a 'good' taxation system that adheres to the above principles is challenging. In general, a balance has to be struck between the competing objectives of equity and efficiency while minimising complexity and raising sufficient revenue. Striking such a balance is not straightforward; for example, an income tax incentive solely targeted at the female labour supply might be more efficient than a population-wide measure but it would not be equitable. Similarly, females, who on average live longer, should perhaps pay more social insurance contributions than males; again, a policy proposal with efficiency merits but with problems when it comes to equity. Conversely, there may be equity merits in having low taxes on food, to assist low-income households to make ends meet; but better-off households will also benefit, raising questions of efficiency. Below, we outline the Irish taxation system and subsequently evaluate it relative to these principles.

3 THE IRISH TAXATION SYSTEM

Throughout this section and the remainder of the chapter various concepts and features of a taxation system are discussed. At the outset, some clarity on the meaning of these phrases is appropriate.

Governments can impose taxes *directly*, through the reduction of an individual's real income and the transfer of that revenue to government, or *indirectly,* through the imposition of consumption taxes or user charges on goods and services. Therefore, direct taxes allow government greater ability to target taxation measures towards particular groups of specified earners and to pursue the aforementioned objective of progressivity. The *tax base* comprises that which is to be taxed and can include income, consumption, property, profits and wealth. A *narrow tax base* will concentrate tax collection across a limited number of these areas, while a *broad tax base* will include many if not all of them.

The *incidence of taxation* measures on whom a tax falls. This can be on producers or consumers, on those at particular income levels or situated in particular industries or regions. In this regard a distinction needs to be made between the legal and effective incidence; for example, brewers may legally have to pay the excise duty on alcohol but in practice it may be fully paid for by the consumer. The *tax rate* captures the scale of the charge imposed by government relative to a good's/ service's price or income level. In income tax, we consider *average tax rates*, also known as *effective tax rates*, which summarise the overall proportion of an individual's income that is paid in taxation. The effective tax rate differs from the *marginal tax rate*, which captures the proportion of the last euro in income that is paid in taxes. As such, marginal rates are always higher than average rates.

Occasionally, governments have chosen to address legacy tax evasion issues by establishing a *tax amnesty*. These tend to be time-defined opportunities for taxpayers to acknowledge hidden liabilities and settle their outstanding tax bills with the tax authorities without fear of prosecution. In behavioural terms, an amnesty offers an attractive opportunity to boost ongoing compliance and allows evaders to legitimatise their position; something that can be of particular relevance in the context of widespread evasion, which would be administratively challenging to address. However, if amnesties become recurring events, they highlight the scale and potential for evasion and can therefore undermine compliance and the effectiveness of the tax administration system.

Tax Revenue: Historical and International Trends
The overall level of tax revenue in Ireland compared to the rest of the Organisation for Economic Co-operation and Development (OECD) and EU member states within the OECD is examined in Table 4.1. As taxation can be levied on all economic activity within a country, GDP is the international benchmark against which to assess the overall taxation burden. Irish data are compared against both GDP and GNP, as these national income measures can diverge by as much as 20 per cent, and given some historical precedents to assess the tax burden against GNP (see Chapter 7). However, to do so only in relation to GNP would exclude some of the national tax base, specifically the profits of multinational corporations, and consequently overstate the comparable scale of the national taxation burden.

The table shows that over the period from 1975 to 2007 there was an international trend towards higher overall taxation levels within the OECD and its EU member states. During that period in Ireland, taxation climbed and then fell, driven by growth and fiscal policies of the 1970s and 1980s and the economic expansion and taxation reductions post 1990. By 2007 Ireland's tax ratio was below average levels in the OECD and the EU. A comparison between the 2007 and 2012 data reveals the impact of the global recession (from 2008) in the OECD, the EU and Ireland. Taxation ratios fell over the period, driven by reductions in taxation revenue which outpaced simultaneous declines in economic activity.

Table 4.1 General Government Tax Revenue as a Percentage of GDP

	1975	1985	1995	2007	2012[1]
Ireland (% GDP)	28.4	34.2	32.1	31.1	28.3
Ireland (% GNP)	28.4	38.2	36.2	36.2	35.0
OECD EU[2]	32.1	37.5	38.6	38.1	37.9
OECD average	29.2	32.4	34.4	35.0	34.6

Source: OECD, *Revenue Statistics 1965–2012*, OECD, Paris 2013.
[1] Estimates.
[2] EU member states that are also OECD members.

Table 4.2 shows the composition of tax revenue in Ireland and the OECD from 1985 to 2011. The major trends across that period have been a shift away from specific consumption taxes such as excise duties, reductions in the proportion of taxes collected from personal incomes and an increase in the contribution to taxation revenue from general consumption taxes (e.g. VAT). In Ireland, the increase in the relative importance of corporate taxes as a revenue source is notable and is reflective of the increasing role of that sector in the economy. Property taxes also increased over the period in Ireland and by 2011 accounted for 7 per cent of total revenues; revenue from this source decreased from a peak in 2007 as the number and value of property transactions declined when Ireland's property bubble burst.

Table 4.2 Composition of Tax Revenue (Percentage of Total)

	1985		2000		2011	
	Ireland	OECD	Ireland	OECD	Ireland	OECD
Personal income tax	31	30	31	25	32	24
Corporate income tax	3	8	12	10	9	9
Social security and payroll taxes	17	23	14	26	17	27
Property taxes (including stamp duty)	4	5	6	6	7	5
General consumption taxes	21	16	22	20	22	20
Specific consumption taxes	22	16	14	12	11	11
Other taxes	2	2	2	3	3	4

Source: OECD, *Revenue Statistics 1965–2012*, OECD, Paris 2013.

Table 4.3 Structure of Ireland's Taxation Revenue, 2014

	%
Income Tax	33.9
Value Added Tax	21.4
Social Insurance (employee and employer)	20.4
Excise Duties	9.6
Corporation Tax	8.7
Stamp Duties	2.9
Local Taxes and Charges (including Local Property Tax)	1.1
Capital Gains Tax	0.8
Capital Acquisitions Tax	0.8
Customs	0.5
Total (€)	€50,276m

Source: Calculated from data in Department of Finance, *Budget 2014*, Stationery Office, Dublin 2013, and annual reports of the Department of Social Protection.

Using budget data on the expected flow of taxation revenue to the exchequer in 2014, Table 4.3 shows that the main sources of taxation revenue in Ireland are those related to personal income (including social insurance contributions by employees and employers), consumption taxes (VAT and excise duties) and corporate taxes. The remainder of this section will examine each of these areas and consider the role of capital taxes, property taxes and other smaller sources of taxation revenue.

Personal Income Taxes
In the current Irish income taxation system, an individual's gross pay from working is reduced by three taxation payments: income tax, the universal social charge (USC) and employees' pay-related social insurance (PRSI).

Income tax is charged at the standard rate of 20 per cent on earnings up to €32,800; above this, income is subject to tax at the higher tax rate of 41 per cent. The USC is structured so that income up to €10,035 is charged at 2 per cent; between €10,036 and €16,016 it is subject to a 4 per cent rate; and all income above this level is charged at a rate of 7 per cent.[3] PRSI is charged at a rate of 4 per cent on all income once earnings exceed €352 per week (€18,304 per annum). Collectively, these three charges sum to the worker's gross taxation level. From this, employees' income tax credits are deducted to establish taxable income.

Employees in the PAYE system are entitled to two tax credits which reduce their income tax liability: a personal credit and a PAYE credit. These can only be used against the employee's income taxation liability and cannot be used against the USC or PRSI. Entitlements to additional tax credits associated with family circumstances and certain tax breaks can further reduce an individual's tax liability. Similarly, non-PAYE workers, such as the self-employed and company directors, will record higher average tax rates as they are only entitled to claim the personal tax credit.

The Social Insurance Fund receives pay-related contributions from employees, the self-employed and employers. These contributions are used to fund the provision of social welfare payments to those in society who need them – jobseekers' benefit, illness benefit, maternity benefit, etc. Where the fund is unable to meet the cost of these payments it is absorbed by the exchequer. As indicated, employees contribute 4 per cent of their earnings to this fund once their income exceeds €352 per week (€18,304 per annum). Those who are self-employed pay 4 per cent of their profits (income) as PRSI once profits exceed €5,000 per annum. Employers also pay to support the provision of social insurance for their employees. Employers' PRSI is charged at a rate of 8.5 per cent of gross pay up to €356 per week and 10.75 per cent of gross pay above this, meaning that the net cost of an employee to an employer is €108.50 or €110.75 for every €100 of gross income.

Consumption Taxes

Value added tax (VAT) is the primary source of consumption taxes in Ireland. Most goods and services are subject to VAT at one of three rates. The standard rate is 23 per cent and this applies to most goods and services. A reduced rate of 13.5 per cent applies to a number of broadly consumed goods including heating fuel and electricity. A third, zero per cent, rate applies to many foods, medicines, books, and children's clothing/footwear. In addition, some goods are deemed to be exempt from VAT and these include many services supplied in the public interest in areas such as health, childcare and education. There is a technical distinction between goods and services that are exempt and those that are charged at zero per cent. This relates to the ability of companies and the self-employed to claim VAT paid against VAT collected on these goods and services.[4]

Excise duties are a further source of consumption tax revenue for the Irish government. These duties, which are strictly regulated within the context of EU free trade rules, are charged in addition to VAT and apply to mineral oils (petrol, diesel, home heating oil), alcohol and tobacco. In the case of each of these goods, the combined charge of VAT and excise duties represents a large proportion of the retail price paid by the consumer. The inelastic nature of their demand also makes them attractive sources for additional exchequer revenue at Budget time. Excise duties are also charged on certain business premises and activities including betting, alcohol sales, restaurants, auctioneers and bookmakers.

Environmental taxes represent a recent and growing area of consumption-related taxation in Ireland. In general these taxes are intended to elicit some behavioural change among consumers by encouraging them to reduce or modify their consumption patterns. A carbon tax was introduced in 2010 at a rate of €15 per tonne of CO_2 equivalent. This means that the rate at which the carbon tax is levied is linked to how much pollution a good produces (see Chapter 10). For example, on its introduction the carbon tax increased petrol prices by 3.5 per cent, natural gas prices by 7 per cent, peat briquette prices by 10.1 per cent and coal prices by 11.8 per cent. Over time, the government has signalled that it will increase the rate per tonne of CO_2 equivalent, which will drive up prices and revenue from this taxation source. Carbon taxes are charged alongside VAT and, where appropriate, excise duties.

User charges, such as commercial and residential water charges, act both as a contribution to the cost of provision and as a form of consumption tax. In particular, adjusting prices from zero to even small nominal amounts tends to alter consumption behaviour and promote the conservation of expensive societally provided and subsidised resources.

Corporation, Capital and Property Taxes

Corporation Tax

The tax rate for most company profits in Ireland is 12.5 per cent. Companies operating in specified natural resource sectors (minerals and petroleum), alongside those who deal in development land, are subject to a higher corporate tax rate of

25 per cent. Companies can reduce their tax liability below these levels through the use of various tax breaks and exemptions (see below).

Capital Taxes

Capital taxes are levied on the value of assets, or the increase in the value of assets. In Ireland there are two main forms of these taxes: capital gains tax (CGT); and capital acquisitions tax (CAT). CGT is charged on the capital gain (profit after associated transaction costs) made on the disposal of any asset and is levied on the person making the disposal. These gains are subject to tax at a rate of 33 per cent and the first €1,270 of annual gains is exempt from the tax.

CAT is levied on the increase in a person's or company's wealth and arises through either gifts or inheritance. The tax is charged at a rate of 33 per cent of the market value of the gain over and above certain specified thresholds. These thresholds depend on the relationship between the person giving the benefit and the beneficiary. Transfers between spouses are exempt from CAT while there are generous thresholds for gifts/inheritances to children with a CAT liability only arising on values above €225,000. These thresholds reduce to €30,015 for transfers between closely related people (near relations and siblings) and to €15,075 where wealth increases come from any other person. Gifts below €3,000 per annum are exempt from CAT. Special provisions also exist for business owners and farmers who wish to transfer assets to family members. CAT does not arise on increases in wealth associated with transfers of the family home, payments for damages or compensation, most redundancy payments or lottery wins.

Property Taxes

For many years Ireland remained an exception in the developed world in that it did not have any form of recurring residential property tax for all dwellings. However, this changed with the introduction of the local property tax (LPT) in 2013. The tax is value-based and levied on the owners of a property as a percentage of the mid-point of the valuation band into which a property falls. For example, in 2014 a property valued at €180,000 would fall into the €150,000–€200,000 valuation band and would be taxed at a rate of 0.18 per cent of the mid-point of that band (€175,000), giving a tax of €315. The rate of the LPT is the same for all dwellings below a value of €1 million. Above that threshold, a so-called 'mansion tax' applies where owners pay 0.25 per cent of the value above €1 million in addition to 0.18 per cent of the first €1 million in value. Over time, the revenue from the LPT is intended to predominantly flow to local government, which will also gain powers to marginally alter the LPT rate applicable in each area. Associating the tax with local government and local service provision is intended as a measure to strengthen local government and was recommended by the Commission on Taxation in its 2009 report.

There are two other forms of property tax: these are charged on property transactions (stamp duty) and businesses via local authority rates. Stamp duties arise on the sale of any residential property and are payable by the purchaser.

Stamp duty is charged at a rate of 1 per cent on the purchase price up to €1 million and 2 per cent on the excess of the price above this threshold. Notionally, the 'stamp duty' is a fee associated with the state's need to record and register these transactions; however, it is predominantly a revenue-raising source for the exchequer.

Local authorities levy businesses that occupy commercial property in their area with an annual rates bill which is based on the value of that property as established by a central government agency, the Valuation Office. Within each local authority the level of the rate (known as the Annual Rate on Valuation or ARV) is determined annually by the elected council as part of its budgetary process. The annual rates bill for commercial premises is calculated by applying this ARV to the valuation of the property concerned and it is levied on the occupier of the building. There are exemptions available for unoccupied units and some educational and charitable institutions. These charges provide almost 35 per cent of the funding for Ireland's local authorities.

Other Taxes

A series of other taxes also provide revenue to the exchequer. The government imposes small rates of stamp duties on bank cards, cheques, stock market share transfers and many insurance policies. Deposit interest retention tax (DIRT) is collected at a rate of 41 per cent on the interest paid or credited on deposits of Irish residents in financial institutions. It is collected at source, meaning the financial institutions deduct the tax from the interest paid and pass these funds to the Revenue Commissioners.

Where a working individual receives some additional non-monetary benefit on top of their salary, they are liable for benefit-in-kind (BIK) tax. These benefits may include the private use of a company car, free or subsidised accommodation, preferential loans received from an employer, free meals and subsidised childcare among others. BIK is levied at a worker's marginal tax rate, thereby treating the benefit in the same way as additional income.

The purchase and annual registration of motor vehicles produces another source of tax revenue for government in the form of vehicle registration tax (VRT) and motor tax. VRT is imposed as a percentage charge on the initial purchase price of a vehicle and since 2008 the levy is based on its CO_2 emissions. There are exemptions and reductions for electric and hybrid vehicles, while rates range from 14 per cent up to 36 per cent for the highest polluting vehicles. Motor tax is an annual charge on all vehicles and is similarly structured with low charges (less than €200) for low polluting and electric vehicles and increasing tax levels associated with higher levels of CO_2 emissions. The payment is collected by local authorities and is unrelated to the usage levels of the vehicle.

Since March 2002, an environmental levy has been charged on plastic shopping bags at the point of sale. The rate of the levy, which is set by the Minister for the Environment, Community and Local Government, stood at 22 cent per bag in 2014. A similar environmental initiative is the Waste Electrical and Electronic Equipment (WEEE) levy, which applies to the sale of most medium- to large-sized electronic goods and is intended to fund the recycling of the product. The WEEE is incorporated by retailers into the selling price of products. Revenue from both these levies is *hypothecated*, or specifically allocated to, an environmental fund to support waste management, litter and other environmental initiatives. These are two of the few sources of tax revenue in Ireland that are hypothecated rather than flowing to the exchequer and being merged into the overall collection and allocation of state revenues.[5]

Two further revenue sources are related to land rezoning and development. In 2010 a windfall gain tax was introduced on the profits derived by landowners where their lands are rezoned as approved for development by local authorities. These decisions, taken in the interest of appropriately planning further urban development, can result in significant increases in the value of land, particularly when it is reclassified from agricultural use to residential or commercial use. As society is making these decisions in the interest of its own development, the tax captures much of these windfall gains for the use of society rather than for the benefit of landowners or land speculators. The tax is charged at a rate of 80 per cent on the amount by which the land increased in value as a result of the rezoning decision and is payable on the disposal of the land.

Development levies are imposed on non-residential developments following a local authority's approval of a planning permission for that development. The levy is based on the public facilities, such as roads, water, sewerage and parks, which the development will benefit from. They are set by each local authority and additional levies can be imposed for developments near certain urban redevelopment and infrastructural projects that are funded by the state and that by their existence will further increase the value and benefits derived from the development.

4 EVALUATION: TAXES ON INCOME

Ireland's income taxes climbed to high levels in the 1980s, then slowly dropped on foot of social partnership agreements and economic growth during the 1990s and early 2000s, before climbing once again as the recession and economic collapse unfolded from 2008 onwards.

Focusing on the years from 1997 to 2014, Table 4.4 reports the effective tax rates faced by two household types at either end of that period and in 2008, the year when income taxation levels reached their lowest point. Overall, the table reflects significant reductions in income tax across the period, with all household types experiencing large income tax cuts up to 2008. Over the eleven years from 1997 to 2008 a single employee on €60,000 received almost €10,000 in income tax cuts with their disposable income rising from €33,660 in 1997 to €43,500 in 2008. Over the same period the post-tax income of a couple earning €60,000 increased by €14,640, almost 25 per cent of their total gross income.

Table 4.4 Effective Taxation Rates on Gross Annual Earnings, 1997, 2008 and 2014 (%)[1]

Income Levels	Single person			Couple: two earners[2]		
	1997	2008	2014	1997	2008	2014
€15,000	23.0	0.0	2.7	11.1	0.0	0.0
€20,000	28.5	4.4	11.1	15.9	0.0	1.6
€25,000	33.7	8.3	15.1	20.3	0.0	1.8
€30,000	37.1	12.9	17.7	22.2	1.7	5.6
€40,000	40.6	18.6	24.8	28.5	3.6	9.8
€60,000	43.9	27.5	33.9	36.6	12.2	17.7
€100,000	46.5	33.8	41.1	42.6	23.8	30.3
€120,000	47.1	35.4	42.9	43.9	27.2	33.8

Source: Author's calculations.
[1] Calculations are for a PAYE employee on full PRSI. Total income taxation includes income tax, PRSI and health and income levies for 1997 and 2008. Levies were replaced by the USC for 2014.
[2] Couple assumes 2 children and 65%/35% income division.

At the lower end of the income distribution, a policy commitment to remove all at or below the minimum wage from paying income tax saw rates reduce to zero per cent. A need to generate additional taxation revenue from Budget 2009 onwards saw a series of reductions in tax bands, cuts to tax credits and the introduction of the USC.[6] Collectively, these changes rapidly raised effective rates once again, although the effective rates for all earners remained well below the levels experienced in 1997.

Behind the overall trends in Table 4.4 are a series of issues on the functioning and impact of the Irish income taxation system, which we will examine in the remainder of this section.

Tax Base

The tax base defines what types and levels of income are to be considered as subject to taxation. Currently, each of the three tax charges on income has a differently defined tax base. This occurs because there are different tax exemptions and reliefs for income taxes, PRSI and the USC. Of these three bases, the USC is the broadest, including most forms of income and offering limited reliefs and exemptions. However, the simultaneous existence of three bases undermines the aforementioned desire for simplicity in the taxation system and policymakers have signalled a desire to consolidate the tax base further, most likely by aligning and eventually merging PRSI and the USC.

The narrowness of the income taxation base has been a subject of increasing attention in recent years. To illustrate this, we can use data from the tax system as structured in 2014. Under that structure, the combined effect of income tax rates and tax credits implies that a PAYE employee only begins to incur an income tax liability once their income has exceeded €16,500 per annum. Up to that point, their income incurs a tax rate of 20 per cent, but this liability is cancelled out by their entitlement to tax credits totalling €3,300 per annum. They are, however, subject to charges under the USC and PRSI. Data from the Revenue Commissioners following Budget 2014 (October 2013) suggest that in that year 39 per cent of income earners were exempt from income tax while 43 per cent paid at the standard rate and 18 per cent paid at the higher rate.[7] While these figures include those in receipt of all types of income, including pensions, they reflect both the narrowness of the income tax base and the fact that a large proportion of the Irish population earns and lives on low incomes.

The structure of the income taxation system is such that not all forms of income face the same marginal tax rates. In particular, income from savings and capital gains are treated differently from earned income. As outlined earlier, DIRT is charged at a rate of 41 per cent and capital gains incur taxation at a rate of 33 per cent. The tax expenditure system (see below) also incorporates generous reliefs which complement these rates and allow investors to write off the capital costs of their investment over short periods of seven to ten years, even when the value of these investments is inflating.

Tax Wedge and Employment
The combined impact of taxation on the take-home pay of workers has impacts on their labour market participation decisions, both at the margin (working additional hours) and at the point of entry and exit. As an employee's income level increases, high marginal taxation rates emerge and form a widening wedge between their gross earnings and their take-home pay.

Using data from the 2014 tax system, Table 4.5 shows that once income passes €32,800 the marginal tax rate reaches 52 per cent, meaning that an employee takes home only €48 out of every additional €100 earned. The table also highlights the existence of a number of steps in the structure of marginal tax rates in the Irish system. These emerge given the structure of tax credits, tax bands, PRSI thresholds and the USC. Self-employed earners with incomes above €100,000 are subject to an additional USC surcharge of 3 per cent on all income above this threshold, bringing their marginal tax rate to 55 per cent.

The existence of high marginal tax rates and the step-effect nature of their increases have knock-on implications for the wider economy. An employee on average earnings (€36,079 in 2012) may find it unattractive to take on additional work hours given these rates.[8] For others, particularly those earning near the marginal tax thresholds, there may be an incentive to reduce work hours or to leave the active labour market and become unemployed − becoming so-called 'discouraged workers'. To reduce the labour market participation disincentive effects experienced by individuals whose spouse/partner is already at work, most tax credits are *individualised*, i.e. they can only be claimed by the person who is entitled to them and they cannot be transferred to another, even within the same household. Consequently, a woman returning to work after having children will start earning with her own PAYE tax credit intact, although she is likely to have shared her personal credit with her partner.

Table 4.5 Composition of Marginal Tax Rates for Irish Workers (2014)[1]

Income Range	Income tax[2]	PRSI[3]	USC[4]	Marginal rate
€0–€10,035	0%	0%	0%	0%
€10,036–€16,016	0%	0%	4%	4%
€16,017–€16,500	0%	0%	7%	7%
€16,501–€18,304	20%	0%	7%	27%
€18,305–€32,800	20%	4%	7%	31%
€32,801+	41%	4%	7%	52%
> €100,000 self-employed[5]	41%	4%	10%	55%

[1] Assumes a single PRSI employee with entitlements to the personal and PAYE tax credit only.
[2] The personal and PAYE tax credit eliminate any income tax liability up to €16,500.
[3] PRSI is charged at a rate of 4 per cent on all income once earnings exceed €352 per week (€18,304 per annum).
[4] Employees who earn less than €10,035 are exempt from the USC; once earning above this level the USC applies to all income starting at a rate of 2 per cent up to €10,035.
[5] Self-employed income above €100,000 is subject to an additional USC surcharge of 3 per cent.

High marginal tax rates may also dampen the entrepreneurial enthusiasm of high-income workers, including the self-employed. Likewise, they can serve as a disincentive in attracting high-skilled migrants to work in Ireland while simultaneously enhancing the attractiveness of emigration for skilled Irish nationals. They also tend to be associated with increasing activity in the shadow or black economy where workers are paid in cash and do not declare their income to the Revenue Commissioners. While the scale of this activity is difficult to measure, the incentive for its emergence and growth is positively related to the marginal tax rate.

For government, it is difficult to avoid many of these marginal tax rate problems in a progressive tax system. Consequently, the challenge for tax policymaking is to balance the necessity of collecting sufficient taxation revenue against the disincentives inherent in high marginal rates, which may undermine economic activity and as a consequence undermine tax revenue.

Reliefs and Exemptions
An individual can decrease their effective and marginal tax rates below the levels in Tables 4.4 and 4.5 by availing of tax reliefs and exemptions. These mechanisms, formally known as tax expenditures, are incorporated by government into the

taxation system as a means of incentivising certain activity or accommodating certain needs. Examples include tax relief on pension contributions; incentives to invest in film-making, small business and property; a tax credit for blind employees; and a tax credit for employing a home carer. A review of the 2010 tax year found that the top 30 tax expenditures cost €17 billion in *revenue forgone* – revenue forgone measures the tax forgone by the exchequer as a result of the tax break.[9] The need to reduce the quantity and scale of these tax breaks and to adopt more formal accounting and economic evaluation methods in recording, reviewing and extending tax breaks has been highlighted.[10]

The largest tax relief is on employee pension contributions, costing €2.5 billion in revenue forgone each year. Employees avail of the relief by making contributions to their personal pension funds from their pre-tax income. Consequently, a higher rate of relief is available to employees on higher income tax levels than those on lower incomes. Overall, the ability to avail of tax breaks is directly linked to higher incomes. The more income a person has the more tax they are liable for and therefore the more tax they have available to be written down against various tax breaks. In 2014 a minimum effective tax rate of 30 per cent of income was set for earners with incomes of more than €125,000 in an attempt to minimise their use of tax breaks to reduce their tax bills – a 30 per cent rate is equivalent to the tax level faced by a single PAYE worker earning €50,000. While there is merit in the provision by government of certain tax breaks, the evidence for many is limited and in some cases it is clear that they lead to unnecessary and arbitrary market distortions.

Equity and Simplicity

As Tables 4.4 and 4.5 show, the Irish income taxation system has a progressive structure. But the equity principle is undermined at the top of the income scale by the quantity and generosity of many tax breaks. Similarly, there are questions at the other end of the income distribution regarding the point at which income taxes should begin to be imposed on earners. The USC initially (Budget 2011) collected tax from all earners on all income once their annual income exceeded €4,004; this was subsequently increased to €10,036 (Budget 2013). Collecting tax at low income levels marked a significant alteration in the approach to income taxation in Ireland, which previously had exempted earners up to the annual value of the minimum wage. The appropriateness of this policy reform can be judged against competing desires to protect the living standards of low-income workers and the need for exchequer revenue collected from a broad income tax base. Undoubtedly, the debate on both these issues is likely to continue for some time.

From a simplicity perspective, the compliance and administrative costs faced by most Irish taxpayers are low. As taxes are deducted from wages before they are paid, most employees have limited need for interaction with the Revenue Commissioners. For the self-employed, directors and other corporate tax payers, sophisticated online tax return systems and electronic cash transfers have made tax returns and compliance considerably simpler than in the past. It is likely that over the next decade the entire administrative side of the tax system will move to exclusively electronic exchanges. However, as we have seen, the Irish income taxation system is far from simple and the existence of multiple bases, thresholds, exemptions and rates makes for a complex system that most taxpayers would be challenged to comprehend.[11]

5 EVALUATION: INDIRECT TAXES, CORPORATION TAXES AND PROPERTY TAXES

While income and social security taxes comprise more than 50 per cent of the tax take (see Table 4.3), almost all of the rest of the exchequer's revenue is derived from taxes on consumption, company profits and property. The performance of each of these taxes in the Irish system is considered in this section.

Indirect Taxes

VAT

As Figure 4.1 shows, VAT is a regressive tax that collects a higher proportion of income from poorer households. In Ireland, as in most countries where VAT or equivalent general sales taxes have been in existence for some time, there are multiple VAT rates. This contrasts with countries, including a number in Eastern Europe, that have over recent decades introduced VAT systems with only one or two rates. The Irish system is characterised by a large number of exemptions and goods and services charged VAT at zero per cent. As a result, the potential base for VAT in Ireland is narrower than it could be and consequently the standard and reduced rate (13.5 per cent) are higher than they might be, given the revenue-raising constraints faced by government when setting these rates.

Figure 4.1 Indirect Taxes as a Proportion of Gross Household Income by Decile, 2009–10

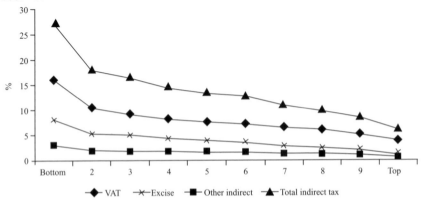

Source: M. Collins and D. Turnbull, 'Estimating the Direct and Indirect Tax Contributions of Households in Ireland', *NERI Working Paper No.8*, NERI, Dublin 2013.

While the progression of VAT rates across categories of goods and services is for the most part negatively related to their necessity, the fact that the consumption of most goods and services increases as income rises results in higher-income households benefiting more in absolute terms from the exemptions, zero-ratings and reduced rates. These benefits further undermine the equity of the tax, and the complexity associated with their implementation and administration reduces the efficiency and simplicity of VAT. In general, such inequities and inefficiencies would make the case for reform of the VAT structure, but the ability of government to do this is limited by strict EU rules which in effect only allow goods and services to be moved to the standard VAT rate irrespective of their current status.

Excise Duties

Excise duties on fuel, alcohol and tobacco serve a dual function for government as both revenue generators and public policy tools to discourage consumption and reduce or minimise externalities such as pollution and health effects. The former is possible given that these goods are characterised by low price elasticities and consequently increases in excise levels produce limited demand effects and sizeable exchequer revenue effects. They are therefore a relatively efficient tax. Similarly, they are simple to operate, with the tax revenue collected from distributors, importers and retailers. However, these taxes do raise a number of questions when considered in terms of equity.

The involuntary nature of some expenditure, such as on fuel to heat the home or because products are addictive, makes excise duties difficult, if not impossible, to avoid. Furthermore, data from the Household Budget Survey shows that households at the lower end of the income distribution spend a greater proportion of their disposable income on fuel, alcohol and tobacco – see Figure 4.1. Therefore, excise duties represent a greater burden to poorer households than better-off ones, implying that these taxes are regressive and violate the vertical equity principle. As the excise duty tax burden falls on households based on their consumption needs and addictions, households with similar incomes may pay significantly different amounts of total excise duties, violating the horizontal equity principle.

In designing taxation policy, government needs to balance the problematic effects of these taxes against the objectives of generating revenue and discouraging certain types of consumption. Setting excise duties is also influenced by levels in neighbouring jurisdictions as relatively high excise duties may result in a loss of the tax base as consumption shifts to purchases made outside the state. In recent years government has limited increasing the excise duties on tobacco and alcohol products as their levels in the Republic of Ireland were greater than those in Northern Ireland and the widening differential over previous years had shifted consumption and undermined the tax base.[12]

Carbon taxes raise similar efficiency and equity issues when considered against the earlier principles, given that they are collected and imposed in a similar way to excise duties. Studies prior to the introduction of the tax in 2010 suggested that the government should recycle some of the revenue from the tax to compensate low-income households whose consumption comprises a greater proportion of goods subject to the carbon tax than was the case for better-off households. It was argued that such an approach would cushion the effect of the policy reform while still encouraging households to alter their carbon consumption patterns. However, a compensating mechanism was not introduced to accompany the policy as the exchequer was unable to afford it in 2010. Similar issues also arise for motor taxation and it can be argued that these taxes fall more heavily on rural households, large households and those living in areas with limited access to public transport.

Overall, for the most part reforms of indirect taxes have been driven by the desire for additional tax revenue rather than some other objective. Comparative European reports have highlighted Ireland as one of the countries that most frequently changes indirect taxation rates.[13] Furthermore, from the perspective of the overall taxation system, the fact that it is difficult to avoid the regressive nature of indirect taxes, irrespective of their design and structure, challenges government to ensure that the other elements of the tax system are characterised by a high degree of progressivity.

Corporation Taxes

The corporate profits of both indigenous and foreign-owned firms in Ireland are taxed at a rate of 12.5 per cent. In international terms, Ireland's headline corporate tax rate is low, with only one other country in the EU or OECD possessing rates below this level – Bulgaria, with a 10 per cent rate. Data for 2013 suggest that the Irish rate is more than ten per cent lower than the EU-27 average of 23.2 per cent and well below the top statutory rates on corporate income in Germany (29.8 per cent), France (the EU's highest rate of 36.1 per cent), the UK (24 per cent) and the USA (39.1 per cent).[14]

The effective tax rate faced by companies in these countries is likely to be below these headline rates as they can avail of various tax breaks such as for research and development, recruiting workers from disadvantaged groups or operating in regional or economically disadvantaged areas. In general, countries with higher headline corporate tax rates provide a greater array of corporate tax breaks. Estimates by the European Commission found that in 2012 the average EU-27 corporate tax rate reduced from a headline figure of 23 per cent to an effective average tax rate of 20.9 per cent. However, even taking account of tax breaks, the Irish corporate tax rate is low in international terms and is regularly highlighted as a key incentive for new foreign direct investment.

In general foreign-owned firms benefit from Ireland's low corporate tax rate by locating a subsidiary in Ireland whose profits are subject to tax in Ireland with no taxes payable in the corporation's home country until the profit is repatriated there (see also Chapter 9). On repatriation, profits are taxed in the home country with a credit given for taxes already paid in Ireland. Companies are free to delay indefinitely the repatriation of these profits and as such benefit from an ability to use in their business the portion of profit yet to be repatriated. Shareholders also benefit from share price inflation associated with these higher profits and the benefits derived from the use of the additional funds. Irish subsidiaries also enjoy almost no restrictions on their ability to engage in *transfer pricing*. This allows multinational companies to artificially value sales between associated companies located in different countries and can be used to maximise the profit realised and taxable in lower-tax jurisdictions such as Ireland. Such sales can comprise actual goods, or payments for intellectual property rights, and can often represent a large proportion of a firm's turnover.

The sustainability of Ireland's current corporate taxation model is under threat from a series of ongoing international reforms (see also Chapter 9). In 2013 the OECD commenced a Base Erosion and Profit Shifting (BEPS) project aimed at investigating and reforming the international corporate tax system. At its core the BEPS has set out to establish whether and why the taxable profits of multinational companies are being allocated to locations different from those where their business activity takes place. Although reform will take some time, it carries notable implications for Ireland's corporate tax revenues.

Complementing the OECD BEPS process, there are a number of other corporate tax reforms with implications for Ireland. The impact of the post-2008 recession on the fiscal balance sheets of countries such as the USA focused attention on the need for governments to minimise tax leakages. As a result, incentives to repatriate profits have been introduced and a harder attitude is being taken to countries and territories that facilitate corporations not paying the tax they would be expected to pay. Simultaneously, in the EU proposals for the establishment of a common consolidated corporate tax base (CCCTB) were made in 2011 by the European Commission after almost a decade of developing the proposal.[15]

While the debate on CCCTB is continuing, its emergence, if agreed, would require firms in all member states of the EU to calculate their profits in the same way, essentially imposing a uniform definition of how corporate income is defined and what can and cannot be discounted against it. The reform is also likely to require firms that operate in multiple countries to apportion their profits between those countries in accordance with a formula that weights the activities of the multinational in the different countries, rather than the company arranging its own internal balance sheet to maximise the profit it realises in the country with the lowest tax rate. While the CCCTB reforms seem logical, they would undermine the ability of firms to shift their profits and tax liabilities to Ireland and consequently reduce the flow of revenue from this sector to the exchequer.

A further international threat comes from reductions in headline corporate tax rates of other EU member states. While Ireland's low corporate taxation rate has been a competitive advantage for some time, an increasing number of EU member states are cutting their rates to compete with Ireland, and others, for foreign direct investment. In the years ahead, it is unlikely that Ireland could fiscally afford to match these reductions.

Finally, given the recent increases, outlined earlier, in income and indirect taxes and the introduction of recurring property taxes and additional user charges, it seems inevitable that attention will turn domestically to the feasibility of raising corporate taxes. Despite the importance accorded to corporate taxes, and near universal political support to leave them untouched, there is limited economic evidence to suggest that there are no deadweight exchequer losses associated with having the rate at 12.5 per cent rather than 15 per cent or 20 per cent.

Property Taxes
A study by the OECD in 2009 used time series data from its members states to establish a hierarchy of taxes with regard to their negative effect on GDP per capita in the following order from the most to the least harmful for growth: (1) corporate income taxes; (2) personal income taxes; (3) consumption taxes; and (4) recurrent taxes on immovable property.[16] Notably, the Irish taxation system has only recently introduced a recurring domestic property tax, despite this being the least harmful form of taxation given the objective of economic growth.

Recommendations from the 2009 Commission on Taxation and requirements of the EU/ECB/International Monetary Fund (IMF) bailout set the context for the introduction of a local property tax (LPT).[17] Political reluctance and fear of such a tax, spanning decades since the abolition of local authority rates on households in 1977, made it challenging for the tax to be implemented. At its most basic, the state did not possess a list of all the dwellings in the country, let alone details of ownership and the amenities they enjoyed. This is despite the fact that the state would have provided many of these households with tax breaks on their purchase, charged stamp duty on their transfer, paid universal transfer payments (child benefit, pensions) to their occupiers and collected various taxes from their occupiers. Despite delays, the commissioning of further reports, and the significant logistical challenges, the tax was implemented from mid 2013. A key attraction of the LPT is that it provides the exchequer with a stable annual flow of resources based on an immovable tax base. This contrasts with the volatile flow of funds from transaction-linked stamp duties which had served as the main source of state property tax revenue.

Judged against the total amount of taxes collected (see Table 4.3) the LPT revenue is small at about 1 per cent of the total (€550m in 2014). While it is likely to grow over time, it is unlikely to quickly exceed 2.5 per cent of the total tax take. There may also be regressive elements to the tax, where property owners are asset-rich but have low incomes; although the LPT has been introduced with a series of exemption and deferral mechanisms to counteract such outcomes. However, the intention is for the tax to fall on property, not income, and provide a flow of resources back to the exchequer and local government to reflect the cost of provision of local services and amenities enjoyed by occupants. An added benefit is that the LPT provides a new policy tool to keep a check on house prices and ensure that they do not diverge from various earnings-to-price benchmark ratios as they did in the early 2000s.

6 DEFERRED TAXATION: PUBLIC DEBT

Imposing taxation on incomes, consumption, profits, and assets is not the only way in which government can access finance to pursue its spending and economic management objectives. It may also borrow money by selling bonds and using the proceeds to finance public spending. In doing so, governments are engaging in *deferred taxation* as implicit in the selling of a bond is a commitment to pay interest over its lifetime and repay its value upon maturity. To do this, governments will have to raise future taxation revenue from current and future taxpayers.

The appropriateness of governments borrowing today on the basis of taxpayers paying in the future is linked to how governments use these borrowings. Where bond revenues are used to finance capital investments, such as hospitals, museums and transport infrastructure, the benefits derived from the provision of these facilities will flow to the future taxpayers who will service and repay the borrowing. As such, deferring taxation so that beneficiaries finance the provision of government investments while they experience their benefits has a logical basis.[18]

Conversely, governments should finance day-to-day, or current, spending from current taxation revenue, thereby balancing the exchequer's current account. Current account deficits, where they occur, should only be associated with attempts to stabilise the economy in the short run and governments should cancel this effect out by running current account surpluses in other periods. Financing current account deficits from borrowing serves as an inappropriate transfer of avoided current taxation burdens on to future taxpayers.

Table 4.6 Government Debt and Financial Balances as % of GDP

	General government gross public debt as % of GDP				
	1980	1987	2000	2007	2015[1]
Ireland	65.8	110.4	37.0	24.9	118.5
Euro Area			69.3	66.4	95.6
	Government financial balances as % of GDP			
	2000	2007	2010	2013
Ireland	4.9	0.2	−30.6	−7.4
Euro Area	−0.1	−0.7	−6.2	−2.9

Source: IMF, *World Economic Outlook Database* (www.imf.org) and OECD, *Economic Outlook Database* (www.oecd.org), both accessed March 2014.
[1] Estimates.

The scale of public debt is measured relative to a country's national income, with the EU and ECB regarding a gross debt to GDP ratio of below 60 per cent as optimal. As Table 4.6 and Figure 4.2 show, over the past four decades Ireland has moved from marginally above this threshold in 1980, to well above it in 1987, to significantly below it in 2007 and back to well above it in 2011. Borrowing to fund the current account deficit drove national debt levels up in the 1980s while strong economic growth and budget surpluses decreased the debt burden up to 2007.

In 2000 Ireland ran a fiscal balance of 4.9 per cent of GDP, meaning that taxation revenues covered all current and capital spending and provided almost 5 per cent of GDP as an exchequer surplus. By 2007 Ireland's debt to GDP ratio reached a level of 25 per cent of GDP; a debt burden regarded as very low and suggesting that the nation's debt was small, manageable and of limited long-term economic significance. If anything, such a low debt level reduced the need for higher future taxes as its servicing and repayment would inflict limited fiscal strain and, given GDP growth, the debt burden would be further eroded.

Figure 4.2 Ireland's National Debt as a Percentage of GDP, 1980–2015

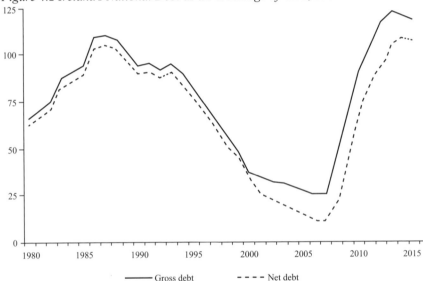

Source: IMF, *World Economic Outlook Database* (www.imf.org), accessed March 2014.

The simultaneous collapse in the construction and banking industries from 2008 had significant knock-on effects for exchequer revenue and spending. Taxation revenue from employees' incomes and spending contracted rapidly, as did revenue from housing-related VAT and stamp duty. The concurrent international recession also decreased trade, corporate activity and corporation profits. Between 2007 and 2009 current taxation revenues fell by almost €15 billion or 31 per cent. Exchequer spending also increased to fund higher social welfare needs and to pay for capital injections into various banks.

By 2010 Ireland's exchequer deficit reached record levels with the nation borrowing over 30 per cent of GDP in one year; a figure associated with both a large exchequer deficit and once-off rescue costs for Anglo Irish Bank. Ongoing budget deficits and low economic growth saw Ireland's gross debt levels peak in 2013 at 123 per cent of GDP. As Figure 4.2 shows, Ireland net debt level peaked at a lower level (108 per cent) a year later. The net debt measure discounts cash balances and other financial assets held by the exchequer, including cash-on-hand at the National Treasury Management Agency (NTMA), which regularly stockpiles borrowing in advance to minimise the exposure of the exchequer to turbulent bond markets.

While Ireland's debt transformation is severe, debt to GDP ratios and exchequer deficits have also increased across the euro area as a response to the recent international recession. In 2009 and 2010 average euro zone budget deficits exceeded 6 per cent of GDP and average debt to GDP ratios climbed more than 30 percentage points to reach 95.6 per cent in 2013.

This growth in debt carries a series of structural and policy implications for Europe and Ireland in the coming years. In a number of countries independent fiscal councils have been established to act as a watchdog for the fiscal health of nations and to comment publicly on the appropriateness of governments' taxation and spending decisions before and after they are announced (see Chapter 3). In Ireland this has seen the creation of the Irish Fiscal Advisory Council (IFAC). However, the fact that Ireland's debt to GDP ratio has climbed to such a high level will necessitate ongoing higher taxation levels relative to those that existed over the decade from 2000. Questions have also been raised regarding the sustainability of retaining and servicing certain elements of this debt, in particular that related to the rescue of banks, given the different European rules that applied to the Irish bank bailouts and subsequent ones in other member states.

The fact that future Irish taxpayers will pay for the fiscal and economic mistakes of the first decade of this century violates the logic of intergenerational deferred taxation discussed at the start of this section. The phenomenon of imposing this debt on future generations has also given rise to a consideration to create constitutional checks on governments' fiscal policy decisions.

7 CONCLUSION

This chapter has provided an overview of Ireland's taxation system, setting it in the context of economic theory, its features and operation and the nation's future liabilities. In a given year the taxation system, including tax expenditures, is a €60–€70 billion system and it is clear that in the years ahead the system will face significant challenges and reforms.

Central to these will be the need to generate the additional revenue required to close Ireland's exchequer deficit and begin to repay the debt accumulated in the years since 2008. As part of the process, this chapter has highlighted the opportunities and needs for a broader tax base and reforms targeted at enhancing the simplicity, efficiency and equality of the tax system. These reforms will also need to address the backdrop of unemployment and tackle any tax-related disincentives to labour market participation and, where possible, use taxation policies to enhance growth, recovery and job creation. A further backdrop will be reforms at a European level relating to corporate taxation structures and the ongoing management and monitoring of fiscal policy (see Chapter 2).

The cumulative effect of revenue needs, deferred taxation, international reforms and economic recovery in the years ahead will necessitate that taxation policy and taxation reform will be recurring public policy themes for the foreseeable future.

Notes

1   A. Smith, *An Inquiry into the Nature and Causes of the Wealth of Nations*, Strahan and Cadell, London 1776.

2   A good overview is provided by T.O. Weber, J. Fooken and B. Herrman, 'Behavioural Economics and Taxation', *European Commission Taxation Papers N.41*, Brussels 2014.

3   The USC does not apply to individuals with a gross annual market income of less than €10,035.

4   There are a total of seven VAT rates in the Irish system. Additional rates of 4.8 per cent apply to agricultural livestock, horses and greyhounds; a rate of 5 per cent applies to certain agricultural outputs; and a rate of 9 per cent applies to a number of labour-intensive and cultural services such as restaurant and catering services, hotel/B&B lettings, hairdressing and admissions to cinemas and theatres.

5   EU proposals for a Financial Transactions Tax (FTT) may in time add to the list of hypothecated taxes with revenue earmarked as a contribution to the EU Budget.

6   The USC was preceded by an income levy and health levy, which were merged in Budget 2011 to create the USC.

7   See Department of Finance, *Budget 2014*, Stationery Office, Dublin 2010.

8   Central Statistics Office, *Earnings and Labour Costs,* Stationery Office, Dublin 2013.

9   M. Collins, 'Income Taxes and Income Tax Options', *NERI Working Paper 2013/5*, NERI, Dublin 2013.

10 M. Collins and M. Walsh, *Ireland's Tax Expenditure System: International Comparisons and a Reform Agenda*, Policy Institute, Trinity College Dublin, Dublin 2010.

11 A comprehensive explanation is available on the websites of the Office of the Revenue Commissioners (www.revenue.ie) and the Irish Taxation Institute (www.taxireland.ie).

12 See P. Reidy and K. Walsh, *Modelling the Market for Cigarettes in Ireland*, Revenue Commissioners, Dublin 2011.

13 See European Commission, *Study to Quantify and Analyse the VAT Gap in the EU-27 Member States*, Brussels 2013.

14 Eurostat, *Taxation Trends in the European Union*, Eurostat, Luxembourg 2013, and OECD Tax Database.

15 See proposals for a CCCTB and background documents on the European Commission website <http://ec.europa.eu/taxation_customs/taxation/company_tax/common_tax_base/index_en.htm>.

16 OECD, *Going for Growth*, OECD, Paris 2009.

17 Commission on Taxation, *Report 2009*, Stationery Office, Dublin 2009; EU/IMF, *Ireland Memorandum of Understanding on Specific Economic Policy Conditionality*, Dublin 2010.
18 See A.L. Hillman, *Public Finance and Public Policy – Responsibilities and Limitations of Government* (2nd edn), Cambridge University Press, New York 2009.

CHAPTER 5

Regulation and Competition

Francis O'Toole*

1 INTRODUCTION

This chapter examines from both the national and international perspective the general policy area of regulation and the specific policy area of competition policy, including the regulatory treatment of natural monopolies.

Broadness of Regulatory Issues

The field of regulation, which spans disciplines such as economics, ethics, law, management, political science, public policy, social administration and sociology, requires a suitably wide definition of regulation, such as 'the intentional use of authority to affect behaviour of a different party according to set standards, involving instruments of information gathering and behaviour modification'.[1] A set of formal rules with respect to health and safety in the workplace provides an example of command and control-type regulation, while the use of taxes (e.g. a carbon tax) and subsidies (e.g. a subsidised flu vaccine for health workers or older people) that aim to alter behaviour provides an example of incentive-based regulation. Informational requirements with respect to whether or not the seller of a particular financial product is a tied agent represents a standard supply of information-type regulation.

However, specific uses of name and shame or nudge techniques by official agencies can also be viewed from a regulatory perspective. In the context of the official use of the name and shame approach, allowing a Financial Services Ombudsman to name offending financial institutions or allowing the relevant Revenue authorities to publish summary details on tax cheats generally raise few major public objections, but opening up the sex offenders register to greater public scrutiny is a much more controversial topic. Similarly, designing the presentation of the school lunch menu in a particular health-friendly manner seems a sensible nudge, as does encouraging organ donor registration and designing tax return forms in as compliance-facilitating a manner as possible, but a government agency being involved in designing campaigns (e.g. letters and emails) so as to maximise private donations to charities (and hence perhaps reducing demands on the public purse) could be seen by some as overstepping some appropriate boundary.

As suggested by the above, the regulatory remit certainly extends well beyond standard economically based examples and into broader social policy-based areas such as: gay marriage; surrogacy; gender X (or intersex); the rights and responsibilities (and even definition) of parents; gene therapy; domestic and foreign adoption (including the rights and responsibilities of gay partners with respect to adoption); genetically modified (GM) foods and food safety issues more generally; internet gambling; and the 'markets' for sexual services or illicit drugs; or even the 'market' for votes and the associated policy debate with respect to limiting corporate or private donations to political parties.[2]

Competition Policy and Natural Monopolies

Competition policy provides one important example of a regulatory policy. At the national level, Irish competition policy aims to ensure that markets produce pro-competitive outcomes such as lower prices and higher-quality products for buyers as well as the appropriate returns for sellers. As such, competition policy discourages anti-competitive practices such as price-fixing or market-sharing and blocks mergers that would lead to a substantial lessening of competition. However, competition policy also encourages pro-competitive agreements such as product standardisation agreements, even when agreed between rivals.

At the European Union level, competition policy is implemented by the European Commission and focuses attention on business practices that may affect cross-border trade within the EU. At the global level, the World Trade Organisation (WTO) provides a stage for the negotiation of trade agreements between governments. The WTO encourages reductions in trade barriers as well as non-discrimination in the implementation of any remaining trade barriers, but also has the authority to interpret and enforce the underlying existing trade agreements that cover goods, services and intellectual property.

An important distinction can be drawn between the traded and non-traded sectors of the economy in terms of competition policy, in that the enforcement of competition policy within the traded sector of the economy is facilitated by the threat as well as the reality of imports, while in contrast the enforcement of competition policy within the non-traded sector of the economy is more dependent on the competition policy agencies and/or national courts. However, the creditability associated with the threat of imports is in turn related to the effective implementation and enforcement of both EU competition policy and WTO trade agreements. In addition, the existence of large-scale imports does not rule out the possible existence of local retail markets; for example, the large-scale importation of many grocery and pharmaceutical items into Ireland does not rule out the possibility that a specific community could be vulnerable to being exploited by one supermarket or one pharmacy, especially in the presence of restrictive planning regulations.

Recent high-profile competition policy issues include: Ryanair's third attempted acquisition of Aer Lingus, which was rejected by the European Commission in February 2013 and the UK Competition Commission's subsequent decision (August 2013) to order Ryanair to reduce its 29.8 per cent shareholding in Aer Lingus to a maximum of 5 per cent; and a proposed ban on the below-cost selling of alcohol products or the introduction of minimum (retail) pricing for alcohol. In the context of the WTO's enforcement of international trade agreements, many disputes fall under the heading of export subsidies and/or dumping (i.e. predatory pricing), whereby products are exported at below cost prices in order to gain market share unfairly.

A natural monopoly exists in a market if it is technically more efficient for one firm, as opposed to two or more firms, to supply any relevant level of output. In particular, there are significant economies of scale and direct (or 'in the market') competition between firms would be inefficient as economies of scale opportunities and hence significant cost savings would be forgone.

The provision of a costly infrastructure such as a natural gas network provides a standard example of a natural monopoly. Recent prominent natural monopoly policy issues include: the appropriate regulation of the collection and disposal of Dublin's household waste, encompassing the controversial Poolbeg incinerator/ waste to energy project; the recent sale of Bord Gáis Energy but not the state-owned natural gas pipeline network; and the setting of retail prices for natural gas by the Commission for Energy Regulation (CER).

Sectoral Regulation

The importance of regulatory and competition policies is felt throughout the economy. For example, the EU Nitrates Directive, which imposes limits on the amount of nitrogen (from animal manure or fertiliser) that can be used in farming, highlights the specific importance of regulatory policies to the agricultural sector (see Chapters 10 and 11). In addition, very significant controversy was caused in Ireland by the imposition of a ban on non-commercial turf-cutting on raised bogs, which arose as a result of EU conservation laws. These two examples also demonstrate the importance of transnational regulatory policy and the need for co-ordination with respect to Irish and EU regulations.

In the manufacturing sector, policies with respect to corporation taxes have been responsible for the location of many foreign-owned manufacturing plants in Ireland, for example in the IT and pharmaceutical sectors. The recent controversies surrounding Ireland's relatively low corporation tax rate (12.5 per cent) and, in particular, Apple's apparently much lower effective tax rate again demonstrates the importance of transnational regulatory policy but also highlights the existence of tensions between the goals of national (i.e. Irish) and international (e.g. EU, USA and Organisation for Economic Co-operation and Development (OECD)) regulations (see Chapters 4 and 9).

In the services sector of the economy, the importance of regulatory policy, both domestic and transnational, was more than aptly demonstrated by Ireland's banking crisis (see Chapter 3). The re-capitalisation and restructuring of the Irish (as well as the UK) banking sector also demonstrates the importance of competition policy, both nationally and internationally. While competition policy was trumped in the short run by the immediate needs of financial stabilisation (e.g., in the Irish context, the merger of AIB and EBS), it is clear that a suitably designed and implemented competition policy offers significant long-run benefits (e.g. protection from a possible banking duopoly).

Chapter Outline

This chapter attempts to address in a systematic manner many of the issues mentioned above. Section 2 provides an overview of regulation, addressing possible explanations and/or justifications for, and theories of, regulation and focuses specific attention on the risk-based approach to regulation. Section 3 explores Ireland's banking crisis from a regulatory policy perspective as the financial services sector has contributed significantly in recent years to the increased realisation of the importance of both domestic and transnational regulatory policy.

Section 4 focuses attention on the specific regulatory policy example of competition policy and provides a number of illustrative examples, while Section 5 addresses the specific policy area that intersects both regulation and competition, namely the regulation of natural monopolies and networks such as the electricity transmission and natural gas grids. Section 6 offers some concluding comments.

The above outline and the previous examples make it clear that an understanding of regulation is essential for an understanding of policy issues in both the Irish market and non-market sectors. As such, it should be no surprise to readers of the rest of this book to encounter many of the above themes, for example in discussions surrounding food safety, labour markets, distributional issues, energy, education and health.

2 REGULATION: PRINCIPLES AND ISSUES

Reasons for Regulation ✳

Information and Co-ordination

There are a number of plausible reasons for the existence of regulations. At a very general level, informational and co-ordination problems could justify, or at least explain, the existence of many regulations. For example, basic fire safety standards are set to protect the vast majority of individual users of, say, cinemas, hotels and public transport as individually very few of these users would be in a position to assess the appropriateness or otherwise of the fire safety precautions taken by others.

A similar argument holds with respect to the existence of regulations regarding, say, maximum taxi fares. For example, a fare of €100 might well be acceptable to an individual (rich) tourist attempting to get from an airport to the city centre on a very cold evening, but it is generally regarded as inappropriate to take advantage of the tourist's initial informational deficiency. Indeed, many forms of regulation are responses to what are seen as informational problems, as it is argued that markets often under-provide relevant information. For example, what is the real price of an advertised 1 cent airfare or how can one individual compare the costs of different loans? The latter question is addressed in the USA by the Truth in Lending Act (2001), which insists that all lenders must quote the annual percentage rate (APR) to potential borrowers; APRs can then be compared across different loan options.

Other regulations surrounding information requirements in at least some jurisdictions insist that car manufacturers provide fuel efficiency information, brewers of beer provide alcohol content information, cigarette packets display graphic health warnings, food products carry nutritional information and league tables of school performance are produced and published. In addition, various regulations insist upon what might be termed minimum standards, as opposed to simply the provision of information, e.g. travel agencies and operators enter into various forms of travel bonds and retail banks must keep a certain proportion of their retail consumers' deposits in liquid assets. These minimum standards are at least arguably a policy response to underlying informational deficiencies.

Spillover Effects
Economists tend naturally to view the existence of (non-priced) spillover effects, or externalities, as providing an explanation for the existence of many regulations. Technically, externalities imply the existence of a divergence between private costs and social costs (or private benefits and social benefits). Taking the standard example of pollution – a negative production externality – without suitable regulations a producer does not have to internalise the cost of the pollution that the production process imposes on others.

A similar argument holds with respect to placing restrictions on the consumption of tobacco products, although of course reasonable people can differ with respect to the appropriate limits of such regulations. For example, should an adult be allowed to smoke at home or in a car in the presence of children, or should adults be allowed to choose between a smoking and non-smoking pub/restaurant? Indeed, the appropriate regulation of electronic cigarettes (e-cigarettes) appears particularly controversial.

Of course, informational and spillover explanations for regulations do not always separate out easily. For example, the requirement for drivers (and businesses more generally) to hold at least third-party insurance is commonly justified by the belief that drivers (and society more generally) should be protected from the results of mistakes of another driver, even if each individual driver is allowed to rationally (or otherwise) decide not to protect himself or herself from his or her own actions. The existence of this regulation can be understood via the information explanation (how would one know which drivers are insured?) and/or by the spillover explanation (why should you have to pay for my mistake?).

Another possible example is provided by retail planning guidelines with respect to the location and scale of various types of retail development (e.g. shopping centres) at or near a town centre which set the rules by which business people make important (and often non-reversible) investment decisions.

Unequal Bargaining Power and Wider Social Policy

The reality of the existence of unequal bargaining power also underlies the existence of many regulations. For example, although at least some users of industrial saws or chainsaws may well be prepared to work without safety guards, many other users would prefer not to be put in a position where they had to actively request the installation of such (perhaps expensive) guards and hence perhaps not be employed in the first place (as a result of their rather 'conservative' approach to safety matters).

Arguably, the same applies with respect to the use of minimum wage legislation; at least some workers and employers would be prepared to transact at a lower wage, but society in effect does not allow such 'voluntary' transactions. However, at least some people might regard the setting of some safety requirements and labour restrictions as being excessively interventionist. Indeed, some might even feel the need for less regulation in the 'markets' for sexual services or so-called recreational drugs, but most would probably feel uncomfortable if a non-interventionist position were used to justify the straightforward buying and selling of votes or vital organs (such as kidneys) or even people (e.g. babies).

More generally, it is clear that many regulations are explained on social policy grounds as opposed to what might be termed market failure grounds. For example, anti-discrimination legislation is difficult to explain on market failure grounds alone; indeed, market proponents might well insist that the market system would eliminate such discrimination. The existence of universal service obligations with respect to a basic daily postal delivery service (at no extra cost to the recipient living alone in a very isolated location) or the proposed new 1 per cent levy on insurance policies in Ireland to cover those most at risk of flood damage (who are currently not offered flood insurance by the insurance market) can also be seen as addressing social policy objectives. Indeed, in at least the latter case, arguably there is no market failure at all as it would be irrational for an insurance business to offer affordable flood insurance if flood damage is almost guaranteed.

Behavioural Economics, Nudging and Paternalism

Behavioural economics uses insights from psychology to analyse how individuals actually make choices and the possible policy implications and applications of these choices. In particular, behavioural economics highlights factors or biases that impact significantly and consistently on the decision-making process, for example anchoring, framing, inertia, loss aversion and myopia.[3] Until recently, the standard economics approach would have ignored these biases, seeing them as short-run phenomena that, in theory at least, must wash out in the long run.

Anchoring focuses on the importance of the order in which questions are asked. For example, consider the possible impact of reversing the order of the following two questions: (1) How happy are you; and (2) How many really close friends do you have? It seems likely that the stated (or perhaps even actual) level of happiness would fall considerably when one is tempted into anchoring the response against a (presumably) smallish number.

Framing highlights the importance of presentation. For example, consider any standard quantity discount system where the mean price paid by the consumer falls as the quantity purchased increases. One can present this scheme as being a *loyalty discount* scheme (where the consumer is *rewarded* for loyalty) or as being a *disloyalty penalty* scheme (where the consumer is *penalised* for being disloyal or unfaithful); it seems very likely that more will be sold using the former marketing approach.

Inertia (or the status quo bias) refers to the tendency to stick to one's original choice, which in many cases is the initial default option. For example, if the default option is that one must actively opt in to organ donation or a basic retirement plan as opposed to actively opting out of organ donation or a basic retirement plan, it seems clear that organ donation and future income will be relatively low.

Loss aversion refers to the, in general, greater level of unhappiness associated with a particular loss (say €100) compared to the happiness associated with the same gain (i.e. €100). For example, it appears that the prospect of winning €200 just about compensates for the (equal) prospect of losing €100.

Myopic (or short-sighted) behaviour refers to the tendency to over-value (under-value) the present (future). For example, a small reward today might be chosen over a much larger reward tomorrow. Many would instinctively defend this choice as being rational (which it may very well be), but an underlying tension or apparent inconsistency of preferences is suggested if the same individual reverses the choice when, say, the same choice is put off for 24 hours: for example, perhaps you would choose €10 today over €12 tomorrow, but would you also choose €12 the day after tomorrow over €10 tomorrow?

Many of these and other similar issues centre on the architecture of choice and, given its obvious potential importance (e.g. in terms of organ donation or retirement pensions), it seems reasonable to nudge people into making decisions that would make them better off by influencing this architecture. Indeed, it is argued that it would be wrong not to respond to the importance of the architecture of choice as this apparent 'non-decision' (i.e. not to 'interfere') would actually represent a decision not to make people better off, i.e. in effect a decision has been made to make people worse off.

For example, if school children tend to pick the first option on the school menu, surely it is reasonable to dedicate that position on the menu to a healthy option? If organ donation is significantly higher under opt-out, as opposed to opt-in, surely it is reasonable to change the default for organ donation? If savers are myopic, surely it is reasonable to push them into increasing their pension contributions automatically as their income increases, as well as opting them into the pension scheme in the first place? This policy approach has been termed 'libertarian paternalism' in that people are being pushed into making decisions that are good for them, into making decisions that they (arguably) would make anyway but for the presence of the above-mentioned imperfections or biases.

For many people, there are limits to this paternalist approach. For example, at least some might feel somewhat uneasy if an official agency had the goal of increasing charitable giving by utilising the insights offered by behavioural economics.[4] Possible mechanisms include: offering individuals the opportunity to opt in to increased future donations; using personalised messages or offering prizes; using prominent individuals as examples to follow; and getting the timing right by, for example, making the request in December. The increased private donations may well reduce the immediate need for public expenditures, but perhaps public expenditure was a more efficient and effective form of support for these (presumably deserving) charities in the first place? Indeed, it is arguably possible that the short-run significant increases in charitable donations might be offset by uncertain long-run reactions by the contributors, as the extra contributions must come from somewhere.

While information, co-ordination, spillover effects, behavioural economics and unequal bargaining power or, more generally, social policy grounds can be used to explain the existence of very many regulations, it is not so easy to explain the existence of many other regulations, such as the ban on private health insurers from offering discounts to non-smokers, without stretching the concepts of co-ordination failures, spillover effects and social policy objectives beyond their usefulness. Indeed, in addition, the above-mentioned proposed explanations may not be able to explain the non-existence of arguably sensible regulations, for example with respect to you being required to inform (up front) any potential partner of at least some of your particular health and personality 'characteristics' before the potential partner has to make a potentially irreversible investment in you. As such, there is much merit in examining plausible over-arching theories of regulation.

Regulation: Theories and Strategies

Theories

There are a number of overlapping theories of regulation. From an economics perspective, it is tempting to focus particular attention on the distinction between, on the one hand, the public interest approach to regulation and, on the other, the interest group and private interest approaches.

The public interest approach to regulation highlights the claimed equivalence between the regulator's interests and the public interest. As such, the regulator may be said, in a somewhat paradoxical sense, to be disinterested; the public interest is somehow ascertained (for example with respect to food safety), and the regulator acts in a purely technical manner so as to achieve the desired end state. In particular, there is no allowance made for any underlying power struggle between, say, the regulated parties (e.g. producers and sellers of food) and the parties for whose benefit the regulations are being put in place (e.g. consumers of food). This approach may be appropriate at least sometimes in the context of basic food safety, but what about the context of the appropriate regulation of genetically modified (GM) foods?

In contrast, the interest group and private interest approaches highlight the private incentives of, respectively, groups and individuals. The interest group approach focuses attention on the relationships between groups and the state.

Within the context of these evolving relationships a competition or battle is seen to take place between various different conceptualisations of the public interest. From an Irish perspective, the evolution of social partnership could be analysed from this perspective.

The private interest approach, also referred to as the economic theory of regulation or public choice, goes further and insists that the individual incentives confronting each rational agent or actor must be considered if regulation is to be understood. For example, it is claimed that regulatory capture, a process in which regulators over time appear to begin to represent the interests of the regulated, as opposed to society more generally, can only be understood if particular attention is paid to the incentives of the employees of regulatory agencies. It is these employees who interact with, and begin to depend on, the regulated entities (e.g. with respect to the provision of data in a particular format by a certain date).

From the public choice perspective, unless particular safeguards are put in place, it is hardly surprising that implicit understandings between these individuals and even their respective organisations begin to develop. For a plausible example, consider at least some aspects of the Irish banking crisis, where the interests of individuals and financial institutions somehow appeared to become blurred with the interests of the state.

In addition to the above interest approaches to regulation, there are other approaches that can be considered on their own merits or in conjunction with the interest approaches. For example, at particular times in history, it is clear that the force of ideas can drive regulatory developments. At a macroeconomic level the Keynesian revolution could be viewed as a prime example of a shift in ideas with significant policy implications, while at a more microeconomic level (albeit one with macroeconomic consequences), there was a shift towards privatisation in the UK and deregulation and market liberalisation in the USA during the early 1980s.

Strategies

Assuming the need for a regulatory response, there are various options with respect to the appropriate form of regulation, for example: command and control (e.g. no smoking indoors in work places); production and/or consumption taxes (e.g. the imposition of a carbon tax); quotas, perhaps supported by a system of tradable permits (e.g. fishing or even pollution); or simply naming and shaming (e.g. tax evaders or negative inspection reports for nursing homes or, albeit perhaps less likely – but more horrifying – evaluation reports by students on individual teachers or lecturers). Even in the context of a standard externality, say insufficient take-up of the flu vaccine or, more controversially, the MMR vaccine, alternative and very different regulatory strategies can be followed, ranging from simple provision of information to subsidising consumption of the vaccine to compulsory vaccination.

In contrast to these various measures, some market enthusiasts simply highlight the need to specify property rights very clearly so as to facilitate negotiations and market-based transactions between all affected parties. For example, if anglers have the right to clean water, anglers will be paid by the polluters for any pollution that the anglers choose to allow and if the polluters have the right to pollute the water, the anglers will pay the polluters so as to restrict the level of pollution to the appropriate level.[5]

Almost all regulatory strategies suffer from some disadvantages. Command and control tends to be inflexible; for example, in the context of pollution reduction, the adoption of a tradable permit system would be more efficient because those most able to reduce pollution could transfer (at an appropriate price) the right to pollute to those least able to reduce pollution. In addition, command and control, as well as other regulatory strategies, can suffer from what is termed creative compliance; for example, the introduction of a maximum waiting period for hospital admission is often closely followed by the introduction of, in effect, a waiting list for the waiting list.

More generally, there has been a move away from regulating by rule (which can be associated with a rather narrow understanding of regulation) and towards what might be termed market-based systems of regulation, e.g. where the regulator highlights the goals and allows maximum flexibility to the regulated with respect to attaining the goals. However, in the presence of serious or catastrophic risk (e.g. nuclear energy or some financial systems), it may not be appropriate to rely simply on the market system and the assumed rationality of all economic actors.

Risk-Based Regulation ➤
The concept of risk has become an organising concept in regulatory matters, particularly with respect to allocating regulatory resources (in terms of the regulators) and perhaps even with respect to compliance efforts (in terms of the regulated). The adoption of a risk-based approach to regulation requires the estimation of both the probability of, in some sense, failure (to achieve the regulatory goal) and the impact of this failure in numerical or financial terms and the appropriate ranking of the subsequent adjusted or weighted risks. The resulting risk ranking varies from 'close to unacceptable' (e.g. nuclear energy) through 'as low as reasonably possible' (e.g. treatment of sex offenders within the community) to 'acceptable' (e.g. speeding). The appropriate regulatory strategy can then be assigned, for example command and control in the context of nuclear energy safety through perhaps mandatory registration in the local police station in the context of sex offenders to perhaps installation of speed cameras and/or speed bumps in the context of speeding.

While the risk-based approach to regulatory strategies has proved useful in dealing with certain types of risk, such as workplace accidents, environment and retail financial services, the approach suffers from a number of implementation problems.

First, there is the underlying fundamental problem of uncertainty versus risk, with the distinction being that only the latter can be estimated in any meaningful manner. Thus uncertainties (perhaps with very significant potential impacts) are often omitted from the analysis. Arguably, GM foods might provide such an example, although the formal recognition of the existence of uncertainty in a particular context should not imply simple prohibition, as for example, it is unlikely that physicists would be able to conclusively prove that the Large Hadron Collider (LHC) at the European Organisation for Nuclear Research (CERN) is absolutely incapable of giving rise to a black hole large enough to consume the earth, the universe and perhaps even itself.

Second, the risk-based approach to regulatory strategies also arguably facilitates what might be termed the blame-shifting game. Take, for example, the mandatory registration of sex offenders at their local police station. In the event of recidivism, to what extent, if any, are those at the local police station responsible? This example also highlights the apparent lack of evidence with respect to the actual rate of recidivism in the first place. Indeed, given the more general absence of evidence, is it really possible to implement the risk-based approach to regulation with any degree of satisfaction in the first place?

Third, and even when there is a significant degree of evidence available, it is clear that society, for good or bad, has not responded fully to the risk-based approach to regulation. For example, it is clear that an excessive amount of impact-adjusted risk is accepted by society with respect to road transport and an insufficient amount of impact-adjusted risk is accepted by society with respect to rail and air travel. Perhaps more controversially, it appears that the same could be said with respect to childhood obesity and radon gas (where society appears to accept too much impact-adjusted risk) and smoking and nuclear energy (where society appears to accept too little impact-adjusted risk, although the juries are still out with respect to the long-term effects of the Fukushima and other nuclear accidents).

3 REGULATORY FAILURE CASE STUDY: IRISH BANKING

Although it is clear that the Irish banking crisis and the associated Irish fiscal crisis need to be considered in their appropriate international context, it is also evident that the underlying Irish property bubble and the associated Irish fiscal and regulatory failures were unique in their scale and impact.[6]

Genesis of the Banking Crisis
The main players in the Irish banking crisis included the Irish and foreign-owned banks and building societies; the two main relevant regulators, namely the Central Bank of Ireland and the Financial Regulator, previously known as the Irish Financial Services Regulatory Authority (IFSRA); the auditors of the banks; a relatively small number of large property developers, who accounted for a significant proportion of lending for property development; the public authorities, such as the Department of Finance and various policymakers; and various legal advisers.

Other parties, including the media and the public (e.g. multiple property owners), also played their role. The role and influence of other internationally based entities such as the International Monetary Fund (IMF), the European Commission, the European Central Bank (ECB) and various purchasers of bonds in the relevant Irish banks (e.g. British and German banks) should, of course, also be considered, particularly with respect to the later stages of the evolving banking crisis.

A significant number of banking practices, particularly with respect to the domestic mortgages market, had already elicited much negative commentary well before the Irish banking crisis broke. For example, loan-to-value thresholds in effect disappeared as first-time buyers were being offered mortgages above 100 per cent. In addition, loan-to-income thresholds were in effect replaced by the much more nebulous concept of 'affordability', which encompassed potential rental income as well as expected annual bonuses/commissions.

To compound matters a very large proportion of these mortgages were offered at fixed small margins above the ECB rate (tracker mortgages) and hence were very vulnerable (from the banks' perspective) to any future difficulties in the wholesale money markets. At the same time, the standard length of a mortgage increased rapidly from 20 years towards and beyond 30 years. Finally, a number of at best shoddy practices with respect to keeping appropriate records and documents in relation to domestic mortgages and commercial lending (e.g. property development) emerged. Decision makers in the financial institutions became more concerned with the amount of lending (which would influence commissions and bonuses) as opposed to the quality of lending.

The focal point of the international financial crisis is generally dated to 15 September 2008, when Lehman Brothers filed for bankruptcy. While it is true that other financial institutions had been bailed out earlier (e.g. Northern Rock in the UK), the contagion effects of the international credit crunch were particularly clear to see after the Lehman Brothers bankruptcy. For example, many financial institutions were left holding assets that consisted directly or indirectly of USA-based sub-prime mortgages or bonds in other vulnerable financial institutions and hence the wholesale money markets quickly dried up.

Although it was initially tempting to blame the evolving Irish banking crisis on the developing international financial crisis, particularly against the backdrop of the negative impact of the freezing of the wholesale money markets with respect to short-term loans to Irish banks, it became clear that the Irish banking crisis was not simply a temporary liquidity crisis but a deep solvency crisis. However, by that stage, the Irish government (and hence the Irish state), in an initially very successful attempt to address the liquidity component of the Irish banking crisis, issued its comprehensive banking guarantee of 30 September 2008.

Although it continues to evoke heated debate, a less comprehensive guarantee that focused its attention on guaranteeing future bank borrowings, as opposed to all existing bank liabilities, would have reduced considerably the cost of the Irish banking crisis to Irish taxpayers, in that more of these costs would have remained with the bank bond-holders. Of course, some of these bank bond-holders would ultimately, albeit indirectly, also have been Irish taxpayers. In addition, it seems clear that the ECB was against burning bond-holders, although this opposition was with respect to reneging on the comprehensive nature of the Irish banking guarantee, once it had been introduced. As such, while the threat posed by the ECB to the Irish economy and society more generally may explain or perhaps even justify the non-removal of the comprehensive bank guarantee, it does not explain or justify its implementation in the first place (see Chapter 3).

Investigations, Reports and Possible Lessons

A number of investigations were launched into the Irish banking crisis, although to date no official investigation has explored the actual night's events that led to the guarantee. Three specific issues related to the Irish banking crisis appear to jump out from at least a regulatory perspective.

First, there was for a number of years a significant level of undisclosed directors' loans within Anglo Irish Bank. It appears that this non-disclosure (involving in at least one year a total sum of well in excess of €100 million) was facilitated by repeated (and timely) transfers of loans to Irish Nationwide Building Society. Second, it appears that a significant short-term deposit (of over €7 billion) was made between Irish Life and Permanent (later to split into Irish Life and Permanent TSB) and Anglo Irish Bank in order to improve significantly the balance sheet of the latter. Third, significant non-recourse loans were made by Anglo Irish Bank to a small number of individual property developers so as to finance their purchase of a significant number of shares in Anglo Irish Bank itself. These loans were made with the intention of reducing one individual's very significant exposure to Anglo Irish Bank shares without flooding the market with Anglo Irish shares.

In each of these cases, it will be important from a regulatory perspective to examine the exact roles of the various regulators and other players such as auditors and legal advisers, both passive (e.g. possession of knowledge) and active (e.g. facilitation and/or encouragement) and to examine the exact role of the existing regulations. Indeed, from a regulatory perspective, it would be particularly 'interesting' if few, if any, formal regulations were broken.

Two substantial specific reports into the Irish banking crisis have already been published: *The Irish Banking Crisis: Regulatory and Financial Stability Policy 2003–2008*, A Report to the Minister for Finance by the Governor of the Central Bank, 31 May 2010 (generally referred to as the Honohan Report), and *Misjudging Risk: Causes of the Systematic Banking Crisis in Ireland*, Report of the Commission of Investigation into the Banking Sector in Ireland, March 2011 (generally referred to as the Nyberg Report). Although much public attention has understandably been focused on decisions related to the above-mentioned specific events and on the guarantee of 30 September 2008 itself, arguably insufficient public attention has been paid to one of the factors explaining the systemic failure of the Central Bank and Financial Services Authority of Ireland as outlined in the Honohan Report (p. 9):

1.13 ... even if armed with the necessary information, to be effective there would have had to be a greater degree of intrusiveness and assertiveness on the part of regulators to challenging the banks. Although management of the FR [Financial Regulator] would not accept that their 'principles-based' approach ever implied 'light touch' regulation, the approach was characterised as being user-friendly in presentations aimed at expanding the export-oriented financial services sector. ... Thus, it would have been known within the FR that intrusive demands from line staff could be and were set aside after direct representations were made to senior regulators. Also, attempts to formalise some of the principles (through Directors' Compliance Statements and a Corporate Governance Code) both came to naught following industry lobbying (and, for the first of these, in the face of concerns expressed by the Department of Finance).

A later reference (p. 51) notes that the Minister for Finance also highlighted possible negative repercussions (of the implementation of the Directors' Compliance Statements) for Ireland's competitiveness. Indeed, the promotion of the Irish financial services sector was at that time (but no longer) one of the statutory objectives of the system of financial regulation in Ireland.

As such, at a general level, while it is important to compare and contrast the USA's overall rules-based approach to financial regulation with the Irish and UK's overall principles-based approach, it is surely far more important to focus attention on the actual implementation and enforcement of the approach chosen as there will always be a need for both rules-based and principles-based regulations. In particular, it seems clear that in Ireland the principles-based approach was implemented and enforced in a rather 'light' manner.

4 COMPETITION POLICY

Competition policy provides one very important example of regulatory policy at both the domestic (Irish competition law) and international level (e.g. EU competition law). Competition policy attempts to regulate competition between businesses by, for example, making cartels illegal and discouraging anti-competitive actions by a dominant firm (e.g. refusal to deal or discriminatory pricing) but encouraging efficiency-enhancing agreements (e.g. product standardisation agreements) even between competitors.[7]

Competition policy enthusiasts do not suggest that unfettered competition between competitors (i.e. the pure market system) is a panacea for all of society's issues of resource allocation. For example, visions of completely uncontrolled competition between, say, competing household waste collection trucks in a housing estate touting for business on a daily basis, competing buses speeding towards the same bus stop and competing hospitals out in ambulances hunting for prospective clients, merely highlight the need for a rational policy approach to, and a specific regulatory framework for, competition, i.e. competition policy must be seen as a subset of regulatory policy.

The most important concept in the area of competition policy is that of (significant) market power (or dominance). From the perspective of an individual firm, the presence of significant market power indicates the ability of the firm to raise price significantly above the cost of production for a significant period of time. In contrast, the absence of significant market power indicates the presence of an effectively competitive market. As such, the role of a suitably designed competition policy is to encourage the existence of competitive markets by discouraging agreements or anti-competitive conduct that give rise to the presence of significant market power (e.g. a merger between the two largest significant competitors).

☛ Perfect Competition, Monopoly and Contestable Markets

There are three market structures that are particularly important for an understanding of the economics of competition policy: perfect competition; monopoly; and contestable markets. Perfectly competitive markets have the characteristic of being (allocatively) efficient, as firms are forced by the pursuit of their own self-interests to price at marginal cost (i.e. $P = MC$) and hence to produce the correct amount from society's perspective. Price (P) represents the economic value placed by society on the marginal or last unit of the product produced, while marginal cost (MC) represents the economic cost to society of producing that marginal or last unit. The equivalence between price and marginal cost suggests, at least in the absence of externalities or other market failures, that the correct amount of the product has been produced.

In contrast, a monopolist produces a level of output at which price is greater than marginal cost ($P > MC$), and hence produces too little when viewed from society's perspective. However, it is also argued that the monopolist's excess economic profits do not just represent a transfer from consumer to producer, as profit-seeking activities (or rent-seeking, as it is generally referred to) dissipate these profits over time. In particular, prior to the creation of the monopoly (e.g. markets for various mobile telephony services), firms will involve themselves in socially unproductive activities in order to increase their chances of being the chosen one, while once installed, the incumbent will involve itself in unproductive activities, when viewed from society's perspective, in order to sustain its monopoly position

Notwithstanding the strength of the above arguments against monopoly, there are also economic arguments in favour of monopoly. First, some economists and other social scientists view monopoly's excess profits as the short-term reward necessary for sustaining the competitive process in the long term; IBM, Microsoft, Intel and Google provide plausible illustrative examples. Second, it is argued that a monopolistic market structure may be more conducive to the pursuit of innovation and research and development, which require significant levels of up-front and risky investments; the pharmaceutical sector is one example. Third, in the presence of significant economies of scale, it may well be appropriate to place a limit on the number of firms allowed to enter a market; indeed, in the extreme case of a natural monopoly, the appropriate number is one (see Section 5 for further details).

More generally, the competitive process is facilitated by the presence of potential competition. Potential competition focuses attention on the ability of potential entrants to dissuade incumbent firms from attempting to take advantage of (i.e. abusing) their market position. In the extreme case of a perfectly contestable market, potential competition can perfectly simulate perfect competition, even in a monopoly situation. The incumbent firm is forced to price at marginal cost, as any divergence between marginal cost and price would allow an equally efficient entrant to enter with a price below the incumbent's price but above marginal cost and to exit if/when the incumbent reacts.

It is sometimes claimed that competing on a specific airline route provides an example of an almost perfectly contestable market, as the entrant's plane and other investments can be withdrawn and used elsewhere at little additional cost. In contrast, it would be difficult for an entrant to withdraw, without incurring substantial sunk costs, after attempting to compete with respect to the provision of a rail network or an electricity grid. The latter examples represent natural monopolies as opposed to contestable markets; natural monopolies, in contrast to contestable markets, require hands-on regulation.

Indicators of Significant Market Power
Price Elasticities and Definition of Market
A firm's own-price elasticity of demand measures the percentage decrease (increase) in demand that would follow from a percentage increase (decrease) in the price of the firm's product. However, a high own-price elasticity of demand (in absolute terms) does not necessarily imply the absence of significant market power as such a situation would only imply that the firm is not able to profitably increase price beyond its current level. It would not, however, prove that the firm has not already increased price significantly above the cost of production.

In practice, economists and, more important, the courts have to proceed on a case-by-case basis. In particular, significant market power can only exist in the context of a particular 'market'. This relevant market, for competition policy purposes, is thought of as representing the minimum set of products over which a (hypothetical) firm would have to have monopoly control before it could be sure of exercising a given degree of market power. In practice, this 'given degree of market power' is perceived as the ability to profitably raise prices by 5 or 10 per cent above competitive levels for a significant period of time (say a year).

For example, a proposed banana 'market' might be rejected under this test if it can be shown or at least successfully argued that a sufficient proportion of banana consumers would switch to other fruits if banana prices increased significantly (above cost); in contrast, a proposed fruit market might be accepted under this test.

In the context of the drinks sector, while lager and stout might be deemed to be in separate product markets, on-trade lager (which mainly encompasses draught and bottled lager) might be deemed to be in the same product market as off-trade lager (which mainly encompasses bottled and canned lager). The ongoing movement from on-trade consumption to off-trade consumption in Ireland provides some support for this proposition, as does the ability of publicans to sidestep the breweries' standard supply lines to publicans via drinks wholesalers by accessing cheaper products in the supermarkets or via so-called parallel imports, i.e. products sourced ultimately from the breweries' foreign counterparts.

Significant market power, in legal terms, is defined as a position of economic strength enjoyed by a firm that enables it to hinder the maintenance of effective competition in the relevant market by allowing it to behave to an appreciable extent independently of competitors and ultimately of consumers.

◈ Market Concentration and Barriers to Entry

Competition authorities have adopted the Herfindahl–Hirschman Index (HHI) for the purpose of measuring market concentration. The HHI is defined as the sum of the squared percentage shares of all firms of the relevant variable (e.g. value of sales) in the market. The HHI ranges from 0 (corresponding to a market with an infinite number of infinitesimally small firms) and 10,000 (corresponding to a market with a single firm, i.e. a pure monopoly). For example, a market consisting of only two equally sized firms would have an HHI of 5,000 (= $50^2 + 50^2$). A market with an HHI below 1,000 is generally regarded as a non-concentrated market and, as such, as a market in which market power or competition policy issues are unlikely to arise. In contrast, a market with an HHI above a level of approximately 2,000 is generally regarded as a concentrated market and, as such, as a market in which market power issues could arise.[8]

Without barriers to entry, any attempt by an incumbent firm to abuse an apparent position of significant market power would simply attract entry by other firms. The so-called *Chicago School* views entry barriers as being restricted to 'costs that must be borne by an entrant that were not incurred by established firms'. In the extreme, Chicago economists only accept restrictive licensing schemes as being valid examples of entry barriers in that early entrants often entered freely, while later entrants may have to buy an existing licence at a significant cost. Prior to the effective deregulation of the Irish taxi industry in 2000 – as a result of a court challenge as opposed to an active policy decision – taxi licences represented an example of just such an entry barrier. Ironically, some argue that new taxi regulations being put in place by the National Transport Authority (and other proposed regulations currently being considered) may create some significant entry barriers.

In contrast to the Chicago School, the so-called *Harvard School* has a much broader definition of entry barriers in mind, namely, 'factors that enable established firms to earn supra-competitive profits without threat of entry'. Economies of scale, excess capacity, lower average costs as a result of experience (i.e. learning by doing), brand proliferation, restrictive distributional agreements, and product differentiation (perhaps as a result of excessive advertising) represent some of the major examples of entry barriers as justified by this broader definition.

In practice, competition authorities and courts appear to feel most comfortable with the approach of the Chicago School towards the formal definition of a barrier to entry, but with the approach of the Harvard School in terms of actually deciding whether or not a specific market feature represents a barrier to entry.

General Competitive Environment

The existence, or otherwise, of a competitive environment within a market must also be considered. In this regard, economists distinguish between unilateral price effects concerns, which arise particularly in differentiated product markets, perhaps in the context of a proposed merger, and co-ordinated price effects concerns, which arise particularly in homogeneous product markets, again perhaps in the context of a proposed merger. Unilateral price effects concerns arise where it is in the joint interests of two merging firms to increase their prices, even if their competitors' prices remained constant, i.e. the firms produce relatively close substitutes. A proposed merger of Bank of Ireland and AIB provides a useful hypothetical example. Prior to the merger, each represented a significant competitive threat to the other and hence restrained each other's prices; post merger, prices would be expected to increase significantly.

Co-ordinated price effects concerns arise where conditions exist that tend to dampen price competition between all competitors. When reviewing the issue of co-ordinated price effects within a market, the relevant competition authority examines the market for the presence, or absence, of the following features (whose presence would tend to be supportive of tacit collusion): symmetry in market shares; stability in market shares; homogeneity of product and/or firm structure; transparency with respect to trading conditions (and, in particular, transparency with respect to input and output prices), low price elasticity of demand (signalling the absence of a strong temptation to 'cheat'); the non-existence of maverick firms; the non-existence of strong buyers (and hence countervailing buyer power); and the non-existence of excess capacity (again, signalling the absence of a strong temptation to cheat).

In summary, both unilateral and co-ordinated price effects concerns can arise even in markets with a relatively large number of firms; closeness of competition and market conditions conducive to tacit collusion represent the respective warning signs. However, it is also possible that the market conditions conducive to tacit collusion may be absent even in a well-defined market with a very small number of firms.

Aircraft design and manufacture represents a plausible example, with Airbus and Boeing providing intense competition to each other, so much so that Boeing was allowed to acquire the only large competitor in the market (McDonnell Douglas) in 1997. However, the existence of very significant countervailing buying power as well as the non-existence of price transparency is crucial in explaining the existence of a highly concentrated yet competitive market. For example, it seems very unlikely that Ryanair's recent deal to purchase 175 new aircraft from Boeing involved Boeing making a significant amount of excess profits, i.e. Ryanair and other large buyers of aircraft appear well able to play Boeing and Airbus off against each other.

Competition Law

Competition law addresses a number of specific concerns. First, and most important, anti-competitive agreements between firms (e.g. price-fixing or market-sharing agreements), are prohibited. In this regard, the courts generally distinguish between horizontal agreements (i.e. agreements between firms at the same level of the production and distribution chain) and vertical agreements (i.e. agreements between firms at different levels of the production and distribution chain). Horizontal agreements are generally discouraged, as the effect of such agreements is to dampen competition, to the almost inevitable detriment of final consumers; allowance is made for considering certain classes of potentially beneficial, or pro-competitive, agreements (e.g. research and development joint ventures or product standardisation agreements). In contrast, vertical agreements are treated on a case-by-case basis, as an agreement between, say, a manufacturer and a retailer that enhances the efficiency of their relationship does not necessarily come at the expense of final consumers; indeed, it seems likely to benefit final consumers.

Second, the anti-competitive creation of a position of market power, or what is formally referred to as a dominant position, as well as the abuse of any existing market power, is also prohibited via abuse of market power or dominance legislation. Third, competition law also contains a proactive approach to proposed mergers, acquisitions or takeovers, as a reactive approach would at times require the equivalent of unscrambling eggs.

EU Competition Law

EU competition law takes precedent over national competition law, provided that there is a significant effect on inter-state trade. This can be of huge practical and political significance as EU competition law arguably has not one but two policy goals: competition; and the pursuit of the single internal market. EU competition law also limits the freedom of member states to intervene in the process of competition, through the actions of public undertakings (e.g. state-owned bodies) or private undertakings granted exclusive rights by member states. The state has limited exemptions from the application of EU competition law but only with respect to 'services of general economic interest'; at present the provision of the traditional postal service (i.e. daily delivery to all addresses) and the standard state pension system offer generally accepted examples of the application of this exemption.

Under the Treaty on the Functioning of the EU (TFEU), member states are also prohibited from granting state aid that would distort competition. Two prominent examples provide proof of the importance of the rules on state aid. First, the continued existence of a special low rate of corporation tax for manufacturing and internationally traded services in Ireland would have fallen foul of these rules on state aids and hence the relatively low rate of 12.5 per cent is applied across all sectors. Second, the various recapitalisations and forced mergers of Irish banks and financial institutions had to be approved on a case-by-case basis by the European Commission as otherwise state-supported financial institutions would arguably have been unfairly advantaged, for example by being able to offer superior deposit rates.

The European Commission enforces EU competition rules, the General Court hears appeals against Commission competition decisions, and the European Court of Justice hears further appeals on points of law. However, in the pursuit of a policy of increased subsidiarity national courts and/or member states' competition authorities have been allowed and encouraged to directly enforce EU competition rules since May 2004; the increased similarity between national competition laws and Community competition law facilitated this shift.

Regulation and Competition Policy Examples ✦

Below-Cost Selling and Minimum Pricing

The Restrictive Practices (Groceries) Order (1987) prohibited retailers from selling many grocery products (e.g. bread, milk, alcohol) at a retail price below the relevant suppliers' net invoice price. Fears of predatory pricing by the large retail multiples, where price wars that would eliminate the smaller competitors would be followed by excessive prices being charged, were used to defend this provision. However, and crucially, off-invoice discounts (e.g. rebates) were not taken into account when defining the net invoice benchmark, i.e. retailers were 'forced' to impose a mark-up that was at least equal in size to off-invoice discounts. Under the Order, the Office of the Director of Consumer Affairs, which was charged with prosecuting breaches of the Groceries Order, fined Dunne's Stores and Tesco over €2,000 for selling baby food products below cost in 2004. The Groceries Order was rescinded in 2006, but only after much debate and recrimination.

A ban on below-cost selling of alcohol, particularly by the multiples, is also one of the policy instruments proposed in the battle against excessive alcohol consumption in Ireland. However, the difficulty in defining cost and the ability of firms that are supplied from abroad (perhaps by their parent companies) to avoid this restriction has moved the policy debate towards the proposed introduction of a minimum retail price for alcohol. This proposal is aimed particularly at cheap, strong alcohol products, sold through off licences and, in particular, the multiples. The proposal is supported by publicans and by those in the off-trade, excluding the multiples.

Scotland recently (2012) legislated for the introduction of a minimum price for alcohol, initially to be set at 50p per unit of alcohol. However, the Scottish Whisky Association is in the process of taking a legal case against this plan. In addition, a number of European wine-exporting countries (e.g. France, Spain and Italy) have claimed that the policy, if implemented, would discriminate against imports in a manner that cannot be justified on public health grounds. As such, it appears that the issue will ultimately be decided in the European Court of Justice. As an alternative to a ban on below-cost selling or the setting of a minimum retail price of alcohol, many economists favour a targeted increase in excise duty with the potential for the extra revenue raised being used for health promotion. In contrast, the introduction of a minimum price of alcohol appears to increase profits within the drinks industry.

Office Supply Stores
Competition authorities encourage the appropriate interrogation of what data may be available in case useful inferences, either positive or negative, can be drawn with respect to the appropriate market definition and the presence, or absence, of significant market power. The most cited case in this regard is the proposed merger of Staples and Office Depot in the USA in 1997, where the crucial issue was whether or not, from a competition policy perspective, the three largest office supplies superstores (Staples, Office Depot and OfficeMax) were in a separate product market from the very many remaining relatively small office supplies stores.[9]

On the basis of a detailed examination of prices and other data across different geographical locations in which different numbers of office supplies stores were present, the USA Federal Trade Commission was satisfied, as ultimately was the relevant court, that the three office supplies superstores were in an office supplies (superstores) market distinct from the wider sector that contained the much smaller office supplies stores. Crucially, using a large volume of retailer scanner data across both geography and time, the Federal Trade Commission demonstrated that product prices were significantly higher (all other factors, e.g. wages, land prices and local incomes, held constant) in geographical locations in which fewer than the three largest office supplies stores were present, but were not influenced by the presence, or absence, of the much smaller office supplies stores. As such, econometric interrogation of the data facilitated the drawing of two strong conclusions: (1) the appropriate product market consisted of various services provided by office supplies superstores; and (2) a decrease in the number of superstores from three to two would be expected to significantly increase prices.

5 REGULATION OF NATURAL MONOPOLY AND NETWORKS

Specific sectoral regulation is required in the case of natural monopolies as the latter represents an extreme form of market failure, in that the relevant market cannot function efficiently without a significant level of direct and ongoing regulation. As previously indicated, a market is said to be a natural monopoly if its total output can be produced more efficiently (i.e. at lower cost) by a single firm than by two or more firms. The provision of a national electricity transmission grid or natural gas grid, a railway network, a national daily delivery postal service and perhaps a national fibre-optic broadband network represent some examples of natural monopolies, many of which have in the past in Ireland been referred to as public utilities. Other possible examples include the provision of a local, regional or national bus service, or a local household waste collection service.

Pricing and Competitive Tendering ⤶

A natural monopoly exists if there are very significant economies of scale. In such a case, an individual firm's marginal cost (MC) and average cost (AC) curves decline continuously and the firm's marginal cost (MC) curve will be below its average cost (AC) curve. As the number of firms increased, the average cost of production would also increase, dramatically. Regulators can apparently achieve allocative efficiency by insisting that the natural monopolist produces a level of output at which price is equal to marginal cost. There are, however, at least two significant problems with this proposed solution.

First, the regulator may not have enough information to be able to determine the output level at which price would be equal to marginal cost and it would not necessarily be in the natural monopolist's interest to provide the regulator with the appropriate information. Second, even if the natural monopolist produces the allocatively efficient level of output, it will sustain losses, as pricing at marginal cost implies pricing below average cost as the marginal cost curve lies below the average cost curve in a natural monopoly.

One possible solution to this latter problem is for the regulator to provide the natural monopolist with a subsidy to offset the losses associated with achieving allocative efficiency. However, these subsidies must be financed by increased taxation elsewhere, which, in turn, causes other inefficiencies. It may also be difficult politically to be seen to provide a monopolist with a subsidy, although in Ireland such subsidies have for many years been provided to public entities such as Bus Éireann and Irish Rail.

Setting price at average cost, where the natural monopolist makes neither excess profits nor losses, avoids the problem of having to subsidise the natural monopolist, but at the expense of sacrificing allocative efficiency. Average-cost pricing regulation also suffers from the problem of dampening cost-reducing incentives. In practice, average-cost pricing is often adapted so as to encourage cost-reducing innovations by allowing scope for some 'excess' profits. This type of regulation, adjusted average-cost pricing, is referred to as rate of return regulation.

Regulators have also adopted the so called CPI-X approach, where CPI represents the inflation rate as measured by the consumer price index and X represents the required decrease in real prices within the relevant market. For example, if X was 2 per cent and inflation was also 2 per cent, there would be no change in nominal prices but a 2 per cent decrease in real prices.

Rather than attempting to regulate the natural monopolist on an ongoing basis, it may be preferable to auction the right to be the natural monopolist; this is often referred to as competition 'for the market' (as opposed to competition 'in the market', which is not efficient in the case of natural monopoly). The auction can be done on the basis of bidders committing to charging a certain price and providing a particular level of service to customers in the future. The results of this process are likely to be close to the results obtained by average-cost pricing regulation, as bidders would find themselves forced to offer lower and lower (quality-adjusted) prices until almost no net excess profits could be expected. A further possibility is for the auction to be done on the basis of a relatively large number of criteria, including price; bidders would then compete on the basis of quality as well as price and other considerations. This latter possibility is generally referred to as a 'beauty contest'; economists tend to prefer a greater emphasis being placed on price than is suggested under a standard beauty contest.

Public Ownership, Privatisation, Market Liberalisation and Regulation

Rather than the state attempting to regulate the natural monopolist, many governments in the past, particularly in Europe, simply elected to be the (natural) monopolist. In an Irish context, airport management, airline ownership, electricity, natural gas and public transportation provided examples of state ownership of enterprise. The distinctive feature (and advantage or disadvantage, depending on one's political perspective) of this approach is that the objective of the natural monopolist is no longer the maximisation of profits or even the covering of costs. Opponents of state ownership of enterprises generally point to this so-called soft budget constraint, with management and workers, it is claimed, being united in their efforts to extract public funds for 'their' enterprises. However, EU restrictions on state aids to public-owned enterprises have removed at least some of the force of this argument.

A movement away from public ownership and towards privatisation began in the early 1980s. The complementary specific experience in the USA in the late 1970s and early 1980s was one of market liberalisation or deregulation, e.g. in aviation, telecommunications and inter-state trucking. Within a European context, the UK government led by Margaret Thatcher was at the forefront of the privatisation movement, e.g. British Telecom (1984) and British Gas (1986), which created a large number of new holders of shares, with the value of these shares increasing significantly (see Chapter 3).

However, many of the large privatisations within the UK were subsequently followed up by the setting up of specialist independent regulatory agencies (e.g. Ofcom), as the process of competition failed to take off in markets that were still characterised by at least some elements of natural monopolies. Indeed, the ultimate lesson from the UK privatisation experience was that the creation of market conditions conducive to competition was at least as important as the formal ownership structure.

In the Irish context, after successfully selling its stake in Irish Life (1991), the Irish state privatised Telecom Éireann (later Eircom). Initially, the privatisation proved to be at least a political success as Eircom's share price increased by over 20 per cent above its flotation price. However, Eircom's share price then fell, and remained, for the rest of its (initial) existence as a public limited company, considerably below its flotation price.

From an economics perspective, the success or otherwise of the privatisation of Eircom should be judged primarily by the effect of the privatisation on the process of competition within the Irish telecommunications market(s) and on the quality-adjusted prices paid by final consumers. However, from a political perspective, the fall in Eircom's share price, combined with Ryanair's attempted acquisition of Aer Lingus only days after Aer Lingus's part-privatisation (2006), had significant repercussions for future possible privatisations in Ireland, e.g. Voluntary Health Insurance (VHI).

More recently, the issue of privatisation became linked to attempts to reduce Ireland's growing national debt as witnessed by the publication of *Report of the Review Group on State Assets and Liabilities* in April 2011 (see Chapter 3). This report, which focused attention on both commercial state bodies (e.g. ESB and Coillte) and intangible state assets (e.g. the radio spectrum and carbon emissions permits) recommended a number of asset sales, but crucially also recommended that, even if these assets were not sold, they should be restructured so as to facilitate the economy's competitiveness.

Much discussion about major asset sales followed (e.g. the proposal to sell Coillte, which was ultimately withdrawn) but to date the sale of Bord Gáis Energy provides the only prominent example of privatisation, outside events associated with the banking crisis. Indeed, developments in the relevant energy markets that resulted in a sale price for Bord Gáis Energy below some market expectations threatens future sales in a similar way that reductions in Eircom's share price severely dampened Ireland's flirtation with privatisation in the 1990s.

The various regulatory agencies in Ireland have ongoing important decisions to make with respect to pricing and investment decisions within the particular elements of markets that are naturally monopolistic, e.g. the Commission for Energy Regulation (CER) and the Commission for Aviation Regulation (CAR). In the context of a downstream natural monopoly (e.g. fixed-line telecommunications in the past), the level of the resulting consumer price was at least highly visible, while in the context of an upstream natural monopoly (e.g. transportation of natural gas or electricity transmission), the level of the access price charged to downstream firms is less visible and hence may be less politically sensitive, but still of crucial importance, particularly if the upstream firm itself also operates in various downstream (e.g. retail) or upstream (e.g. power generation) markets.

The recent creation of Irish Water and its subsequent regulation will represent a most interesting case study. Irish Water (while technically a subsidiary of Bord Gáis Éireann) is a vertically integrated semi-state company which will provide public water and wastewater services nationally; Irish Water is in the process of taking over these responsibilities from over 30 local authorities. The CER will be the economic regulator of the water sector and hence of Irish Water; Irish Water will also be accountable to the Environmental Protection Agency (EPA). The task of the CER will be particularly sensitive from a political perspective as domestic water charges will be introduced in 2015 (albeit levied towards the end of 2014). Given the need for significant investments in the water infrastructure, it is clear that future regulatory interactions between Irish Water and the CER will be particularly important.

On a related matter, the appropriate link between regulators and other public authorities needs to be considered carefully. In this regard, the *Government Statement on Regulatory Reform* (October 2009) appeared to be proposing a significant reduction in regulators' independence, as opposed to improving the currently available mechanisms with respect to accountability and transparency.

6 CONCLUDING COMMENTS

The purpose of this chapter has been to provide the reader with a broad overview of the area of regulatory policy. In particular, it has attempted to address various explanations for regulations, theories of regulation and approaches to regulation or regulatory strategies while at the same time discussing a number of specific types or examples of regulations in Ireland and the EU, including competition policy and the regulation of natural monopolies and networks. The chapter concludes with some brief comments on the evolving EU regulatory context and on the balance between the rules-based and principles-based approaches to regulation.

EU Regulatory Context
In many regulatory policy areas such as the environment, agriculture, health and safety, competition and public utilities, the most important regulatory forum has moved from member states to the EU. As such, the discussion above is increasingly conducted at, and relevant to, an EU and even wider-level debate (e.g. international trade negotiations). The growth of the European regulatory state has been facilitated by both demand and supply side factors. On the demand side, multinational firms increasingly sought out a one-stop regulatory shop, for example with respect to environmental regulations; while on the supply side, national regulations required an international forum in order to address regulatory spillover effects, for example with respect to environmental policy.

The EU Parliament's increasing powers with respect to the other two EU political institutions (the Commission and the Council of Ministers) appears to have increased the EU's legislative mandate. In addition, the existence and decisions of the Court of Justice as well as the ongoing rebalancing of powers between the Parliament, Commission and Council of Ministers have increased accountability and control within the EU and have to at least some extent addressed past accusations of a democratic deficit at the heart of the EU.

There are now a significant number of European regulatory agencies, which in general deal with narrowly defined policy areas, similar in standing to the European Food Safety Authority (EFSA), established in 2002. The current highly Europeanised food safety regime has EFSA at the hub of the equivalent national organisations. EFSA champions food traceability and food science more generally and conducts prior risk analysis on behalf of the Commission, with the latter body being responsible for formal decision making. For another example of Europeanised regulation, see the discussion above with respect to EU competition law, although it should be noted that in that context EU competition law can be implemented/enforced by the national courts, i.e. enforcement can take place in the locality although the policy is decided at the centre.

Rules-Based or Principles-Based Regulation?

There are lessons to be taken from Ireland's recent regulatory experiences and in particular the Irish banking crisis. While interesting debates can be held between followers of a rules-based approach to regulation and followers of a principles-based approach, it is crucial that such a debate be informed by specific details of the proposed implementation of either approach. For example, given that a principles-based approach confers a significant level of discretion on the regulators and on the regulated entities, it is imperative that issues such as regulatory capture be considered.

Similarly the adoption of a rules-based approach does not avoid the need to consider important issues such as creative compliance. In addition, while the need for evidence-based policy decision making is generally supported at least at a theoretical level, it seems less well recognised that its application may be in some tension with the desire to eliminate apparently unnecessary 'red tape' by reducing the need for, and amount of, form-filling. However, perhaps the biggest regulatory lesson from Ireland's recent experiences with the banking and fiscal crises is that in the absence of certain minimum agreed ethical standards very few assumptions of the 'public interest' kind can be made with respect to how interested parties may behave.

Notes

* The author acknowledges many very helpful comments and suggestions by Carol Newman and John O'Hagan, and their patience. Any remaining errors and all views expressed remain the responsibility of the author.

1 J. Black, quoted in R. Baldwin, M. Cave and M. Lodge (eds), *The Oxford Handbook of Regulation*, Oxford University Press, Oxford 2010, p. 12. For an excellent textbook on regulation, see R. Baldwin, M. Cave and M. Lodge, *Understanding Regulation: Theory, Strategy and Practice* (2nd edn), Oxford University Press, Oxford 2012.

2 Sandel questions the moral limit of markets by highlighting some provocative USA-based examples of the current reach of markets, e.g. $6,250 ($25,000) for the use of a surrogate mother in India (in the USA); $20 per hour to get someone (e.g. a homeless

person) to represent you in a queue at Congress; $2 given to a child for each book read; and a unknown 'donation' for admission to a prestigious university. See M. Sandel, *What Money Can't Buy: The Moral Limits of Markets*, Farrar, Straus and Giroux, New York 2012.

3 See R. Thaler and C. Sunstein, *Nudge: Improving Decisions About Health, Wealth and Happiness*, Penguin Books, New York 2009; and D. Kahneman, *Thinking, Fast and Slow*, Allen Lane, New York 2011.

4 See Cabinet Office and Behavioural Insights Team (UK), *Applying Behavioural Insights to Charitable Giving*, 28 May 2013. Perhaps ironically, the Behavioural Insights Team, generally referred to as the Nudge Team, has since been part-privatised.

5 See R. Coase, 'The problem of social cost', *Journal of Law and Economics*, Vol. 60, 1960.

6 See K. Whelan, 'Ireland's economic crisis: the good, the bad and the ugly', UCD Centre for Economic Research, WP13/06, July 2013 (*Journal of Macroeconomics*, forthcoming).

7 For a comprehensive review of the economics of competition policy (also known as antitrust economics), see S. Bishop and M. Walker, *The Economics of EC Competition Law: Concepts, Application and Measurement* (3rd edn), Sweet & Maxwell, London 2010.

8 See the Competition Authority's *Guidelines for Merger Analysis*, N/12/001, 2013 (www.tca.ie) for further details of the practical application of the HHI.

9 See S. Dalkir and F. Warren-Boulton, 'Prices, market definition and the effects of merger: Staples–Office Depot', in J. Kwoka and L. White (eds), *The Antitrust Revolution: Economics, Competition and Policy* (5th edn), Oxford University Press, Oxford 2010, Case 7.

POLICY ISSUES AT A NATIONAL LEVEL

CHAPTER 6

Population, Employment and Unemployment

John O'Hagan and Tara McIndoe-Calder

1 INTRODUCTION

The experience with regard to employment and unemployment has been the truly remarkable 'story' of the Irish economy in the last 25 years or so. Table 6.1 illustrates clearly the dramatic changes that have taken place since 1990. Who could have predicted the scale of the change in the time between then and 2008? Employment in 1990 was just 107,000 higher than in 1961; the only period in which there was a significant increase in employment up to this was during the 1970s, when over 100,000 net new jobs were created. Between 1990 and 2000, however, 525,000 net new jobs were created, quite a phenomenal increase in employment in such a short period. It did not stop there, though, as a further 462,000 jobs were created between 2000 and 2008, bringing to almost one million the total number of net new jobs created between 1990 and 2008. The decrease in unemployment during the same period, as seen in Table 6.1, was equally remarkable.

However, equally dramatic was the decline in employment between 2008 and 2012. Over 310,000 net jobs were lost in this short period with the unemployment rate rising from 5.7 per cent in 2008 to 15.0 per cent in 2012. The level of employment in 2012, though, was way above that applying in 1995 and its level by early 2014 was similar to that in 2005: as such the huge gains between 1995 and 2005 have not been lost.

The increase in employment was the main force behind the extraordinary increase in output in the economy in the 1990 to 2008 period. Definitionally:

$$(1) \qquad\qquad Q = (Q/E) \cdot E$$

That is, the output of an economy (Q) can be expressed as the product of the average productivity of those in employment (Q/E) and the level of employment (E). As we will see later, the level of employment in Ireland in some years increased by over 6 per cent; this alone would have pushed up Q by 6 per cent assuming no change in productivity. Thus, increases in E were the main factor explaining the exceptional growth in Q in the period 1993 to 2008. Productivity, though, was also increasing during this period, hence ensuring a much faster increase in Q than in E; the causes of this growth in productivity are the subject matter of Chapter 7. The growth in productivity in the 1990s and 2000s, however, was lower than that in the 1960s and not much higher than that in the 1970s and 1980s. The remarkable thing is that the huge increase in employment was not accompanied by any decrease in the growth of productivity.

Table 6.1 Employment and Unemployment: Ireland's Changing Fortunes

	Employment (millions)	Unemployment rate (%)
1961	1.053	5.0
1971	1.049	5.5
1980	1.156	7.3
1986	1.095	17.1
1990	1.160	12.9
1995	1.282	12.2
2000	1.685	4.6
2005	1.945	4.7
2008	2.147	5.7
2010	1.894	13.9
2012	1.836	15.0
2014[1]	1.918	12.4

Source: Central Statistics Office (CSO), *Quarterly National Household Survey* (*QNHS*), Stationery Office, Dublin, various issues.
[1] Forecast.

Just as employment increases drove the increase in output in the boom years, decreases in employment drove the huge decline in output between 2008 and 2012, with the large employment increase in 2013 in turn driving the increase in national output in that year. Thus swings in employment, and not productivity, are the driving force behind the huge swings in output in Ireland over the last 25 years.

Sections 2 and 3 in this chapter examine the issues of population and labour supply and emphasise the critical role that migration plays in this regard, a factor that marks Ireland apart from other Organisation for Economic Co-operation and Development (OECD) countries. Section 4 looks at the issue of employment, its growth and composition, and compares Ireland's performance to that of a number of other countries. The huge reliance on employment growth in the construction sector in the 2000s is highlighted. Section 5 does likewise in relation to unemployment. The rest of the chapter examines the various factors that may influence the level of employment, and hence the level of unemployment, in a small open economy such as that of Ireland. Section 6 will examine three factors that impinge on job creation, arising from the single European market and globalisation: increased competition for goods; increased mobility and migration of labour across national boundaries; and technological change. As the section highlights, the adaptability and skill levels of the labour force are the key issues in responding to these global pressures.

A major reason perhaps for the different responses in different countries to the phenomena of migration, technological change and the globalisation of trade relates to the *flexibility* of the labour market, and this is the subject matter of Section 7. Issues such as the wage-setting process and the effects of employment legislation on employment creation are discussed in some detail. The effects of prolonged payment of unemployment and related benefits and the effectiveness or otherwise of active labour market policies in dealing with unemployment are also examined in Section 7. Section 8 concludes the chapter.

2 POPULATION

Population Change and its Components

The size of the population has major emotive significance in Ireland; not surprisingly given the huge reduction in population in Ireland following the Famine (see Chapter 1). As a result, the size of the population has in a sense become an objective of policy in itself (for a discussion of this see Chapter 2). Table 6.2 outlines the trends in population dating back to 1841. The population of the Republic of Ireland in pre-Famine days was over 6.5 million. The decline in this population size in the post-Famine period is all too obvious: a fall of over two million in 20 years. Given the high birth rate at the time the population should in fact have increased substantially were it not for death and emigration.

Population continued to decline up to 1926; almost 50 years later there was no increase on the 1926 level; in 1971 the population still stood at only 2.978 million. Since then population size has increased by almost 1.7 million, with most of this increase occurring between 1991 and 2014; the population in 2008 in fact exceeded its 1861 level for the first time.

This for many is seen as a very positive development and reflects a reversal of a demoralising decline that had persisted for almost a century and a half. It is noteworthy that even during the recession years population continued to increase, up by almost 300,000 between 2006 and 2014.

The total population of a country depends on three factors: the number of births, the number of deaths and the level of net migration. The difference between the number of births and deaths is known as the natural increase and in most countries the natural increase translates directly into a population increase. This has not been the case in Ireland, where in the past the change in population has 'tracked' much more closely the trend in migration than that of the natural increase.

Table 6.2 Population, Republic of Ireland, 1841 to 2014 (millions)

Years	Population	Years	Population
1841	6.529	1961	2.818
1851	5.112	1971	2.978
1861	4.402	1981	3.443
1871	4.053	1991	3.526
1881	3.870	2002	3.917
1891	3.469	2006	4.323
1901	3.222	2011	4.575
1911	3.140	2013[1]	4.593
1926	2.972	2014[2]	4.621
1951	2.961	–	–

Sources: CSO, *Statistical Yearbook 2013,* Stationery Office, Dublin 2013, Table 1.1; CSO, *Population and Migration Estimates*, Stationery Office, Dublin 2013, Table 1; *Regional Population Projections 2011–2031*, Stationery Office, Dublin 2013, Table 1.
Note: Up to and including 2005, the annual population estimates are on a de facto basis. From 2006 onwards the concept of usual residence is used. The 2006 population using the de facto definition is lower than shown above, at 4.240 million.
[1] Preliminary. [2] Forecast.

Table 6.3 Components of Population Change, Selected Intervals (annual average in '000s)

	Total births	Total deaths	Natural increase	Population change	Estimated net migration
1926–36	58	42	16	0	−17
1951–56	63	36	27	−12	−39
1956–61	61	34	26	−16	−42
1961–66	63	33	29	13	−16
1966–71	63	33	30	19	−11
1971–79	69	33	35	49	14
1981–86	67	33	34	19	−14
1986–91	56	32	24	−3	−27
1991–96	50	31	18	20	2
1996–02	54	31	23	49	26
2002–06	61	28	33	81	48
2006–11	73	29	45	70	25
2011–13[1]	73	29	44	13	−32

Sources: CSO, *Statistical Yearbook 2013*, Stationery Office, Dublin 2013, Table 1.2; CSO, *Population and Migration Estimates,* Stationery Office, Dublin 2013, Table 1.
[1] Preliminary.

143

As seen in Table 6.3, the number of births per annum reached a peak in the 1970s and declined significantly after that; it increased again in the 2002–2006 period, and reached a new peak in the period 2006–2011, but this was more a reflection of the increase in the size of the child-bearing female population than of any large increase in the birth rate. This means that the natural increase in the population is now averaging around 44,000 per annum.

Migration
While there have been significant changes in the natural increase, they are slight compared to the huge swings in net migration that can occur: 40,000 per annum throughout the whole of the 1950s, a similar number in some years in the 1980s, to net annual immigration of 2,000 in the early 1990s, around 26,000 in the late 1990s and 48,000 in the 2000s, with net out migration again in recent years of 30,000 per annum or more.

The *net* immigration figure is the balance between two flows, *gross* outflows and gross inflows of people. Looking first at gross inflows, as can be seen in Table 6.4 immigration increased steadily, up from 40,000 in 1996 to over 105,000 per annum between 2006 and 2008. The figure fell after this but throughout the recession years significant in-migration continued, with an inflow of nearly 56,000 in 2013.

Initially the increase was due primarily to returning Irish nationals, who accounted for around half of total gross immigration between 1996 and 2000. In absolute terms the immigration of Irish nationals continued after 2000 at the levels of the period 1996 to 2000, but there was also a large inflow of non-Irish nationals, initially from 'Rest of the World' (mainly Africa, Nigeria in particular) and, since the enlargement of the EU in 2004, a further huge increase of non-Irish nationals from 'Rest of EU', mainly Poland. This was the most obvious change in Irish society in this period, i.e. the increasing number of non-Irish nationals who to this day make up a significant share of the country's population and labour force. The evidence for this is clear to see, not only in Dublin but across the country, including many small rural towns. Even in the years 2010 to 2013 there were substantial inflows of people from outside Ireland and the UK.

There was substantial out-migration also over the entire period. It was of course until recently less than gross in-migration and substantially so in some years, but nonetheless the persistence of out-migration during the boom years is noteworthy. For example, even in 2006 there was out-migration of 36,000 people, over 15,000 of them Irish nationals (Table 6.4). Between 2006 and 2010 the level of out-migration nearly doubled and increased further in the following two years. Out-migration by Irish nationals rose to almost 28,000 in 2010, but as mentioned there was in-migration of Irish nationals of over 13,000 in the same period, meaning that there was *net* immigration of less than 15,000. In 2013, though, this net figure for Irish nationals rose to over 35,000, with out-migration of 50,000 and in-migration of 15,000.

Table 6.4 Estimated Migration Classified by Nationality, 1996–2013 (percentage of total)

	Irish	UK	Rest of EU	Rest of world	Total (000s)
			Immigration		
1996	45.2	21.2	12.8	20.9	39.2
2006	17.5	9.2	58.1	15.2	107.8
2010	42.8	6.0	37.1	14.4	41.8
2013[1]	28.1	8.8	32.7	30.6	55.9
			Emigration		
2006	42.5	6.1	34.2	17.2	36.0
2010	41.8	4.3	40.5	13.4	69.2
2013[1]	57.2	4.4	26.9	11.6	89.0

Source: CSO, *Population and Migration Estimates*, Stationery Office, Dublin 2013, Tables 2 and 3.
Note: Figures for nationality of emigrants not available prior to 2006.
[1] Preliminary.

Table 6.5 provides an age breakdown of migrants over the period 2002 to 2013, which is of relevance to our later discussion. The most remarkable feature up to 2008 was the huge proportion of total immigrants in the active age groups of 15–24 and in particular 25–44. This means that the vast bulk of the immigrants came here for work, with few young dependents. Most of the dependents were probably attached to Irish nationals returning home, with small numbers associated with the immigration of non-Irish nationals. This means that, unless they had children since they arrived in Ireland, many immigrant workers have no family ties to Ireland and hence are still highly mobile, reinforcing the point made earlier that many of the immigrants could go elsewhere if and when employment prospects turn down, something that is borne out in Tables 6.4 and 6.5.

It is apparent that well over half of the out-migration between 2008 and late 2010 was accounted for by non-nationals, mostly from 'Rest of EU', and that the vast bulk of this occurred in the active age groups of 15–24 and 25–44. It is interesting to note in fact that even in 2006 around 30,000 people in these age groups emigrated, but of course there were around 90,000 immigrants in that year, thereby reflecting a very fluid migration situation in these age groups.

Table 6.5 Estimated Migration Classified by Age Group, 2002–2013 (percentage of total)

	0–14	15–24	25–44	45–64	65 and over	Total ('000s)
			Immigration			
2000	13.5	31.9	44.5	7.6	2.3	52.6
2005	9.5	28.8	53	7.2	1.4	84.6
2010	4.3	41.4	45	4.8	4.6	41.8
2013[1]	16.6	23.1	51.2	8.2	0.7	55.9
			Emigration			
2000	0.0	80.5	17.3	0.4	2.3	26.6
2005	7.1	48.6	36.1	5.1	3.1	29.4
2010	2.9	38.6	52.7	4.2	1.6	69.2
2013[1]	7.6	39.1	46.1	6.4	0.8	89.0

Source: CSO, *Population and Migration Estimates*, Stationery Office, Dublin 2013, Table 4.
[1] Preliminary.

Another interesting dimension to migration patterns relates to the educational level of the migrants. ESRI research has shown that over the whole recession period there was a net inflow of people with third-level education, in response to an *increase* in employment in every year for those with such a level of education.[1] Thus the bulk of the net migration in the recession years was among the less well-educated groups, in response chiefly to the huge decline in employment in construction (see later).

3 LABOUR SUPPLY

Labour supply in any country depends on three factors: the total size of the population; the proportion of that population of working age; and the proportion of the working-age population seeking or in work. This is illustrated by the identity:

$$(2) \qquad L = (P) . (Pa /P) . (L/Pa)$$

where L is the size of the labour force, P the size of the population, and Pa the size of the population of working age. The labour force, in turn, consists of those in employment (E) and those unemployed (UE). Hence:

$$(3) \qquad L = E + UE$$

146

Two further identities of interest to this discussion are the following:

(4) $Q/P = (Q/E) . (E/P)$

(5)   where $E/P = (E/L) . (L/Pa) . (Pa/P)$

Equation (4) links the demographic factors back to (1). It states that output per person employed and the proportion of the population employed determine output per head of population. We saw in Equation (1) that increases in E were the most important factor accounting for record increases in Q in Ireland in the ten years after 1990; E/P also increased at a record rate in this decade, thereby pushing up Q/P (our measure of living standards, as seen in Chapter 2) to record levels.

E/P (the proportion of the population in employment), as can be seen from Equation (5), is influenced by three factors, all of which increased in the 15 years up to 2007; E/L (the proportion of the labour force in employment) increased as unemployment decreased, Pa/P (the proportion of the population of working age), as shall be seen later, increased because of demographic factors and L/Pa (the proportion of the working population in the labour force) increased principally because of increased participation by married females in the labour force. These very favourable demographic trends, in terms of their impact on living standards, became known as Ireland's 'demographic dividend' in the 1990s and early 2000s. Since 2008, though, there has been a decline in E/P, largely due to a decline in E/L, but also perhaps Pa/P.

Working-Age Population
As a result of the fall in the birth rate in the 1980s and 1990s, there was a later fall in the population aged 15 and under. However, because of the high birth rate prior to this, and more important the trends in migration observed above, there was a large increase in the population aged 15–64, and especially in the prime working-age population, 25–64. As seen, a large proportion of the immigrants were of prime working age, thereby pushing up the population in this age group disproportionately. The number of people aged 25–64 rose from 2.18 million in 1991 to over 2.91 million by the year 2006; this is a very large increase in such a short period and had a marked effect on Ireland's age dependency ratios.

Table 6.6 highlights these changes in the composition of the population. In 1981, those aged under 15 years accounted for 51.4 per cent of those aged 15–64, but in just over 20 years this had dropped by almost 21 percentage points. At the same time, the population aged 65 and over, expressed as a proportion of the 15–64 population, also declined, albeit slightly.

Table 6.6 Percentage Age Dependency Ratios,[1] 1981 to 2013

	Young	Old	Total
1981	51.4	18.2	69.6
1991	43.4	18.5	61.9
2001	30.4	15.8	46.2
2011	31.8	17.3	49.2
2013	33.4	18.8	52.2

Sources: CSO, *Census 2006 – Principal Demographic Results*, Stationery Office, Dublin, various issues; CSO, *Population and Migration Estimates*, Stationery Office, Dublin 2013, Table 5.
[1] The ratios in the first two columns are obtained by dividing the population aged 0–14 and 65 years and over by the population aged 15–64. The final column is the sum of these two.

As Table 6.6 illustrates, these favourable demographic trends have now run their course; importantly, though, there will be no worsening of the demographic situation until after 2021, when the percentage classified as 'old' begins to rise significantly. These projections depend very much on what happens with regard to migration over the next decade or so. The 'young' ratio has crept up a little in recent years but is still well below the levels of 20 years ago.

Participation in the Labour Force
An important factor when examining the employment situation in any country is the proportion of the working-age population that actually seeks work. This is known as the labour force participation rate.

Table 6.7 provides data for Ireland, a number of other small EU countries, two countries of particular interest to Ireland (namely the UK and the USA) and the OECD average; where possible these will also be used as the comparator countries in the other tables in this chapter.[2] As can be seen in Table 6.7, the labour force participation rate for males in Ireland in 2012 was below the OECD average, but that for females (while considerably lower than for males) was at the OECD average. The variation across countries, though, is marked: for example, the figure for females for Ireland was 62.2 per cent, compared to a figure of 58.4 per cent in Greece (the lowest rate), 71.0 per cent in the UK, and 75.9 per cent in Norway (the highest rate).

A noteworthy feature is that female participation rates are increasing in most countries, Ireland being no exception. Following a substantial increase up to 1994, the rate increased further in Ireland, up from 45.8 to 62.2 per cent, a large rise in such a short period. By 2012 the rate for Ireland exceeded the OECD average but, as discussed above, was still well below that in some key comparator countries, in particular the UK. It is difficult to predict how much further this participation rate will grow in Ireland, but with the lower birth rate, and if employment prospects improve in the 2010s, it could increase to British levels if not to those in Denmark and Norway. If this happened, it would lead to a large increase in the labour force arising from this factor alone.

Table 6.7 Percentage Labour Force Participation Rates[1] in Selected OECD Countries, 1994 and 2012

	Males		Females	
	1994	2012	1994	2012
Belgium	72.0	72.5	51.2	61.3
Denmark	83.7	81.4	73.8	75.8
Greece	77.0	77.4	43.2	58.4
Ireland	*76.2*	*76.7*	*45.8*	*62.2*
Netherlands	79.6	84.2	57.3	74.3
Norway	81.6	80.7	70.9	75.9
OECD	81.4	79.7	57.8	62.3
UK	85.1	83.2	67.1	71.0
USA	84.3	78.8	69.4	67.6

Source: OECD, *Employment Outlook*, OECD, Paris 2010 and 2013, Tables B and C.
[1] Ratios refer to persons aged 15–64 years who are in the labour force divided by the total population aged 15–64.

Conclusion

A consideration of migration trends is central to any discussion of labour supply in Ireland. It, more than any other factor, determines changes in the size of the population and the growth of the labour force. As seen from Table 6.3, more than half of those added to the Irish population on an annual average basis between 1996 and 2008 were as a result of net inward migration. Between 2008 and 2013 the trend of net outward migration began to exert a marked downward pressure on population growth and for the years ahead it will be what happens on the migration front that will largely determine labour supply. The increases in the labour force participation rates of females aged 25 to 64 may be dwarfed by the changes in net migration, but in themselves they are very significant changes which, after the effects of net migration are removed, could also have a marked bearing on the growth of the labour force in years to come.

4 EMPLOYMENT: GROWTH AND COMPOSITION

Overall Employment

The first point worth noting from Table 6.8 is the tiny size of the workforce in Ireland: around 1.8 million in 2012, as opposed to 8.3 million in the Netherlands, 28.5 million in the UK and 135.2 million in the USA. Given that there is an effective common labour market between Ireland and the UK, it is very important for labour policy purposes to bear in mind the relative sizes of these two labour markets in particular.

The most striking fact in relation to employment in Ireland up to 2008 had been its growth relative to other countries. In the ten years to 2004, employment grew on average by 4.1 per cent per annum in Ireland compared to less than 1 per cent growth in many countries; the Netherlands had, at 1.6 per cent, the nearest rate of growth to Ireland's. This is remarkable given that employment in Ireland had actually declined in the 1980–86 period and had not managed to rise significantly over the entire decade spanning the years 1980–1990 (see Table 6.1).

The growth of employment continued to outpace all of the countries listed in Table 6.8 up to 2008. This means that for 15 years Ireland had managed to outperform the smaller European countries as well as the UK and the USA in the employment growth stakes. As seen in Table 6.1, employment then decreased substantially between 2008 and 2011 but since then has increased again, markedly so in 2013.

Table 6.8 Employment and Proportion of Active Age Group in Employment in Selected OECD Countries

| | Employed (millions) | E/Pa (%) | | |
	2012	2000	2006	2012
Belgium	4.5	60.5	61.0	61.8
Denmark	2.6	76.3	77.4	72.6
Greece	3.7	56.5	61.0	51.3
Ireland	*1.8*	*65.2*	*68.7*	*58.8*
Netherlands	8.3	72.9	74.3	75.1
Norway	2.5	77.5	75.4	75.7
OECD	530.2	67.2	66.0	65.0
UK	28.5	71.2	71.6	70.1
USA	135.2	74.1	72.0	67.1

Sources: OECD, *Labour Force Statistics 1989–2009*, OECD, Paris 2010, Part 1; OECD, *Directorate for Employment Labour and Social Affairs*, Online Database, 2013.

Ireland, of course, had up to 2005 a much greater increase in potential labour supply than any of the other countries and hence unemployment would have remained at a very high level and the position of net immigration might have been translated into substantial net emigration without this growth in employment. Much of the early immigration, after all, was due to the return of people who had emigrated in the depressed labour market conditions of the 1980s. Much of the immigration in the 2000s, though, as seen earlier, was due to immigration of non-Irish nationals.

The last three columns in Table 6.8 show the ratio of total employment to population size aged 15–64 years for each of the countries listed. Despite the rapid growth of employment in Ireland up to 2006, just 68.7 per cent of the population aged 15–64 were in employment in 2006, a lower figure than that experienced by many OECD countries in the same year; the figure for the USA was 72.0 per cent, the UK 71.6 per cent and those for Norway and Denmark as high as 75.4 and 77.4 per cent respectively.

It could be argued therefore that the employment increase in Ireland in the ten years up to 2006 was strongly associated with a huge increase in the labour force, an increase that was simply bringing Ireland up to just below international norms in terms of the proportion of the total working-age population in employment.

The changes in the E/Pa ratios since 2006 have been quite dramatic, across many countries. The most striking case is the USA, where E/Pa decreased from 72.0 to 67.1 per cent, with the figure having been as high as 74.1 per cent as recently as 2000.[3] In contrast, it went up for some EU countries shown in Table 6.8, but in the Irish case it declined, to as low as 58.8 per cent in 2012. This is well below the OECD average and the lowest for all countries shown in the table bar Greece. The contrast between Ireland and the Netherlands and Norway is particularly striking, where both have E/Pa ratios almost 20 percentage points above those for Ireland.

Part-Time and Temporary Employment

An important issue relating to employment in some countries, including Ireland, is the extent to which it consists of part-time employment and/or temporary employment. The available data suggest (Table 6.9) that the level of part-time employment as a proportion of total employment is low throughout the countries examined. In this regard Ireland is not out of line with its OECD counterparts. Similarly, there appears to have been no significant increase in part-time employment, especially among males, in the period up to 2012.

There is a marked gender difference in relation to part-time employment, as may be seen in Table 6.9. Only 13.1 per cent of total male employment in Ireland in 2012 was part time, whereas 37.5 per cent of female employment was part time. These percentages vary considerably from country to country, but on balance the position in Ireland was not unusual.

What is more important, perhaps, is the extent to which part-time employment is involuntary, i.e. chosen by the individual only because they cannot get full-time work. The evidence suggests that most part-time employment is in fact voluntary, reflecting therefore a desire for such employment; largely, it seems, from female employees entering the labour force and with a preference for part-time work as it fits better with family and other commitments.

A different but related issue is the extent to which employment is in temporary work.[4] This is a much-debated topic in labour market economics as some economists believe that an increasing proportion of jobs will have to be temporary if labour markets, especially in Europe, are to be sufficiently flexible to cope with an employment crisis, a topic that will be returned to later.

Table 6.9 Incidence and Composition of Part-time Employment[1] in Selected OECD Countries, 2012

	Part-time employment (% of total employment)			Temporary employment (% of dependent employment)
	Men	Women	Total	Total
Belgium	7.1	32.1	18.7	8.1
Denmark	14.4	24.9	19.4	8.5
Greece	6.0	15.1	9.7	10.0
Ireland	*13.1*	*37.5*	*25.0*	*10.2*
Netherlands	18.0	60.7	37.8	19.5
Norway	11.5	29.1	19.8	8.4
OECD	9.3	26.4	16.9	11.8
UK	12.2	39.4	24.9	6.3
USA	8.7	18.3	13.4	–

Sources: OECD, *Employment Outlook*, OECD, Paris 2010 and 2013, Tables H and I;
OECD Directorate for Employment Labour and Social Affairs, Online Database, 2013.
[1] Part-time is usual hours of work of less than 30 per week.

As seen in Table 6.9, temporary employment in Ireland in 2012 accounted for 10.2 per cent of dependent employment. This compares to figures of 8.5 per cent in Denmark, 19.5 per cent in the Netherlands, 6.3 per cent in the UK, and a weighted OECD average of 11.8 per cent. Thus there is no evidence that employment here was overly based on part-time employment.

Although experiences across the OECD vary, it does appear that younger and less educated workers disproportionately fill temporary jobs. On the other hand, temporary workers are a diverse group who work in a wide range of occupations and sectors. There is no evidence, though (as mentioned), that this is a particularly acute problem in the Irish context, and this may be due to the weakness of employment protection laws in Ireland whereby employers have sufficient flexibility not to need to resort to temporary contracts (see later).

Sectoral Composition of Employment
Table 6.10 outlines the composition of employment in Ireland from 1994 to 2013; while the data are not strictly comparable the table shows some broad trends in this composition in the period.

The once central position of the agriculture sector has truly diminished (see Chapter 1) and now accounts for just 5.5 per cent of total employment (down from over 12.0 per cent only 19 years ago). There are now more people employed in accommodation and food services than in the total agricultural sector, reflecting the increased importance of tourism to the Irish economy and the marked trend towards eating out among Irish people. More people are employed in the health sector than in manufacturing in total, and almost 50 per cent more people are employed in education than in agriculture.

The services sector as a whole is over four times the size of the industrial sector and six times that of the manufacturing sector (other production services). As can be seen in the final column in Table 6.10, employment in all of the services sub-sectors grew between 1994 and 2008, but in particular in transport, storage and communication, and health. Between 2008 and 2013 there were further increases in employment in some services sectors but in particular in health, whereas there were declines in most other sub-sectors.

Table 6.10 Employment by Sector, Ireland

	('000s)			
	1994	2004	2008	2013
Agriculture, Forestry and Fishing	*147.0*	*113.8*	*116.0*	*103.4*
Industry	*343.3*	*492.0*	*537.5*	*341.1*
of which:				
Other production services	251.8	294.3	291.4	238.4
Construction	91.5	197.7	246.1	102.7
Services	*730.2*	*1,394.4*	*1,486.3*	*1,424.2*
of which:				
Wholesale and retail trade	169.2	259.5	314.8	271.5
Accommodation and food services	68.4	107.2	128.7	129.6
Transport, storage and communication	55.9	152.1	166.3	166.4
Financial and other business services	114.3	148.0	184.9	156.9
Public administration and defence	66.4	90.1	103.5	95.1
Education	80.5	121.4	147.4	150.3
Health	101.0	177.4	222.8	244.6
Other	74.5	190.7	225.3	209.8
Total	*1,220.6*	*1,902.3*	*2,147.3*	*1,869.9*

Source: CSO, *Quarterly National Household Survey (QNHS)*, Stationery Office, Dublin, various issues.

The figures in relation to employment in construction though tell the story of the overall economy: 91.5 thousand in 1994, 197.7 thousand in 2004, 246.1 in

2008 and back to 102.7 thousand in 2013. This is truly a roller-coaster in employment terms which in turn is reflected in the overall employment situation.

5 UNEMPLOYMENT: EXTENT AND FEATURES

International Comparisons

Table 6.11 provides the key information on recorded unemployment rates in Ireland and selected OECD countries, including, as mentioned earlier, some small EU countries, since 1995. The unemployment rate is given by $E/(E + UE)$ and the picture is fairly clear.

Between 1995 and 2006, all countries bar Greece experienced significant declines in unemployment, with the OECD average declining from 7.3 per cent in 1995 to 6.1 per cent in 2006. The most dramatic decline was in Ireland, down from 12.3 per cent to 4.5 per cent in the same period. Between 2006 and 2012, though, unemployment in the OECD area increased from 6.1 per cent to 8.0 per cent, with a much more dramatic increase in Ireland, up from 4.5 per cent to 14.7 per cent in 2012. In contrast, unemployment in Belgium and Norway declined. The success story in terms of employment since 2009 has in fact been Germany (not included in tables), with large drops in unemployment experienced there, and standing in early 2014 at under 6 per cent.

Table 6.11 Standardised Unemployment Rates in Selected OECD Countries[1]

| | As a percentage of the labour force | | | |
	1995	2000	2006	2012
Belgium	9.7	6.9	8.3	7.6
Denmark	6.7	4.3	3.9	7.5
Greece	8.8	11.2	8.9	24.3
Ireland	*12.3*	*4.2*	*4.5*	*14.7*
Netherlands	7.1	3.1	4.3	5.3
Norway	4.9	3.2	3.4	3.2
OECD	7.3	6.1	6.1	8.0
UK	8.5	5.4	5.4	7.9
USA	5.6	4.0	4.6	8.1

Source: OECD, *Employment Outlook*, OECD, Paris 2010 and 2013, Table A.
[1] All series are benchmarked to labour force survey-based estimates and have been adjusted to ensure comparability over time.

Comparison/Measurement Problems
Standardised Unemployment Rates

The discussion above is based on the assumption that the data can be used for valid comparison both across countries and over time. Is this the case? There are three main issues of concern here. The first is whether or not all countries are using the same methods of defining and compiling data on unemployment; the second is whether or not there is a consistent series over time for Ireland; the last is whether or not there are certain categories of persons that are not, and perhaps cannot be, included by any country but who should be included in any discussion of labour market slack (i.e. where labour demand is less than labour supply) in an economy.

International comparison of unemployment rates is fraught with difficulty, despite the best efforts of the OECD and the EU. Nonetheless, there are reasonably reliable comparative data for the EU member states, if not for most of the OECD countries, and these are the data that inform comparative studies and international policy debate.

In relation to Ireland, there are two main sources of data on unemployment: the Quarterly National Household Survey (QNHS) and the Live Register. The QNHS gives two measures of unemployment: the International Labour Office (ILO) measure and the Principal Economic Status (PES) measure. The first of these is the internationally recognised measure of unemployment and defines somebody as 'unemployed' if their response in the survey makes it clear that they did not work even for one hour for payments or profit in the previous week; that they actively sought work in the previous four weeks; and that they are available to start work within two weeks. It does not include so-called discouraged workers, those who have given up hope on the job search, a phenomenon which can vary in its impact in different countries and hence disguises comparison of the 'true' level of unemployment.

The ILO definition is, then, a strict measure of unemployment and much stricter than the Live Register measure. The latter counts each month all those in receipt of unemployment benefit or unemployment assistance (now called jobseeker's allowance, but the more generic terms will be used throughout this chapter), plus those who, though entitled to no payment, wish to have social insurance contributions 'credited' to them; in addition, casual and part-time workers who work for not more than three days in the week may be entitled to register on account of the days they do not work. There is little doubt, therefore, that the Live Register figure gives an overstatement of the number unemployed in the normal sense of the term.

It is the ILO data, therefore, that are used for international comparison, as the methods used in arriving at these data are considered to give the more accurate indicator of the underlying level of unemployment in a country. These data are also used in this chapter, unless indicated otherwise. It is important to remember that the ILO definition is quite a restrictive measure of unemployment and gives perhaps the most favourable picture of the unemployment problem in a country.

It excludes, for example, many who are in involuntary part-time work and also, as mentioned, those described as discouraged and marginalised workers.

Invalidity/Disability Benefit Issue
There are also many people unable to work through invalidity or disability; the proportion of the working-age group in this category has grown significantly in some EU countries in recent years, with some commentators suggesting that some of the decrease in unemployment in the 2000s, in the Netherlands and the UK in particular, could be linked to this development. For example, in the UK a major programme has been put in place to get many of these people back to work, on the lines of the policies used to bring the long-term unemployed back into the labour force in the UK in earlier years.

As the OECD states, too many workers leave the labour market permanently due to health problems and, indeed, expenditures on disability programmes in many OECD countries far exceed expenditures on other income-replacement programmes for working-age persons (such as unemployment benefits).[5] A large number of OECD countries have seen substantial increases in the share of disability beneficiaries in the working-age population. It appears that vulnerable groups such as women, young individuals and the low-skilled are most affected by this trend.

Helping disabled people find and keep jobs is a major challenge for all OECD countries, including Ireland, especially given that the potential personal, social and financial benefits are huge. Although it is costly to leave disabled people outside the labour force, no country has so far been successful in crafting policies that will help disabled people return to work. The OECD suggests various broad areas for improvement, including: individual benefit packages with job search support, rehabilitation and vocational training; new obligations for disabled people, including, for those who are capable, a requirement to look for work; involving employers and trade unions in reintegration efforts; and more flexible cash benefits, depending on job capabilities and changes in an individual's disability over time.

Long-Term and Youth Unemployment
Apart from the level of unemployment, its composition is also of considerable interest to economists, for reasons alluded to already. Perhaps the most important consideration in this regard relates to the comparison between short-term (less than 12 months) and long-term (12 months or more) unemployment.

Long-term unemployment (LTU) in Ireland rose significantly between 1980 and 1990. The LTU rate was only 2.8 per cent of the labour force in 1980, rising to 8.3 per cent in 1990. As Table 6.12 shows, a marked decline took place in LTU between 1990 and 2000. The reductions were remarkable: the numbers in absolute terms were down to just over a quarter of their level in 1990; and the drop in the LTU rate is even more dramatic, falling from 8.3 to 1.6 per cent, below the level pertaining in 1980.

Table 6.12 Long-Term Unemployment (LTU) in Ireland, 1990–2013

	Number ('000s)	Unemployment rate (%)	LTU rate (%)
1990	110.2	12.9	8.3
2000	28.6	4.6	1.6
2005	31.6	4.7	1.5
2010	140.2	13.9	6.4
2011	178.1	14.6	8.2
2012	199.6	15.0	9.2
2013	175.0	13.9	8.1

Sources: CSO, *Quarterly National Household Survey (QNHS)*, Stationery Office, Dublin, various issues; CSO, *Statistical Yearbook of Ireland*, CSO, Dublin 2000.

This picture remained largely unchanged up to 2008, when the first rise in LTU on all counts was recorded. Between 2008 and 2012 there was a dramatic worsening of the situation, with the LTU rate rising from 1.5 per cent to 9.2 per cent in four years and the numbers in LTU increasing over sixfold. The LTU problem of the 1980s and early 1990s had returned to Ireland in a few short years, although some decline did take place in 2013. This in many ways could be the most worrying legacy of the economic crisis of the last six years.

Table 6.13 Long-Term Unemployment in Selected OECD Countries (percentage of total unemployment)

	2000	2006	2012
Belgium	56.3	51.2	44.7
Denmark	20.0	20.8	28.0
Greece	56.4	54.3	59.3
Ireland	*33.1[1]*	*31.6*	*61.7*
Netherlands	–	43.0	33.7
Norway	5.3	14.5	8.7
OECD	30.8	31.4	34.3
UK	28.0	22.3	34.8
USA	6.0	10.0	29.3

Source: OECD Directorate for Employment Labour and Social Affairs, Online Database, 2013.

[1] 2001 figure.

Table 6.13 provides data on LTU for the countries shown. Arguably the most striking trend in the table relates to the USA, with the share of long-term unemployment in total unemployment rising steadily from 6.0 per cent in 2000 to

29.3 per cent in 2012. The figure for Ireland declined between 2000 and 2006 but then almost doubled between 2006 and 2012, with the figure of 61.7 per cent in that year being the highest by far for any country shown in the table, bar Greece. Norway had a figure of only 8.7 per cent. This confirms that the LTU problem is very serious indeed in Ireland, both in an absolute and relative sense.

Another major worry with regard to the composition of unemployment relates to youth unemployment (see Table 6.14). These data relate the number of people in the age groups 15–19 and 20–24 who are not in employment, education or training. Thus, they include not just those unemployed but also those on disability benefit, those doing domestic unpaid work and discouraged workers.

Table 6.14 Percentage of Youth Inactivity (neither employed nor in education or training)

	15–19-year-olds		20–24-year-olds	
	2000	2011	2000	2011
Belgium	6.5	6.1	16.0	17.1
Denmark	2.7	5.3	6.6	11.9
Greece	9.3	8.3	25.9	24.3
Ireland	*4.4*	*9.4*	*9.7*	*26.4*
Netherlands	3.7	3.4	8.2	6.9
Norway	–	3.2	8.0	10.4
OECD	9.4	8.2	17.7	18.5
UK	8.0	9.5	15.4	19.1
USA	7.0	7.1	14.4	18.5

Source: *OECD Directorate for Employment Labour and Social Affairs*, Online Database, 2013.

What is shown is not unemployment rates but 'inactivity rates'. These are more meaningful than unemployment rates, which relate the number unemployed to the sum of those unemployed and those in employment, and not to the total population in that age group. Thus, figures for youth unemployment rates in, say, Greece can be calculated as over 55 per cent, whereas, as seen in Table 6.14, fewer than 25 per cent of that age group are not in employment, education or training.[6] In fact the number of those aged 20 to 24 unemployed in Greece probably account for not much more than 12 per cent of the population in that age group.

The data presented in Table 6.14 are quite striking. Over a quarter of all those aged 20–24 in Ireland are not in education, training or employment, a higher figure than that for Greece. The figure for Ireland increased dramatically between 2000 and 2011, from 9.7 per cent to 26.4 per cent. In the Netherlands the figure is as low as 6.9 per cent, but the figures for the UK and USA are also high, with increases in inactivity in the 20–24-year-old group in the USA between 2000 and

2011. The great worry, of course, is that some of these people have been out of the labour market for more than a year and hence already belong to the LTU or disabled.

6 ADAPTING TO NEW TECHNOLOGY, AND INCREASED TRADE AND MIGRATION

What causes employment levels to rise and fall in any country, including Ireland? First, there are arguments relating to global factors such as increased competition in international trade, technological change and greater freedom of movement of labour, especially in the EU, and hence a potentially large increase in migration. These are factors that would affect every country in Europe, but they affect some to a greater extent than others. How each country fares largely depends on the skill level and adaptability of its labour force in the new circumstances. These issues will be discussed in this section. Second, there are structural arguments relating to such issues as the role of unions and wage bargaining/setting, employment protection legislation and the taxation and social welfare systems. These issues will be discussed in Section 7.

Single Market, Trade, and Technological Change

Given the extent of Ireland's trade, and factor and corporate links with the world economy, it is inevitable that the increasing globalisation of economic activity has, and will have, a major effect on economic activity and employment in Ireland (see later chapters). Added to this is the deepening of the single European market and the removal of barriers to free trade in services, mergers and acquisitions, and capital flows with the consequential implications for economic activity, competition and employment in Ireland. Ireland's entry into the euro zone in the late 1990s was a further major commitment to the benefits and challenges of the single market. It appears that these challenges were never properly understood at the time and that this was a key cause of the drop in employment after 2008.

It is generally believed by economists that an increasing intensity of trade and integration will lead to higher incomes, but that it will also lead to the displacement of labour in some activities and the expansion of labour in others.[7] The net impact on employment should be negligible as long as labour and product markets function well and wages are reasonably flexible. Thus, if decreased overall employment should result from increased trade intensity and competition it is not trade or competition *per se* that is causing the problem, but the functioning of the labour and product markets, a topic that will be returned to in a later section. The evidence, according to the OECD, supports such an argument. This indeed is the reason why Ireland has adopted such a pro-trade liberalisation, pro-competition stance in the last 40 years.

Increasing international trade and economic integration may also have an impact on innovation and the absorption of technological change. It is argued by some that labour-saving technologies are, at least in part, introduced in anticipation of and/or in response to the increased competition both on domestic and foreign markets that arises from the increased globalisation of trade and European integration. As such, the effects of increased international integration and of technological change are difficult to separate in practice.

Technology is central to the process of growth (see Chapters 7 and 9): it allows increases in productivity and thereby real incomes. But does it destroy jobs and in the process create unemployment?

Fears about widespread job losses associated with the emergence of new technology are not new and are in the aggregate largely unfounded.[8] They date back to at least the time of the Industrial Revolution in the early nineteenth century, when the Luddite movement in England destroyed new machinery for fear of job losses. It is true that technological change involves a process of job destruction in some older occupations, firms and industries, but it also involves a parallel process of job creation in new and emerging sectors and occupations. There are many historical examples of predictions of large-scale technological unemployment being followed in fact by large net expansions of jobs, the experience in the last two decades or so with regard to the information technology (IT) sector in the USA being the most recent striking example.

Technology and trade, then, do not lead to a decrease in the level of employment, but they allow for a decrease in the annual hours of work per employee, thereby allowing for increased per capita incomes *and* increased voluntary leisure time. The average working year has declined steadily over the last 100 years and this trend is continuing, as seen in Table 6.15.

Table 6.15 Average Annual Working Time in Selected OECD Countries (hours per worker)

	2000	2006	2012
Belgium	1,545	1,566	1,574
Denmark	1,581	1,586	1,546
Greece	2,130	2,066	2,034
Ireland	*1,719*	*1,644*	*1,529*
Netherlands	1,435	1,392	1,381
Norway	1,455	1,420	1,420
OECD	1,844	1,802	1,765
UK	1,700	1,669	1,654
USA	1,836	1,800	1,790

Source: *OECD Directorate for Employment Labour and Social Affairs*, Online Database, 2013.

For all countries listed, bar Belgium, average annual working time decreased between 2000 and 2012, and markedly so in Ireland. The other striking finding revealed in Table 6.15 is the significant variation across even developed countries in the average annual working time. In particular, it can be seen that it was 1,790 hours in the USA, more than 17 per cent higher than the figure for Ireland, and almost 30 per cent more than in the Netherlands. This is an issue that is discussed in the examination of comparative living standards Chapter 7. From a labour supply point of view the question is to what extent the variation in hours is a reflection of work preferences or of a slack labour demand. Those supporting the USA model argue for the latter, whereas Europeans tend to argue that the former applies.

While Ireland's adoption of new technology will be discussed in later chapters, particularly Chapter 9, it is worth noting here that there are four key technology areas that will influence the country's success in IT: infrastructure; competitive market conditions; education and training; and access for all. It has been, and will be, the country's ability to take appropriate action on all four fronts that will allow us to absorb and adapt to the new technology: our ability to do this will in turn be the key to employment, not only in manufacturing but perhaps more importantly, given its scale, in the services sector as well (see Chapters 9 and 13).

Labour Market Integration

Labour market integration is a highly contentious aspect of economic integration in Europe. Popular opinion, especially in periods of high unemployment, holds immigrants responsible for high unemployment, abuse of social welfare programmes, street crime and the deterioration of neighbourhoods. Economic theory predicts that in a world of no unemployment there will be both winners and losers resulting from labour migration. Without migration, however, the worldwide allocation of productive factors is inefficient. Improving the overall efficiency of the world economy through migration, then, leads to a net gain which must be split between the home and foreign country.

In the situation where there is no unemployment and workers initially earn better wages in the domestic economy than in the foreign economy, migration will result in labour flowing from the foreign to the domestic economy. This may push down wages at home, harming domestic workers while benefiting domestic consumers. The opposite happens in the foreign economy. Wages there tend to rise as some foreign labour moves to the domestic economy; thus, remaining foreign workers are better off while foreign consumers are made worse off. The net outcome is positive for the efficiency reasons outlined above, but serious distributional issues can arise.

For most European economies labour comprises both highly skilled and low-skilled workers. Recognising this distinction allows a more nuanced under-standing of the dynamics of labour market integration under net inward or net outward migration. It is in this context that one may view immigrant labour as a complement or substitute for domestic labour. If immigrant labour is a complement to native workers, immigration will raise the demand for native workers, resulting in higher wages, higher employment, and an unambiguously favourable impact on unemployment.

The empirical evidence for Ireland suggests that although the skill make-up of immigrants was higher than that of the native population, immigrants tended to fill low-skilled jobs and thus acted as complements to the skilled Irish workforce, even if this meant that migrants achieved a low occupational attainment relative to their educational attainment. It remains to be seen whether the favourable impact of migration on the Irish labour market will continue when the economy is growing much more slowly. Preliminary evidence suggests (see Table 6.5) that recent immigrants are still highly mobile and that many have returned to their home countries as employment in construction collapsed. In this way the ease of movement between Ireland and the new European member states helped to ease the adverse unemployment impacts of the downturn in Ireland between 2008 and 2012.[9]

Education, Training and Skills Adaptability

Over the last 20 years the structure of work in the industrialised world has, for the reasons mentioned above, been changing. There has been a shift in demand away from low-skilled, low-wage jobs towards high-skilled, high-wage jobs. The change in the nature of work arises not only from the transformation of jobs by technology and international trade but also from the 'natural' sectoral changes that have occurred with regard to employment (see Table 6.10). Allied to this, because of immigration, there was a marked transformation in labour supply in many sectors.

The skills required in services are different from those needed in industry and hence the declining industrial workforce cannot be automatically transplanted into services jobs. The new wave of employment creation leads, as mentioned earlier, to a transformation of the competencies required from the workforce. Not only do they need different qualifications and skills but the continuously changing nature of work also requires them to have a high degree of flexibility that was not necessary in the past when permanent, stable positions were the norm.

The skills of the labour force, then, have to be altered to take account of the changing environment and nature of work. In the absence of this adjustment, mismatch can, and may have, become a serious problem in the labour market.[10] Evidence for this is reflected in repeated statements of serious skills shortages in parts of the EU.

It is for these reasons that the EU has placed special emphasis on upgrading the skills and competencies of the labour force, as part of the search for a solution to maintaining and increasing employment. Not all persons have acquired adequate initial education and training before they enter the labour market and these are the people most likely to experience long-term unemployment in Ireland and elsewhere in Europe. The first priority, then, must be to reduce through preventive and remedial measures the number of young people who leave school without some qualification (see Chapter 13).

The next concern is to ensure that those who have acquired satisfactory initial qualifications make the transition to employment and this may be assisted by a more employer-led approach to education, particularly vocational education. Last, and of most relevance perhaps in relation to the issues discussed in this section, is the need to emphasise continuing education and training (see Chapter 13), as individuals need the opportunity to upgrade their knowledge and competencies to prepare themselves for the changes brought about by increasing international trade, migration and technological change. The challenges in 2014 are pressing in identifying the areas for employment growth and ensuring that the skill levels of the Irish labour force match the resulting employment opportunities.[11]

7 FLEXIBILITY IN THE LABOUR MARKET

It has been mentioned already that structural rigidities in labour markets, especially in those of many countries in Europe, may largely explain why unemployment was and is at such high levels in these countries. Putting it more positively, it is argued that it is the countries with flexible labour markets that have experienced the lowest rates of unemployment in the 2010s. There are several dimensions to the structural rigidity and labour market flexibility arguments and some of the key ones are looked at here.

First, wage and price adjustments are examined, with attention devoted to industrial relations and product market competition. Second, quantity adjustments (which refers to barriers facing the movement of people in and out of jobs) are analysed. Policies to enhance quantity adjustment include reforms of employment protection legislation and active labour market policies. Last, the effect of the tax and social welfare system on the working of the labour market will be examined briefly.

Wage Adjustments
Price formation in the labour market is, by necessity, different from that in other markets. This is because wages are not simply a price of one type of product among others, but determine to a large extent the well-being of the majority of people in modern society. Societies' concern about social justice and the distribution of income therefore becomes integrally linked to wage-setting. Because of this, distinct social arrangements and institutions intervene in every country in the market-clearing role of wage adjustments. However, even if the operation of the price system for labour is different from that for products, the effects of prices being too high are the same, i.e. wages above market-clearing levels will result in excess supply and therefore lower levels of employment than would otherwise be the case.

Industrial Relations

The response of wages to market conditions has to be seen against the background of the institutional arrangements, particularly those relating to industrial relations and the role of trade unions, in the labour market in each particular country. These arrangements have been partly designed to encourage stable employment relationships and to avert the income insecurity that can accompany rapid price adjustments in the market for labour, as happened in the USA in the 1980s. However, in so doing, these arrangements may encourage anti-competitive behaviour in the labour market and, as in all markets, this will result in lower demand because prices are not set at their clearing rate. This of course must be set against the advantages for employees of the protective industrial relations arrangements and the potential advantages for employers, in that these arrangements may strengthen co-operation by workers and prevent the harmful behaviour that may be inherent in a more atomistic wage-setting environment.

Given the above, it is generally recognised that income restraint by trade unions and individual workers is essential to employment creation in Ireland and that there *is* a trade-off between pay and employment. In the multinational high-tech sector of the economy, pay moderation can lead to more employment in the medium to longer term, through increased profitability and its effect on investment location decisions. In the more traditional labour-intensive parts of the traded sector there is likely to be a substantial trade-off between pay and employment, as in many cases pay moderation is essential in this sector simply to retain existing jobs. In the sheltered private sector, pay moderation is necessary to underpin the competitiveness of the traded sector and also to generate increased employment in this sector. Last, in the public sector, given a fixed budget, there is a very direct and almost immediate trade-off between pay and employment.

Table 6.16 Union Membership in Selected OECD Countries (percentage of employees)

	1999	2005	2011
Belgium	50.9	52.9	50.4
Denmark	74.9	71.7	–
Greece	26.8	24.6	25.4
Ireland	*38.9*	*33.7*	*35.1*
Netherlands	*23.6*	*21.4*	19.0
Norway	54.8	54.9	54.6
OECD	–	–	–
UK	30.5	27.1	–
USA[1]	13.4	12.0	11.3

Source: OECD Directorate for Employment Labour and Social Affairs, Online Database, 2013.

[1] Survey data rather than administrative data used.

The usual indicator of perceived industrial relations problems is the level of unionisation of the labour force in a country. There are a number of interesting facts in this regard emerging from Table 6.16. First is the huge variation in trade union membership across countries, from as low as 11.3 per cent in the USA to 54.6 per cent in Norway and 71.7 per cent in Denmark. Surprisingly, perhaps, trade union membership is very low in the Netherlands, well below that in the UK. As such, it is almost impossible to draw any firm conclusions between the rate of unionisation and unemployment. The other striking thing is that there was little decline in the unionisation rate in the countries shown between 1999 and 2011.

In relation to the wage-bargaining process, there is a degree of corporatism in the Irish labour market with a large proportion of wages having being determined by national wage agreements up until recently (see Chapter 3). Ireland therefore appeared to have adopted the preferable system of wage bargaining (i.e. centralised) for such a small country where participants are more likely to take wider economic interests into account.

The OECD, though, warned in general against too little differentiation of relative wages by skill, region, or other dimensions. It also acknowledges that it might be best to accept the variation in national industrial relations and practices evident across member states and concentrate instead on 'identifying policies that increase wage flexibility in the presence of such structures ... and that greater allowance be made for the potential contribution of centrally co-ordinated bargaining to achieving aggregate wage restraint, at least in those countries whose histories and structures are compatible with such an approach'.[12]

In recent years, though, the position in Ireland has changed dramatically and many now question the desirability of centralised wage setting, at least if it does not recognise the reality of competition in product markets in a single currency area and thereby the limitations of passing on wage increases into prices (see Chapter 3). Nationwide collective bargaining has been effectively abandoned, although it still applies across the public sector, with the so-called Croke Park and Haddington Road agreements put in place in recent years.

Competition in Product Markets
Imperfect competition in product markets can also affect the wage level and thereby the level of employment and unemployment. If there is an absence of competition in product markets, firms have an option of choosing 'supra-normal' profits ahead of increased employment. They also have the option of retaining the entire surplus for themselves or sharing it with existing employees. The latter will happen if the workers have bargaining strength or the rents may be willingly shared with workers to encourage efficiency and to boost work motivation, i.e. the employers may be prepared to pay what are called 'efficiency wages'.

The solution to reducing the distortionary effects of imperfect product market competition on labour market outcomes is clearly to remove the opportunity for producers to earn rent, and this calls for a strict and tough competition regime, a topic that was covered at some length in Chapter 4. More important, the opening

165

of the EU market to increased competition, internal and external, has greatly reduced the potential for such imperfect competition. Besides, entry into the euro zone has removed the exchange rate option for dealing with excessive wage rises: employers and employees must now 'live' with the euro exchange rate, which is in turn determined by market conditions. The potential benefits of course are reduced exchange rate risk, more transparency of prices, fewer transactions costs and increased employment levels overall.

The main concern now relates to the public sector, where for some time the tax price of its services can be shielded from any immediate effect on employment in the public sector. In time, though, the higher tax price for public services must be paid for out of taxation, thus impacting on Irish competitiveness and ultimately therefore on Irish employment, tax revenue and public sector employment. Wage negotiations still take place at the level of the whole public sector and in recent years there has been a realisation that in return for this, much greater work flexibility and public sector reform will be required.

Minimum Wage
A national minimum wage (NMW) was introduced in Ireland in 2000. Although the ESRI predicted that this would decrease employment and increase unemployment and inflation, 95 per cent of firms surveyed a year later viewed the NMW as having had no impact on the number of employees they had subsequently hired. Those paid less than the NMW are concentrated in sales and personal services, which reflects a wider concern that younger female and non-Irish national workers are most likely to experience low pay.

Table 6.17 Ratio of Minimum to Median Wage in Selected OECD Countries

	2000	2006	2012
Belgium	0.53	0.50	0.51
Denmark	–	–	–
Greece	0.47	0.45	0.43
Ireland	*0.68*	*0.52*	*0.48*
Netherlands	0.51	0.47	0.47
Norway	–	–	–
UK	0.41	0.45	0.47
USA	0.36	0.31	0.38

Source: OECD Directorate for Employment Labour and Social Affairs, Online Database, 2013.

Many studies have shown that the adverse impact of minimum wages on employment is modest.[13] This, however, depends on the level of the minimum wage and how it interacts with the tax system. The important thing in this regard is to ensure that work pays better than remaining on social welfare benefits and also that high rates of labour taxation do not apply at low income levels (see Chapter 4). An employer considering hiring a low-skilled or inexperienced worker is likely to compare the worker's expected productivity with the *sum* of the minimum wage and employer-paid social security contributions when deciding whether or not to hire.

The minimum wage, relative to median income, is about average in Ireland. As shown in Table 6.17, in 2012 this ratio was 0.48 for Ireland, compared to 0.47 in the UK (our main competitor market), and 0.38 in the USA. This ratio has, however, come down significantly for Ireland between 2000 and 2012, much more so than for any other country listed.

Employment Protection Legislation

Employment protection relates to the 'firing and hiring' rules governing unfair dismissal, lay-off for economic reasons, severance payments, minimum notice periods, administrative authorisation for dismissals and prior discussion with labour representatives. A number of benefits are alleged to justify employment protection legislation: encouraging increased investment in firm-specific human capital; reducing contracting costs by setting general rules and standards; and early notification of job loss to allow job search prior to being laid off. As against this, employment protection legislation imposes constraints on firms' behaviour that can raise labour costs and adversely affect hiring decisions. It may also provide strong incentives for employers to use forms of employment (e.g. short-term contracts) that do not involve high firing costs.

Labour security legislation does not only affect the actions of employers, it also influences the bargaining power and, hence, strategy of the insiders. With the legislation in place, workers' fear of job loss will be greatly diminished and they will push for higher real wages. This will then have an impact on labour demand. Labour security legislation therefore could cause labour demand to be inflexible both directly (i.e. through employers' immediate decisions) and indirectly (i.e. through its promotion of higher real wages). In fact, employment protection laws are thought by many to be a key factor in generating labour market inflexibility.

It appears that a certain level of employment protection is justified to protect workers from arbitrary or discriminatory dismissals. However, the OECD believes that dismissals that are required on economic grounds must be allowed and that the provision of more explicit, long-term commitments to job security should not be imposed on all firms but decided on a firm-by-firm basis. Whether and to what extent reform is required clearly depends on the country-specific circumstances.

A related issue is that the emphasis is now increasingly on employment security rather than job security, that is on guaranteed employment as opposed to employment in a specific job. The best way to ensure this is to increase adaptability and employability, as discussed earlier. After all, labour reallocation is an important driver of productivity growth, in that less productive firms tend to destroy jobs and more productive ones create jobs; and empirical evidence shows that the process of firm birth and death, as well as the reallocation of resources from declining to expanding firms, contribute significantly to productivity and output growth.

Attempts have been made to construct various summary indicators to describe the 'strictness' of employment protection in each country, including Ireland. Given the complexity of constructing such indicators, they are inevitably somewhat arbitrary, but nonetheless are indicative. An OECD study ranking countries according to 'strictness' of protection in the areas of individual dismissals of regular workers, fixed-term contracts and employment through temporary employment agencies showed in 2013 that employment protection was ranked relatively low as a problem in Ireland (see Table 6.18). This, as can be seen, applied in particular to temporary employment and less so to regular employment.

However, compared to the USA, Ireland, and indeed most of Europe, have much more strict employment protection, with scores of 0.26 for the USA in relation to regular employment in 2013 (0.25 for temporary employment), against figures of 1.81 and 2.38 in Belgium, 2.82 and 0.94 in the Netherlands, and 2.20 and 1.38 in Denmark. Indeed the important figure relates to regular employment, where the figure of 1.4 for Ireland is much higher than in the USA and most important perhaps the UK (1.03). Over time it can be seen that the level of employment protection in Ireland has remained the same for regular employment but increased significantly for temporary employment, up from 0.25 in 2000 to 0.63 in 2013.

Table 6.18 Employment Protection in Selected OECD Countries (strictness indicators, 0–6)

	Regular employment		Temporary employment	
	2000	2013	2000	2013
Belgium	1.76	1.81	2.38	2.38
Denmark	2.13	2.20	1.38	1.38
Greece	2.80	2.12	4.75	2.25
Ireland	*1.44*	*1.40*	*0.25*	*0.63*
Netherlands	2.88	2.82	0.94	0.94
Norway	2.33	2.33	3.00	3.00
OECD	–	2.04	–	1.72
UK	1.20	1.03	0.25	0.38
USA	0.26	0.26	0.25	0.25

Source: *OECD Directorate for Employment Labour and Social Affairs*, Online Database, 2013.

Taxation
Payroll taxes, such as employers' social security contributions, raise the costs of employing labour over and above the wage paid. Income taxes and employees'

social security contributions reduce the return to working. These taxes therefore are important because they directly affect the rate of return from decisions to enter the labour market and thereby affect the supply of labour. They may also influence the choice between working in the black economy and in declared paid employment.

These taxes may have an even greater impact on employment and unemployment through their influence on wage determination and therefore on the demand for labour. Cuts in real wages through the imposition of increased personal income taxes or social security contributions may be resisted by workers and compensated for by higher nominal wages – but at the cost of higher unemployment. Likewise, an increase in employers' social security contributions can also result in unemployment when workers resist offsetting wage cuts. In the light of increased competition, both within the EU single market and globally, though the scope for such resistance by trade unions and workers is significantly reduced, as discussed earlier.

Reductions in average tax rates at low levels of earnings are clearly an important way of increasing the income differential between being in and out of work, for the groups for which this is the most serious problem (see earlier). It appears that particular attention needs to be devoted to social security contributions in this regard; not just to the level of these contributions but also their structure: employers' taxation not only influences the amount of people that are employed but may also influence the type of worker who is hired.

The level at which social benefits are withdrawn, as seen in Chapter 4, is also another important aspect of the problem. A feature of many tax and benefit systems, including that in Ireland, is that they can embody very high marginal tax rates for those on low incomes, especially those with large families, as benefits are reduced and earnings are taxed.

A key objective, then, of *A Strategy for Growth: Medium-Term Economic Strategy 2014–2020* is to ensure that there is a strong benefit to the unemployed from returning to work, with an Advisory Group on Tax and Social Welfare established in 2013. However, in the time since 2008 this may not have been the case for many and it may be asked why it took so long for significant action to be taken on this front. The lack of action may have contributed to the build-up of long-term unemployment and, given the nature of such unemployment, the later that action is taken, the more difficult the task of reducing it becomes (see later).

Unemployment Payments

The rationale for unemployment insurance payments is 'to relieve people who have lost a job through no fault of their own from immediate financial concerns, and thus allow efficient job search. Insurance benefits, therefore, have an economic efficiency as well as a social equity objective.'[14] In relation to unemployment assistance payments, which apply in Ireland after 12 months and effectively for an indefinite period, the social or equity role, in reducing poverty among unemployed people and cushioning the adverse effects of high and rising unemployment, becomes paramount.

As a result of the above, there would be strong political objections to resist any cuts in unemployment benefits or assistance and this clearly 'flavours' any debate on the causal connection between unemployment benefit/assistance and unemployment. However, the possibility of such a causal connection, and its extent, must be addressed, as it has been recently in countries such as France, Germany and Italy, where unemployment persisted at high levels for more than a decade and led to a build-up of large-scale long-term unemployment and a 'hand-out' dependency. A similar problem has arisen in Ireland since 2008.

Few economists question the fact that there *is* a link between the benefit system and unemployment. At the simplest level, unemployment payments may create an option of leisure and low income, which some people might choose in preference to full-time work and a higher income. However, such payments could affect employment in many other ways. First, receipt of such payments may prolong intervals of job search, even for those who want to work. Second, because unemployment payments reduce the cost of becoming unemployed, employed people may take a tougher stance in industrial relations disputes or in collective bargaining over wages (see earlier), thereby exacerbating the high real wage problem. Last, payments may increase employment in high turnover and seasonal industries, by subsidising these industries relative to those that provide long-term contract jobs.

Table 6.19 Unemployment Payments in Selected OECD Countries (unemployment benefit/previous earnings)

	2001	2005	2011
Belgium	0.35	0.37	0.37
Denmark	0.54	0.55	0.32
Greece	0.10	0.08	0.12
Ireland	*0.29*	*0.34*	*0.38*
Netherlands	0.50	0.35	0.33
Norway	0.56	0.55	0.31
UK	0.12	0.11	0.11
USA	0.08	0.09	0.23

Sources: OECD Directorate for Employment Labour and Social Affairs, Online Database, 2013; OECD, Tax Benefits Models, OECD, Paris 2013.

As seen in Table 6.19, unemployment benefits as a percentage of previous earnings increased markedly in Ireland between 2001 and 2011: the figure for Ireland is much higher than for the USA and in particular for the UK. On the other hand it is not much higher than for Denmark, the Netherlands and Norway, low unemployment countries. So again the evidence of the employment effects of unemployment payments is mixed. It is noteworthy though that the ratio for

Ireland has increased so much while for several countries listed the ratio has declined, and markedly so for Denmark, the Netherlands and Norway. Thus Ireland on the basis of this evidence appears to have increasingly generous unemployment payment levels, with the highest listed for 2011.

The adverse effects of unemployment payments may, however, result not so much from the existence and level of these payments, but more from the entitlement conditions, the administration of the system and other institutional background factors. For example, payment of unemployment benefits is conditional upon the claimant being available for, and willing to take, full-time work. If this condition is not effectively implemented, people *not* in the labour force (i.e. not available for or not seeking work) may register as unemployed simply to collect unemployment payments. If this condition is strictly enforced and payments stopped if it is not met, then many of the distortionary effects of unemployment payments could be substantially reduced. A related issue is that the employment agency must not only enforce this condition but must also facilitate effective job search, the final topic to which we now turn.

Active Labour Market Policies[15]

Issues

The OECD was as far back as 1994 unequivocal concerning the changes that needed to be effected in benefit administration. It suggested, for example, much more in-depth verification of eligibility, much better matching of workers to job vacancies and fieldwork investigation of concealed earnings and related fraud. A more fundamental problem they claimed was making unemployment payments, especially to the long-term unemployed, effectively conditional on availability for existing vacancies. In particular, they stressed that the long-term unemployed should be expected to take, and unemployment payments made conditional on taking, even low-status jobs. As the OECD noted, much may depend upon achieving a social, political and analytical consensus on this, rejecting the opposite idea that modern economies should be able to afford to make work optional.

The real concern here is that if people are allowed to drift into long-term unemployment, as happened in Ireland in the 1980s and the early 1990s, and again since 2008, that the problem becomes more difficult to overcome. At an individual level long-term unemployment may lead to significant de-skilling and demotivation. At a macroeconomic level, and partly as a result of this, the long-term unemployed may not be regarded as 'employable' and in a sense may cease to be part of the labour market. Thus in effect they exert no downward pressure on the wage-setting process that might bring about equilibrium in the labour market.

A similar problem has arisen in recent years in relation to groups receiving *non-employment* benefits. As discussed earlier, the numbers on some non-employment benefits have grown. These benefit recipients represent a large share of the potential workforce and if their numbers are not reduced employment rates will remain low for years to come in many OECD countries. The pattern in relation to non-employment benefit recipients suggests, the OECD argues, that there could be a high pay-off to extending activation measures, currently available to the unemployed, to persons receiving these non-employment benefits. Recent experience demonstrates that there is considerable scope to apply activation strategies to persons receiving non-employment benefits, albeit with appropriate modifications for the specific characteristics of each group.

Solutions

What was being suggested above is effectively a much more active approach to labour market policy on behalf of the employment service in each country. The purpose of active labour market policies is threefold: first to mobilise labour supply, second to improve the quality of the labour force, and third to strengthen the search process in the labour market. They are particularly appropriate for those experiencing long-term unemployment (and many of those on long-term disability benefit), because, as mentioned, many of them are effectively not participating in the labour force. Because of the de-skilling and demotivation that has taken place, they need assistance with education and training; and because of demotivation and the indefinite nature of unemployment and related payments, the search for jobs may not be as active as might be desired.

Active labour market policies can be classified into four categories: first, there are state employment services (e.g. placement and counselling); second, there is labour market training (i.e. for unemployed and employed adults); third, there are youth measures (e.g. remedial education, training or work experience for disadvantaged young people); and last, subsidised employment (i.e. subsidies to increase employment in the private sector, support for unemployed persons starting their own enterprises and direct job creation in either the public or non-profit sector).

In the last decade or so many countries increased both the number and variety of instruments used to activate jobseekers. Job placement efforts have been enhanced; there is a greater emphasis on testing and monitoring work availability; there is earlier intervention in the unemployment spell and participation in programmes is compulsory; and there is more efficient administration of public employment services. There is considerable evidence that these measures have made a significant impact on the numbers in long-term unemployment in several countries, including Ireland in the past. However, such measures are costly, and on-going evaluation of the cost-effectiveness of each programme needs to be undertaken.

The OECD in 2009 carried out a comprehensive evaluation of active labour market policies in Ireland.[16] The report was very critical of certain aspects of the unemployment service and also commented on the tendency for the implementation of administrative reforms to be slow. While dealing with the banking and fiscal deficit problems understandably took precedence in economic policy between 2008 and 2012, it is noteworthy that no serious action was taken until 2013 to deal with the long-term unemployment problem, a policy failure that may dog the country for some years to come.

Helping the Unemployed Back to Work is a key policy objective of the recent *Strategy for Growth: Medium-Term Economic Strategy 2014–2020*. There is certainly a clear recognition of the scale of the long-term unemployment problem, but is the action too little, too late? The *Pathways to Work* initiative, the report claims, is 'transforming the Department (of Social Protection) from a passive benefits provider to a public employment service that is actively assisting job seekers to return to work' (p. 50). A new Intreo one-stop shop for job seekers, combining employment and income support services, will, it is claimed, be in place by end 2014. Complementary to the work of Intreo, the report states that the Department of Social Protection will outsource by end 2014 a new labour market activation service called Job Path to provide monthly engagement with the long-term unemployed. The other flagship project in this regard is the Youth Guarantee, aimed to be introduced over 2014 and 2015, ensuring that young people under the age of 25 'who are unemployed or who are leaving education will receive an offer of employment, continued education, an apprenticeship or a traineeship' (p. 50).

These are all worthy objectives, but one wonders why these measures were not put in place in the 1990s following the huge rise in long-term unemployment then, and why they are only being introduced when the long-term unemployment problem has already been with us for a few years and hence will prove extremely difficult to reverse, no matter what new measures are taken.

8 CONCLUSION

The outstanding economic policy failure in the last 40 years in Ireland was the inability to increase employment in the 1980s, despite the huge increase in the potential labour force in this period. The result of this failure was a dramatic increase in the unemployment rate and the emigration of almost 200,000 people. More seriously, perhaps, the sustained failure to increase employment meant not only that the high level of unemployment persisted into the mid 1990s, but also that an increasing proportion of that total drifted into long-term unemployment and therefore, in many cases, effectively left the labour market.

The outstanding policy success of the last 40 years, on the other hand, indeed of the whole post-independence era, was the increase in employment between 1993 and 2004, and the corresponding huge reductions in unemployment and the dramatic switch from large-scale emigration to significant immigration. In a very short period the disastrous failures of the 1980s had been turned around into one of the most remarkable success stories in terms of employment growth in the Western world.

A variety of explanations for this have been looked at in this chapter, with further insights to follow in Chapter 7. There are no simple explanations, though. The policy of attracting foreign investment, much of it in the high-tech sectors, allowed Ireland to cope with the trade and technological effects of globalisation (see Chapter 9). The positive policy stance to trade in general, and the EU and the euro zone in particular, may have helped in this regard (see Chapters 1, 7 and 9). The advent of the 'borderless' economy meant that Ireland's peripheral location mattered much less than before (see Chapter 9). The increased emphasis on competition in the non-traded sector of the economy added to Ireland's competitiveness (Chapters 5 and 9), while the centralised wage bargaining process appears to have delivered on competitive wage setting and a good industrial relations climate (Chapter 3).

Past policies on education also appear to have been a factor (see Chapters 7 and 13) and the relatively flexible employment protection environment that was in place would have assisted in the huge employment increase that the above facilitated. Ireland also appears to have had a relatively 'entrepreneur-friendly' climate, as measured by relative cost, length of time and minimum charter capital required to form a private limited liability company (see Chapter 7). Finally, changes in taxation and the increased emphasis on active labour market policies made inroads into the most intractable unemployment problem that Ireland faced in the mid 1990s, namely long-term unemployment.

The employment growth between 2004 and 2008 appears now to have been illusory, based as it was on unsustainable increases in building activity. Between 2008 and end 2010 all of the employment increases of this period had been reversed. The credit-based building boom could not be maintained and a large drop in employment in construction and related activities was inevitable; it was the speed and scale of the decline that surprised commentators most. Besides, since the early 2000s, Ireland steadily lost competitiveness, especially in terms of wage costs. By 2008 this loss of competitiveness had become acute, especially in the context of Ireland being a member of the euro zone. Problems on this front, which had been disguised during the credit-fuelled boom between 2004 and 2008, came home to roost in 2009.

The boom in employment in the 1993 to 2004 period of course followed decades of failure to provide jobs for Irish people, the result being large-scale emigration in the 1950s and again in the 1980s. This resulted also in extraordinarily high unemployment levels in the decade 1985 to 1995. Potential labour supply had been increasing rapidly in Ireland from 1980 and a large employment increase was required to absorb this growth in supply; without it there was initially, and would continued to have been, large-scale emigration and high levels of unemployment.

The country, in other words, for the first time in its history provided employment to those who needed it. This has for decades been the norm in other small European countries such as Denmark, the Netherlands and Norway. Indeed, the unemployment rate in Ireland was in 2007, and is still, higher than in these three countries and the proportion of those of working age in employment in Ireland lags well behind that for these countries. Much progress has been made, but more has to be achieved and the failures of the past on the employment front must not be repeated.

That is the challenge that lies ahead. The employment gains of the decade up to 2004 have not been reversed, but the gains between 2004 and 2008 have been almost totally wiped out. As unemployment, and particularly LTU, spiralled between 2008 and 2012, net emigration resumed and fears of a repeat of the decade of the 1980s re-emerged. The spectre of emigration still haunts the Irish psyche, and has done so ever since Famine times. The costs of emigration now of course do not compare with then, or even the 1950s and 1980s, yet the question remains: why can an independent state like Ireland not provide employment for its own nationals? It is true that emigration of Irish nationals continued during the period 1993 to 2004 and many emigrants returned with enhanced experience and skills. The scale of the out-migration of Irish nationals has increased substantially, though, since 2008 and the worry is that many of these people will not return unless there is a very significant upturn in employment.

That upturn, as seen earlier, began in 2013 and is projected to continue into 2014 and beyond. As such, this chapter can conclude on a much more positive note than was the case in 2011. The challenges ahead, though, are enormous if long-term unemployment is to be reduced to acceptable levels and the proportion of the active population age group in employment brought up to levels applying in many EU countries.

Notes

1   'Research contradicts brain drain narrative of emigration', *Irish Times*, 18 December 2013.

2   The OECD does outstanding research work in relation to data on employment and related matters, and employment policies, both in general and by member country, and this chapter draws extensively on such work. Its key publication is the annual *Employment Outlook*, which includes general chapters, detailed research reports and detailed statistical tables.

3   For a discussion of this phenomenon, see 'Unemployment in Europe equals US', *Financial Times*, 17 February 2014.

4   OECD, 'Taking the Measure of Temporary Employment', *Employment Outlook*, OECD, Paris 2002.

5   OECD, *Employment Outlook*, OECD, Paris 2009.

6   See the Public Policy.ie website for a good discussion of this topic and indeed other aspects of labour market policy in Ireland, especially at http://www.publicpolicy. ie/?s=Unemployment.

7   See OECD, 'Institutional and policy determinants of labour market flows', *Employment Outlook*, Paris 2010, for a good discussion of this issue.

8   For a review of the implications for employment of recent dramatic technological change, see 'The future of jobs: the onrushing wave', *The Economist*, 18 January 2014.

9   Extensive work on various aspects of immigration in Ireland is undertaken by the ESRI. See, for example, its publications at: http://www.esri.ie/publications/search_ for_a_publication/search_results/index.xml? TopicSearch=9

10 For detailed empirical evidence, see OECD, 'Right for the job: over-qualified or under-skilled?', *Employment Outlook*, OECD, Paris 2011.

11 See Department of Finance, *A Strategy for Growth: Medium-Term Economic Strategy 2014–2020*, Department of Finance, Dublin 2013.

12 OECD, *Employment Outlook*, OECD, Paris 2006, p.88. This report contains a good review of wage-setting institutions and policies in OECD member states.

13 See 'Free exchange: the minimum wage and the state of microeconomics', *The Economist*, 18 January 2014, for a good discussion of and references on this issue.

14 OECD, *Jobs Study: Part II*, OECD, Paris 1994, p.171.

15 A comprehensive review of these policies is contained in OECD, 'Activating the unemployed: what countries do', *Employment Outlook*, OECD, Paris 2007.

16 OECD, *Activation Policies in Ireland*, OECD Social, Employment and Migration Working Papers No. 75, OECD, Paris 2009.

CHAPTER 7

Growth in Living Standards and Output

Jonathan Haughton

1 THE CELTIC TIGER

Two decades ago, Ireland was one of the poorer countries of Western Europe, a small peripheral island with a mediocre record of economic growth. Employment, at 1.2 million, had hardly risen in 50 years.

Then, quite unexpectedly, the Irish economy took off, and the Celtic Tiger was born. In the subsequent decade and a half, real gross domestic product (GDP) rose two and a half-fold, employment grew to 2.1 million, and Ireland's economic and social indicators caught up with, and in some cases surpassed, those of its Western European peers. By the standards of its neighbours, this growth was remarkable, although somewhat less so when considered in a broader global context.

The second half of the boom was largely built on sand, and could not be sustained. GDP per capita has fallen every year since its peak in 2007, and is only now (in 2014) set to rise again.

The central question we address in this chapter is this: what explains the rise of the modern Irish economy, and its subsequent stumble? And what, if anything, does this imply for the ability of the country to maintain, and even expand, its current level of affluence?

We begin by looking at the numbers: how rich is Ireland, and how have the measures of well-being evolved over time? We then try to explain these changes, first in a mechanical way, and then by asking about deeper causes. To anticipate the argument: Ireland's economic growth in the late 1990s and 2000s was real and impressive and the country is indeed very rich, if not quite as affluent as the GDP per capita numbers imply. Taking a long view, most of Ireland's recent growth may be thought of as an overdue catch-up. The retrogression since 2008 began as a domestic correction related to the housing bubble, and was exacerbated by the worst global recession since the 1930s: 2009 was the first year in half a century when world real GDP actually declined.

The recession, and foreign pressure, shook Ireland out of a creeping complacency – fiscal discipline had weakened, the minimum wage was (and still is) one of the highest in the world, rising prices and wages led to an erosion in competitiveness, so foreign direct investment went elsewhere and exports flagged, and the banking system became insolvent. Having made important structural changes, Ireland is now poised to grow again, at least as quickly as other EU countries, given its fundamental strengths, including a young, well-educated and relatively hard-working labour force. But the challenge of managing a small, open, affluent economy that is inevitably vulnerable to outside shocks is increasingly daunting.

2 HOW AFFLUENT IS IRELAND?

Output and Income

By most economic and social measures, Ireland has caught up with its peers in Western Europe, although not with the USA. This is shown clearly in Figure 7.1, which compares the evolution of Irish per capita output since 1980 with those of the USA, Denmark, and the UK. Denmark is included here because it is, like Ireland, a small open economy, and has often been held up as a role model for Ireland to emulate.

Figure 7.1 Irish GDP and GNP Per Capita in Context, 1980–2012

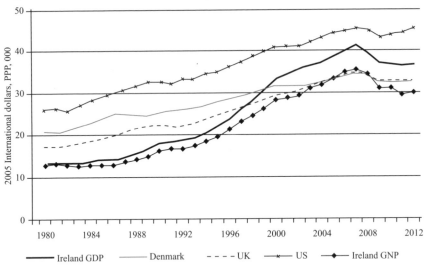

Source: World Bank, *World Development Indicators* (http://data.worldbank.org/data-catalog/world-development-indicators), accessed April 2014.

Two measures of Irish affluence are shown in Figure 7.1. The first is GDP per capita, which measures the money value of goods and services produced and marketed in the economy in a year; it represents the value added by economic activity within the geographic borders of a country, and is the most commonly used indicator of economic activity. There was a clear acceleration in the growth of Irish GDP per capita starting in about 1994, with slower but still robust increases after 2000, and a sharp downturn after 2007.

In order to compare output across countries, the measures of GDP per capita in Figure 7.1 are shown in 'international dollars' in the prices of 2005. A serious problem in cross-country comparisons of this sort is that prices differ substantially from one country to the next: a euro in Ireland barely buys a cup of coffee, but converted into rupees and spent in India, it would buy a whole meal. So if the exchange rate were used to convert India's GDP into euros, it would understate the true purchasing power of India's GDP. The standard solution is to recompute every country's GDP using a common set of 'international' prices, giving a measure of purchasing power parity (PPP) GDP that is reasonably comparable across countries. By this measure, GDP per capita in Ireland in 2007 approached the US level, and it remains well above the levels of the UK or Denmark.

However, in the Irish case, GDP is not a particularly good indicator of affluence. Not all of the goods and services produced in Ireland accrue to Irish citizens or residents; for instance, profit that is repatriated does not contribute to local incomes. A more satisfactory measure of the output that stays in Ireland is gross national product (GNP), which is conceptually the same thing as gross national income (GNI): it starts with GDP and adds net factor income from the rest of the world (NFIROW). In 2013 these amounts, in billions of euros, were as follows:

$$GNP = GDP + NFIROW$$
$$137.5 = 162.3 + -24.8$$

The most striking feature of these numbers is the uncommonly large value of net transfer payments out of Ireland, mainly the repatriation of profits by foreign firms operating in Ireland. Much of this is attributable to the pharmaceutical industry, which accounted for a remarkable 48 per cent of exports and 12 per cent of GDP in 2012, but just 2 per cent of employment. The expiration of patents, and hence the lower export price for drugs, is believed to have contributed to almost all of the 5 per cent drop in Irish exports seen in 2013. This also helps us understand the contradictory growth signals in 2013: GDP fell by 0.3 per cent, signifying recession, while GNP rose by 3.4 per cent, reflecting robust growth, and consistent with the expansion of employment in 2013.

An unknown part of factor income flows may be attributable to profit outflows that reflect transfer pricing, as some corporations overstate their exports and understate their imports in order to book their profits in low-tax Ireland (see Chapters 4 and 9) – the corporation income tax is just 12.5 per cent, compared to 35 per cent in the USA. As a result of this measurement error, reported GDP may overstate 'true' GDP by as much as 10 per cent.

This makes a difference: using GNP rather than GDP per capita, Ireland just caught up with the UK and Danish levels a decade ago, and has since slipped back, as Figure 7.1 shows clearly.

Other Measures of Well-Being

It is sometimes argued that the focus on per capita incomes is an unhealthy obsession, a reflection perhaps of the crass materialism of economists (see also Chapter 2). In an oft-quoted speech, Robert Kennedy in 1968 said, 'we will find neither national purpose nor personal satisfaction in an endless amassing of worldly goods ... the gross national product measures neither our wit nor our courage, neither our wisdom nor our learning, neither our compassion nor our devotion to country. It measures everything, in short, except that which makes life worthwhile.'

Quality of Life Indicators

We might respond to Kennedy's critique by looking at other measures that presumably contribute to making life worthwhile. A selection of such variables is shown in Table 7.1 for Ireland and, to provide more context, the EU and USA.

Ireland's life expectancy continues to rise, and surpasses the EU average for both men and women. The infant mortality rate – defined as the number of deaths of infants up to six months old per 1,000 population – is very low by historical standards, and is now well below the EU average. These measures, considered to be good indicators of health outcomes in general, show that Ireland has now caught up with the standards that prevail in Western Europe (see also Chapter 12).

GNP represents an annual flow of final goods and services; even when GNP rises, it can take time to build up a good stock of assets – cars, houses and fine roads. This helps explain why Irish visitors to France, for instance, are often struck by the high quality of the infrastructure, in a country whose consumption per capita is now appreciably lower than that of Ireland. However, Table 7.1 shows evidence of catch-up: car ownership per capita almost doubled between 1990 and 2011, a measure that goes a long way towards explaining the increasingly high levels of congestion on Irish roads.

House building rose above the long-term sustainable level after 2001; where Ireland had 330 houses per thousand people in 1990, this figure had risen to 440 by 2007, despite a 22 per cent increase in the population over the same period, bringing Ireland close to the EU average of 450 houses per thousand people. According to the OECD's 'better life' project, housing is now better in Ireland than anywhere else in Europe, and ranks behind only the USA and Canada in international comparisons.

Ireland is also connecting fast. Almost four out of five households are connected to the internet, similar to the proportion found in the USA; and there are more mobile phones than people! Five times as many people flew into Ireland in 2011 as in 1990.

By US, but not European, standards, Ireland has a low level of reported crime. The incarceration rate is in line with European norms.

Tourism operators boast of Ireland's wild and open beauty (the woodlands were cleared by the sixteenth century!) and its clean air and water. While water is relatively clean, and the levels of particulates in Irish urban areas are lower than in any other EU country, emissions of CO_2, the main 'greenhouse gas', exceed the EU-15 average. Besides, Irish firms and households generate 660kg of municipal waste per person per year, the highest level in the EU, and close to the 720kg level of the USA (see Chapter 10).

Table 7.1 Indicators of the Quality of Life

	Ireland			EU	USA	EU-27 best
	1970	1990	2012	2012	2012	2011
Health						
Infant mortality rate	20	8	3.8	4.5	5.2	2.6
Life expectancy, F	74	77	83.2	83.1	82.2	85.5
Life expectancy, M	69	72	78.7	77.5	77.4	79.9
Crime						
Prisoners/100,000	–	–	94	135	716	60
Homicides/millions	–	6	12	16	48	6
Environment						
CO_2/capita, t	6	9	7.8	8.7	17.6	3.8
Municip. waste, kg/cap	–	–	660	540	720	310
Particulate matter (10)	–	–	12.6	28.1	–	12.6
Connectivity						
% hh, internet	–		79	75	81	94
Airline pass, m	1.5	4.8	24	832	646	–
Mobile phones/100	0	0.7	107	126	98	173
Human resources						
Third-level education	–	–	52	37	36	52
Total fertility rate	–	–	2.0	1.6	2.0	1.3
Assets						
Houses/1,000	280	330	420	450	428	–
Cars/1,000	–	227	434	446	423	665

Sources: World Bank, *World Development Indicators* (www.worldbank.org); Eurostat.

Human Development Index

There is another interesting way to evaluate Irish levels of affluence. The United Nations Development Programme (UNDP) annually constructs its Human Development Index (HDI), which combines measures of life expectancy, educational achievement (mean years of schooling of adults aged 25 and over; and expected years of schooling for those of school-going age), and the log of GDP per capita (in PPP terms) into a single index. The most recent figures refer to 2012, and rank Ireland seventh in the world with a score of 0.916 (out of a maximum possible 1.000). Ireland's HDI has risen rapidly since 1980, as Table 7.2 shows.

Table 7.2 Human Development Index for Ireland

1980	1985	1990	1995	2000	2005	2010	2012
0.720	0.739	0.768	0.799	0.855	0.886	0.895	0.916

Source: United Nations Development Programme (UNDP), *Human Development Index (HDI)*, http://hdr.undp.org/en/statistics/hdi, accessed March 2014.

An unsurprising consequence of the increase in real incomes and consumption has been a drop in absolute poverty, particularly since the late 1980s. Using a poverty line set at 60 per cent of average income in 1987, the proportion of the population in poverty was then 16 per cent, falling to 15 per cent by 1994, 8 per cent by 1998 and 5 per cent by 2001 (see Chapter 8). The stagnation in wages, and rise in the unemployment rate, since 2007 have contributed to a recent rise in poverty: six-sevenths of the poor do not have employment. Social welfare payments have helped keep as much as a third of the population from falling into poverty (as measured by the EU norms).

Employment and Population

An economy's success could also be measured by its ability to provide employment for those who want it, and to sustain a larger population. Between 1960 and 1986 the rise in employment was negligible, from 1.05 to 1.09 million. Then came a remarkable, and historically unprecedented, burst of job creation, pushing employment up to 2.12 million by 2007, as shown in Figure 7.2 (see also Chapter 6), before dropping sharply to 1.85 million as of the end of 2010, since when it has risen to 1.91 million as of December 2013.

Migration flows have mirrored the changes in employment, albeit with a lag of a few years. There was immigration in the 1970s, when Irish economic growth was higher than elsewhere in Europe. Emigration resumed in the early 1980s, peaking at 44,000 (1.3 per cent of the population) in 1989. In due course the pendulum swung back, and about 150,000 people migrated into Ireland in the course of the 1990s, with a further 375,000 net arrivals between 2000 and 2008, although by 2009 there was net emigration once again (see also Chapter 6).

The 2011 census showed that Ireland was one of the most cosmopolitan countries in Europe, as 17 per cent of the population was born outside the Republic. This is substantially higher than in most other high-income countries, including the USA (12 per cent), and the EU (9 per cent), but lower than the proportions in Australia (24 per cent) or Canada (21 per cent).

The importance of the inflow of migrants can hardly be understated. Between 1997 and 2006 the total population rose by 609,000; during this same period a total of 575,000 people moved to Ireland. There were similar waves of immigration into France and Germany when they grew rapidly in the 1960s. Four-fifths of the annual growth of the population of the EU is now attributable to in-migration.

Figure 7.2 Labour Force and Employment, 1960–2013

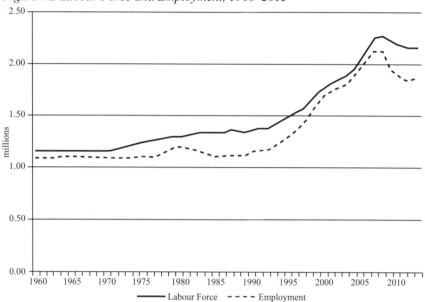

Source: World Bank, *World Development Indicators*, http://data.worldbank.org/data-catalog/world-development-indicators, accessed April 2011; Central Statistics Office (CSO), www.cso.ie, accessed March 2014.

The unemployment rate, 5 per cent in 1960 and 7 per cent in 1980, surged to 17 per cent by 1986, remaining in double digits for a decade before falling very rapidly in the late 1990s to a low of 3.7 per cent in 2001, after which it edged up again slightly, reaching 6.0 per cent in 2008 and jumping to 14.7 per cent in 2012 before declining to 12 per cent by early 2014. The high unemployment rate of the 1980s was a consequence of slow economic growth, coming at a time of diminished employment opportunities abroad (particularly in the UK), a rapid increase in the working-age population, and a system of taxes and subsidies that made working unremunerative for many low-skilled workers. The surge in unemployment after 2007 was a direct consequence of the end of the boom and onset of recession.

Measures of Happiness
It is clear that most measures of living standards are correlated strongly, if not perfectly, with GNP per capita. That is one of the reasons why economists and others tend to use GNP per capita as their primary measure of welfare. But perhaps the only way to respond to Robert Kennedy's challenge is to ask people how satisfied they are with their lives, and then to determine whether these subjective evaluations are linked to GNP per capita (see also Chapter 2). The recent *World Happiness Report* summarises the results of a number of surveys of happiness, from Gallup World Polls and from the World Values Surveys.

In almost all cases Ireland is ranked among the top ten countries, generally behind Denmark but ahead of most other members of the EU. Commenting on an earlier international comparison of subjective wellbeing, Alber and Fahey write, 'the comparisons of countries across Europe ... [show that] the level of GDP per capita in the country in which the individual lives turns out to be the best predictor of individual life-satisfaction.'[1]

In short, Robert Kennedy overstates the case: GNP may not measure personal satisfaction, but it is closely correlated with it, in which case it is indeed a useful guide to happiness!

We are left with the conclusion that Ireland is indeed a comparatively rich and happy country. The interesting question, to which we now turn, is: how did it get there?

3 IRISH GROWTH EXPERIENCE

We have established that Ireland has closed the gap with Western Europe by almost all measures of affluence, and that most of the catch-up occurred since the mid 1990s. We now need to ask what explains this recent success, and why, by 2008, the episode of rapid growth had come to an end.

Decomposing Growth in GNP per Person
As we have seen, economic growth performance is typically measured by looking at changes in GNP (or GDP) per capita. Mechanically, this may be decomposed into increases in *labour productivity* (i.e. output per hour or per worker), and changes in the participation rate. This decomposition is set out in more detail in Table 7.3, which breaks down annual real GNP per capita *growth* into its component parts, and also shows the annual (log) percentage growth rate of each component for three distinct periods – the growth spurt between 1994 and 2000, when per capita GNP rose by 8.1 per cent per year, the housing expansion years (2000–2007), and the recession years (2007–2013) during which GNP per capita fell by an average of two per cent annually.

The first thing to note in Table 7.3 is that output per hour worked has continued to rise, even through the recent recession. This is the single largest source of economic growth in every period, and the only source of rising incomes that can be sustained indefinitely; we examine the sources of productivity growth in more detail below. The rise in labour productivity even during the recession might seem surprising, but there are a number of plausible explanations: the least-productive workers may have lost their jobs; the least-productive firms may have been the first to fail; job losses may have been concentrated in a low-productivity sector (housing); workers may have put in more effort, lest they lose their jobs; and technical change may have continued to raise output per worker.

Table 7.3 Decomposition of GNP Per Capita Growth

	$\dfrac{\text{GNP}}{\text{population}} \equiv$	$\dfrac{\text{GNP}}{\text{hour}} \times$	$\dfrac{\text{hour}}{\text{worker}} \times$	$\dfrac{\text{worker}}{\text{labour force}} \times$	$\dfrac{\text{labour force}}{\text{adults 15–64}} \times$	$\dfrac{\text{adults 15–64}}{\text{population}}$
1994–2000	8.1	3.3	0.2	2.0	1.6	1.0
	100%	40%	2%	24%	20%	13%
2000–2007	2.0	0.5	0.2	−0.1	1.3	0.1
	100%	23%	10%	−3%	63%	3%
2007–2013	−2.0	1.7	−0.8	−1.5	−0.9	−0.5
	100%	−86%	41%	75%	47%	25%

Source: World Bank, *World Development Indicators* (www.worldbank.org); Eurostat.
Note: totals may not add up due to rounding and approximation errors.

Among the noteworthy features of the 1994 to 2000 period are the sustained increases in the proportion of the labour force that was working (meaning that the unemployment rate was falling), the substantial rise in the share of adults in the labour force (mainly due to greater female participation), and the rise in the share of adults in the total population (due in part to substantial immigration of adults, not children) (see also Chapter 6).

These factors, which were unusually favourable in the late 1990s, are sometimes referred to as the 'demographic dividend', although in earlier years the need to create jobs was seen as a demographic drag! Together they accounted for over half of the rise in GNP per capita during Ireland's growth spurt, and during the much slower growth seen during the 2000 to 2007 period. The important point is that these factors will contribute far less to growth in the years ahead, as the population ages, and labour force participation reaches a plateau.

Components of Economic Growth
Over the long run, incomes mainly rise because labour productivity goes up. Mechanically, we may write:

(1) $$Q = (Q/E) \times E$$

where Q refers to output (i.e. GNP) and E to employment. Expressed in growth terms we have

(2) $$g_Q = g_{Q/E} + g_E$$

This says that the growth of GNP comes from growth in labour productivity plus growth in employment. Table 7.4 (the key table for later discussion) shows the record of growth of these components, going back to 1960, separating out the key periods, including the 1960s (output growth without employment growth), the period between the two main oil shocks, the stagnation of the early 1980s that was accompanied by very high unemployment rates, the subsequent slow recovery (1986–94), the primary boom when both employment and living standards grew quickly (1994–2000), the secondary boom when employment still rose and population expanded fast but consumption per capita grew more modestly (2000–2007), and the recent recession. The episodes of rapid expansion were associated with substantial growth in the stock of productive capital, rising employment, and faster growth of GDP than GNP.

Table 7.4 Measures of Recent Performance

	1960–73	1973–79	1979–86	1986–94	1994–2000	2000–7	2007–13
				(annual growth rates, %)			
Output							
Real GDP	4.4	4.2	1.8	4.2	10.2	5.0	−1.3
Real GNP	4.2	4.2	1.1	3.8	9.1	4.2	−1.2
First decomposition							
Real GNP/worker	4.2	2.8	1.8	2.4	3.4	0.7	0.9
Employment	0.0	1.3	−0.7	1.4	5.5	3.4	−2.1
Second decomposition							
Real GNP/capital stock	–	–	–	1.8	3.9	−1.8	−3.7[1]
Capital stock	–	–	–	2.0	5.1	6.0	1.7[1]
Memo items							
Real consumption/capita	3.2	2.7	−0.1	2.7	6.7	3.1	−2.2
Capital: equipment, etc.	–	–	–	1.6	7.3	5.7	0.3
Investment/GDP	–	25.0	23.0	17.1	21.3	20.2	14.3
Housing investment/GDP	–	–	–	–	5.5	7.5	4.3[1]
Output per capita							
Real GDP/capita	3.7	3.3	1.5	4.0	9.2	2.9	−2.1
Real GNP/capita	3.5	2.6	0.4	3.7	8.1	2.0	−2.0
				(levels in end year)			
Employment (millions)	1.06	1.15	1.09	1.20	1.69	2.12	1.88
Population (millions)	3.07	3.37	3.54	3.57	3.81	4.39	4.59
Unemployment rate	5.9	7.1	17.2	14.8	4.3	4.6	13.0

Sources: World Bank, *World Development Indicators* (www.worldbank.org); Eurostat.
Note: some totals do not match due to rounding errors.
[1] 2007–12.

Interestingly, output per worker grew rapidly in the 1960s, and again between 1994 and 2000. Certainly we need to explain this, but clearly something else was happening during the growth spurt: how was Ireland able to increase employment during the 1994 to 2007 period when it hardly managed to do so before or since? This will be returned to in Section 5.

International Comparisons

Table 7.5 shows the increase in GDP over a long period (1989–2013) for a selection of countries. During the span of this generation, GDP growth in Ireland was easily the highest in Western Europe, which is certainly impressive. It was also faster than world GDP growth, which totalled 143 per cent over this period. However, it was exceeded by 34 of the 119 countries included in the study. These included Chile and Singapore, which are also small, open, relatively affluent economies. While comparisons such as these are sensitive to the choice of starting and ending dates, the point remains that recent Irish economic growth is only exceptional when compared to other countries in its neighbourhood.

Table 7.5 Productivity Growth: an International Perspective

	GDP growth (%) 1989–2013	GDP/E growth (%) 1989–2013	Contribution of productivity growth (%)
Ireland	*180*	*115*	*64*
Denmark	40	34	87
Germany	43	47	111
Estonia[1]	104	133	128
USA	78	49	63
Japan	30	49	164
Chile	208	125	57
Singapore	306	95	31
World	143	73	51

Source: Conference Board, *Total Economy Database*, January 2014 (http://www.conference-board.org/data/economydatabase/), accessed April 2014.
[1] 1992–2013

Almost two-thirds of economic growth in Ireland, the USA and Chile came from improvements in labour productivity, the rest being due to rises in employment. In Germany, Estonia and Japan, employment actually shrank during this time – mainly due to population decline – and in these cases labour productivity growth outstripped the rise in GDP. We now turn to a systematic exploration of the factors that drive labour productivity.

4 EXPLAINING GROWTH IN OUTPUT PER WORKER

Two things now need to be explained: what drives economic growth over the long term; and why this growth occurs in fits and starts such as the boom of the late 1990s and stagnation since 2007.

We argued in the previous section that over a long period of time it is essential to focus on what drives output per worker. In the words of Paul Krugman, 'Productivity isn't everything, but in the long run it is almost everything. A country's ability to improve its standard of living over time depends almost entirely on its ability to raise its output per worker.'[2]

General Production Function

To organise our ideas, it is useful to start with a *production function*, which links inputs to output. A straightforward version looks like this:

$$(3) \qquad Q = A(I) \, F(E, H, K)$$

where the function F(.) is increasing in its arguments. Output will be larger if more people are employed (E), they have more education or other human capital (H), or they work with greater quantities of information and communication technology and are equipped with more capital of other kinds, such as equipment and machinery (K).

The term A(I) is often taken to represent 'technology', but this should be interpreted broadly to include everything that enhances the productivity of inputs, including such things as better managerial techniques, suddenly higher prices for outputs, boom or recession, or regulatory changes that spur competition; the I refers to 'institutions', and reminds us that economic productivity is strongly influenced by the fundamental structure of economic organisations. Economic historian Douglas North won a Nobel Prize largely on the strength of his work emphasising the importance of institutional change – such as the development of private property rights, or patent law – in enhancing economic growth over time.

The A(I) term is referred to as a measure of *total factor productivity*, because it may be written as a ratio of output to an index of inputs (i.e. as Q/F(.)); it cannot be observed directly, so is generally computed as a residual – indeed it has been termed a 'coefficient of ignorance' because it captures the effects of everything we cannot measure!

In Equation 3, if inputs are doubled, it is reasonable to suppose that output would also double; more generally, this allows us to write:

$$(4) \qquad q \equiv Q/E = A(I).F(1, H/E, K/E) = A(I).f(h,k)$$

Used creatively, Equation (4) can be illuminating. It implies that output per employed worker (q) will rise if there is more capital; if workers acquire education, training and experience, and enjoy good health, since this raises h; and if technical advance, innovation and institutional change occur, since these increase A. These are useful, if rather obvious, conclusions, but it is possible to make the analysis much more interesting.

Solow Growth Model

The 'workhorse' for understanding the role played by investment and these other factors of production in economic growth is the model developed by MIT professor and Nobel laureate Robert Solow. Here we develop the model graphically and apply it to the Irish case.

The production function in Equation 4 may be graphed as the curve 0–q in Figure 7.3. It curves because of the 'law' of diminishing marginal returns: as the amount of capital per worker (k) rises, output per employed worker (q) also rises, but less and less quickly.

Figure 7.3 Solow Growth Model

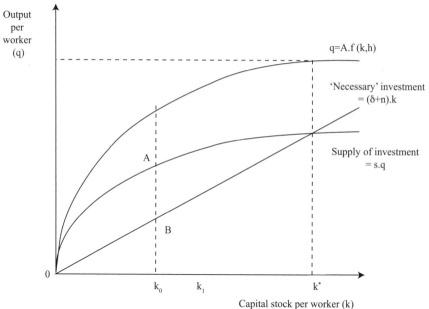

Now assume that a constant fraction, s, of output is invested. This gives the investment supply curve 0–s.q, which has the same shape as the production function but is only s per cent as high.

To complete the story we may add a line that reflects the investment that would be necessary to prevent k (and therefore q) from falling. Simply to maintain the capital stock per employed worker, we need to:

- invest enough to replace the wear and tear ('depreciation') of the capital stock; represented by δ: this is of the order of 3–5 per cent per annum in most economies;

189

- invest enough to equip new workers, otherwise their arrival would dilute the capital stock and capital per worker (k) would fall. An n per cent rise in the labour force thus requires n per cent more capital for this purpose.

Taken together, 'necessary' investment per employed worker thus represents $(n+\delta).k$, and is shown by the straight line in Figure 7.3.

A poor country will have a low stock of capital per worker, such as k_0. At this point, the supply of investment (s.q) exceeds necessary investment $((n+\delta).k)$, leaving an investment surplus that will serve to deepen the stock of capital. Thus by the next year, the stock of capital will rise to k_1, and so on.

There is an important implication. Poor countries should be able to grow faster than rich ones, because their investment 'surpluses' are larger relative to Q/E.

Note that the process stops at k^*. In other words, investment alone can raise k to k^*, and therefore output per worker to q^*, but then growth stops – unless, of course, other influences can be brought to bear.

This has an immediate and interesting implication: economies should experience (conditional) convergence. For a given savings rate (s), technology $(A.f(.))$, employment growth rate (n) and depreciation rate (δ), all countries should converge on the same k^* and hence the same level of output per worker.

Has Ireland Converged?
It is natural to ask whether recent Irish economic growth follows the predictions of the Solow model, in effect causing the Irish economy to converge to those of the rest of the EU.

Figure 7.4 Initial Income and Subsequent Growth: 1960–2012

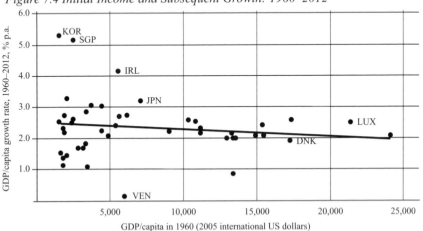

Sources: World Bank, *World Development Indicators* (www.worldbank.org); Eurostat.
Note: countries include all those at or above the GDP per capita level of South Korea in 1960.

This question may be addressed with the help of Figure 7.4, which shows GDP per worker in 1960 (in 2005 international PPP US dollars) on the horizontal axis and the annual percentage growth rate of GDP per worker from 1960 to 2012 on the vertical axis, for all countries that were at least as well-off as South Korea in 1960. In 1960 Ireland was relatively poor, grouped with Greece, Spain, Japan and Mexico.

The Solow model predicts that poorer countries should grow faster than richer ones, until they have caught up: thus South Korea (initially poor) should grow faster than Denmark (initially rich). It follows that we would expect the observations in Figure 7.4 to fall along a line that slopes downwards to the right, which is indeed what we see, although the effect is not particularly strong (and disappears if the sample includes most developing countries).

The interesting feature of Figure 7.4 is that Ireland is at the upper edge of these observations, suggesting that its economic growth (per worker) was somewhat higher than one would have expected. Thus the Solow model alone is not sufficient to explain the Irish growth experience. However, it can be used to help us understand in more detail the factors that have influenced the growth of GNI (or GDP) per employed worker, which is what we discuss next.

Applying the Solow Model

Investment (K/E)

In the Solow model, a higher savings rate, by allowing more investment, would cause an acceleration of economic growth in the short run, and allow growth to continue longer *but not indefinitely*. In other words, even if Ireland were to invest a higher proportion of its GNP, it would not permanently grow faster than other countries.

Between 1994 and 2007 Ireland's investment rate was slightly higher than the EU average of about 20 per cent of GDP. The share of investment going to housing rose from a quarter of investment between 1994 and 2000 to a third between 2000 and 2007. The housing market is highly cyclical: this is clear from Figure 7.5, which graphs the number of new houses completed annually from 1970 to 2013. About 30,000 new households are formed annually, which gives a rough measure of the steady-state demand for housing; but in 2006, completions were three times this level, clearly an unsustainable situation. It has taken some time for the overhang of unoccupied houses to be put into use, but spending on construction did eventually rise sharply, in 2013.

The investment rate fell when the housing boom ended. This need not be fatal: the USA has had an investment rate lower than the Irish rate for over half a century, but this has not prevented the USA from maintaining its position of affluence. The trick is to use the investment productively, and this requires complementary inputs of skilled labour and technology – topics to which we now turn.

Figure 7.5 House Completions, 1970–2013

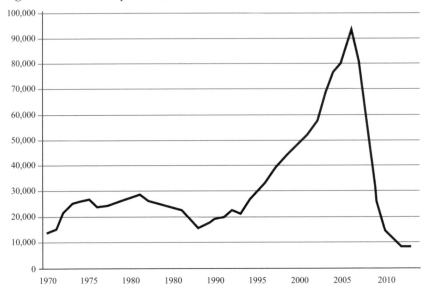

Source: Department of Environment, Community and Local Government, *Housing Statistics*, April 2011.

Human Capital (H/E)

Education, training, experience and good health make workers more productive, and more employable. Thus increases in 'human capital' can boost economic growth. In the Solow model, there are diminishing returns to additional human capital, which means that the effect, at the margin, on economic growth will eventually become negligible. Formally, an increase in human capital per worker (h) will shift the curves 0–q and 0–s.q in Figure 7.3 upwards, pushing the steady state capital–labour ratio (k*) to the right. More recent models of 'endogenous growth' allow human capital to contribute to growth without diminishing returns, but these remain controversial.

Universal secondary education was only introduced in Ireland in 1968, and older workers are not particularly well educated by Western European standards (see Chapter 13). However, the recent expansion of higher education has created a well-educated cohort of young people; 52 per cent of those aged 30–34 had some third-level education in 2012, the highest rate in the EU and well above the EU rate of 37 per cent. In passing it is worth noting that women are substantially more likely than men to go on to tertiary education in Ireland, as in all other countries of the EU, but the gap is wider in Ireland than in most European countries.

On average, the Irish educational system provides a solid if not spectacular base (see Chapter 13). A standardised test administered to 15-year-olds in OECD countries in 2012 found that Irish students scored 523 in reading literacy (compared to an OECD average of 496), 501 in mathematics and 522 in science (compared to OECD averages of 494 and 501). Only Finnish students performed (marginally) better at reading – perhaps Ireland is a literary society – but Irish students were in the middle of the pack when judged by their performance in mathematics and science. The improvement in the quantity of human capital did coincide substantially with the growth spurt of the late 1990s and 2000s, but growth accounting exercises show that improvements in human capital have rarely contributed more than a tenth of overall growth.

Technological and Institutional Change (A(I))
Logically, within the framework of the Solow model, the only potentially persistent source of growth is technological change, including institutional progress. Formally, this raises the total factor productivity (i.e. A) parameter year after year, which shifts upwards the 0–q curve (see Figure 7.3) and hence also the 0–s.q curve. That technological change is the only durable source of economic growth is not surprising; 'modern' economic growth, with its concomitant rise in popular living standards, only began with the Industrial Revolution in the late eighteenth century.[3]

Technology may be created or acquired. A narrow view of technology would focus on the creation and application of technology through spending on research and development (R&D). The numbers in Table 7.6 show that Irish spending on R&D, as a proportion of GDP, is modest enough by EU standards, although it is rising. This level of spending is too low to explain much of Ireland's economic growth. But until recently, Ireland was a 'follower' country that, like China, could still acquire technology that had been created elsewhere.

As in other European countries, Ireland has increased the number of students who are pursuing doctorates in science and technology, from 0.34 per cent of the 20–29 age group in 2006 to 0.57 per cent in 2011; in the EU the proportion rose from 0.27 to 0.49 per cent over the same period, although Ireland still falls short of the leaders, notably Finland (1.3 per cent) and Germany (0.99 per cent).

Table 7.6 Research and Development Spending as a Proportion of GDP, 1991–2010

	Ireland				EU-27	EU maximum: Finland	EU minimum: Romania
	1991	1996	2001	2010	2010	2010	2010
R&D/GDP (%)	0.93	1.32	1.09	1.79	2.00	3.87	0.47

Source: Eurostat.

The acquisition of technology is helped if a society and economy is highly open – to trade (making it easy to import goods, including investment goods, that incorporate improved technology), to ideas (so managerial, organisational and institutional changes can be learned and copied), to foreign direct investment (so that international firms can bring best-practice technology and skills), to allowing labour-market flexibility (so resistance to technological change is low), and to competition (forcing firms to stay on their toes).

By such measures, Ireland has become a truly open society. Exports rose exceptionally quickly during the boom years – by 125 per cent between 1995 and 2000 – and then slowed to an expansion of just 29 per cent in the following five years as rising domestic prices eroded Ireland's competitiveness. Since 2007, relatively low inflation has led to an improvement in Ireland's international competitiveness, so that by 2012 exports of goods and services were equivalent to 108 per cent of GDP, having risen by 83 per cent since 2007.

Ireland is very receptive to foreign investment, which flowed in to the tune of 20 per cent of GDP as recently as 2002. By 2006 the flows had reversed, and Ireland had become an important source of investment abroad, but the pendulum has swung back, and inflows of foreign direct investment in 2012 came to $29.3 billion, well in excess of outflows (of $19.0 billion), confirming Ireland's continued attractiveness as a destination for foreign capital (see Chapter 9).

Ireland's march towards openness is not new. It began in earnest in the 1960s with the Anglo-Irish Free Trade Agreement, and was boosted by EU membership (1973) and the advent of the European single market (1992). The Irish growth spurt of the late 1990s and 2000s may have required such openness, but Ireland was not unique among European countries – including those that grew far less quickly – in this respect.

5 THE EMPLOYMENT ENIGMA

While the framework of the Solow model helps us understand why output per worker has risen over time, it does not answer a much greater puzzle: How is it that employment in Ireland rose by three-quarters between 1994 and 2007? (See also Chapter 6 and earlier in this chapter.)

It is a puzzle for several reasons. First, the historical record of job creation was abysmal: over the previous half-century, employment in Ireland had hardly risen at all, and no one in 1994 anticipated that this record would change radically. Second, there was no substantial surge in the investment rate, which the Solow model would lead us to believe is necessary in order to equip all the new workers so that they are highly productive.

While there were improvements in education and technology, these were not sudden enough to explain the surge in hiring. As a member of the EU and the European Monetary System, Ireland in the 1990s had almost no scope for changing fiscal, monetary or exchange rate policy, so these do not explain the change. And agricultural employment, which stood at 12 per cent of the workforce in 1994, was expected to continue to decline, putting downward pressure on overall employment.

A Suggested Narrative

The simple solution to the enigma runs something like this: with relatively low taxes and macroeconomic stability, and the implementation of the EU 'single market' by 1992 that assured the easy movement of most goods and services within the EU, Ireland by the early 1990s was an attractive destination for US companies wishing to serve the EU market. During the first phase of the boom (1994–2000) investment flowed into export-oriented manufacturing and then into financial services, where it had a quick payoff, raising output and employment very rapidly. Given the initial high unemployment rates, a large pool of relatively well-educated labour was readily available. As more households could count on steady earnings, the demand for services, including public services, rose quickly, so employment spread to other sectors too.

The employment data in Table 7.7 provide some support for this narrative. The data come from the Survey of Earnings, Hours, and Employment Costs, but the series only goes back to 1998. In the three years beginning in early 1998, employment rose by 219,000, but less than ten per cent of the increase was attributable to jobs in industry. All the rest of the job creation was in construction (a quarter of new jobs) or the services sector. This is consistent with the idea that growth in an 'autonomous' sector leads to higher employment both in businesses that supply it ('indirect employment') and in sectors on which the newly flush employees spend their money ('induced employment'). The export-led investment boom appears to have primed a remarkably responsive employment pump, and to have done so more effectively in the 1990s than in any other periods.

Table 7.7 Sectoral Changes in Employment ('000s), 1994–2013

	Total	Change in employment				Change
	1998 Q1	1998– 2001	2001– 7	2007– 12	2012– 13	1998– 2013
Agriculture	134	−13	−7	−24	27	−17
Industry	296	20	−31	−48	6	−52
Construction	118	51	97	−163	0	−15
Trade, transport, accommodation	369	61	117	−66	15	127
Finance, insurance, real estate	60	17	28	−3	−6	37
Professional, scientific, ICT	114	27	44	0	12	84
Administrative and public sector	207	28	93	−23	2	100
Health and social work	111	27	84	24	4	138
Total	*1,408*	*219*	*426*	*−304*	*61*	*402*

Source: Central Statistics Office (CSO) database, accessed April 2014.

Note: 1998 and 2001 refer to first quarter; other dates refer to fourth quarter.

The initial boom might have run its course sooner had Ireland not joined the euro area in 1999. This pushed the real interest rate down essentially to zero, fuelled in part by funds flowing into Irish financial institutions from Germany and elsewhere. In this second phase (2000–7), consumers reacted to the cheap credit by taking out mortgages and expanding their use of credit. Over-exuberant developers built excessive numbers of houses, insouciant households were willing to borrow and to pay high prices for their homes, over-confident bankers were prepared to extend credit without adequate due diligence, and short-sighted governments threw spending caution to the wind. The supply of labour needed for this continued expansion was met entirely by immigration, mainly from Eastern Europe, which kept labour costs in check. Although rising prices made the Irish industrial sector less competitive – industrial employment contracted during this period – the expansion in the financial sector, made easier by the use of the euro, offset this to some extent.

The employment data in Table 7.7 reflect these forces rather well. Construction and public services each added nearly 100,000 jobs during the 2001 to 2007 period, and jobs in finance and the professions also grew strongly. The large trade, transport, accommodation and food services sector simply responded: it tends to rise and fall with the rest of the economy, accounting for about a quarter of all jobs in good times and bad.

The inevitable correction began in 2008 as the construction sector collapsed: half of the more than 300,000 jobs lost between 2007 and 2012 were in construction. House prices and wages did not adjust downwards very quickly, and Ireland remained uncompetitive in export markets for a number of years. The European Central Bank (ECB) publishes a monthly 'harmonised competitiveness indicator' for its member countries, which is a measure of the real effective exchange rate. From a base of 100 in early 1999, Ireland's indicator rose to 126 by mid 2007, reflecting a serious loss of competitiveness, especially as the indicator then stood at 106 for the euro countries as a group.

Since then Ireland's indicator has fallen to 108 (as of February 2014), as wages and house prices have fallen (see also Chapters 2 and 9). International companies supported by IDA Ireland added a net 7,100 jobs in 2013, and indigenous export-oriented businesses supported by Enterprise Ireland added a further 5,400 jobs, but as in the past, most of the 61,000 new jobs created in 2013 were not in these sectors.

Growth Environment
The story we have told so far is coherent, but one important element is lacking: why Ireland? In other words, what made Ireland, rather than, say, Scotland or Italy or a region of Germany, such a fast-growing part of the world in the late 1990s? A possible answer is that since about 1990 there are four areas where Ireland, wittingly or not, has espoused pro-growth strategies, or has been just lucky – in the role of the state, attitudinal changes, social protections, and the US factor.

Role of the State

Like the USA, UK and Japan, but unlike most of the richer EU countries, the government sector in Ireland is relatively small (see Chapter 3) – if the recent bailouts of the banking system are not included. The low tax burden helps limit distortions to the choices that households make about work, consumption and investment (see Chapter 4). Internationally, Ireland is known for its regime of low tax rates on corporate income, which make the country attractive to foreign investors (and as a tax haven): the effective marginal tax rate on the profits generated by foreign investments in Ireland is estimated at 13 per cent, well below the OECD mean of 21 per cent;[4] formally, the corporation tax rate is just 12.5 per cent, compared with an EU average of 31 per cent and a US rate of 35 per cent – although these overstate the difference, because other countries tend to provide more tax breaks of one kind or another. Ireland has a score of 0.04 on the OECD's Index of FDI Regulatory Restrictiveness, lower (i.e. less restrictive) than the OECD average of 0.09, but somewhat more restrictive than in countries such as Portugal, the Netherlands and Germany.

The relatively light weight of the state sector is possible in part because of low military costs, and health and educational systems that are inexpensive relative to their outputs (see Chapter 3), and are not yet burdened by a high proportion of old people. One might point to 1987 as the turning point: in national discussions, the government promised to lower taxes if wages were restrained and labour peace restored. Thus began a dynamic that differed sharply from the European norm where governments typically promised more welfare payments, rather than lower taxes, in return for wage restraint. This is reflected in the structure of personal income taxes: an 'average' production worker who is married with two children would have disposable income equal to 103 per cent of gross pay in Ireland, compared to 96 per cent in the USA and 83 per cent in the EU (see Chapters 3 and 4). The comparatively modest size of the public sector – civil servants are not numerous (and class sizes are large), even if they are comparatively well paid – has also kept in check the proportion of the public with a vested interest in raising taxes.

Some argue that much of the credit for the rise in employment in the 1990s and 2000s should go to national wage agreements that kept labour costs low and bought labour peace; they point to a reduction in strikes since 1987 – there were only six industrial disputes in 2007 – as evidence of the success of these efforts. However, this argument is not entirely compelling: labour unrest abated in most of Western Europe at the same time, without a corresponding rise in employment; and in practice, actual wage increases bore little relation to the rates negotiated in national agreements – hardly surprising given that Ireland's labour market is integrated with that of the UK and, increasingly, the rest of the EU.

One may also measure the weight of government by the extent of rules and regulations. Like the UK and USA, but in contrast with most of continental Europe, Irish rules protecting employment and product markets are relatively light, again a feature that endears the country to investors (see Chapters 3 and 4). The 1990s also saw a new government commitment to fostering competition (see Chapters 3 and 9), with changes that were particularly successful in the airline industry but have yet to affect some expensive and cosseted groups, such as lawyers.

Every year the World Bank publishes an 'Ease of Doing Business' ranking (see Chapter 9); in the 2014 version, Ireland was ranked 15th out of 189 countries, behind Denmark (5th) and the UK (10th), but ahead of Germany (21st), France (38th), Greece (72nd) and China (96th). The median rank for the EU countries was 36. Although Ireland was among the top 20 countries in six of the ten dimensions that are used to compute this ranking, it scored very poorly in the way it handles construction permits (115th), enables one to get electricity (100th), enforces contracts (62nd), and registers property (57th).

Attitudes
Although it is hard to quantify, there appears to have been a change in attitudes over the past three decades, a change that favours economic growth. In the 1970s, college students tended to aspire to jobs in the Foreign Service, or as employees in well-established firms. Now they are more likely to want to be entrepreneurs. According to the Global Entrepreneurship Monitor, in 2013, 9.3 per cent of Irish adults were either nascent entrepreneurs or managers of new companies, a rate higher than in France (4.6 per cent) and Italy (3.4 per cent) but lower than in the USA (12.7 per cent) and in the Baltic republics.

There is no better metaphor for the transformation than the relative decline of staid, state-owned Aer Lingus and the rise of tough, profitable, private and entrepreneurial Ryanair, although this story has a twist because Aer Lingus has responded by re-inventing itself as a budget carrier. By the 1990s Ireland's fertility rate, once the highest in Western Europe, had fallen close to that of a number of other EU countries, a symptom of changing attitudes, including an increasing disregard for some of the teachings of the Catholic Church. As recently as 1984 an estimated 90 per cent of Roman Catholics went to mass every Sunday; this number is now less than 25 per cent.

It is difficult to account for the change in attitudes, but a case can be made that high unemployment in the UK and the USA made emigration less attractive in the early 1990s; forced to stay at home, but unable to find wage-paying work, many young, increasingly well-educated people started to improvise, learned to like the change, and began to succeed. With greater opportunities for success, attitudinal change was strengthened. At the same time Ireland became better informed about, and more closely attuned to, attitudes prevalent in continental Europe.

Social Protection
The comparatively small government sector has a price too – less social protection, including relatively modest spending on health, education and pensions, and fewer national cultural institutions. On the other hand, government pensions and transfers (such as unemployment assistance) appear to have been more important in Ireland than in most EU countries in preventing people from

sinking into poverty over the past few years. The relatively hard-nosed attitude towards social protection has probably helped economic growth. A decade ago, the structure of taxes and subsidies was such that, for low-skilled workers, it did not pay to go to work. This structure has now been reformed faster than in countries such as France – although it is still the case that about one in ten unemployed people would be worse off working because, in the jargon of the trade, they face a replacement rate of more than 100 per cent.

US Factor

If the USA did not exist, Ireland would not have experienced a growth spurt in the 1990s, although since 2000 most of the economic growth has been home-grown, and much of the most recent wave of foreign direct investment has come from Europe. In the 1990s, four-fifths of foreign direct investment originated in the USA, and US firms now account for a quarter of manufacturing employment and about a half of manufacturing output and exports (see Chapter 9). The high-tech wave that lifted the US economy in the 1990s and 2000s washed over Ireland too, but not over most of the rest of Europe. The point is not that US investors raised the Irish investment rate, but rather that the investments that they made, and the associated learning and external economies of scale, had a large and immediate effect on output, and employment.

It may now be more realistic to think of the Irish economy not as a region of Europe, but as an outpost of the USA attached to the edge of the EU.

We still need to ask why US investors steered so much of their investment to Ireland rather than, say, Scotland or Greece or Portugal or India. In part the answer is because Ireland made them welcome, with low taxes and other benefits. But Ireland has historically had close links with the USA; there are strong cultural similarities between the two countries; and they share a common language. The single market act of 1992 confirmed the stability of Ireland as a platform for serving the EU, and the promise of its adhesion to the euro also worked in its favour, by lowering transaction costs.

According to the UNCTAD *World Investment Report*, by 2012 foreign investors owned assets in Ireland equivalent to $65,100 per capita, four times the level in the EU countries ($15,500). Irish companies have begun to return the favour, and in the same year they held assets internationally to the tune of $78,100 per capita, well above the EU mean of $19,500 and higher than the US level of $16,600 (see Chapter 9).

The Combination

In a nutshell, the Irish growth spurt occurred because all the economic planets came into alignment at the same time. The key elements: a booming US economy providing firms there with the profits to invest abroad; a 10 per cent tax on manufacturing profits to attract them to Ireland, coupled with relatively light regulation of labour and product markets; the lure of a pool of well-educated and English-speaking workers; the creation of a single European market that could be served efficiently from Ireland; a credible and conservative macroeconomic stance; wage restraint due to the inertia built into early rounds of national agreements; and a new-found attitude favourable to entrepreneurial activity.

Once the boom began, it led to a virtuous circle, raising the demand for housing and other construction, as well as for a wide array of services such as restaurants, banks and accountants.

A recent book on spatial economics presents a model of 'punctuated equilibria' that matches the Irish case rather well.[5] Consider a region that exports some good. Part of the export earnings are spent and re-spent locally; the computer exporter pays local workers, who buy restaurant meals from chefs, who spend their money buying haircuts, and so on. Now suppose that as the region grows, the proportion of export spending that goes into local purchases rises, which is plausible. Then it can be shown that as exports rise, local income will rise too, at first fairly slowly, then increasingly quickly, and then it will suddenly jump from one equilibrium path to another, before resuming a slower and steadier rise. Ireland jumped a decade ago.

The Crash

This chapter is fundamentally about long-term growth, but a few further comments are in order about the painful recession that began in 2008. This exacerbated the slowdown that would have been inevitable in response to the end of the housing bubble, first by reducing demand for exports, and second by reducing inflows of foreign direct investment.

Two serious imbalances emerged very quickly. The first is the turnaround in public finances, from a general government balance of 0.2 per cent of GDP in 2007 to a general government deficit of 7.3 per cent in 2008 (compared to the EU-27 average deficit of 2.3 per cent of GDP), 14.4 per cent in 2009, and a truly stunning 31.9 per cent in 2010. A corollary has been a rapid rise in government debt, from 25 per cent of GDP in 2007 to 125 per cent by the end of 2013, although the rate has now begun to fall gently. This may be compared to the average debt to GDP burden of 87 per cent in the EU; the Irish relative debt burden is only exceeded by those of Greece, Italy, and Portugal.

In retrospect, it is clear that part of this unravelling of government finances was due to an excessive reliance on taxes with a volatile base – such as on corporate profits, and stamp duty, which melted away in recession – and inadequate spending restraint in the boom years. Although it was not obvious at the time, the government had been running a structural deficit since about 2000; the words of billionaire investor Warren Buffet certainly apply: 'you only find out who is swimming naked when the tide goes out.'

The second major imbalance is in the banking sector, which was bankrupt by 2007. Over the past decade the major banks, flush with inflows from financial houses in Germany and elsewhere, were too aggressive in lending, particularly for property; for instance, the average new housing loan rose from €75,000 in 1998 to €266,000 by 2007. The most dramatic case was that of Anglo Irish Bank, which grew particularly rapidly, but manipulated loans to directors and had close links with property developers (see Chapter 5); when its loans turned sour, it was nationalised in January 2009 and delisted on the Irish and London Stock Exchanges, at which point its shares were valued at just 2 per cent of their peak price.

But the two largest banks were not in much better shape: Government injections of €3.5 billion into Bank of Ireland (March 2009) and Allied Irish Bank (AIB) (May 2009) had little effect on their share prices, implying that the market considered them to be insolvent (see Chapters 2, 3 and 5). Private credit grew by 20 per cent annually from 2000 to 2007 during the go-go years, but fell by 5.5 per cent per year between 2009 and 2010, when the banks' ability to lend was far less (and demand for credit low).

The collapse of the housing market and onset of recession left the banks with large quantities of non-performing loans ('toxic assets'). As long as these remain on the banks' balance sheets, the banks are restricted in the amounts they can lend safely, even for legitimate business needs. The government established the National Assets Management Agency (NAMA) to buy the toxic assets from the banks. This has left the banks in private hands while providing them with enough capital to lend. NAMA issued bonds to pay just over €30 billion to acquire property loans with a face value of €72 billion.

It has begun to sell off the property, to the tune of more than €10 billion by March 2014, and is hopeful that the rising property prices will enable it to turn a profit. The rapid rise in government debt was due in part to the need to borrow in order to acquire the banks' toxic assets. The situation was complicated by the fact that the banks could only be recapitalised adequately if the government overpaid for the toxic assets (or nationalised the banks, which would also amount to paying too much (i.e. €0) for institutions with negative net worth).

Other countries have weathered financial and economic crises comparable to that now faced by Ireland. Sweden saw a surge in private lending in the late 1980s, and asset prices rose by over 125 per cent in the second half of that decade, eroding competitiveness and weakening exports. Between mid 1990 and mid 1993, GDP fell by 6 per cent, unemployment rose from 3 per cent to 12 per cent, the public sector deficit ballooned to 12 per cent of GDP, and there was a 'tidal wave' of bank bankruptcies. In 1992 the government provided a guarantee to bank depositors, but forced the banks to write down valuations quickly and to liquidate bad debts, and required bank shareholders to accept losses ('take a haircut'), before injecting capital equivalent to about 4 per cent of GDP. The cost to the Irish government is far larger than it was in Sweden, but the point is that even difficult financial crises do have solutions. The IMF argues that Ireland is on the right track with its commitment to NAMA and to budget restraint, but that it will need patience and that 'the task ahead is formidable'.

Banking crises can take on a life of their own. Due to a lack of confidence in the country's financial institutions, there were large withdrawals of bank deposits by late 2010. To prevent a collapse of the banking system, the government was effectively forced to agree to an €85 billion 'rescue package' from the IMF, the

EU, UK, Denmark and Sweden. By absorbing the bank losses, the government has taken on an enormous risk; if economic growth falters, and the state finds itself with insufficient revenues, there would be a sovereign debt crisis.

On the other hand, Ireland has so far been a model pupil at getting its public finances in order, and has been rewarded by improved access to world credit markets, and by early 2014 the government was able to borrow on international markets at an interest rate of just 3.5 per cent. In December 2013 the formal monitoring of government financial decisions by the 'troika' of the IMF, European Central Bank, and European Commission came to an end, leaving Ireland with slightly more room for manoeuvre in handling its public finances.

6 WILL GROWTH CONTINUE?

The period of rapid economic growth is now over. The relevant question for the future is whether Ireland will be able to maintain its position as one of the most productive and affluent countries in the world. Sweden, once one of the most affluent countries in Europe, experienced a relative decline after about 1980, as did Japan after 1989. Can Ireland expect the same?

'Forecasting is difficult', wrote Nobelist Niels Bohr, 'especially about the future.' Even so, some things are clear.

On the positive side, an interesting feature of the 'punctuated-equilibria' model is that even if exports fall, the economy will not decline as quickly as it grew. Having reached a higher plateau, the economy will be able to remain there relatively easily. This helps explain why the IMF expects Irish GDP growth to reach 1.8 per cent in 2014, above the EU average of 1.3 per cent, but half the world average of 3.6 per cent. Moreover, corporate income tax rates remain low, entrepreneurialism is alive and well, and anticipated improvements in infrastructure and the regulatory environment are likely to help sustain growth.

Against this, the decomposition of Section 4 indicates that the 'demographic dividend' is essentially over, although in the short run there is a pool of unemployed labour that is available to be employed.

Second, the Solow framework predicts that the *growth* in GNP per worker will eventually fall, although continued external economies and ongoing improvements in human capital and technology could postpone this somewhat. Such a fall has already occurred: labour productivity grew by 3.4 per cent annually from 1994 to 2000, but since then has risen by just 0.8 per cent per year.

Third, some of the economic planets discussed in Section 5 are going out of alignment: perhaps the most important is the rise of the EU members of Eastern Europe, which have quite explicitly tried to emulate the 'Irish model' and still offer relatively cheap entry points to the EU market, much as Ireland did a decade and a half ago.

And fourth, Ireland became a victim of its own success. By 2007 it was a high-cost destination for investors, as the boom ended. While competitiveness has improved since then, it has not returned to its pre-boom level.

Even staying near the top of the GNP per capita ranking will be challenging. Irish education is good, not extraordinary; government regulatory policies are fairly light, but the public sector is not universally honest, transparent or efficient (as the OECD points out).[6] The World Economic Forum ranked Ireland 28th worldwide in 2013–14 in its 'global competitiveness index', and the *World Competitiveness Yearbook* ranks it 17th; whatever one may think of rankings of this nature (see Chapters 2 and 9), these do not point to overwhelming international confidence in the growth prospects of the Irish economy.

Moreover, if investment and jobs can flow rapidly into Ireland, they can vanish quickly too. In 2013, firms supported by IDA Ireland and Enterprise Ireland added 31,000 jobs, but cut 19,000 jobs, for a net gain of 12,000. Given the rapidity of turnover of industrial jobs, the sector could shrink rapidly if external conditions were to worsen.

For now, the danger of complacency has receded, and it is useful to remember that Ireland has resilience. People are not afraid of working: at 64.1, the average retirement age is the second highest in the EU, compared to an EU average of 61.2. More young people (aged 30–34) have acquired a higher education than in any other EU country. The air and water continue to become cleaner. GDP per capita is still well above the EU-27 average (in purchasing power terms). Labour markets are open, and workers will continue to flow into and out of the country with ease. Export competitiveness has already improved sharply. One can take heart in the fact that both Japan and Sweden, after making adjustments, have seen a resurgence in their economic performance over the past few years.

Notes

1 J. Alber and T. Fahey, *Perceptions of Living Conditions in an Enlarged Europe*, European Foundation for the Improvement of Living and Working Conditions, and European Commission, Luxembourg 2004, p. 51.

2 P. Krugman, *The Age of Diminished Expectations*, MIT Press, Cambridge MA 1990.

3 The term 'modern economic growth' was coined by Nobel laureate Simon Kuznets, whose *magnum opus* traced the growth of the UK and USA over the past two centuries.

4 K. Yoo, 'Corporate Taxation of Foreign Direct Investment Income 1991–2001', OECD Working Paper UnECO/WKP(2003)19, Paris 2003.

5 M. Fujita, P. Krugman and A. Venables, *The Spatial Economy*, MIT Press, Cambridge MA 1999.

6 OECD, *Economic Surveys: Ireland*, OECD, Paris 2003.

CHAPTER 8

Social Justice: Distribution, Poverty and Policy Responses

Michael King

1 INTRODUCTION

Reducing inequality and eradicating poverty are key policy objectives for a small open economy like Ireland, both from a competitiveness angle and a quality of life perspective. Greater levels of equity and lower incidences of poverty afford more Irish citizens the opportunity to participate in the modern economy, reduce costly social problems and foster trust, co-operation and a greater sense of community.

Yet Ireland is characterised by significant inequalities and deep-rooted poverty. As Ireland emerges from the financial crisis, 16 per cent of Irish adults earned less than 60 per cent of the median income in 2011, the amount deemed necessary to participate fully in society. When we consider the most vulnerable groups, we find that Ireland experiences one of the highest rates of child poverty in Europe, and significant poverty among the elderly. In terms of inequality, while Ireland is not exceptional by international standards, there are significant inequalities, not just in income and wealth but in education and health status.

The extent of inequality within countries varies significantly. Data from the United Nations illustrate that the ratio of income of the top 10 per cent of earners to the bottom 10 per cent of earners ranges between over 50 in Bolivia, Colombia and Honduras, countries with extreme income inequality and weak welfare systems, to less than 10 in many developed countries. In Ireland, the ratio of income of the top 10 per cent of households to the bottom 10 per cent of earners is around 13.5, but in the absence of taxation and transfers the ratio would be 161.

Research suggests that there is greater income inequality between countries than within countries. Estimates from the International Monetary Fund (IMF) in 2012 suggest that gross national income (GNI) per person is 154 times higher in Luxembourg, the world's richest economy, and 91 times higher in Ireland than in the Democratic Republic of the Congo. The contrasts in income inequality are mirrored in areas such as health and education. Women are expected to live to the age of 84 in euro zone countries compared with 45 in Sierra Leone and 48 in Swaziland. Literacy rates for over 15-year-olds range from very close to 100 per cent for most developed countries to 25 per cent and 31 per cent for Guinea and Mali respectively.

A child born in rural Chad is likely to live to the age of 50 without the opportunity to become truly literate and survive with lifetime earnings of €35,000, whereas a European child born into a middle- to high-income family will most likely enjoy third-level education of some kind, have an opportunity to live into their 80s and enjoy life earnings of approximately €3,000,000. While the contrasts may be less extreme, statistics show that children born on the same day in different parts of the same Irish city will enjoy different life expectancies, education opportunities, and future income possibilities. This brings us to the question, 'What is fairness?' To help answer this question we start with the concept of social justice.

Social justice can be seen as the extension of the legal concepts of equality and fairness into the wider aspects of society and the economy. Recognising the dignity of every human being, social justice seeks greater levels of equality and solidarity in society. But how exactly do we define fairness? This, of course, is open to interpretation. At the core there are two approaches in thinking about social justice; equality of outcome and equality of opportunity. Achieving equality of outcome would mean the equalisation of income or wealth, and while the absolute equality of outcomes was tried in communist regimes in the 20th century, all rich countries move somewhat in this direction through redistributive policies.

We can turn to the American philosopher John Rawls for the rationale for seeking equality of outcome (see also discussion in Chapter 2). He argued that to maximise social justice the welfare of the worst-off person in society should be increased. Rawls specifically argued that in calculating total societal welfare we should be solely concerned with the outcome for the poorest individual or family. Designing policy from this perspective would lead to very radical policy conclusions aimed at equalising income.

The second concept is the idea of equality of opportunity. Equality of opportunity is attained when all citizens enjoy an agreed norm of education and healthcare that opens up the opportunity for all citizens to participate and succeed in society. When accompanied with a basic level of income support for the poorest in society, achieving equality of opportunity is often the centrepiece of government policy.

The focus on equality of opportunity with modest income supports was endorsed by the World Bank's 2006 *World Development Report*. The report defined fairness (equity) as a situation where individuals should have equal opportunities to pursue a life of their choosing, where a person's life achievements should be determined primarily by his or her talents and efforts, rather than by pre-determined circumstances such as race, gender, social or family background, and be spared from extreme deprivation in outcomes, particularly in health, education and consumption levels.

This chapter is structured as follows. Section 2 explores the historical reasons for the development of inequality and poverty. Section 3 outlines the case for and against pursuing greater equality and poverty reduction, illustrating the trade-offs that can be present. Section 4 discusses the nature and trajectory of inequality and poverty in Ireland and Section 5 describes the political economy of redistribution, placing the Irish welfare system in an international context. Section 6 describes Ireland's policies that are aimed at reducing inequality and poverty, focusing on some practical examples. Section 7 concludes the chapter.

2 CAUSES OF INEQUALITY AND POVERTY

Across Countries

The obvious question for many is why is there so much poverty in the world? Why are some countries over a hundred times richer than others? A better way of asking these questions is perhaps to ask why some countries are rich. The reality of human history is that for approximately 200,000 years humans survived day to day initially by hunting and gathering plants and berries, before progressing to small-scale farming in some regions of the world around 10,000 years ago. While some regions enjoyed concentrated but ultimately modest increases in economic well-being in the last 3,000 to 4,000 years (Egypt, Greece, the Roman Empire and the Italian city states) due to innovations in finance, the development of trade routes and the concentration of political power, significant increases in income levels only began around 200 years ago.

Modern economic growth began in the 1800s when the Industrial Revolution facilitated the division and specialisation of labour and began the process of urbanisation. Initially, only a small number of European countries, North America and other European colonies enjoyed the higher living standards that accompanied the Industrial Revolution.

Hence, the birth of significant global inequalities was not the result of some regions doing so badly, but others doing so extraordinarily well. Economic histories continue to debate the reasons why economic growth took hold in some regions of the world and not others. While undoubtedly conditions such as abundance of natural resources, population density and proximity to trading routes and markets play important roles, it is often argued that the quality of national and local institutions, and their conduciveness to trade and investment activities, determine the relative economic performance of countries. During the last 50 years, some regions of the world, most notably significant parts of Asia, have followed the path to modernity and high incomes, but others, particularly Africa, have failed to join the transformation due to a combination of geographic isolation, poor government institutions and local conflicts.

Within Countries and Across Individuals

Does this historical process tell us anything about inequality and poverty within countries such as Ireland? The answer is yes. The free market capitalism that drove the Industrial Revolution led to wage differentials within countries, between people of different levels of education, experience and skills. As a result, significant income inequality can occur within a developed country when there are differences in skill levels, health outcomes, or indeed any characteristic that is highly rewarded in modern economies, such as motivation, dependability and conscientiousness. For example, research in the USA attributed the rise in inequality since 1970 to the increase in wages for skilled workers which came about due to technological change, increasing trade and the decline of manufacturing.

Inequality from wage differentials can be deepened by unequal ownership of capital (wealth) in the form of financial or physical assets. Income inequalities in the past can cement current inequalities through the enjoyment of significant income from investments. The evidence suggests that the importance in inequality of labour and non-labour income differs by region. In Western Europe, non-labour income is the most important factor driving inequality, whereas in North America labour income is a more important driver.

At the individual level we know a lot about inequality. We know that level of education and type of occupation are strong predictors of higher income. However, we can ask a deeper question: what accounts for differences in educational outcomes and levels of professional achievement? The answer to this question has four parts.

First, we know that everyone is born with different abilities and talents, and these play a central role in determining future success. A large body of research shows that cognitive ability is a powerful determinant of wages, schooling, participation in crime, and success in many aspects of social and economic life. In addition, recent research by Nobel Prize-winning economist James Heckman documents how non-cognitive abilities (perseverance, motivation, time preference, risk aversion, self-esteem, self-control, preference for leisure) have direct effects on wages (controlling for schooling), schooling, teenage pregnancy, smoking, crime, performance on achievement tests, and many other aspects of social and economic life.

Second, who your parents are and how you are cared for in early childhood determines success in life. Empirical research shows that being born into a household with working, health-conscious, educated and education-focused parents increases the likelihood of achieving higher levels of education and income. These environmental effects start in the womb. Research documents that pre-natal interventions that reduce foetal exposure to alcohol and nicotine have long-term positive effects on cognition, socio-emotional skills (such as attentiveness, motivation and self-confidence) and health. Indeed, James Heckman argues that the reason children of low-income parents often grow up to be low income has little to do with genetics and innate abilities and everything to do with the impact of the socio-emotional environment in early childhood on long-run abilities.

Third, peer and network effects play an important role in shaping the ambitions of and opportunities enjoyed by different children. Whether school or neighbourhood based, education and health-conscious peers can improve a child's education and income outcomes. In addition, the availability of parental, neighbourhood or school-based networks can change career trajectory and deepen the initial inequality caused by early childhood environmental factors.

Fourth, luck in life is not evenly distributed. Some people are extremely unlucky to endure debilitating health issues that undermine their ability to reach their potential, while others are extremely lucky to secure high-paying jobs. Of course, an individual's ability to overcome bad luck is determined by the availability of private insurance, an option not open to low-income groups, and luck in achieving a high-paying job may in fact be related to proximity to networks.

Over the life cycle inequality can also emerge when households have different attitudes to saving and investing. For example, a household that saves a sizeable proportion of income on a yearly basis can develop income from investments that raises their long-term income above and beyond the sum of their labour income. Whether invested in a dedicated pension plan or not, such savings can help the household maintain a high level of consumption in their retirement years. Thus, inequality can emerge because of different financial management strategies pursued by households for given levels of income.

Evolution of Inequality over Time

Does the nature of economic growth mean that inequality will continue to rise? In a seminal paper, the Russian-American economist Simon Kuznets argued that economic inequality increases over time while a country is developing, and then after a certain average income is attained, inequality begins to decrease.[1] The prediction of changes in inequality as a country develops is depicted in what is known as the Kuznets curve (see Figure 8.1). Among many suggestions as to why this might be the case is the idea that owners of capital and workers in sectors with rising productivity benefit disproportionally in the early stages of development. As the capabilities of the state increase, however, improving education and health opportunities for all citizens, the emergence of redistributive policies gradually reduces the inequality.

Up until 1980 there was evidence for the Kuznets curve. In the USA inequality rose in the second half of the nineteenth century and declined over the twentieth, until the 1970s, when it started increasing again. In the UK inequality also rose after 1977, after almost a century of declines following the initial rise during the Industrial Revolution. Recent data suggest that there is in fact a natural tendency for capitalist economies to lead to *Downton Abbey* (high) levels of inequality, contradicting the predictions of the Kuznets curve.[2] It is argued that pre-World War I economies in Western Europe were characterised by significant inequalities, before the two wars and the great depression dragged levels of wealth back down to earth through physical destruction, capital losses and inflation.

Figure 8.1 The Kuznets Curve

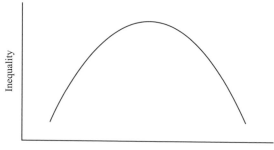

However, since the 1970s the ratio of wealth to income has increased together with income inequality and is now approaching levels last seen before World War I. *The Economist* recently argued that the inverted U of the Kuznets curve has turned into something closer to an italicised *N*, with the final stroke pointing menacingly upwards.[3]

The central role that policy plays in determining the trajectory of inequality cannot be underestimated. Right-of-centre governments in the UK and the USA in the 1980s and early 1990s deliberately pursued policies of lower taxation and lower redistribution that increased inequality, undermining the predictions of the Kuznets curve. In contrast, left-of-centre governments in the UK after World War II and during the Great Depression in the USA (1930s) reduced inequality through pioneering reforms in the areas of pensions and social welfare.[4]

3 ARGUMENTS FOR AND AGAINST REDUCING INEQUALITY AND POVERTY

Arguments For

If everyone has a basic standard of living, is inequality something to worry about? The answer for many is yes; and economists and political leaders from Adam Smith to Barack Obama have been exercised by the corrosive impact inequality can have in society.[5] In examining the case for reducing inequality and poverty, inspiration can be taken from philosophy, economics and political science.

As mentioned in the introduction and discussed in Chapter 2, John Rawls (1921–2002) provided a philosophical justification for significant efforts at reducing inequality. In his 1971 book *A Theory of Justice*, Rawls argued that in the pursuit of social justice the welfare of the worst-off groups in society should be emphasised and policy should focus on increasing the welfare of low-income groups. Rawls argues that we would all opt for a more equal society rather than an unequal one if behind a metaphorical 'veil of ignorance' we did not know what our position in society will be. This appealing 'thought experiment' provides a strong philosophical rationale for the pursuit of greater equality; although it could be argued that as voters know their relative position on the income distribution spectrum when they vote, the attractiveness of the idea may be trumped by economic self-interest at the ballot box.

Perhaps an even more convincing argument can be derived from the proposition of *diminishing marginal utility of income*. The proposition states that the effect on well-being (utility) of an additional €1 of income becomes progressively smaller as income rises. In other words, if the richest person in Ireland won €5,000 his/her well-being would not increase nearly as much compared with a low-income person winning the same amount. In terms of policy, diminishing marginal utility suggests that raising the income of poor people will raise their well-being considerably, while reducing the income of the rich by an equal amount will have comparatively little effect on their well-being. Thus redistributing from rich to poor maximises overall societal welfare; a noble objective for policymakers.

High levels of inequality also lead to externalities that undermine both well-being and income levels of not just low-income groups but all in society, including the wealthy. Intuitively, it is easy to understand how the quality of social relations can deteriorate in a more unequal society. Inequality affects our ability to identify with and empathise with other people. The literature suggests that health and social problems are closely related to levels of inequality, not average income levels, in developed countries; rates of mental illness are five times higher in the most unequal societies.[6] Similarly, in more unequal societies people are five times as likely to be imprisoned and six times as likely to be clinically obese. It is important to note that while this evidence cannot be strictly considered as causal, the data are suggestive of an important link. Dealing with greater levels of crime and healthcare costs will affect the tax burdens of high-income groups and can lead to an inefficient waste of human talent.

In addition, levels of societal trust and sense of community are demonstrably higher in more equal societies, and while both are important to quality of life, they both play a key role in facilitating economic growth. Throughout history the societies that have flourished are those where economic transactions have taken place based on a person's word. In the absence of trust, complex business deals are no longer feasible and individuals expect betrayal in business transactions; this increases the cost of ensuring business transactions through time, resources spent on monitoring others and the need for contingency planning, reducing the likelihood that the transaction will occur in the first place.

Economic inequalities have important consequences for democracy. Nobel Prize-winning economist Paul Krugman lamented, 'Extreme concentration of income is incompatible with real democracy. Can anyone seriously deny that our political system is being warped by the influence of big money, and that the warping is getting worse as the wealth of a few grows ever larger?' Political science theory suggests that political policies chosen in a democracy should reflect the preferences of the 'median voter' or average voter and thereby allow majorities to dictate policy. However, there is evidence to suggest that tax policy of the last decade and post-crises financial sector reform fail to reflect the interests of the majority of citizens but instead have been overly influenced by wealthy individuals and corporations respectively.

In summary, strong economic arguments exist for reducing inequality and poverty in Ireland. As a small open economy, Ireland must remain competitive and succeed in export markets. First, as Ireland competes internationally on the quality of our labour force, a meritocratic society with full equality of opportunity reduces the losses from poverty when individuals do not reach their true potential. Second, Ireland needs to continue to attract the best international talent from around Europe. While high incomes undoubtedly attract some non-nationals to Ireland, the quality of life, such as low levels of crime and social cohesion, are also important.

Arguments Against

The benefits of inequality cannot be considered without reference to the costs associated with government policies designed to reduce inequality. There are costs to society incurred in the pursuit of greater equality, and concern over these costs go a long way to explaining why we do not see concerted political efforts to reduce inequality. Indeed, the history of the 20th century is littered with examples of poorly designed policies pursued in the name of equality of outcomes that seriously harmed economic growth prospects by ignoring the costs of taxation and redistribution. Economists call these costs the *excess burden of taxation*, *diminishing returns to high tax rates* and *disincentive effects* (see Chapter 4).

The excess burden of taxation, also known as the distortionary cost of taxation, is the economic loss that society suffers as a result of a tax. First discussed by Adam Smith in the 18th century, the excess burden of taxation occurs because individuals or firms change their behaviour when a tax is imposed. An income tax, for example, reduces the return to working an additional hour, and thereby makes it more likely that the worker will choose to enjoy leisure instead of working for some part of the week. In business, the taxation of company profits reduces the return to investment, making it less likely that the firm will undertake a project. A sales tax such as value added tax (VAT) is perhaps an even more intuitive example. A sales tax on goods and services will increase the cost of the goods at the point of purchase, and hence by the basic laws of supply and demand will reduce the number of units purchased. These are hidden losses to taxation, hence the term *excess burden of taxation*.

The level of excess burden for a given tax will differ between countries. For example, if citizens have a strong work ethic, a tax on labour income will lead to a smaller reduction in the number of hours worked. High work ethic has been cited as a reason why some countries, such as the Scandinavian countries, can prosper with high levels of income tax without significant losses to economic activity.

At very high levels of taxation, the excess burden of taxation can lead to diminishing returns to tax authorities. If the government increases tax rates beyond a certain point the tax base will begin to disappear. At very high rates of income taxation, people will simply choose not to work, will work in the informal economy, or will fail to declare their income to the authorities.

In a globalised world, where capital can freely move between countries, taxation on capital or company profits is perhaps the most obvious example of diminishing returns to high tax rates. If taxes on capital or company profits are increased to a high level, the capital can simply move jurisdictions. As a result, the presence of the excess burden of taxation and diminishing returns to high tax rates limits the ability of governments to tax.

An additional cost to high levels of redistribution can occur when transfers to the unemployed cause a proportion of welfare recipients to reduce their efforts to be self-reliant. Such transfers can in some cases act as a disincentive to finding paid employment. There is little disagreement that welfare payments are warranted for people who suffer from bad luck such as job loss or illness. However, welfare programmes need to be careful not to discourage the pursuit of paid employment among recipients. Any change in behaviour due to this disincentive effect is an economic loss to society.

To counter Rawls' philosophical arguments for greater redistribution, another American philosopher, Robert Nozick (1938–2002), published a retort in his 1974 book *Anarchy, State and Utopia*. Nozick's theory of justice claims that whether a distribution of income, wealth or property is just or not depends entirely on how it came about. If income or wealth has been created by the fruits of individual effort, then to take property away from people in order to redistribute it violates their rights. Further discussion of Nozick's ideas can be found in Chapter 2.

Nozick favoured the pursuit of social justice through voluntary donations, thereby avoiding the violation of ownership rights and the losses to taxation implicit in government-led redistributive policies. Mankind has the potential to be altruistic. Adam Smith, in his book *Theory of Moral Sentiments* (1759), observed that human nature leads people to be altruistically concerned about the well-being of others.

The World Giving Index monitors the proportion of people in each country who give money to charity. In 2013, 76 per cent of adults in the UK and 70 per cent of adults in Ireland (4th place in the world) donated money to charity. In contrast, some European countries, such as Russia (6 per cent), Greece (6 per cent), Ukraine (8 per cent) and Croatia (10 per cent), do not have a tradition of giving to charity. The USA is often cited as the most generous country for the amount of private giving, with about $316 billion given to charities in 2012. This represents, though, just 2 per cent of GDP and is significantly below the level of redistribution in many developed economies.

One reason why private giving is small can be characterised by the prisoners' dilemma of private income transfers when each person prefers that the other gives. Let's imagine a three-person society; two potential donors and one low-income individual. Both potential donors care about the welfare of the third person but would rather not bear the cost of the income transfer themselves. Each potential donor prefers the scenario where the other donor provides the income transfer to the low-income individual. This dilemma can lead to a free rider problem and will ultimately result in neither donor choosing to donate and acts as rationale for government involvement in redistribution.

4 INEQUALITY AND POVERTY IN IRELAND

In this section we explore the different dimensions of inequality and poverty, discuss different approaches to their measurement, and provide a full picture of the nature and extent of economic inequality and poverty in Ireland. We focus specifically on the concepts of equality of outcome and equality of opportunity defined in Section 1. For an alternative approach, we discuss the capabilities approach developed by the Indian economist Amartya Sen. Throughout our analysis, an attempt is made to highlight the life-cycle approach to poverty, and urban and rural differences that exist in Ireland.

Dimensions of Inequality and Poverty
Poverty and inequality can exist across four dimensions: economic, political, social, and affective (see Table 8.1). The economic sphere encompasses income, wealth, and access to services; the political sphere is associated with the distribution of influence in the political process; the social sphere is concerned with the distribution of recognition and respect in the community and finally the affective sphere concerns the distribution of love, care, and solidarity. There is a tendency for social scientists to focus on the economic and the political dimensions, and this is due in part to the availability of data on these aspects, but also due to the intangible nature of the social and affective spheres.

Table 8.1 The Dimensions of Inequality and Poverty

Economic	Income, wealth and access to services
Political	Representation and power relations
Social	Recognition and respect
Affective	Love, care and solidarity

Before focusing on the economic dimension, it is worth making a few important observations about the interconnections between the dimensions. Even within modern democracies, with the established principle of 'one person one vote', economic inequalities can lead to imbalances in access to political influence. This is particularly the case when private donations to political parties are not sufficiently regulated.

The relationship between income level and enjoyment of love, care and solidarity is less straightforward. Low-income communities can be characterised by high levels of community spirit and strong family relationships. Conversely, we know that wealth does not necessarily lead to personal happiness. Finally, the distribution of respect and recognition in society differs between cultures and ultimately depends on what is valued in society. In modern consumer societies, traditional reasons for respect such as integrity and community involvement can be overtaken by displays of wealth and exclusive memberships.

Inequality Outcomes

Measurement

When we consider equality of outcomes, we typically think of income. In Section 1, a measure of income inequality was mentioned, namely the ratio of the income share of the top 10 per cent of earners to the income share of the bottom 10 per cent of earners. While this represents a good starting point, the measurement of inequality can be taken a step further with the development of a Lorenz curve. Developed by the American economist Max Lorenz in 1905, the Lorenz curve is drawn with the cumulative percentage of wealth measured along the y-axis and the cumulative percentage of households measured along the x-axis. To draw the Lorenz curve, the proportion of income earned by the poorest 10 per cent of the population is calculated, followed by each additional 10 per cent of the population until the point is reached where 100 per cent of wealth is owned by 100 per cent of the population.

Figure 8.2 The Lorenz Curve

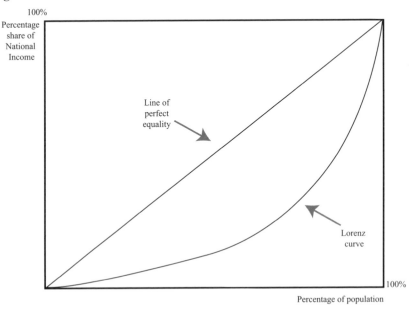

The Lorenz curve simply joins the points on the graph that represent how much income is earned by each additional 10 per cent of the population. If income is equally distributed each additional 10 per cent of the population will earn an additional 10 per cent of income and since we are looking at cumulative percentages, the Lorenz curve would be a straight line emanating from the origin. This is known as the line of absolute equality and will have a slope of 45 degrees. When we plot the data for a particular country, the Lorenz curve will bow away from the line of absolute equality down to the right. The more unequal a society is, the further it will deviate away from the line of absolute equality. Changes in the Lorenz curve over time illustrate the evolution of inequality in a country.

A related measure of inequality is the Gini coefficient. It is calculated as the ratio of the area between the Lorenz curve and the line of absolute equality (numerator) and the whole area under the line of absolute equality (denominator). The extreme values of the Gini coefficient are 0 and 1, although they are often presented as percentages, between 0 and 100 per cent respectively. A low Gini coefficient indicates greater equality in society, with absolute equality represented by a Gini of zero. Conversely, a Gini of 100 per cent means that the top 10 per cent of income earners enjoy 100 per cent of all income in society. The Lorenz curve is most often used to depict the distribution of income; if data are available it can also be used to illustrate the distribution of wealth.

Income Distribution

How does Ireland perform using these different measures of inequality? Table 8.2 provides the data necessary to draw Lorenz curves for Ireland for different years. The table shows the distribution of disposable household income after taxation and transfers in Ireland between 1980 and 2010. Overall, there is a remarkable degree of consistency, with the percentage of disposable income earned by each decile of the population remaining broadly constant over the 25-year period.

When the income shares of the top 20 per cent to the bottom 20 per cent are compared over time a number of points are worth noting. The ratio fell during the economically depressed 1980s but rose through the economic expansion of the 1990s. This can be attributed to an increase in the share of income enjoyed by the top 20 per cent of earners. After 2004, however, the income share of the bottom 20 per cent increased as the welfare state expanded, and as a result the ratio fell. The ratio fell further between 2007 and 2009, but this time because of a fall in the share of income enjoyed by the top 20 per cent of earners. In 2010, a higher level of inequality was recorded as welfare cuts became operational and the top 20 per cent of households was the only decile that increased its income share between 2009 and 2010.

Table 8.2 Distribution of Disposable Household Income (1980–2010), Percentage of Total Household Income

	1980	1987	1999/ 2000	2004	2007	2009	2010
Bottom	1.7	2.3	1.9	2.1	2.2	2.4	2.1
2nd	3.5	3.7	3.2	3.0	3.5	3.6	3.4
3rd	5.1	5.1	4.5	4.3	4.9	5.0	4.8
4th	6.6	6.4	6.0	5.7	6.2	6.3	6.0
5th	7.9	7.7	7.7	7.4	7.7	7.7	7.3
6th	9.3	9.2	9.3	9.2	9.4	9.1	8.7
7th	11.0	11.2	11.2	11.1	11.5	11.0	10.5
8th	13.0	13.4	13.5	13.6	13.8	12.9	12.7
9th	16.2	16.5	16.8	16.5	16.9	16.2	16.0
Top	25.7	24.5	25.9	27.1	28.3	25.8	28.5
Ratio of top 20% to bottom 20%:	8.1	6.8	8.4	8.5	7.9	7.0	8.1

Source: Household Budget Surveys; Central Statistics Office (CSO), *Survey on Income and Living Conditions* (EU-SILC), various issues.

Given the relationship between the Lorenz curve and the Gini coefficient, it is unsurprising that these changes are also reflected in changes in the Gini coefficient. Ireland's Gini coefficient fell from 31.9 in 2005 to 28.8 in 2009, before rising again to 29.8 in 2011. Based on these measures, there is reason to believe that inequality behaved in a counter-cyclical manner in Ireland since 1980, but that cuts in transfer payments led to increasing inequality between 2009 and 2011. The data for more recent years are not available and hence the position since 2011 is unknown.

Table 8.3 places Ireland's performance in an international context, comparing Gini coefficients (after taxes and transfers) for 12 European countries, ranked by the 2011 Gini coefficient. The period was characterised by significant economic volatility, rising unemployment and destruction of wealth in many European countries. For most of the last two decades, Ireland experienced higher levels of inequality than many central European and Scandinavian countries. This seems to have moderated to some degree as the decline in Ireland's Gini between 2005 and 2011 has meant that Ireland has fallen from 4th place to 8th place in the group of 12 countries considered.

Table 8.3 European Comparison of Gini Coefficients (after taxes and transfers)

Country	2005	2009	2011	Change 2005–2011
Portugal	38.1	35.4	35.4	−2.7
Denmark	23.9	27.0	35.4	11.5
Spain	31.8	32.3	34.5	2.7
Greece	33.2	33.1	33.5	0.3
UK	34.6	32.4	33.0	−1.6
EU 15	29.9	30.3	30.9	1.0
France	27.7	29.8	30.8	3.1
Ireland	*31.9*	*28.8*	*29.8*	*−2.1*
Germany	26.1	29.1	29.0	2.9
Netherlands	26.9	27.2	25.8	−1.1
Finland	26.0	25.9	25.8	−0.2
Sweden	23.4	24.8	24.4	1.0

Source: Eurostat Online database 2011.

Regional and Life-Cycle Inequalities

Regional inequalities exist within Ireland, although these have fallen since 2000. According to the Central Statistics Office (CSO), data for 2010 show that residents of Dublin enjoy disposable income (after taxes and transfers) that is 11 per cent higher than the national average, while residents of the southern and eastern regions enjoy disposable income that is 3 per cent higher than the national average. This is balanced by 8.3 per cent lower than average disposable income in the border, western and midland regions.

At county level, Donegal and Offaly are the counties with the lowest levels of average disposable income; Dublin, Cork, Kildare, and Limerick are the only four counties with disposable income above the national average. Differences in standards of living are likely to be smaller when differences in the cost of living between the counties are taken into consideration. There is also a rural/urban dimension to inequality with extensive rural development policies in place to deal not only with this but also to prevent the decline of rural areas due to migration (see Chapter 9).

Inequalities can emerge at different points in the life cycle. For children, students in full-time education and the elderly, opportunities to earn money are limited and consumption is financed by parental support or the drawing down of accumulated financial wealth such as pensions.

It has been shown that in Ireland and around the world, low-income households tend to have more children. This can lead to the situation where a small number of children have access to significant resources when growing up, while more modest resources are spread more thinly over a larger number of

217

children. Such inequality is likely to lead to very real differences in education and health status between socio-economic groups.

A second inequality related to the life cycle occurs when households fail to adequately save for their retirement. This can occur as people prioritise immediate consumption while working or fail to adequately anticipate their retirement needs. This latter issue has been exacerbated by the sizeable losses incurred by private pension funds during the recent financial crisis.

Wealth Distribution
Unlike many OECD countries, Ireland does not yet have a reliable survey of household wealth, although this will change when Ireland publishes the results of its first survey on household finance and consumption that was conducted in 2013. We do know that the explosion in asset prices, up to the end of 2007, resulted in significant increases in household wealth for those with financial assets and those who owned property.

Estimates from 2007 suggest that Ireland ranked second only to Japan in terms of personal wealth in 2006.[7] Estimates also suggest that the top 1 per cent of the Irish population hold 20 per cent of the wealth, the top 2 per cent control 30 per cent, and the top 5 per cent disposed of 40 per cent of private assets. When the value of housing is excluded, the distribution of financial wealth is more unequal, with the top 1 per cent controlling 34 per cent of all wealth. These numbers suggest that wealth is more unevenly distributed than income in Ireland and this conclusion is consistent with international experience; even in countries with relatively equal income distributions such as Germany and Sweden, the distribution of wealth is very unequal.

Despite the fact that some older people in Ireland tend to suffer from relative poverty, a second group of older people enjoy significant personal wealth, such divergence reflecting the outcome of a lifetime of divergent income paths and investment decisions. This divergence occurred during Ireland's economic expansion between 1994 and 2007 as significant increases in returns to employment occurred in some professions and at management level in the private sector, while stock market and property investments early in the period produced very high returns. As property prices and the stock market have fallen significantly since 2007, inequality in wealth will have reduced somewhat in Ireland.

Poverty Outcomes
Absolute Poverty
Poverty can be described as the state of not having enough money to take care of basic needs such as food, clothing and shelter. At a broad level, poverty can be measured in either absolute or relative terms and is generally calculated as a head count indicator; the fraction of the population falling below a minimum standard of income. Absolute poverty is defined as the fraction of the population below some threshold of income. The simplicity of absolute poverty, and its specified

income level, is undermined by the need to change the threshold income level as countries grow and the cost of living rises. For example, a measure of absolute poverty in 1960s Ireland would be out of date in the 21st century.

The theoretical distinction between inequality and poverty is worth noting. In our measures of inequality, some households (exactly 10 per cent) must be by definition located in the bottom 10 per cent of the income distribution. As a result, stagnant inequality is consistent with falling absolute poverty, where the poorer members of society are able to enjoy a superior standard of living.

The most famous examples of absolute poverty lines are the US$1.25 a day and US$2 a day used as part of the Millennium Development Goals (MDGs). Each year, the United Nations estimates the proportion of people living under these thresholds across the globe and it has been estimated that in 2010, 1.2 billion people lived on US$1.25 a day and 2.4 billion lived on less than US$2 a day.

As the absolute income thresholds of the MDGs hold little relevance for high-income countries, nationally income thresholds are established that appropriately reflect expectations about the minimum standard of living. In the USA, the Census Bureau adjusts the absolute poverty threshold each year. In 2012, an income threshold of approximately $23,300 for a family of two adults and two children under the age of 18 was used.

Relative Poverty
The alternative approach, relative poverty, occurs when people fall behind, by more than a certain degree, from the average income and lifestyle enjoyed by the rest of the society. An advantage of a relative measure of poverty is that it does not need to be adjusted as average earnings change. Ireland's first official poverty measure, the 'at risk of poverty rate', is a measure of relative poverty and refers to all individuals who earn less than the threshold of 60 per cent of the median income. This measure is used by the National Action Plan for Social Inclusion and by the EU.

Each of these poverty measures focuses on income and such an approach can be criticised in a number of ways. First, there are limitations to income as a single identifier of poverty. Focusing on income alone fails to take into consideration household characteristics such as savings or outstanding debts. For example, monthly income may fluctuate from year to year and thus poorly represent long-term income. Second, the level of past investment in consumer durables and household assets influences the extent to which current income is available for immediate needs. Third, households may be in receipt of non-cash benefits and services from the state or non-state organisations that would not be reflected in a measure of poverty based on income alone. Fourth, the non-consideration of work-related expenses such as transport and childcare may also affect the net income actually available to support living standards and avoidance of deprivation. Finally, regional differences are also important. Where prices are considerably higher in one part of the country than another, deprivation in high-cost regions may not be captured by a simple income-based indicator.

Reflecting these concerns, social scientists developed an approach to poverty measurement based on access to basic necessities. Basic necessities include food, heating, clothes, shelter and furniture as well as an ability to engage in family and social life. Ireland's second official poverty measure, known as 'consistent poverty', is a hybrid of this approach and the at-risk of poverty rate described above. Households and individuals who are at risk of poverty (earn less than the threshold of 60 per cent of the median), and experience an enforced absence of at least two items from the official deprivation list of 11 items (presented in Table 8.4), are deemed to be in consistent poverty.

Table 8.4 Eleven-Item Basic Deprivation Scale

Two pairs of strong shoes
A warm waterproof overcoat
Buy new rather than second-hand clothes
Eat meals with meat, chicken, fish (or vegetarian equivalent) every second day
Have a roast joint (or equivalent) once a week
Gone without heating during the last 12 months
Able to keep the home adequately warm
Replace any worn-out furniture
Buy presents for friends once a year
Have family or friends for a drink or meal once a month
Have a morning, afternoon or evening out in the past fortnight for entertainment

The absolute and relative measures of poverty discussed so far simply measure the *proportion* of the population falling below a minimum standard of income. They are, however, insensitive to the *depth* of poverty in the sense that transfers from the least poor to the most poor do not reduce poverty, but transfers from the most poor to the least poor may bring some households out of poverty. In this latter scenario, poverty may have been reduced but we cannot claim that social welfare has increased. This is known as a violation of Dalton's Principle of Transfers.[8] An alternative measure, which takes into consideration the depth of poverty, is the poverty-gap measure. It weights the head count measure by how far below the poverty line a given household is and has the advantage of not violating Dalton's Principle of Transfers.

Evidence
How has Ireland performed against these various measures of poverty in recent years? Ireland experienced a decline in the 'at risk of poverty' rate (threshold of 60 per cent of median income) from 20 per cent in 2003 to 14 per cent in 2009, before rising to 16 per cent in 2011 (see Table 8.5). A similar trend was found for consistent poverty which fell from 8.8 per cent in 2003 to 5.5 per cent in 2009, before rising to 6.9 per cent in 2011. The data suggest that the recent financial

crisis and associated increases in unemployment have led to an increase in poverty. Alarmingly, if the social welfare system were stopped, the at risk of poverty rate would be over 50 per cent.

Table 8.5 Key National Indicators of Poverty and Social Exclusion (% of individuals)

	2003	2005	2007	2009	2011
At risk of poverty rate: [1]					
Including transfers	19.7	18.5	16.5	14.1	16.0
Excluding transfers	39.8	40.1	41.0	46.2	50.7
Consistent poverty	8.8	7.0	5.1	5.5	6.9
Poverty gap (EU definition)	22.4	20.6	17.4	16.2	19.6

Source: EU-SILC Surveys 2003–9.
[1] Refers to the 60 per cent threshold.

Research on the socio-demographic characteristics of households in poverty found similar types of household suffering from consistent poverty and being at risk of poverty. The importance of education as a buffer against poverty is evident; those without formal educational qualifications accounted for half of income-poor households in 2007. Families headed by a person ill or disabled formed an increasing share of consistently poor households over the decade.

When we consider poverty over the life cycle, important results are revealed. The period of economic growth up to 2007 was characterised by falls in poverty among children, the working-age population, and the elderly. However, child poverty remains a serious problem in Ireland. By EU standards Ireland in 2010 had among the highest rates of child poverty, with 8.1 per cent of children (93,000) experiencing consistent poverty and 19.5 per cent (224,000) in income poverty.

Inequality and Equality of Opportunity

A focus on equality of opportunity is consistent with the natural dispersion of talent and motivation in society, and with a philosophy that economic outcomes should not reflect predetermined circumstances such as gender, race, place of birth, family endowments of wealth or ethnic group.

We can measure equality of opportunity with a measure of intergenerational socio-economic mobility that captures how people fare in life relative to their parents. Equality of opportunity in education, healthcare and access to employment would mean that young people's outcomes such as income or education are not determined by their parent's outcomes. If this were the case we would say there is high economic mobility between generations. We measure economic mobility with an elasticity measure, where 0 represents the desirable scenario of complete economic mobility between generations and 1 represents a complete absence of economic mobility, a situation where a child is destined for the same outcomes as their parents.

221

Studies of the relationship between the income levels of fathers and sons in high-income countries suggest significant differences. Elasticity estimates for the Scandinavian countries and Canada range from 0.13 to 0.28 depending on the methodology used, suggesting significant levels of economic mobility between generations. In contrast, elasticity estimates for the UK and the USA range between 0.4 and 0.6. It is no surprise that countries with more generous welfare systems and superior state services in health and education enjoy greater levels of socio-economic mobility.

Recent data from the World Bank show that a high proportion of total inequality in Ireland can be attributable to inequality of opportunity when compared with other EU countries. In Ireland 22 per cent of inequality can be attributed to factors over which people have no control: race, gender, birthplace, parents' education and occupation. This compares with 21 per cent in the UK, 19 per cent in the USA, 18 per cent in Germany, 13 per cent in France and 2 per cent in Norway.

Capability Approach to Poverty and Inequality
So far our measures of poverty and inequality have been based on access to resources. Amartya Sen's 1979 essay 'Equality of What?' challenged the focus on economic outcomes and access to resources.[9] Sen argues that these approaches do not consider a range of important aspects of deprivation such as natural/social environment characteristics (pollution and crime levels, for example), personal characteristics (illness which can reduce the ability to participate in society and enjoy material wealth, for example), and freedoms in the political and social sphere. Instead, Sen suggests that poverty be considered as the absence of capabilities or states of being such as being nourished, being loved, being able to work, having an ability to participate in democratic decision making or an ability to pursue one's dreams (see earlier discussion of various dimensions of inequality and poverty).

We can consider a number of examples that vindicate Sen's approach, such as an elderly person with considerable material wealth who is not looked after properly, reducing unnecessarily her range of capabilities; or a malnourished child with a parasitic infection, who may have access to sufficient levels of food but remains malnourished. The merits of the capability approach are undermined by the challenges faced in adhering to Sen's ideas in a practical sense. However, it is worth keeping in mind that it remains an important critique of the more orthodox approaches discussed in this chapter.

5 POLITICAL ECONOMY OF POVERTY AND INEQUALITY REDUCTION

Political Preferences and Systems
Political preferences for redistribution and poverty reduction vary both across and within countries. Political theory suggests that as democracies emerge, there will be an increasing constituency favourably disposed to redistribution. This

occurs because the small number of people who enjoy very high incomes will be out-voted by the majority of voters who earn less than the average income. An alternative theory points to an opposing force, where the initially wealthy use their disproportionate economic resources to influence political outcomes, preventing efforts towards redistribution. Cultural norms of solidarity and work ethic will also play an important role. As discussed in Section 3, political preferences for redistribution will depend not only on an understanding of the benefits of equality but also on sensitivities to the disincentive effects of high taxation and social transfers. Each of these forces combines to define a country's unique set of preferences for redistribution.

Perceptions of inequality can be garnered from globally comparable surveys such as the *World Values Survey*. The survey is conducted across a range of countries and asks respondents in 56 countries whether they believe that incomes should be made more or less equal. The results are striking; in only eight countries the mean preference was in favour of greater income equality, with 46 of the remaining 48 countries characterised by a greater preference for larger income differences as an incentive for individual effort.

The countries that favour more equal incomes include Switzerland, Iran, Germany, Chile, Slovenia, Romania and India. These countries' Gini coefficients range from 0.28 in Germany to 0.52 in Chile, suggesting that a preference for greater income inequality is not necessarily related to current levels of income inequality. A number of developing countries and Eastern European countries, such as Ghana, Mali, Peru, Indonesia and Thailand, as well as Russia and Ukraine, report significant preferences for larger income differences as an incentive for individual effort.

In many societies, people have a strong preference for equality of opportunity over equality of outcome. When presented with the statement, '*It's fair if people have more money or wealth, but only if there are equal opportunities*', the majority of respondents agree. In Britain, the USA and Germany, over 70 per cent more people agree than disagree with that statement.

It is possible to observe the outcome of 200 years of political preferences for redistribution in the welfare states across Europe. We distinguish between four different models.

First, the Scandinavian or 'social democratic model' has a strong focus on social rights and a high degree of universality, and is financed through general taxation and social insurance contributions. The Scandinavian model is considered the most generous welfare state and is associated with high levels of taxation.

Second, the 'continental' or 'social capitalism model' is also characterised by generous welfare benefits, the difference being that benefits rights are often enjoyed by those who contribute through work-based social insurance schemes.

Third, the Anglo-Saxon/UK model is primarily needs-based and combines modest universal schemes and extensive means-tested assistance.

The fourth model, known as the southern European model, involves a more basic system of income redistribution, where the primary source of welfare is often a combination of the family, private charity and the Church, rather than the state. This type of model is in operation in Portugal, Spain and Greece. The USA would be characterised as being at the less generous end, similar to the southern European model.

We can place these four welfare systems into a simplified left–right political spectrum. Ignoring for our purposes consideration of personal freedoms, we define the political right as a low-tax and low redistribution platform and the political left as a high-tax and generous redistribution platform. Referring to our approach taken in Section 3, the political right is more sensitive to moral hazard and welfare dependency, whereas the political left is more sensitive to those who are genuinely in need of state support. The Scandinavian and continental models could be characterised as more left-of-centre welfare models, while the Anglo-Saxon and Southern European models, with their more modest levels of taxation, could be considered to the right of the political spectrum.

Evidence and Position of Ireland

Categorising the Irish welfare model within the four models is less than straightforward. During the economic expansion in the 2000s, Ireland was able to pursue the joint objectives of increases in welfare benefits and a reduction in taxes. Conversely, with the economic downturn of 2008 and the ensuing budget deficits, Ireland was faced with the prospect of tax increases and welfare cuts. In normal economic circumstances, governments operate under a resource constraint and the typical policy choice is between low taxation and low welfare or high taxation and generous welfare. In terms of the four European models, Ireland is best described as a hybrid between the Anglo-Saxon model and the southern European model.

Using indicators of service effort (benefits in kind as a proportion of GDP) and transfer effort (cash benefits as a proportion of GDP), Ireland, along with Greece, Spain and Portugal, can be characterised as having a low-service and transfer effort. Within each category a distinction can be made between transfers that are means tested and those that are not. Ireland fits most comfortably with the Anglo-Saxon model insofar as it aims to provide universal minimum protection with an emphasis on means testing and flat-rate rather than earnings-related provision. Ireland and the UK are both exceptional in the EU for the high proportion of means testing. In Ireland in 2008, 25 per cent of all social expenditure was means tested.

Preferences Over Time

When we compare welfare systems internationally a striking stylised fact emerges. Most countries' chosen balance between taxation and redistribution endures over time. Preferences seem to emanate from deeply held convictions that change very slowly over time. Through survey data we can gain an understanding of the convictions of voters in different countries. In the USA only 29 per cent of respondents surveyed believe that the poor are trapped in poverty.

This contrasts to 60 per cent of Europeans who share this belief. In addition, 60 per cent of Americans believe the poor are lazy, while only 26 per cent of Europeans share this belief. In fact there is no reason to believe that this is the case.[10] It was found that 60 per cent of the members of the bottom quintile of the income distribution in the USA in 1984 remained in that quintile in 1993, while only 46 per cent of Germans in the bottom quintile of their income distribution remained in that bottom quintile nine years later. Besides, there is reason to believe that those in the bottom quintile of the US income distribution work far more hours than their counterparts in many European countries

Despite the consistency in preferences for the welfare system, changes can occur. The deepening of the welfare state has historically been associated with the sweeping to power of left-of-centre governments, often during times of great economic and political challenge such as the Great Depression or emerging from World War II. In the USA, one component of the policies pursued by Franklin Delano Roosevelt between 1933 and 1936, collectively known as the New Deal, comprised the Social Security Act of 1935. The Act enshrined in US law for the first time the right to benefits for retirees and the unemployed. In the UK, following World War II, Clement Attlee's Labour Party government not only established a universal public healthcare system, the National Health Service, but introduced significant welfare benefits such as flat-rate pensions, sickness benefit, unemployment benefit, child benefit and funeral benefit.

Reverses to the welfare system are also possible. As noted in Section 2, the emergence of centre right governments in the early 1980s in the USA and the UK led to an increase in inequality as welfare states were weakened and taxes reduced.

In Ireland, the domination of centrist populist political parties since the foundation of the state has meant the slow evolution of the welfare state and the absence of revolutionary reform. The current crisis may have provided the opportunity for a radical revision of the Irish welfare state, either a strengthening of its reach or its reduction to lessen the excess burden of taxation and disincentive effects. In the watershed election of 2011, Ireland elected a centrist coalition, and with a high likelihood of both increased taxes and reductions in state benefits due to fiscal tightening, it seems unlikely that significant reform in either direction will be possible in the foreseeable future. Nevertheless, the 2011 election saw a historical peak in first preferences for left-wing parties and independents.

As Ireland emerges from the current downturn, a very serious underlying political economy issue will take centre stage in Irish politics and that is the issue of an ageing population who will make up an even bigger proportion of the voting public. The ageing population who have paid taxes right through their working lives will expect that, even in challenging times for the public finances, old age pensions are maintained at reasonable levels. As the Irish population ages and people live longer, the influence of pensioners in the Irish political system will increase over time.

6 POLICY EFFORTS AND CHALLENGES

In the pursuit of social justice a number of alternative approaches can be taken by governments. The legislative framework provides the rules that underpin equal opportunity. However, the achievement of equal opportunity takes considerably more effort than the existence of legal rights. The provision of public minimum levels of education and healthcare needs to be supplemented by a minimum standard of living for all citizens to ensure that social mobility between generations is possible and that people are fully rewarded for their talents and efforts irrespective of social background. This section describes Ireland's policies aimed at reducing inequality and poverty and focuses on Ireland's policy responses, social transfers in particular, towards vulnerable groups. It is worth noting that the public provision of healthcare and education remain essential to the pursuit of equality of opportunity and this aspect of health and education policies is covered in detail in Chapters 12 and 13.

Equality Legislation
The starting point for pursuing equality of opportunity is legislation. There have been several important policy and legislative changes to progress equality in Ireland over the last number of years. These include the adoption of equality legislation, namely the Employment Equality Act 1998, and the Equal Status Act 2000, and the establishment of equality institutions, namely the Equality Authority and the Office of the Director of Equality Investigations. The Employment Equality Act outlaws discrimination in employment on nine distinct grounds – gender, family status, marital status, age, disability, sexual orientation, religion, race, or being a member of the traveller community. The Equal Status Act goes a step further, providing comprehensive legal protection against discrimination in the delivery of goods and services, whether provided by the state or private sector. Further, the establishment of the Disability Authority and the Human Rights Commission are developments with potential to contribute to reducing poverty, inequality and discrimination.

Social Transfers
Social transfers represent the foundation of the modern welfare state (see Chapter 3) and they come in various guises, each with different effects on incentives and social justice. Transfers can differ in coverage levels, either universal or targeted, and form taken – money or in-kind transfers.

Universal payments are paid regardless of a person's income or social insurance record. Universal cash entitlements can be simple to administer, but fail to discriminate between deserving and non-deserving cases. An excellent example of a universal entitlement is child benefit, which was introduced in 1944.

Effective targeting of entitlements can be considered more socially just, particularly when the savings from targeting outweighs the administrative costs of means testing. Examples of targeted benefits provided to citizens once a means test is satisfied include the family income supplement for the low paid and the one-parent family payment. The jobseeker's allowance involves a different form of conditionality. To receive the jobseeker's allowance one must be unemployed but available for and genuinely seeking work. The weekly benefit is €188. In Budget 2010 this was reduced for those under the age of 25 to encourage engagement in training and further education (see also Chapter 6).

Table 8.6 Summary of the Irish Welfare System

Group Served	Government Intervention (Type)	Complementary Policies
Unemployed	Unemployment insurance, known as jobseeker's allowance (targeted) Back to work programmes (targeted)	Rent supplement Mortgage interest supplement Fuel allowance (means tested)
Low paid	Family income supplement (targeted and means tested)	Minimum wage laws Fuel allowance (means tested)
Children	Child benefit (universal) Early childhood care and education (both universal and targeted) Back to school clothing and footwear allowance (targeted and means tested)	Child protection laws
Lone parents	One-parent family payment (targeted and means tested)	Fuel allowance (means tested)
Elderly	Contributory pensions (conditional on PRSI contributions) Non-contributory pensions (means tested)	Free travel (universal) Fuel allowance (means tested)
Widow, widower or surviving civil partner (WWSCP)	WWSCP contributory pensions (conditional on PRSI contributions) WWSCP non-contributory pensions (means tested)	Bereavement grant (conditional on PRSI contributions)
Illness	Illness benefit (targeted) Blind and invalidity pension (targeted, means tested) Back to work programmes (targeted)	Fuel allowance (means tested)
Special groups	Disability insurance Carer's allowance (targeted, means tested)	Affirmative action for minorities Fuel allowance (means tested)

Economic theory suggests that cash transfers are preferred by recipients because it allows them to choose their preferred basket of goods. In contrast, in-kind transfers allow a paternalistic state to tilt recipients' expenditure patterns towards goods and services, such as fuel and education, the consumption of which is deemed in their interest. Examples in Ireland of in-kind entitlements include the fuel allowance given to the elderly as well as the public provision of healthcare and education (see Chapters 12 and 13). If the recipient does not derive much satisfaction from the in-kind transfer provided, they would have been better off receiving the transfer in cash to spend on goods of their choosing.

Table 8.6 outlines the multifaceted nature of the Irish welfare system. Social transfers exist for a variety of groups who have experienced adverse outcomes such as the unemployed, the low paid, individuals who experience illness or disability, and bereaved partners. Groups at risk of poverty, such as the elderly and lone parents, are also provided for. A number of transfer schemes, such as the family income supplement, the carer's allowance and the fuel allowance, as well as the non-contributory pension, are subjected to a means test on income or wealth. Another set of benefits are provided conditional on a record of Pay Related Social Insurance (PRSI) contributions made while in previous paid employment. This chapter now delves into policies focused on two of the most vulnerable groups at risk of poverty, namely children and the elderly.

Children

As children represent the future of Ireland, government intervention is essential to reduce the high poverty rates among the young. Table 8.6 details four different policies aimed at increasing equality of opportunity and reducing child poverty in Ireland, two of which will now be discussed (the others relate to education policy).

Child Benefit

As a universal entitlement, child benefit is paid to all parents in the state towards the cost of rearing a child and was increased significantly during the 2000s. The cost of child benefit to the state rose from 6 per cent of all social welfare spending to 10 per cent over the 20 years from 1993 to 2014. In 2014, the rate for the first and second child is €130 per child per month. With the need to reduce government expenditure a key priority, many have advocated that child benefit become a means-tested payment. From the perspective of social justice, this would seem to be an appropriate course of action, yet the administrative and perhaps political challenges of doing so have so far prevented such a change.

Lone Parents

In 2006, the government published a discussion paper on proposals for reforming the way the welfare system supports lone parents that is still relevant.[11] The report pointed to the fact that children of lone parents have a high probability of experiencing poverty. According to the EU-SILC survey of Ireland in 2011 almost 50 per cent of individuals in single-parent families are at risk of poverty, while 30 per cent experience consistent poverty. This is much higher than the national figure and compares unfavourably to rates of poverty in two-parent families. To address this phenomenon, in 1997 the government introduced the one-parent family payment (OFP), which provides a payment for men and women who are bringing up children without the support of a partner.

To qualify for the lone-parent payment one must be a parent or legal guardian, not living with a spouse or civil partner or cohabiting, have an income of less than €425 per week and satisfy a means test. In 2014, the OFP provided a weekly payment of €188 for those unemployed or earning less than €90 per week, and €29.80 for each dependent child. If a parent or guardian is in receipt of the OFP, they cannot also be in receipt of the jobseeker's allowance. There are two main differences between the OFP and the jobseeker's allowance. OFP recipients receive additional payments for each child and, unlike recipients of jobseeker's allowance, do not have to prove that they are looking for work or engage in back-to-work training.

The 2006 Discussion Paper recommended that reform was required to re-orientate the incentives to encourage lone parents to enter the workforce. The report argued that passive income supports alone were not sufficient to comprehensively address poverty. There were perhaps good reasons to argue that encouraging lone parents into the workplace would lead to an increase in household income and act as a good example to children and their peer group. However, one might also take the alternative view that lone parents experience significant parenting pressures and provide an important caring role and should not be pushed into the workplace. As many of the recommendations of the 2006 report have not yet been implemented, the subtle debate over whether the current OFP involves disincentive effects that ultimately condemn many one-parent families to unemployment will continue.

Elderly Population
Pensions Provision
As the Irish population becomes older in the next 50 years, issues of intergenerational equity will take centre stage in policy debates. At present a significant part of the Irish pension system is paid for by present-day taxpayers, whereby taxes paid by the working generation finance the consumption of retired generations. This is known as a pay as you go system and aptly describes the public component or first pillar of the Irish pension system as well as the generous pension scheme for public sector workers involving a commitment of a monthly pension of 50 per cent of final salary (adjusted over time). From the perspective of poverty reduction, the non-contributory pension provides a minimum standard of living for elderly people in the state.

The second pillar of the Irish pension system comprises private voluntary pensions and while just over 50 per cent of the workforce have enrolled in private pensions, their financial depth even before the recent financial crisis was insufficient. It has been estimated that middle-income earners would have to save an additional 10 per cent of income per year to provide a pension of 50 per cent of pre-retirement income. The third pillar typically refers to non-pension wealth such as other financial assets or property assets that can be wound down in retirement to fund consumption.

Part of the reason for the unsustainable public pension costs and insufficient private saving for retirement involves underlying demographic changes and each raises important issues of intergenerational equity. The OECD predicts that old-age dependency rates, the ratio of old-age dependents to working-age population, will increase in Ireland from an average of 20 per cent in 1990 to 45 per cent by 2050. This means that where the taxes of five workers were available to pay the cost of each elderly person in 1990, by 2050 OECD countries will have to rely on the taxes of two workers for each elderly person. Ireland will reach an old-age dependency ratio of 45 per cent about 20 years after the majority of western European countries, because of our high birth rates in the 1980s and significant immigration between 1993 and 2008.

In addition, the cost of healthcare has been rising faster than the overall cost of living (see Chapter 12): between 1994 and 2013, healthcare costs rose by 57 per cent compared with cumulative inflation of 36 per cent. As medical treatments become increasingly sophisticated, this trend is likely to continue, putting further pressure on the standard of living of the elderly population.

Intra- and Intergenerational Inequity

The unsustainable public pension costs, the insufficient private savings, and the high personal wealth of a small number of elderly people will lead to significant issues of intra-generational and intergenerational equity in future years. Public sector workers recruited before 2013 enjoy a guaranteed pension of 50 per cent of final salary, compared with significantly lower pension provision for the vast majority of workers with private pensions. In addition, the recent financial crisis has devastated many private pension funds, reducing further the monthly payments, while public sector pension funds have been unaffected. For private sector workers without private pensions, the contributory pension will only offer 20 per cent of final income if their final salary is twice the average income.

In essence, the taxpayers of today are paying taxes today for the currently retired, but the pension benefits are unequally split between retired public and private sector workers. In the medium term, as the old-age dependency rate rises to EU levels, Ireland will be faced with a significant transfer of resources from a shrinking working population to a growing elderly population. If public sector pensions are maintained at current levels, and the non-contributory pension remains at 34 per cent of gross annual industrial earnings (GAIE), significantly higher taxation, and associated costs, will be required to keep the promises made to the growing elderly population.

Looming Pensions Crisis

A number of policy options exist to help Ireland deal with the looming pensions crisis and associated inequities, each with implications for social justice. These include increasing the pension age, encouraging private saving for retirement and reducing pension entitlements.

First, increasing the pension age helps reduce the old-age dependency rate by increasing the number of people in paid employment. For those looking forward to retirement this may not be a welcome prospect, but efforts in this direction have already begun. In the National Pensions Framework published in 2010, plans to increase to 66 the eligibility age for the state pension were announced. A commitment to gradually increase the state pension age to 68 by 2028 was also given. If you are currently under the age of 25, it would be prudent to assume that you will not receive the state pension until 70 years of age.

Second, the government can use tax policy to encourage people to save for their own retirement through private voluntary pensions. At present, taxpayers can avail of tax relief at their personal marginal rate of tax when they divert a proportion of their earnings into a private pension scheme. The current system discriminates against low earners. High earners can enjoy tax relief on pension contributions at the higher rate of tax, whereas low earners who pay tax at the lower rate can only avail of tax relief of 20 per cent.

To deal with this inequity, the National Pensions Framework has proposed that the current tax relief scheme be replaced by a state contribution equal to 33 per cent tax relief for all private pension contributions, but as of 2014 this has not been introduced. A complementary policy, introduced in recent years, is the mandatory offering of private pension schemes to all private sector workers over a certain minimum age.

The third approach, the reduction in state pension levels, is perhaps the most controversial from the perspective of social justice, but is nevertheless a real possibility. With an estimated 10.1 per cent of GNP diverted to state pensions in 2056, if the 34 per cent of GAIE is honoured, the likelihood exists, however painful, that the state pension will have to fall. Increasing the pension age will reduce this cost to some degree, but the cost may still prove too great.

The fourth option is to renege on promises to public servants and reduce public sector pension entitlements. While this is a challenging reform from a political and legal perspective, it should be considered a viable approach. The political obstacles to reforming the public sector pension system have meant that most changes are only relevant for new entrants to the public sector.

The final policy option involves a deliberate attempt to increase the size of the working-age population in paid employment through immigration or an increase in the fertility rate. Such policies will help reduce the old-age dependency rate and provide much-needed revenue to pay for pension costs, but their usefulness is dependent on the availability of paid employment. The long-term solution to the looming pension crisis will likely be some combination of all four policies.

7 CONCLUSION

In most developed countries a broad political consensus prevails; policy should seek to ensure equality of opportunity accompanied by a minimum standard of living for all. As a result, political competition and debate generally focuses on modest proposals, aimed at either deepening the welfare system in the pursuit of greater equality or the strengthening of individual incentives through tax reductions and smaller state benefits. Today's consensus is based both on notions of social justice that inspire redistribution and provision of public services and lessons about the distortionary effects of high levels of taxation laid bare by the failed communist political experiments of the 20th century.

Behind the consensus, the level of redistribution varies across countries, and these differences can be observed in the depth of the welfare state and the associated level of taxation preferred by voters. When we compared Ireland with other countries in Section 5, we noted that Ireland is characterised by low taxation and modest levels of redistribution by European standards.

However, it is worth noting that the policy of modest social transfers and the public provision of basic services is unlikely to lead to dramatic reductions in inequality and relative poverty within countries, for two reasons. First, even when high-quality education and healthcare are provided to all citizens, modest social transfers fail to provide a level playing field for children in the face of significant inequalities in income and, especially, wealth. The cross-country evidence suggests that higher levels of redistribution are an essential ingredient, along with the provision of public services, to achieve high levels of social mobility between generations. Second, as it is possible for some members of society to reject government provision of education and healthcare, opting instead for often higher-quality alternatives in private markets, the option to reject undermines attempts at achieving inequality of opportunity.

In the lead-up to the economic crisis, Ireland was in the fortunate and unique position of having sufficient resources to increase social transfers while reducing taxation. While this was unlikely to continue indefinitely, the speed of Ireland's downturn after 2007 and depth of the subsequent fiscal crisis has cast doubt on Ireland's ability to afford the current welfare system. The continued need to reduce Ireland's fiscal deficit is likely to overshadow concerns of inequality and poverty in the short to medium term.

Nevertheless, while trying to balance the books Ireland should tread carefully. Lower inequality and poverty is an important cornerstone for Ireland's competitiveness, while reducing the long-term fiscal burden of challenging social problems. Of course, the primary objective of government is not to help build a high-income and successful economy as an end in itself, but as a means to supporting a trusting, co-operative and self-actualised society.

Section 2 noted how more equal societies are specifically characterised by higher levels of trust and co-operation. It could be argued that now that Ireland has become one of the richest countries in the world, government policy should shift to building a more equal society with more meaningful levels of equality of opportunity. Voters will ultimately decide if this is a priority objective for Ireland in the coming years.

As Ireland emerges from the fiscal crisis, election after election the Irish people will be asked to adjudicate on proposed changes to taxation and redistribution levels that will affect the degree of inequality and poverty experienced in society. On each occasion, a full understanding of the benefits of lower inequality and poverty as well as the costs to economic efficiency from higher taxation will be the starting point for debate as we ponder our future direction.

Notes

1   S. Kuznets, 'Economic growth and income inequality', *American Economic Review*, Vol. 45, No. 1, 1955.

2   T. Piketty, *Capitalism in the Twenty-First Century*, Harvard University Press, Cambridge MA 2014.

3   'For richer, for poorer', *The Economist*, 13 October 2012.

4   R. Kanbur, 'Income distribution and development', in A. Atkinson and F. Bourguignon (eds), *Handbook of Income Distribution*, North Holland, Amsterdam 2000.

5   See for example J. Stiglitz, *The Price of Inequality: How Today's Divided Society Endangers our Future*, Norton, New York 2012.

6   R. Wilkinson, and K. Pickett, *The Spirit Level: How More Equal Societies Almost Always Do Better*, Allen Lane, London 2009.

7   Bank of Ireland, *Wealth of the Nation*, Bank of Ireland, Dublin 2007.

8   H. Dalton, 'The measurement of the inequality of incomes', *Economic Journal*, Vol. 30, 1920.

9   A. Sen, 'Equality of What?', Tanner Lecture on Human Values, delivered at Stanford University, 22 May 1979.

10 E. Glaeser, 'Inequality', National Bureau of Economic Research (NBER) Working Paper 11511, Boston 2005.

11 Government of Ireland, *Proposals for Supporting Lone Parents*, Department of Social Protection, Dublin 2006.

Policy Issues in the Market Sector

CHAPTER 9

Manufacturing and Internationally Traded Services

Carol Newman*

1 INTRODUCTION

A Process of Continuous Structural Change

As history demonstrates, economic development brings a gradual process of structural change whereby a dependence on the agricultural sector in the early stages of development is replaced by a process of industrialisation creating a strong and vibrant manufacturing sector. Recent developments in the world economy have changed the very nature of industry and service provision.

Globalisation and the liberalisation of trade, particularly in developing countries, has led to a fragmentation of production processes which has changed the way goods are produced and the nature of trade itself. Countries compete vigorously for investment from multinational companies (MNCs) which seek out the most competitive locations for the various components of their activities. For developing countries this is usually the low-skilled manufacturing component of the production process. High-income countries, such as Ireland, are attractive because of their high-skilled labour force, but competition between countries for investment in the higher value-added manufacturing and the services components of MNC activities is still fierce. Low-tax regimes are therefore an important attraction for MNCs.

The fragmentation of production means that trade between countries is increasingly characterised by trade between firms, not in final goods but in tasks, with each task performed along the production process, adding further value to the global supply chain.[1] This creates challenges for global governance structures, particularly in relation to taxation and capital flows.

These changes have meant that most developed economies have experienced a decline in the share of output and employment attributable to the manufacturing sector and a corresponding increase in the role and importance of services. Ireland is no exception, with the contribution of manufacturing to output declining from 34 per cent in the late 1990s to 26 per cent in recent years, a large proportion of which consists of outflows of profits of MNCs. Rising costs have led to many manufacturing firms, including Irish-owned firms, seeking alternative production locations. This has happened to such an extent that recently Ireland has become a net investor abroad. As a result emphasis has shifted away from traditional manufacturing sectors towards high value-added activities such as high-skilled manufacturing and internationally traded services. This structural change will have consequences for Irish economic growth given the historical importance of the manufacturing sector in terms of its contribution to employment, internationally traded activities, and aggregate productivity growth.

Focus of the Chapter

This chapter focuses on the key features of the manufacturing and internationally traded services sectors in Ireland. Both sectors contribute significantly to output, employment and exports, but both are dependent on the world economy, which makes them particularly vulnerable to world market conditions and unfavourable changes in domestic competitiveness. Increasingly the boundaries between what is classed as manufacturing industry and what is classed as services are blurred, making it difficult to discuss one sector without making significant reference to the other.

In this chapter, a clear distinction is made between the modern and the traditional manufacturing sectors, the former covering all high-technology enterprises, most of which are MNCs, and the latter including all other sectors, the vast majority of which are indigenous. Small and medium-sized enterprises (SMEs) have received renewed attention in the aftermath of the financial crisis, in Ireland and elsewhere, due to their employment intensity and importance for the generation of real economic activity. The success of the SME sector in Germany and its role in cushioning the German economy during the crisis has also added fuel to this renewed emphasis.

Non-traded and traded services are also differentiated in this chapter. Non-traded services are those which must be consumed at the point of purchase, such as retail trade or hospitality, while traded services are those that can transcend borders; they rely to a large extent on sophisticated technology and telecommunications networks. In this chapter we focus on the latter – the former are covered elsewhere in the book (see Chapters 5, 11, 12 and 13).

While the focus is on long-run trends in manufacturing and internationally traded services, the consequences of the current economic crisis for these sectors, although transient in nature, cannot be ignored. During a recession depressed world markets will reduce the demand for all goods and services, including Irish exports, and given the outward focus of the manufacturing and traded services sectors in Ireland is likely to have significant short-term implications for their performance.

Ireland's export performance is discussed, with evidence suggesting that Ireland has weathered this particular storm well, for the most part due to the strong performance of the internationally traded services sector. The collapse of the banking sector also had effects on enterprise development in Ireland by severely limiting the availability of credit to SMEs, thus stifling entrepreneurship and the growth of indigenous firms. Despite the inclusion of provisions in the Programme for Government for ensuring access to finance for viable SMEs, they continue to be credit constrained, and to an even greater extent than in the rest of Europe. The most significant, potentially long-term, consequence of the current crisis for the manufacturing and internationally traded services sectors is the deterioration of the public finances, leading to rising taxes on employment and limited funding available for providing the types of service enterprises need to grow and prosper. In particular, a major concern in relation to the public finances is the extent to which government support for education, technology, innovation and research can continue into the future.

The collapse in employment levels since the onset of the crisis, particularly in the construction sector, will have consequences for the manufacturing and internationally traded sectors if the displaced workers do not have the skills demanded (see Chapters 6 and 13). Moreover, Ireland's ability to innovate and engage in research and development (R&D) activities will be crucial if new opportunities in the high value-added technology and services sectors are to be exploited. It appears, at least for now, that these parts of government expenditure have been ring-fenced and are an important component of the government's recovery strategy, but the sustainability of high levels of investment is in question.

There have also been some positive aspects to the current crisis for manufacturing and internationally traded services sectors that are worth mentioning. Ireland's performance in relation to cost competitiveness has improved leading to falling costs of production for the first time in over a decade. Furthermore, with excess labour supply there are real opportunities for improvements in labour productivity at a new lower equilibrium wage.

While it is clear that the impact of the crisis cannot be ignored, the discussion here is more concerned with the nature and importance of the manufacturing and internationally traded sectors and the broader issues of relevance to their growth and development. The remainder of the chapter is structured as follows.

Section 2 begins by discussing the rationale for government supports for the manufacturing and internationally traded services sectors and discusses the role that direct interventions in the form of fiscal incentives and grants have played in Irish industrial policy. A brief discussion of the role of regional policy initiatives and the future policy agenda for Irish government is also provided. Section 3 looks at the nature and importance of the manufacturing sector by analysing trends in output, employment, productivity and exports. Section 4 describes the internationally traded services sector and its contribution to the Irish economy. In Section 5, the role of foreign direct investment (FDI), the major component of manufacturing and internationally traded services in Ireland, is explored, with emphasis on the importance of productivity spillovers for economic growth. The increasing levels of outward direct investment (ODI) are also given some attention. Section 6 concludes the chapter with a discussion of some emerging issues relating to the strategic development of manufacturing and internationally traded services in Ireland.

2 ROLE AND EVOLUTION OF INDUSTRIAL POLICY

Rationale for Government Intervention

Industrial policy covers all government interventions that affect the activities of firms operating in the industrial sector. The types of policy aimed at supporting industry are wide-reaching, ranging from policies that affect the ability of firms to trade and compete on world markets to the direct provision of financial assistance to firms in the form of grants or tax incentives. The primary aim of industrial policy is to promote economic growth through creating jobs and facilitating productivity improvements.

Modern industrial policy is increasingly relevant to firms operating in the traded services sector, which behave very much like modern manufacturing firms in terms of their ability to trade internationally, innovate and experience productivity improvements. This is reflected in the recent change in terminology used in Ireland from *industrial* policy to *enterprise* policy. Regional development policy, as shall be discussed later, also plays a role in fulfilling equity objectives through redistributing resources to disadvantaged areas. In particular, promoting economic activity in rural locations affected by the decline in the importance of the agricultural sector has been a key feature of Irish and EU industrial policy objectives.

Aside from equity considerations, the rationale for state intervention in the manufacturing and internationally traded services sectors is justifiable where market failure occurs. Thus, the role for government in the provision of infrastructure, the education and training of the labour force and the promotion of R&D activities, all of which improve competitiveness and thus the productivity of firms and their ability to compete, is clear and economically justifiable. Infrastructural investments can be justified on public good grounds (see Chapter 3). R&D expenditures confer positive external effects in the form of productivity spillovers; the social return exceeds the private return, making private investment alone sub-optimal, thus justifying public R&D investments. Investment in education and training are covered by a number of justifications, including public good and equity arguments but also information and credit market failures (see Chapter 13).

Direct financial supports to specific firms and industries are more difficult to justify on economic grounds. For example, providing supports to sectors that are in decline as a result of an inability to compete on world markets is not justifiable as no market failure has occurred. In contrast, government intervention to support a particular activity that is not taking place due to information failures is economically justifiable, for example the promotion of environmental awareness. Moreover, the productivity spillovers associated with high-technology activities form the key rationale for financial supports aimed at promoting R&D investments by the private sector and in attracting technology-intensive MNCs.

In fulfilling economic growth objectives, industrial policy increasingly focuses on creating favourable economic conditions so that firms can efficiently operate and effectively compete. Both the theoretical and empirical economics literature propose that a key determinant of growth is the extent of openness of economies in terms of both trade and capital markets. The past two decades have seen an increasingly integrated world economy primarily through the expansion, both in scope and membership, of the World Trade Organisation (WTO). The role of industrial policy has thus moved away from providing direct financial assistance and towards removing constraints to competition; facilitating productivity improvements through creating a low-cost environment, good physical infrastructure and encouraging R&D investments and productivity spillovers; and promoting trade and foreign investment.

Key Features of Industrial Policy in Ireland

Ireland's approach to industrial policy has involved a combination of direct interventions in the form of capital grants and tax incentives for industry, and policies aimed at creating the right conditions for these sectors to evolve, including labour market policies, policies aimed at encouraging exports and inward investment, and regional development policies. In fact, the most often cited contributing factor to Ireland's growth performance over the last two decades was the change in policy emphasis, dating back to the 1960s, towards an outward-looking focus, particularly in the manufacturing sector (see Chapters 1 and 7).

The key development that changed the nature of industrial policy in Ireland was Ireland's entry into the European Union in 1973 and subsequent commitment to free trade within the EU internal market. Not only did this add to the attractiveness of Ireland as a location for foreign investors, but it also expanded the size of the market for domestic firms. Ireland also benefited from the macro-economic policy discipline imposed by signing up to the Maastricht Treaty in 1992 and by structural and cohesion funds which were invested in the public infrastructure system and rural development initiatives.

These measures were important in improving Ireland's competitiveness and making it an attractive place to do business. The evolution of industrial policy in Ireland is discussed in detail in Chapter 1 and policy issues relating to labour markets, human capital investments and regulation, all of which fall under the umbrella of industrial policy, are covered elsewhere in the book (see Chapters 5, 6, 7 and 13). Here we focus on two direct policy intervention tools which, despite the lack of a clear economic rationale for their use, have proved instrumental to the success of the manufacturing sector, and to a lesser extent internationally traded services. The first is fiscal incentives in the form of low corporation profits taxes and the possibilities for double non-taxation by MNCs to which low taxes give rise. The second is direct capital grants to firms. The regional dimension of industrial policy in Ireland is briefly addressed with particular emphasis on the role of the EU in this regard.

Corporation Taxes

The importance of corporation taxes in attracting FDI is well documented in the literature and is one of the key factors contributing to Ireland's attractiveness as a place to invest.[2] In the early stages of EU membership, in an effort to promote inward foreign investment and indigenous exports, the Irish government introduced full corporate tax relief on profits generated through export sales. Coupled with the other favourable conditions for investment, including free access to the large EU market, an English-speaking, relatively low-cost labour supply and strong cultural connections with the USA, Ireland became one of the most FDI-intensive countries in Europe.

A strategy of low rates of profit taxes has since been an important feature of Irish industrial policy. However, pressure from the EU Commission to harmonise taxes across all EU countries since the late 1970s has continually threatened to eliminate Ireland's competitive advantage in this regard. In response to changes in EU legislation, in 1978 export profit tax relief was phased out and replaced by a 10 per cent rate for all manufacturing and some internationally traded services. Subsequent pressures to harmonise taxes across sectors led in 1993 to Ireland introducing a 12.5 per cent rate for all sectors. This rate, however, still remains substantially below the average for Western Europe but pressures to increase the rate as part of the EU bail-out package have been met with considerable concern and objection from Ireland (see Chapter 4).

Double Non-taxation

In the aftermath of the financial crisis, tax avoidance by MNCs has received significant attention in the media and by international organisations, such as the OECD and the IMF, and national-level governments. While tax avoidance is legal it is undesirable for a number of reasons. It substantially reduces government tax revenue and is regressive in that it allows the very large corporations to end up paying very little, or in some cases no, tax on their profits. It is also harmful to small businesses that compete with large MNCs who pay substantially less tax and so have a lower cost base.

Tax avoidance by MNCs is made possible by an unco-ordinated international tax framework that allows corporations to manipulate the system, in often very complex ways, in order to avoid paying tax. It is commonly termed 'double non-taxation' given that it involves MNCs finding loopholes in double taxation agreements. The latter are bilateral or multilateral agreements that are in place to prevent companies being taxed twice. This is an issue for the manufacturing and internationally traded services sectors in Ireland since some of the major investors – Google and Apple, among others – have received considerable media attention regarding how little corporation tax they actually pay. Aggressive tax planning strategies of MNCs most commonly involve tax base erosion and profit switching (or 'BEPS' in the terminology of the Organisation for Economic Co-operation and Development (OECD)). This involves moving profits across borders to take advantage of lower tax rates. It results in profits being booked in low-tax countries without any real economic activity taking place there.

There are a number of different mechanisms that MNCs can use to avoid paying tax in this way. In the Irish case transfer pricing is a commonly used tool;

it involves the MNC setting the prices of goods and services that its various parts buy from and sell to each other in such a way that the profits are artificially shifted to the low-tax jurisdiction. This is often done, for example, through the transfer of intangibles such as intellectual property, copyrights and patents. Ireland's low corporation tax rate makes it an attractive destination for these artificial profits.

Other tools include the establishment of special-purpose entities which have no real presence in a country but act as a holding company or group financing entity, and hybrids which have dual residence and attempt to have the same money treated differently for tax purposes in different countries. In practice tax avoidance schemes are complex and usually involve a variety of different tools to move money around in such a way as to pay the minimum tax possible.[3]

It is likely that this issue will receive even more attention in the years to come. In 2013 the OECD produced a 15-point Action Plan for addressing BEPS within the international tax framework. This will involve increased co-operation between countries on tax policy, which is likely to be politically difficult given that many of the loopholes in place are not unintentional and will lead to a loss in competitive advantage in attracting FDI for some countries, including Ireland.[4]

Capital Grants

Capital grants have played an important role in the support and evolution of the manufacturing sector in Ireland. Since the 1950s grants have been made available to firms in the manufacturing sector for capital investments. These grants were for all companies producing manufactured goods for export. In the early stages of EU membership financial assistance was also given to domestic companies prepared to restructure following the introduction to free trade. The Industrial Development Authority (IDA), established in 1949, was responsible for the provision of grants; it was later split into IDA Ireland, which became responsible for grant provision to foreign companies, and Enterprise Ireland (formerly Forbairt), which became responsible for supports to Irish companies.

Over time, the awarding of grants became more aligned with strategic priorities for the sector and grants were extended to cover a range of activities including training and R&D as well as loan guarantees, among others. In the 1970s, for example, priority was given to the development of high value-added sectors including electronics, chemicals, pharmaceuticals and healthcare through the process of attracting foreign multinational market leaders in these sectors. These policies were considered a success, particularly given the agglomeration effects observed in these sectors in subsequent years when competition for investment intensified. Ireland was a tried and tested location for high value-added sectors and an increasing number of firms wanted to be a part of this emerging hub of high value-added economic activity.

A number of developments over the course of the 1980s and 1990s further changed the way in which grants were awarded. The *Telesis Report* in 1984 called for a change in emphasis toward developing domestic industry while the

Culliton Report in 1992 called for a reduction in the use of grants and a shift in focus toward policies aimed at improving competitiveness more generally. Furthermore, from 1994, EU state aid rules determined the permissible size of grants awarded. As a result, grants are now awarded on the basis of geographical location, the skill levels of the people employed, and the nature of the activities being carried out. Emphasis is placed on activities in the high-tech sector, which increasingly covers service-type activities.

Overall, the role of grant supports has been important to the evolution of the industrial sector in Ireland with strong empirical evidence to support their association with employment generation. However, since 2006, changes to EU limits have further restricted the extent to which state aid can be provided. Consequentially, the government must look to other means of maintaining Ireland's competitive position in terms of attracting FDI and promoting sectors of strategic importance.

Regional Development Policy
The decline in the importance of the agricultural sector will generally lead to a gradual outward migration from rural areas to urban centres. The earliest forms of industrial grant in Ireland were given to companies, both foreign- and Irish-owned, to establish in peripheral locations that were disadvantaged in resources as a result of this process of structural change. An important dimension of the IDA's development strategy has been focused on achieving an even redistribution of manufacturing employment throughout Ireland.

Regional development policy objectives have also been facilitated to a large extent by EU Structural Funds, created to help underdeveloped regions within the EU in a number of different ways aimed at promoting regional industrial development. There is some evidence that these policies were successful, given that the levels of migration from rural to urban areas observed in most developing countries did not materialise in Ireland. However, the most successful regional locations are those located around urban centres where industrial clusters, and the benefits that go with them, such as increasing returns to scale and productivity spillovers, for example, were already well developed.

While the regional flavour to industrial policy has diminished considerably, particularly due to the widespread acknowledgement of the benefits of agglomeration, most direct financial supports provided to firms are decided on a case-by-case basis and as such a certain regional dimension still remains in Irish industrial policy. The spatial dimension to economic development is now explicitly incorporated into the National Development Plan, under the Rural Social and Economic Development Programme and covers a range of Irish- and EU-funded initiatives such as LEADER and INTERREG.

Future Policy Agenda
The most significant industrial policy developments at an EU level in recent times are set out in the Lisbon Agenda, which was established by the European

Council in 2000 with the aim of making the EU 'the most dynamic and competitive knowledge-based economy in the world capable of sustainable economic growth with more and better jobs and greater social cohesion, and respect for the environment by 2010'. Its successor, Europe 2020, launched in 2010, placed greater emphasis on addressing the challenges of the economic crisis while continuing with the principal aim of its predecessor to transform the EU into a 'smart, sustainable and inclusive economy'.

For Ireland, the National Reform Programme sets out five national targets relating to employment, R&D, climate change, education and poverty. Progress towards achieving these targets is updated annually and submitted to the European Commission. The crisis has meant that progress has been slow, although as outlined in the National Reform Programme 2013, Ireland has begun to gain some ground as the economy begins to emerge on the other side of a slow and difficult recovery process.[5]

Since 2008, the Irish government has been committed to developing the smart economy and policies aimed at promoting research and innovation. The strategy consisted of prioritising innovation-driven enterprise and high-quality employment. Particular emphasis was placed on a number of sectors, including: key services sectors, such as health informatics, financial analytics and digital lifestyle management; tourism; the food sector; life sciences; software; the creative arts; next generation network-enabled sectors; the internationalisation of domestic construction expertise; and developing technologies to support the lifestyles of an ageing population.[6] Recently, the emphasis has shifted towards job creation more generally with the publication of the *Action Plan for Jobs* under the newly named Department of Jobs, Enterprise and Innovation in 2012. The action plan is co-ordinated by Forfás and aims to mobilise all government departments to work towards creating jobs.[7]

Of critical importance to the job creation process is the creation of a more competitive business environment. This is particularly the case given the increasing levels of competition for investment from China and Central and Eastern European countries and the challenge of sustaining high levels of investment in education, R&D and infrastructure amidst a public finance crisis. Competitiveness continues to be at the heart of the government's strategy for job creation and growth.

3 NATURE AND IMPORTANCE OF THE MANUFACTURING SECTOR

This section reviews the trends in output and employment in the manufacturing sector over the last two decades. An important indicator of performance is productivity and given that the manufacturing sector is the main productive sector of the economy, understanding the constraints to productivity growth within the sector is crucial in any evaluation of the contribution and prospects of the sector. This section also examines the contribution of international trade in manufactured goods to the economy.

Output and Employment

As discussed in the introduction, manufacturing can be divided between modern and traditional sectors. The modern manufacturing sector covers all high-technology multinational enterprises (chemicals and chemical products; basic pharmaceutical products and pharmaceutical preparations; computer, electronic and optical products, electrical equipment; the reproduction of recorded media; and medical and dental instruments and supplies) while the traditional manufacturing sector encompasses all other sectors. In 2011, the year for which the most recent disaggregated statistics are available, modern manufacturing accounted for 68 per cent of gross value added of the sector and 34 per cent of employment.

Table 9.1 presents net output and employment levels in the manufacturing sector in Ireland for 2008 and 2011. Net output of the manufacturing sector in Ireland amounted to €64 billion in 2011 (2009 prices) and the sector employed approximately 190,000 people. Up to 2000, the increase in output was primarily accounted for by the modern sector, which experienced fast growth in the late 1990s, but which has slowed in recent years. Growth in output of the traditional manufacturing sector was also strong up to 2000 but since then has also stagnated. It should be noted, however, that output figures, particularly in the modern manufacturing sector where foreign-owned firms dominate (see later), may be distorted by foreign multinational firms switching profits from subsidiaries located in other countries to avail of lower corporation profit taxes in Ireland (see earlier).

The more recent trend in industrial output growth is captured by the industrial output indices presented in the second panel of the table. These indices are based on a monthly survey of manufacturing firms with more than 20 employees and so are not directly comparable to the value of output figures presented. Of particular note is the contraction in output in the sector between 2010 and 2013.

Employment in manufacturing is also in decline. While in the 1990s many jobs were created in the manufacturing sector, since 2000 there has been a continual decline in the numbers employed in the sector. This trend has continued in recent years with the loss of almost 30,000 jobs net between 2008 and 2011. This loss in employment can be partly attributed to productivity growth (evidenced by the fact that output has simultaneously increased over this period, at least up to 2010, particularly for the modern manufacturing sector) but also to the off-shoring of manufacturing production to more competitive locations leading to plant closures and job losses.

Table 9.1 Net Output and Employment in the Manufacturing Sector in Ireland 2008 and 2011 and Industrial Output Indices 1995–2013

	Net output (€bn)[1]		Employment ('000s)	
	2008	2011	2008	2011
Manufacturing	61	64	219	190
Modern[1]	40	44	72	64
Traditional	21	20	147	126
	Industrial output indices (base 2005=100)[2]			
	1995	2000	2005	2010	2013
Manufacturing	35.9	74.3	100.0	110.1	107.1
Modern[1]	24.3	67.3	100.0	124.7	120.1
Traditional	78.1	94.5	100.0	88.3	86.1

Sources: Central Statistics Office (CSO), Census of Industrial Production (local units), Database Direct, various years; CSO, *Industrial Production and Turnover*, CSO, 2014. See www.cso.ie.
[1] Values in 2009 prices adjusted using the Industrial Price Index (CSO).
[2] Note that the NACE system of classification was revised in 2008 with many manufacturing activities reclassified as services activities. Differences in values pre and post 2008 should therefore be treated with some caution as they may reflect the change in classification as opposed to actual changes in values.

The decline in employment in traditional sectors such as textiles is common across all OECD countries with low-cost non-OECD countries attracting this kind of investment to their shores. This trend is likely to continue into the future as more and more developing countries sign up to the WTO, making them increasingly attractive as locations for labour-intensive manufacturing activities. In contrast, however, Ireland maintains a comparative advantage in certain high-skilled manufacturing activities which are unlikely to be off-shored, particularly if productivity improvements are sustainable.

As highlighted in the introduction to this chapter, manufacturing's share in total employment and output of the economy has declined sharply since 1999. An increasing share of economic activity is now attributable to the services sector. The favourable profile of the manufacturing sector in terms of growth prospects implies that this structural change may have implications for future economic growth. First, manufacturing is a high-productivity sector and aggregate productivity growth in Ireland over the last decades has largely been attributable to the manufacturing sector. Second, manufacturing, up to recently, has been the main internationally traded activity and as such a weakening of the sector will have implications for exports, a key driver of economic growth, unless alternative export opportunities are found.

Productivity and Cost Competitiveness

A vibrant manufacturing sector is an important source of productivity growth given that productivity improvements are generally harder to achieve in more labour-intensive sectors such as the services sector. Productivity is one component of competitiveness and refers generally to the efficiency with which factors of production are converted into outputs. Productivity gains can be attained through a wide variety of means, ranging from decisions made by individual firms in relation to management practices, R&D and technology adoption, to government policies that support investment, entrepreneurship, competition and innovation.

At near full employment during the late 1990s and early 2000s, productivity growth was a key driver of the Irish economy, particularly in the modern sector. Since 2005, however, productivity growth has slowed, lagging far behind that of emerging economies such as South Korea, Poland and Hungary. This is a worrying trend, particularly since these countries are competitors with Ireland for foreign investment.

A more general indicator of the potential performance of the manufacturing sector is cost competitiveness. Cost competitiveness refers to the general environment within which the sector operates rather than the behaviour or performance of the firm specifically. Like productivity it is a relative concept in that it measures the extent to which the cost of doing business in Ireland is lower or higher than our main trading partners.

One silver lining to the current economic crisis is that for the first time in a decade Ireland's cost competitiveness has improved. This is due to both favourable movements in the exchange rate and falling prices. Labour costs have declined as well as non-pay costs such as rental of commercial property, the cost of utilities and some business services. The fact remains, though, that Ireland still remains expensive relative to many other countries, suggesting that it has only endured part of the adjustment process to a lower cost base.

International Trade

The link between economic growth and export expansion has long been established. Exports fuel economic growth directly by bringing additional income into the economy that increases domestic demand, and indirectly through the productivity improvements that result from exposure to competitive pressures. The latter may occur through more efficient allocations of resources or the adoption of new technologies required to compete on world markets, for example. While there is much debate in the literature on the direction of causality (are exporting firms more productive *a priori* or do they become more efficient once exposed to world markets?), there is no doubt that firms that export are more productive than those that do not.

Ireland has a long tradition of export-led growth, which can explain much of Ireland's phenomenal growth rate in the 1990s (see Chapters 1 and 7). In recent years, however, Ireland's share of the world market for merchandise goods has slipped: Ireland fell from being ranked 22nd in the world for goods exports in 2000 to 35th in 2012.[8] Table 9.2 illustrates the proportion of total gross output of the manufacturing sector attributable to exports.

Table 9.2 Percentage Contribution of Manufacturing to Exports and Export Destinations for Ireland

	Output	UK	Other EU	USA	Elsewhere
2000	79.0	19.0	50.4	13.9	16.7
2007	86.2	17.1	52.5	16.8	13.6
2009	82.5	14.7	41.9	27.0	16.4
2011	82.0	11.5	38.1	39.6	19.7

Source: CSO, Census of Industrial Production (local units), Database Direct, various years.

In 2007, 86 per cent of output in the manufacturing sector was exported, up from 79 per cent in 2000. Since then, however, the proportion of output exported has declined, to 82 per cent in 2009, where it has remained stable over the last few years. In terms of the destination of exports, the share going to the UK has declined in all sectors since 2000, and significantly so since 2007. This is consistent with the general trend observed throughout the 1990s. Declines in the proportion of exports going to other EU countries have also been observed. While the EU remains an important destination for exports, the proportion of exports to the USA increased to almost 40 per cent in 2011 with the proportion going to the rest of the world increasing to almost 20 per cent.

The contribution of the Irish manufacturing sector to Ireland's export base is paramount in understanding its economic success story of the last two decades. However, the dependence of the manufacturing sector on export markets leaves it vulnerable to world market conditions. Any international developments that depress demand will have consequences for the Irish manufacturing sector. Furthermore, the declining role of the sector is of concern if the sectors that replace it do not generate significant export activity. Thus a key challenge for Irish policymakers is the promotion of alternative export-based sectors. A sector presenting significant development opportunities in this regard is the internationally traded services sector, to which we now turn our attention.

4 INTERNATIONALLY TRADED SERVICES

For most developed economies, the last number of years has seen a significant structural shift away from agricultural and manufacturing production towards service activities. Ireland is no exception with services accounting for 67 per cent of gross value added in 2012.

A number of factors have contributed to the growth of the sector over the last two decades. First, the rapid pace of advancement in information and communications technology (ICT) has made it significantly easier for services companies to trade internationally. Second, the fragmentation of the production process means that an increasing number of services (for example logistics, IT, etc.) are required to monitor and control the production process within corporations. Third, firms increasingly find it more efficient to outsource many of their service activities, leading to these activities being reclassified from manufacturing to services. Finally, the distinction between manufacturing and services is increasingly blurred with manufacturing firms often providing services with the products that they sell (for example, products are often sold with training and support services or financial packages provided through the manufacturers themselves).

In this section we focus on internationally traded services. Other services sectors, such as retail, hospitality, health and education are covered elsewhere (see Chapters 11, 12 and 13). This section first addresses how trade in services is defined before moving on to analyse the contribution of internationally traded services to the economy.

Definition and Governance

The growing importance of trade in services worldwide has prompted national governments to come together to negotiate the rules that will govern the internationally traded services sector in the future. The two most notable reforms to emerge from this process are, at a regional level, the EU 2006 Directive on Services in the Internal Market, and, at international level, the General Agreement on Trade in Services (GATS).

GATS is the services counterpart to the well-known General Agreement on Tariffs and Trade negotiated in Uruguay in 1986. The GATS defines trade in services to encompass four different modes of service delivery.[9] Mode 1 is *cross-border trade*, which covers service flows across countries, for example an Irish university providing online courses that can be taken by students around the world. Mode 2, *consumption abroad*, covers situations where the consumer of a service physically travels to another country to avail of that service, for example an Irish tourist holidaying in Spain or an Irish patient travelling to the USA to avail of medical treatment. Mode 3 requires a *commercial presence* and refers to situations where the supplier of the service establishes a commercial presence in the country where the service is being provided, for example subsidiaries of an Irish insurance company setting up a branch in the UK. Mode 4 refers to *the presence of natural* persons and covers situations where an individual must travel to another country to supply a service, for example an Irish engineer building a hotel in Dubai. The sectors classed as internationally traded are described in Table 9.3.

Table 9.3 Sectoral Classification of Internationally Traded Services

---

Business services and professional services

Construction and related services

Distribution services

Education services

Energy services

Environmental services

Health and social services

Communication services

Tourism services

Transport services

Movement of natural persons

Source: WTO, General Agreement on Trade in Services, services sectoral classification list, available at www.wto.org.

The generation of an internal EU market for services and further liberalisation of services internationally through GATS negotiations are expected to have positive benefits for Ireland with the services sector predicted to grow in response to the new liberalisation measures, in terms of output, exports and employment. These benefits, however, are contingent on labour supply matching the skill set required (see Chapters 6 and 13). Indirect benefits are also expected. For example, by providing easier access to the international market, the internationally traded services sector will be exposed to greater competition, leading to lower prices. This will benefit final consumers, including Irish consumers, of services but will also improve cost competitiveness for other firms, such as those in the manufacturing sector, that use these services.

Contribution of Internationally Traded Services
Table 9.4 presents the value of Irish services exports for the period 2003 to 2011 (expressed in constant 2009 prices). In 2011 exports of services amounted to over €87 billion, more than doubling on 2003 levels in real terms. According to the WTO, Ireland ranks 11th in the world in terms of services exports. What makes the fast pace of growth of services exports even more remarkable is when it is interpreted against the backdrop of the financial crisis and worldwide recession which has led to depressed demand conditions, and the fact that the value of merchandise exported fell during this time.

Table 9.4 also illustrates the proportion of exports by destination. The EU is the most important destination for our services exports, with the UK and Germany being of particular importance. In the last few years the importance of the USA as a destination has increased to pre-crisis levels. Services exports to the rest of the world are also growing in importance.

Table 9.4 Value of Internationally Traded Services

	2003	2005	2007	2009	2011	2012
Services exports (€bn)[1]	35.3	47.3	67.6	69.3	82.1	87.2
% UK	25.2	25.3	22.0	20.2	18.4	19.2
% Germany	9.4	12.1	9.9	9.8	9.4	8.9
% Rest of EU	27.8	29.6	30.9	33.3	30.4	28.8
% USA	13.5	7.9	6.4	6.3	7.0	8.8
% Rest of world	24.1	25.0	30.8	30.5	34.8	34.3

Source: CSO, *Service Exports and Imports*, various years, available at www.cso.ie.
[1] Values are expressed in 2009 constant prices deflated using the Industrial Price Index.

A disaggregation of the sectors that are important for services exports is presented in Table 9.5. The most important contributing sectors to services exports are computer services and other business services which together account for over 70 per cent of total services exports. While financial services and insurance are also of importance, their relative share has declined, particularly in recent years, hardly surprising given the impact that the financial crisis had on these sectors. Tourism has also declined in importance.

A large share of global trade consists of intra-firm trade, in other words the transfer of goods and services, often termed trade in tasks, within multinational corporations across borders usually for the purpose of avoiding taxes. As already mentioned, this practice can significantly distort sectoral output statistics but can also distort trade statistics since goods and services are simply imported by firms for immediate re-export.

Table 9.5 Proportion of Gross Exports of Services (%) and Level of Net Exports (€m) by Disaggregated Sectors

	2004	2006	2008	2011	2012	Net exports[1] 2012
Transport	4.3	3.4	3.6	5.3	5.1	2,902
Tourism, travel and communications	9.6	6.8	5.9	4.3	4.0	−2,027
Financial services and insurance	28.0	21.6	17.9	18.0	17.7	5,059
Computer services	34.3	26.5	28.9	38.6	39.5	34,948
Other business services	19.1	23.4	25.6	33.1	33.0	−38,068

Source: CSO, *Service Exports and Imports*, various years, available at www.cso.ie.
[1] Values are expressed in 2009 constant prices deflated using the Industrial Price Index.

As discussed in Section 2, Ireland has a low rate of corporation profit taxes (see also Chapter 4) and so it is thought that intra-firm trade of this kind is common among MNCs in Ireland. As such, gross exports for sectors with a large presence of foreign-owned firms, such as financial services and computer services, for example, should be treated with considerable caution given that some of these exports could simply be imports that are re-exported for the purpose of avoiding tax.

A crude check on the extent of the distortion to the export statistics as a result of intra-firm trade is to look at the value of net exports (gross exports minus gross imports) at a particular point in time. Although this will not fully pick up the extent of transfer pricing, it will give some indication of the overall contribution of the different sub-sectors. Net exports by sub-sector for 2012 are presented in the last column of Table 9.5. While financial services and insurance remain net exporters, their impact on the trade balance is much less than what the gross export figures would suggest due to high levels of imports of these services into Ireland.

This is even more so the case for other business services which have a large negative trade balance, which coupled with the high gross export figures for this sub-sector, is suggestive of transfer-pricing activities. Computer services are the single most important sub-sector of the internationally traded services sector with net exports valued at almost €35 million in 2012 and a negligible level of gross imports. It is also of interest to note that there is a deficit in tourism exports meaning that more Irish tourists holidayed abroad in 2012 than visited Ireland.

5 FOREIGN DIRECT INVESTMENT

Policies aimed at attracting FDI are based on the logic that FDI brings new investment to the economy that directly boosts national income and leads to the creation of employment. It is also expected that FDI will bring an inflow of knowledge and technology that leads to productivity spillovers to the domestic manufacturing sector. FDI is of huge importance to the Irish economy and in particular to the manufacturing sector and internationally traded services. In this section, we first examine the contribution of foreign-owned firms to output and employment in Ireland and compare Ireland's FDI flows to other countries in Europe. Second, we explore the extent to which productivity spillovers, one of the main arguments for industrial policy aimed at attracting FDI, have materialised. We conclude the section with a discussion of the increasing role of ODI and what this means for Ireland.

Inward Foreign Direct Investment[10]
Since the 1960s, Ireland's industrial policy has focused on facilitating inward FDI. This yielded substantial rewards for Ireland in terms of economic growth in the latter half of the last century. Of particular importance have been growth-

enhancing economic policies such as fiscal stability, labour market flexibility and science-oriented human capital formation as well as a low corporation tax regime. As a result, Ireland has the most FDI-intensive manufacturing sector of all countries in Europe.

In 2011, foreign-owned firms accounted for 48 per cent of manufacturing employment and almost 80 per cent of output. Approximately 94 per cent of the output in the modern manufacturing sector is attributable to foreign-owned firms. They are also crucial to Ireland's export base. Foreign firms exported 94 per cent of their output in 2011 compared with only 55 per cent for domestic firms. This highlights the importance of foreign investment to trade flows in Ireland. It should be noted, however, that domestic firms are exporting more over time: in 2007 only 47 per cent of the output of domestic firms was exported.

When the extent of FDI into Ireland is set in a European context its relevance and importance for the manufacturing and internationally traded sectors becomes even more apparent. As illustrated in Table 9.6, in 2012 the stock of inward FDI as a percentage of GDP amounted to 142 per cent compared with an average of 47 per cent for the EU. Over the course of the 1990s the ratio of inward FDI stock to GDP grew considerably despite rapid increases in GDP during this period. Since 2000, however, the overall stock of inward FDI (relative to GDP) has remained relatively stable.

This is partly due to the outflow of foreign investors in the early 2000s and is also in line with the decline in the overall importance of the manufacturing sector in terms of output and employment since 2000. This trend can be explained by the increasing attractiveness of developing countries such as China, India, and Central and Eastern European countries as locations for investors in labour-intensive manufacturing sectors. In more recent years, positive inflows have returned but at a more moderate level. These are attributable to an increasing number of investments in high-tech manufacturing sectors and services. The recent global economic downturn is also evident in the ratio of FDI inflows to outflows. In 2000 inflows were 5.6 times the level of outflows. By 2012 the ratio had declined to 1.5 and was similar to pre-boom levels.

Table 9.6 FDI Stocks and Flows for Ireland, the UK and the EU

	FDI stocks as a percentage of GDP			FDI inflows/FDI outflows		
	1990	2000	2012	1990	2000	2012
Ireland	78.8	130.4	142.1	1.7	5.6	1.5
UK	20.1	31.4	54.4	1.7	0.5	0.9
EU	10.5	27.7	46.6	0.7	0.9	0.8

Source: UN Conference on Trade and Development (UNCTAD), *World Investment Report 2013*, UN, Geneva 2013.

There is no doubt that FDI into Ireland over the last two decades has been on a large scale and this has reshaped the manufacturing sector in Ireland in a significant way. According to IDA Ireland, over 1,000 foreign firms have chosen Ireland as their European base in a variety of different sectors including engineering, financial and international services, information communications technologies, medical technologies and pharmaceuticals. In addition to Intel, Apple and IBM, other overseas companies with large operations in Ireland include Amazon, Google, HP, Microsoft and Yahoo. In 2008, the internet social networking site Facebook established its European headquarters in Dublin and in 2010, internet professional networking site LinkedIn announced that it too was to use Dublin as the base for its international headquarters.

Productivity Spillovers
As discussed in Section 2, a key rationale for industrial policy aimed at promoting FDI is the fact that foreign MNCs establishing in Ireland bring with them knowledge and technology that will spill over to the domestic industrial sector. The extent to which FDI yields benefits to the economy above and beyond the direct contribution to output and employment is an issue that has been extensively debated in the economics literature. The evidence is clear on the fact that foreign-owned firms are larger, have higher labour productivity, higher profits, are more export intensive, employ more skilled workers and spend more on R&D than their domestic counterparts. Thus there is no doubt that the presence of foreign companies in Ireland has contributed to higher aggregate productivity levels and growth rates than would otherwise have been possible.

The measurement of productivity spillovers is a more complex matter, however, with no consensus about the most appropriate approach. Productivity spillovers can be horizontal (within a defined sub-sector of manufacturing) or vertical (through input–output linkages). While there is some evidence that the presence of MNCs in Ireland has led to the establishment of an indigenous downstream sector for some industries, most of the empirical literature on the presence of spillovers is concerned with the measurement of horizontal spillovers. In the Irish case this means spillovers from MNCs to Irish firms operating in the same sector. The evidence on the presence of horizontal spillovers for Ireland is mixed, however, with positive spillovers only evident when sectors are narrowly defined. The strongest evidence for the importance of spillovers is found in high-tech sectors.

In order for Irish firms to benefit from productivity spillovers they need to have innovative capacity. Ireland performs well by international standards on a range of comparative innovation measures, with a high proportion of firms involved in innovation activity.[11] However, innovation is concentrated among larger, foreign-owned firms, with smaller indigenous firms lagging far behind. Overall, the returns to innovations are lower in Ireland than the EU average, suggesting that there are some inefficiencies in the way in which R&D resources are being deployed within enterprises.

In a more general context, the key to innovation is the improvement of the absorption capacity of firms so that they can benefit from technology spillovers. This can be achieved through appropriate education and training policies to ensure that the labour force is equipped with the necessary skills to innovate effectively. The Department of Jobs, Enterprise and Innovation, through Forfás, regularly produces reports on the skills needs of various sectors of the economy to highlight the gaps and action plans for addressing these needs (see, for example, the recently published *ICT Skills Action Plan*).

It is clear that FDI has played a crucial role in the success of the Irish manufacturing sector not only in terms of output and employment but also in terms of its impact on the domestic industrial sector. Higher than average productivity levels of MNCs has raised aggregate productivity levels for the sector as a whole and productivity spillovers, particularly in the high-tech sector, have also benefited Irish firms. There is also evidence to suggest that the presence of MNCs has increased domestic firm survival rates and encouraged start-up firms in many upstream supply industries.

In the face of declining flows of FDI, the challenge for Irish industrial policymakers is not only how to continue to attract foreign investment into Ireland and to hold on to the MNCs that are already here, but how better to develop linkages between MNCs and domestic firms in an attempt to fully exploit productivity spillovers. This is an even greater challenge in the face of increasing pressure from the EU to harmonise corporation tax rates and increased restrictions on the provision of grants: two important policy tool options in relation to FDI for the Irish government in the past. Of even more importance, however, is the possibility that changes will be made to the corporation profit tax base and the international rules governing the payment of taxation by MNCs (see Section 2).

For example, if firms are forced to pay taxes on profits in the country where they are earned and can no longer process profits through Irish subsidiaries, not only will it have implications for Irish tax revenues but it may also reduce the attractiveness of Ireland as a place to invest. However, it is also possible that having a low corporation tax in an environment where transfer pricing is no longer permitted could increase the level of actual economic activity that takes place in Ireland, given that firms will be forced to site their real activity in Ireland to avail of the low tax rate. As discussed in Section 2, efforts by the OECD for better tax co-ordination to reduce the incidence of BEPS is a clear sign that policy is moving in this direction. As well as creating an extra administrative burden on MNCs located in Ireland it will inevitably erode the advantages of transfer pricing for MNCs. For reasons mentioned, the overall effect that this will have on foreign investment in Ireland is not clear.

Outward Direct Investment[12]

A key concern for many developed economies is the extent to which the manufacturing sector can survive in the face of emerging low-cost economies offering an attractive base for manufacturing investment in terms of low input costs and liberal trade and investment policies. In 2012, developing economies surpassed developed economies as recipients of FDI for the first time, receiving 52 per cent of global FDI flows.

Also in Ireland, ODI is increasingly important, as illustrated in Table 9.7. In 2012, the stock of investment by Irish companies abroad amounted to over 170 per cent of GDP with dramatic increases in the flow of ODI experienced since the early 1990s. This ratio is well above the EU average and greater than that of the UK. It can in part be explained by the fall in GDP in Ireland in recent years but this does not change the fact that the stock of ODI now accounts for a greater proportion of GDP than the stock of inward FDI (see Table 9.6).

In the mid-2000s, the bulk of manufacturing ODI from Ireland was attributable to a small proportion of long-established Irish companies in the traditional industrial sectors (for example, Cement Roadstone Holdings and Greencore). Intuitively, one would expect that, as is the case for foreign-owned firms operating in Ireland, high labour costs make sourcing labour-intensive parts of the production process in Ireland very costly and so sourcing this part of the production chain abroad will improve the competitiveness of Irish producers. Yet, early flows of Irish ODI were mainly concentrated in the UK and the USA.

It is estimated that Irish companies in the USA employed almost 65,000 people in 1999 compared with just over 100,000 workers employed by US companies in Ireland in the same year. This suggests that low labour costs may not have been the only driver of the decision for Irish firms to invest abroad. Recently, there appears to have been a shift in the type of Irish ODI. The majority of new Irish investment abroad is in the services sector and in particular in green energy projects (examples include NTR and Mainstream Renewable Power).

Table 9.7 ODI Stocks for Ireland, the UK and the EU

	ODI stocks as a percentage of GDP		
	1990	2000	2012
Ireland	31.0	28.7	170.5
UK	22.6	62.6	74.4
EU	11.2	41.4	58.8

Source: UN Conference on Trade and Development (UNCTAD), *World Investment Report 2013*, UN, Geneva 2013.

A key concern in the face of rising levels of ODI is that it will have a negative impact on the domestic economy in terms of investment, exports, and employment. Evidence from countries with a history of ODI suggests that these concerns are unfounded and that high levels of ODI can lead to economic growth. For example, there is evidence to suggest that high levels of ODI are complementary to a strong export base. Traditional exports of finished goods are replaced with exports of high value-added intermediate goods (as has been the case in Ireland in recent years) and the provision of highly skilled services to overseas foreign affiliates by head offices based in the domestic country.

The discussion in Section 3 shows that there is evidence to suggest that this type of restructuring away from low-tech employment to high value-added activities, with corresponding higher wages, is taking place in Ireland. An additional advantage of ODI is that portfolio diversification of this kind may help protect the economy from regional economic downturns at an aggregate level and alleviate some of the pressures associated with export dependence. Moreover, high levels of ODI are generally associated with high levels of R&D investment.

Given these advantages, government policy aimed at facilitating outward investments should aim to remove tax and regulatory barriers to investment flows. This can be achieved through an expansion of Ireland's network of international agreements on double taxation and through support for WTO multilateral agreements on investment rules. An expansion of Enterprise Ireland's current supports to companies wishing to invest abroad, such as overseas network, overseas incubator facilities, acquisition service, outsourcing missions, and foreign trade and investment missions, would also facilitate this process. Ultimately, however, policies aimed at improving Ireland's competitiveness will remain most important, and should aim to re-skill those displaced by these changes and promote high value-added activities in manufacturing and services into the future.

6 CONCLUDING COMMENTS

Major structural change is occurring in the Irish economy: the manufacturing sector, once the backbone of Ireland's economy, is diminishing in importance to be replaced by a vibrant internationally traded services sector. This raises significant challenges, particularly in the aftermath of an unprecedented economic crisis of a scale never before experienced in the history of the state.

The pace of growth of the internationally traded services sector presents real opportunities for growth and job creation as a means of economic recovery. The government's strategy for a smart economy set the stage for Irish entrepreneurs and foreign investors to engage in emerging sectors such as green technology (see Chapter 10) or advanced computer software industries like cloud computing. A growing internationally traded services sector raises its own sets of challenges that need to be carefully considered, for example the fact that rules governing trade liberalisation are yet to be negotiated or that the dearth in language skills within the labour force may compromise Ireland's ability to attract high-end service companies.

The indigenous sector is also at risk. The banking crisis has had a significant impact on the availability of credit for SMEs in Ireland, despite recent government efforts to address access to finance issues (see also Chapters 5 and 7). This will have, and may already have had, serious implications for entrepreneurship in Ireland given that it will result in missed opportunities for new ventures and the postponement of investment in existing enterprises, and may ultimately lead to company closures for enterprises experiencing difficult times.

Lack of access to credit may also lead to a domino effect in the supply chain: for example, if one firm in a vertically integrated chain of firms has difficulty accessing credit to pay one of its suppliers lower down the chain, this can cause cash flow problems for that supplier, who may in turn also be unable to access credit. It will take some time before credit markets are effective in supporting the development of the SME sector, and this could have long-term consequences for economic recovery.

Ultimately, for all sectors to survive, improving competitiveness is of fundamental importance. Falling prices and excess labour supply should help improve Ireland's competitive position, but more is required. For example, an environment must be fostered that promotes innovation and R&D with greater linkages to the university sector. The issue of human capital also looms large, especially if the Irish labour force is to have the right skills to move up the 'value chain' of production in years to come (see Chapters 6 and 13). A strong pro-competition stance must also be maintained in labour markets (see Chapter 6) and product markets (see Chapter 5), for the benefit of both Irish consumers and Irish businesses.

FDI investment flows into Ireland have been critical over the last two decades in terms of increased employment and bringing much-needed technological and managerial skills that eventually pass into other sectors of the economy. Such success was based partly on special tax breaks, something which may have to end as other countries become involved in similar competitive tax-cutting exercises. Such a situation will lead to a zero-sum game overall, with national governments the losers and large MNCs the winners. There is also now the phenomenon of large investment overseas by Irish companies and this process, as this chapter has emphasised, will have to be managed with care.

There will continue to be a rationale for state support of the manufacturing and internationally traded services sectors, but the nature of that support is changing and will have to change even more in years to come. The emphasis is shifting from tax breaks and direct grants to providing the correct competitive environment in which businesses can, without any direct state aid or tax breaks, flourish.

Notes

* This chapter builds on Chapter 9 from the 11th edition of this book and previous studies in this area cited in that chapter. My thanks to John O'Hagan for useful comments and feedback on an earlier draft of this chapter.

1 For seminal work in this area see G. Grossman and E. Rossi-Hansberg, 'Trading tasks: a simple theory of offshoring', *American Economic Review*, Vol. 98, No. 5, 2008.

2 The discussion here draws on F. Barry, 'Foreign direct investment and institutional co-evolution in Ireland', *Scandinavian Economic History Review*, Vol. 55, No. 3, 2007.

3 The extent of the complexity of some of the schemes used by companies is perhaps best illustrated by the 'Double Irish Dutch sandwich' described in International Monetary Fund, *Fiscal Monitor October 2013: Taxing Times*, IMF, Washington 2013, Box 5, pp. 47–8.

4 For a detailed discussion on this issue see: OECD, 'What is BEPS and how can you stop it?', *OECD Insights*, 19 July 2013; IMF, *op cit.*; and OECD, *Action Plan on Base Erosion and Profit Shifting*, OECD, Paris 2013.

5 Department of the Taoiseach, *National Reform Programme 2013 Update*, Department of the Taoiseach, Dublin 2013.

6 Forfás, *Making it Happen: Growing Enterprise for Ireland*, Forfás, Dublin 2010; Department of Enterprise, Trade and Innovation, *Trading and Investing in a Smart Economy, A Strategy and Action Plan for Irish Trade, Tourism and Investment to 2015*, DETI, Dublin 2010.

7 Forfás, *Action Plan for Jobs 2014*, Forfás, Dublin 2014.

8 WTO, *International Trade Statistics 2013*, WTO 2013.

9 The discussion presented in this section draws on Forfás, *Input to the Services Directive: Regulatory Impact Analysis*, Forfás, Dublin 2010.

10 The discussion in this section draws on F. Barry, 'Export-platform foreign direct investment: the Irish experience', *EIB Papers*, Vol. 9, No. 2, 2004; the statistics presented in the text are taken from CSO, *Manufacturing Enterprises by Industry Sector, Country of Ownership*, Database Direct (available at www.cso.ie).

11 Forfás, *Analysis of Ireland's Innovation Performance*, Forfás, Dublin 2011.

12 For a recent account of ODI from Ireland see L. Brennan and R. Verma, 'Outward FDI from Ireland and its policy context', *Columbia FDI Profiles*, 12 February 2013.

CHAPTER 10

Energy Sector and Environmental Issues

Eleanor Denny

1 INTRODUCTION

Energy and the environment are strongly interlinked and are critical policy concerns for governments around the world. Energy plays a role in almost every facet of society, from industry to transport to domestic use, yet it is also responsible for over 80 per cent of global greenhouse gas emissions. The environment is a strategic and valuable asset and as such it must be protected and proactively managed to ensure that it forms the basis of economic welfare and a healthy society. Balancing these two, often competing, policy agendas is at the crux of global energy policy and will be the focus of this chapter.

Since the 1800s the role of energy in modern society has evolved and today energy is an essential input into almost every aspect of daily life, both for consumption and as an input to production. From lighting, heating and transport at the residential level to production processes, IT systems, communications networks, and retail and services provision, energy is considered a vital necessity without which any developed economy would grind to a halt. In fact, a reliable and safe energy supply at a sustainable cost is considered a basic necessity for economic development.

Ensuring a secure energy supply also has a critical political aspect, from a local perspective, with the development of national energy projects and infrastructure, to high-profile international politics. Conflict over the control of valuable oil supplies has been a persistent feature of international affairs since the beginning of the 20th century. Such conflict varies in nature, from territorial disputes over the possession of oil-laden regions to struggles among the leaders of oil-rich countries to major inter-state wars over the control of vital oil zones. As oil reserves continue to be depleted, the frequency and severity of such conflict is likely to increase.

Coupled with the necessity for a safe and secure energy supply is the protection of the environment, including air, water and land quality and the sustainability of natural habitats and species. A sustainable environment is a critical component of high quality of life, with clean air and safe water being two of the most basic human needs. Given the enormous pressure the energy system places on the environment (for example through the release of harmful emissions, the consumption of vast quantities of water, the creation of harmful waste such as nuclear waste, and the impact of energy and transport infrastructure on the natural environment), it is imprudent to consider energy in isolation from environmental concerns. For this reason, this chapter considers both the energy sector and some key environmental aspects.

This chapter examines energy and environmental issues and policy in Ireland in the context of European and global pressures. Section 2 looks at the structure of energy demand in Ireland, highlighting the three main sectors, electricity, heating and transport. A detailed discussion of the role of the state in the energy sector is also provided in addition to an analysis of the political nature of energy supplies. Section 3 looks at energy supply, its diversity and security. The discussion covers energy infrastructure and renewable energy sources, in addition to contentious topics such as nuclear energy and fracking, all of which have obvious environmental dimensions. Section 4 looks at the issue of pricing and competition in the energy sector, relating back to issues discussed in Chapter 5. Section 5 is devoted to four major environmental concerns: air quality, water pollution, waste disposal and biodiversity. Addressing the potentially disastrous consequences of global warming is the responsibility of all nations, including Ireland. Our obligations under the Kyoto Protocol and, in particular, EU agreements are extensively covered. Apart from having safe drinking water, there is also the issue of the supply of drinking water, which in the case of Ireland will require substantial new expenditure on infrastructure. The same applies to waste disposal, an issue which raises environmental and infrastructural provision issues.

2 ENERGY SECTOR: IMPORTANCE AND PROVISION

One of the most significant infrastructural challenges facing the state is the provision of a secure and sustainable energy supply into the future. This requires not only investment in the underlying capital resources, for example in power stations and networks, but also in the security of energy supply, for example in indigenous fossil fuel production and renewable energy. Both of these areas, the provision of the energy sector physical infrastructure and the security of energy fuel supplies, result in the state traditionally playing a large and important role in the energy sector. This section will first introduce the energy sector and its characteristics. It will then elaborate on the importance of the role of the state in the sector and finally discuss some geopolitical issues relating to energy security.

Importance and Nature of Energy Sector and Demand
Energy is generally classified by its mode of application: for electricity, heating/cooling (of space and water) or for transportation. In Ireland, the energy

landscape in each of these sectors has changed significantly over the last century as Ireland has grown from a largely agricultural society to a service, industrial and manufacturing driven economy.

Electricity

The original driver for electricity arose from a desire for people to light their homes cheaply and safely. The subsequent challenge was to develop an electricity system that could create electricity in a central location (at a power plant) and carry it to people's homes (across a network). In 1882 the first power plant in the world was constructed in New York and it supplied 85 customers with electricity to light their homes. It wasn't until over 20 years later, in 1903, that Ireland's first power station was built at the Pigeon House in Dublin to supply power to the street lights around Dublin city.

In 1922 discussions began on a proposal to dam the River Shannon and by 1925 construction had begun on Ireland's first bulk power station, a hydro-electric plant in Ardnacrusha in Co. Clare, to supply electricity to the towns and cities of Ireland. Today the island of Ireland has over 30 power stations operated on coal, gas, oil and peat, 206 wind farms and a range of smaller installations at businesses and homes. In 2012, electricity accounted for 34 per cent of all energy used in Ireland.

Heating

In relation to energy for heating, Ireland has a strong tradition of open fires in domestic dwellings, which has resulted in coal and peat remaining important heat sources in the residential sector over the past century. Open fires typically have low efficiency and in order to heat the entire house are usually supplemented by oil, electric and, increasingly, gas heating systems. Significant upgrades in building regulations have led to improvements in the efficiency of the building stock in Ireland, with a house built in 2010 typically using one-third of the heating energy of the average existing home.

However, Ireland still has a large stock of inefficient residential dwellings with energy use per dwelling 5 per cent above the UK average and 26 per cent above the EU-27 average in 2010. Comparisons with the UK provide a good benchmark as the climate in both countries is similar. Other EU countries would have a much higher air-conditioning demand than Ireland so they tend to have a peak thermal energy demand in the summer months, whereas Ireland has its peak demand in winter.[1]

Reasons for Ireland's poor performance when compared to the UK and the rest of the EU include larger average dwelling sizes, a higher proportion of solid fuel use and a lack of district heating initiatives. District heating allows heat to be generated efficiently in a central location and then circulated to residential and commercial premises. District heating is prevalent throughout Europe, but its uptake in Ireland has been slow. However, advances in technology and environmental drivers are likely to see an increase in the use of district heating in

Ireland into the future. Residential heat demand represents approximately 45 per cent of total heat demand in Ireland, with the remainder from industry, services and agriculture. In 2012, heat demand accounted for 34 per cent of all energy use in Ireland.

Transport
The final third of energy demand is accounted for by the transportation sector, a sector which has seen huge change in the past two decades. Economic activity is the main driver of transport demand and an increase of 190 per cent in economic output in the 1990 to 2007 period saw transport energy demand increase by 181 per cent in the same period. Much of this increase was seen in freight transportation for the construction industry and an increase in aviation demand, but the residential sector also contributed significantly. In the same period, the number of licensed private cars increased from 796,408 in 1990 to 1,882,901 in 2007, an increase of 136 per cent.

Role of the State
Large infrastructural projects often necessitate the intervention of the state due to their significant capital costs and the importance of the assets to sustaining economic growth. The expected lifetime of investments in the energy sector is 40 years or more, thus the wisdom of any investment decisions, for example investment in a coal-fired power station versus a nuclear station, must be considered within a similar time frame. Investments in the underlying network have even longer lifetimes. Similarly, policy decisions that aim to increase competitiveness or decrease emissions today must take account of the long-term legacy of these decisions.[2] The energy sector displays many types of market failure, such as monopolies, externalities and public goods, each of which prompts a role for the state in the sector.

Monopolies
The first form of market failure in the energy sector is the presence of monopolies. Due to the importance of maintaining the security of energy supply, the state traditionally took a role in sourcing, generating, transmitting, and supplying electricity and gas to end-users. In other words, the state created state-owned vertically integrated monopolies such as the Electricity Supply Board (ESB) and Bord Gáis Éireann (BGE). While the energy sector has evolved significantly in recent years with the introduction of new players and increased competition (see also Chapter 5), the state continues to have a large role in all aspects of the energy industry.

Across Europe, the provision of electricity and gas require extensive network infrastructure and, because of the significant economies of scale, these networks are considered to be natural monopolies. In 1996 the EU initiated common rules on the internal markets for electricity and gas, intended to open electricity and gas markets up to competition in all the member states.

However, these EU directives recognise that the networks element of the industry is a natural monopoly and so allow member states to continue to have a monopoly in network provision, but this company cannot participate in any other aspects of the industry. Thus, the electricity and gas networks are now separated from the traditional vertically integrated monopolies and are operated by companies which are ring-fenced from other aspects of the industry. In Ireland, these companies are Eirgrid (high-voltage electricity network), ESB Networks (low-voltage electricity networks), and Bord Gáis Networks (gas interconnectors and network).

While Eirgrid, ESB Networks, and Bord Gáis Networks are now independent companies, they continue to remain under the ownership of the state. In fact, among the recommendations of a recent report were that the high voltage electricity and gas networks should remain under state ownership, as these are the most critical elements of the energy infrastructure.[3]

While the electricity and gas networks are recognised to be natural monopolies, the EU directive does require an increase in competition in the generation of electricity and the supply of both electricity and gas to end-users. With this in mind, Ireland has seen a number of new independent participants enter the electricity and gas markets in recent years, such as SSE Airtricity and Flogas (competition in the energy sector is discussed further in Section 4 and also in Chapter 5). However, the state remains the dominant player in both sectors.

In fact, the ESB remains by a significant margin the largest undertaking in state ownership, accounting for one half of the state's commercial sector when measured by net assets. State participation in the energy sector also includes Bord Gáis (through the gas infrastructure but also in the electricity sector and more recently in wind power developments), Bord na Móna (with involvement in peat production, power generation and wind) and also in Coillte (which provides wood to the power generation sector and has also begun to develop interests in wind farms). Thus, the state owns three companies (ESB, Bord Gáis and Bord na Móna) that have competing interests in the electricity generation sector and one (Coillte) which is developing interests in this area.

While state participation in the energy sector was traditionally required in all aspects of the industry to ensure the provision of a secure energy supply, the necessity to have such a large and competing involvement is now questionable. With this in mind, and with a view to raising additional revenues for the state, a recent report recommends that ESB, Bord Gáis, Bord na Móna and Coillte should all be privatised.

While formerly dominated by vertically integrated monopolies, the energy sector now displays increased competition (see also Chapter 5). However, it is far from perfectly competitive. Natural monopolies remain in the network aspect of the energy sector and the generation and supply elements of the industry are more like oligopolies (which retain a high level of state ownership). The potential for strategic behaviour on the part of participants in the sector remains high and thus the sector must be heavily regulated.

The state-run Commission for Energy Regulation (CER) in Ireland undertakes this role in both the electricity and gas sectors. In fact, the energy sector is one of the most highly regulated of all industrial sectors. Thus, while the state's role in the provision of electricity and gas may diminish in the coming years through the sale of state assets, it will continue to play an important role in the networks element of the sector and crucially in the regulation of all aspects of the industry.

Externalities

A second reason for the involvement of the state in the energy sector is due to the fact that the energy sector is the largest contributor to greenhouse gas emissions in Ireland. The presence of externalities, such as emissions, prompts a role for government in the energy sector. In Ireland this has taken the form of subsidies for renewable generation and energy efficiency measures as well as penalties for producers of carbon dioxide (such as carbon taxes and mandatory participation in the EU Emissions Trading Scheme). Environmental issues are discussed later in Section 5.

Public Goods

A third reason for the involvement of the state in the energy sector is that the security of energy supply is an example of a marketable public good. Energy supply is considered a basic necessity and when provided for all promotes greater standards of living for all. A secure energy supply results in a lower risk of blackouts and supply interruptions, which is a necessity to promote commercial activity and economic development. Thus, the benefits of a secure energy supply are enjoyed by all, even those who do not pay directly for it.

However, investments in energy infrastructure have long lead times (of up to ten years when planning delays are taken into account) and exceptionally high capital costs. Once a power station is built it improves the security of energy supply for all but the cost is so high that no individual customer can afford to pay to incentivise an increase in generation capacity. In addition, providing energy from a single source (e.g. oil) is a threat to supply security, whereas providing energy from a diverse range of sources reduces the risk of supply interruption and increases energy security. However, market incentives are unlikely to be present to encourage private investment in a diverse range of fuels.

All of these factors prompt a role for government in securing the provision of energy security from a diverse range of fuel sources. This can be done by direct involvement through the establishment of state-run vertically integrated monopolies or through regulation and incentive schemes.

Energy and Spatial Planning

In examining Ireland's energy consumption patterns, the state's role in spatial planning is a key issue. Compared to other EU countries, Ireland's planning legacy has resulted in a historical trend of low-density housing resulting in urban sprawl around major cities and large numbers of one-off housing in rural areas. In

2009, just 3.1 per cent of Ireland's population lived in apartments, the lowest in the EU-27, where the average is 41.7 per cent.[4] This planning legacy of low density and one-off housing has important knock-on implications for energy usage in all sectors.

The most obvious implication is for the transport sector; when people live closer to their workplace, commuting distances are shorter, and a public transport system can be optimised to meet the needs of the population more efficiently. In the electricity sector, our dispersed population has led to Ireland having four times the EU average length of power lines per customer.[5] While unsightly and more costly to construct, longer lines also have the disadvantage that more energy is lost in transmission. A history of poor spatial planning decisions also has consequences for the development of new power stations, with the routing of power lines more challenging when houses are distributed widely outside towns and villages. In the heating sector, our distributed housing impacts on the availability of mainline gas, one of the most efficient fuels available for domestic use. One-off and dispersed housing also reduces the potential for district heating.

The provision of electricity, heating and transportation is considered to be a basic necessity in any developed society. Thus, in an era of rising oil prices, environmental concerns and competitive pressures, energy policy is a critical concern for policymakers and decisions in this area have far-reaching consequences. Energy policy is generally driven by three main goals: security of supply, sustainability of prices for end-users, and environmental concerns. Each of these components will be discussed in detail in Section 3.

The Politics of Energy Security

Ireland imports 85 per cent of fuel required for energy provision, of which the majority is oil and gas. Ireland is thus highly exposed to international price and supply fluctuations in these vital resources. While not a major player on the world stage in either supply of or demand for these fuels, our high import dependence and remote location leave Ireland particularly vulnerable to international fuel markets and therefore fuel politics.

Oil is the world's major source of primary energy, accounting for approximately 40 per cent of global energy consumption. Because it plays such a critical role in fuelling the world economy, any prolonged shortage in oil supplies can feed into a global economic recession, as occurred in 1974 (following the Arab oil embargo), 1979 (following the Iranian revolution), and 1990 (following the Iraqi invasion of Kuwait).

Petroleum is also a vital factor in the military strength of nations, as it supplies most of the energy used to power tanks, planes, missiles, ships, armoured vehicles, and other instruments of war. Vast amounts of petroleum are consumed in modern combat operations; for example, during the 1991 Gulf War, US and allied forces consumed an average of 19 million gallons of oil per day – this is equivalent to the total daily consumption of Argentina. Because of its strategic importance in the conduct of warfare, its possession has been termed a 'national security' matter by the USA and other countries, meaning that it is something that may require the use of military force to protect.[6]

This close connection between oil, economic growth and national security has resulted in oil-fuelled political conflict since the early stages of the industrial era. Oil-driven conflict can be seen to derive from two essential features of petroleum: its vital importance to the economy and military power of nations; and its irregular geographic distribution.

Natural petroleum does not occur randomly across the globe but is highly concentrated in a few large reservoirs. The largest of these, containing approximately two-thirds of the world's oil reserves, is located in the Persian Gulf area, which comprises Saudi Arabia, Iran, Iraq, Kuwait, Qatar and the United Arab Emirates (UAE). Large reservoirs are also found in the USA, Canada, Mexico, Colombia, Venezuela, the North Sea basin (Norway and the UK), Russia, Azerbaijan, Kazakhstan, Algeria, Angola, Libya, Nigeria, China and Indonesia. Together, these 22 countries possess more than 90 per cent of the world's conventional oil reserves

For all of these reasons, the risk of armed conflict over valuable oil supplies is liable to grow in the years to come. Such conflict could take the form of conventional warfare involving the military forces of the major powers, as in the 1991 Persian Gulf War, or internal power struggles between competing political, ethnic, and tribal factions. Indeed, throughout the last decade, oil-related conflict of one sort or another was under way in Bolivia, Colombia, Iraq, Georgia, Indonesia, Nigeria, Saudi Arabia and Venezuela.

In addition to exposure to conflict in oil-fuelled nations, Europe is also open to natural gas price and supply risk. While natural gas is more geographically spread than oil reserves, Europe remains heavily reliant on imported Russian gas, with Gazprom, the Russian gas monopoly, currently supplying over a quarter of all European gas supplies. This dependence has been brought into the spotlight in recent months in light of the Ukrainian conflict and the fact that over 50 per cent of Europe's imported Russian gas travels through Ukrainian gas pipelines.

On the flip side, however, Europe accounts for approximately one-third of Gazprom's total gas sales, and around half of Russia's total budget revenue comes from oil and gas. Moscow depends on Europe for this source of revenue, and most energy analysts seem to agree that Russian leadership is unlikely to jeopardise this key income stream. Short of an actual war, the consensus appears to be, Europe's gas supplies are unlikely to be seriously threatened in the short to medium term.

Ireland has a high reliance on imported fossil fuels, which will be discussed further in Section 3. While it is unlikely that Ireland will ever be immune to international geopolitical issues surrounding fossil fuel supplies, the growth of indigenous renewable generation and energy efficiency measures are important strategies to ameliorate this risk.

3 ENERGY SUPPLY: PERFORMANCE AND POLICY ISSUES

As one of the key inputs to economic activity, the security of energy supply into the future is a key concern. Interruptions in supply, even for short periods of time, can have very serious economic consequences. Security of supply can be considered under a number of metrics: for example, how reliant is the country on an individual fuel source, and how diverse are its energy fuel needs? How dependent is the country on imported fuel and as a result how exposed is it to price fluctuations and interruptions in imported fuel supplies? Does the country have the physical infrastructure in place to ensure delivery of energy to the end-user into the future?

Fuel Diversity
Table 10.1 illustrates the breakdown of energy demand in Ireland in 2012 by fuel type. It can be seen that Ireland's dominant fuel source is oil, which accounts for around 45 per cent of total energy use. This demand is primarily driven by the transport and heating sectors. Natural gas is increasing in importance, mainly driven by its use in electricity generation and domestic heating.

Table 10.1 Ireland's Percentage Energy Usage by Type in 2012

	Total	Electricity	Heating	Transport
Oil[1]	45	1	45	98
Natural gas	30	49	38	–
Coal	11	25	7	–
Peat	6	12	5	–
Renewable sources	6	11	5	2
Electricity imports	0.5	1	–	–

Source: Sustainable Energy Authority of Ireland (SEAI), *Energy in Ireland Key Statistics 2013*, Energy Policy Statistical Support Unit, 2013.
[1] Oil includes oil products such as diesel, petrol and kerosene.

As mentioned in Section 2, policymakers generally try to encourage as much diversity as possible so that each sector is protected should there be an interruption in the supply of one fuel source. In each of the energy sectors, though, Ireland has a heavy reliance on at least one fuel type. This is particularly pertinent for the transport sector where 98 per cent of fuels are oil based, and thus this sector is heavily exposed to any potential interruptions in oil supply.

The electricity sector, as can be seen in Table 10.1, has the most diverse range of fuel types, although it has a heavy and growing reliance on natural gas. The existing oil-fired power stations are gradually being decommissioned due to age and any new fossil fuel based power stations planned are expected to be natural gas fired. While coal and oil can be stored (albeit at a cost), natural gas storage is much more complex. Thus, this heavy reliance on natural gas for electricity production can be seen as a threat to supply security into the future. The sources of energy for the heating sector are more diversified and reflect that of the economy as a whole (see earlier), with a heavy dependence likewise on oil.

Indigenous Fuels and Import Dependency

Twinned with the challenge of diversity of fuel supplies is the reliance of a country on imported fuels. When a country can produce energy locally it provides a hedge against fluctuations in international fuel prices and interruptions in fuel supplies. It also saves on important foreign exchange outlays. Thus, policymakers try as much as possible to encourage the production of energy domestically.

Ireland had an import dependency of 84.7 per cent in 2012, the fourth highest dependency in the EU-27 and well above the EU average. The trend has been upward, the figure having been around 70 per cent 20 years ago, and reflects the fact that Ireland is not endowed with significant indigenous fossil fuel resources and has, to date, not harnessed significant quantities of renewable resources.

Oil, as seen in Table 10.1, of which 100 per cent is imported, is by far the most dominant energy source in Ireland. The transport sector has the heaviest reliance on imported fuels. The bulk of Ireland's oil, though, is sourced from politically stable countries such as the UK, Norway and Denmark. The UK continues to have ample oil potential, with proven and probable reserve estimates of 4,353 million tons in 2012. Actual oil production in 2012 was 45 million tons.[7]

Arising from membership of the EU and the International Energy Agency (IEA), Ireland must hold 90 days of oil stocks based on the previous year's imports. Under the European Communities (Minimum Stocks of Petroleum Oils) Regulations, this responsibility has been vested in an Irish state body called the National Oil Reserves Agency (NORA). NORA receives no exchequer funding and its ongoing activities are 100 per cent funded by a levy imposed on certain oil products.

According to the Department of Communications, Energy and Natural Resources, if there were a 10 per cent reduction in world oil supplies (a level of disruption unprecedented since the Suez War of 1956–1957), it is estimated that the required 90-day reserves would last over two years, even without taking into account any demand-reduction measures.[8] Thus, in the short term, Ireland is hedged against fluctuations in oil supply. However, in the medium to long term, in order to protect itself from fluctuating supply and prices, Ireland needs to diversify further its energy mix away from oil, particularly in the transport and heating sectors.

Given Ireland's large oil stocks, interruptions to gas supply are of greater concern in the short to medium term. In 2012, just 14 per cent of Ireland's gas was produced domestically (at the Kinsale gas field) with the remaining 86 per cent imported via a pipeline to Britain. The majority of Ireland's imported gas is sourced from politically stable locations in the North Sea. It is anticipated that Ireland's production of natural gas will increase in the coming years through the completion of the development of the Corrib gas field and a proposed liquefied natural gas development in Co. Clare. A number of gas storage facilities are planned in Larne and Ballycotton.

In addition to domestic gas, Ireland also has an indigenous peat resource, which is currently used to generate electricity at three power stations. The Irish government supports the use of peat for electricity generation through a public service obligation (PSO) levy on all electricity bills (see later). The justification for this support is for security of supply reasons (to reduce Ireland's dependence on imported fuels) and to support jobs in rural areas.

In a further effort to reduce Ireland's reliance on imported fuels (as well as for environmental and sustainability reasons), the Irish government has set targets for renewable energy in each of the energy consumption sectors. In the electricity sector Ireland has an ambitious target of achieving 40 per cent electricity from renewable sources by 2020, exceeding the targets of any other country worldwide. In the heating sector the target is 12 per cent by 2020 and for transport 10 per cent. Given the centralised nature of electricity supply, it is relatively easier to integrate renewable sources into this sector, hence the higher target.

Renewable Energy

Hydro generation was the earliest renewable technology used for electricity generation and it underwent rapid development throughout the last century. Across the developed world few, if any, suitable economic sites remain for the further development of hydro electricity. After hydro, wind generation is one of the most advanced forms of renewable energy and output has grown rapidly in the last 15 years. As the market for wind energy has grown, the costs have reduced dramatically. Ambitious renewable energy targets, together with reducing costs and successes to date, are likely to ensure that wind energy continues to grow in electricity networks worldwide.

Given its location on the edge of the Atlantic Ocean, Ireland has a vast wind resource potential. It is anticipated that the bulk of Ireland's renewable target in the electricity sector will be met through wind generation. In 2012, wind generation represented over 11 per cent of electricity generation and the island of Ireland, as a single synchronous power system, has arguably the largest penetrations of wind power in the world at present.

Solar technology for electricity generation requires direct sunlight, and as such is not considered an economically viable option for Ireland. Ireland does, however, have large ocean energy resources for the development of wave and tidal turbines. Nevertheless, the development of ocean technology has been relatively slow with just a small number of devices at the commercial prototype stage. While the vast majority of wind turbines follow the same general design (three blades on a vertical tower), no single ocean device has emerged as the leading design. Operational challenges and access issues in the marine environment have been among the main barriers to ocean energy development to date.

Renewable technologies such as wind generation, solar, tidal and wave generation have a 'variable' output. The output of these units depends on weather conditions, which cannot be controlled by the operator of the generator. For example, the amount of electricity generated by a wind turbine fluctuates as wind speed changes and that of a solar panel with the intensity of sunlight. Thus, the control of their output is limited. When significant penetrations of these forms of generation are connected to an electricity network, it can increase the challenge of providing a secure and reliable electricity supply at all times. This is a challenge that must be addressed by electricity system operators into the future as wind and other renewable energy sources increase further.

In the heating and transport sectors, the integration of renewable sources of energy is more challenging as these sectors do not generally use centralised energy supplies. For heating just 5.1 per cent of energy in 2012 was from renewable sources with the main contributor being the use of waste wood biomass. In the transport sector, renewable energy represented 2.2 per cent of transport energy in 2012. The share of biofuels in transport continues to grow year on year following the introduction of tax breaks in 2006. The use of electricity in the transport sector (for the Dart and Luas) is also considered to be 'renewable' as the electricity can be generated through renewable sources.

Energy Infrastructure

In order to ensure the security of energy supply it is important to examine not only the sustainability of the fuels used (renewable versus fossil fuel) but also the adequacy of the energy infrastructure. As mentioned in Section 2, adequate infrastructure requires the intervention of the state, not only in incentivising the provision of infrastructure but also through regulation.

The main infrastructural challenges in the heating energy sector are the poor-quality existing housing stock and the availability of mains gas. While advances have been made in recent years regarding the energy usage of new-build housing (for example Part L of the Building Regulations 2008), unfortunately in many cases it was too late and did not apply to houses built at the height of the housing boom. Retrofitting existing houses with improved insulation, glazing and efficient boilers is likely to be the predominant source of infrastructural improvements in residential heating in the future.

Natural gas is one of the most efficient forms of heating. However, access to the natural gas network is required. Gas supply in Ireland is delivered via a network of approximately 12,300km of pipelines. There are two main gas entry points, one at Inch in Co. Cork to service the Kinsale and Seven Heads gas fields and the other from Moffat in western Scotland, which connects Ireland to the main British gas network. The primary source of future indigenous production of gas is from the Corrib gas field in Co. Mayo. To date, five oil wells are completed and ready for production at the Corrib site and the 83km offshore pipeline was completed in 2009.

The final section of the pipeline is onshore and it has led to much local opposition. Planning permission for this final onshore section was granted in January 2011 and tunnelling for the onshore pipeline commenced in January 2013. Assuming no further delays, the Corrib gas field is expected to be online in 2014–15, leading to a third entry point. When operational, the output of this gas field is anticipated to meet approximately 60 per cent of Irish annual gas demand at peak production.[9]

In the *electricity* sector, 'generation adequacy' is used to measure the relationship between the output of electricity that can be supplied, and predicted demand. A statistic known as the 'loss of load expectation' (LOLE) measures any imbalance between projected supply and demand. In Ireland, the accepted LOLE is eight hours per year. In other words, Ireland is considered to have enough supply potential (power stations, renewable generators, etc.) to meet demand if the predicted number of hours when customers lose power is equal to or less than eight hours per year. When examining future demand and supply options, we must ensure that this LOLE criterion continues to be met.

Currently Ireland has two electrical interconnectors to the system in Britain: one to Scotland and one to Wales. This second interconnector to Wales, known as the EastWest Interconnector, which was completed in 2012, is approximately 260km in length and has the capacity to transport enough electricity to power 300,000 homes. These two interconnectors allow Ireland to import electricity when needed and to export power when Ireland has excess generation. They significantly enhance the reliability of the Irish electricity system and allow for continued operation with an LOLE of eight hours per annum.

The electricity system operator of Ireland, Eirgrid, predicts that the adequacy situation is strongly positive until at least 2016. A surplus of electricity supply is predicted for each year with a LOLE of not more than eight hours per year being comfortably met. This is due to projected investment in new generation capacity (both conventional and renewable), network upgrades and developments, and low demand growth, arising from the marked slow-down in economic activity.

It should be noted, however, that any new generation capacity will require the servicing and upgrade of the existing electricity network. To this end, in 2010 the CER announced plans to invest €3.76 billion in the Irish electricity network. The purpose of this investment is to improve the quality of electricity to customers, to allow for the development of new energy projects (such as remote wind farms) and to help attract new foreign direct investment into regions which would traditionally have been poorly serviced by the electricity network. This network upgrade plan will be financed through revenues earned by ESB networks and Eirgrid. Again, the issue of spatial planning arises in regard to the upgrade of the electricity network. Ireland's legacy of ribbon development greatly increases the challenge of routing power lines, often resulting in lengthy planning delays.

Nuclear Energy

A highly controversial topic relating to energy supply security and energy infrastructure is the potential for nuclear energy in Ireland. The international nuclear debate has heightened in recent years following the events in 2011 at the Fukushima nuclear plant in Japan with widespread re-evaluation of nuclear programmes. Current Irish legislation bans the generation of electricity from nuclear sources, and it is unlikely that any Irish government would be elected with a mandate for nuclear energy in the foreseeable future. The infrastructural aspects of nuclear power for Ireland will be discussed in this section and the environmental aspects in a later section.

Nuclear fission energy is the energy that is released when an atom is split in two. In most nuclear power stations, the atom that is split is a uranium atom. The splitting uranium atoms react with each other to split more atoms, creating a chain reaction. Each of these reactions releases energy in the form of heat, which can then be used to generate electricity. Uranium is in abundant supply across the world, with large stocks in politically stable countries such as Canada and Australia.

The infrastructural requirements of integrating nuclear energy into the Irish electricity system are very challenging. First, the majority of nuclear power stations are large at over 1,000MW. A power station of this size would represent 22 per cent of Ireland's peak electricity demand in 2013. In order to operate the electricity system in a reliable fashion, the system operator is required to carry a certain amount of electricity in 'back-up' mode to prevent against any contingencies (similar to having a doctor 'on call'). This 'back-up' electricity is known as reserve and the amount carried is equal to the size of the largest unit on the system. Currently the largest unit is at Poolbeg in Dublin and is 460MW in size. The introduction of a nuclear unit would increase the amount of back-up capacity required to 1,000MW, which would have significant cost and operational implications. In addition, any power station of 1,000MW in size would require significant electricity network reinforcement.

Another infrastructural challenge of nuclear generation is that it is relatively inflexible in nature. Once a nuclear plant is in operation its output cannot be varied easily due to safety concerns. This lack of flexibility would cause a challenge for the reliable operation of the Irish electricity system. With a large and growing wind penetration, what Ireland needs are flexible power stations to accommodate the variable wind output, i.e. power stations which can increase their output when renewable generation is low and decrease output when renewable generation is high. Thus, as Ireland is actively pursuing the promotion of renewable energy, it needs   complementary flexible conventional power stations. Nuclear power stations are not flexible in their operation and thus are not complementary to renewable generation on a small isolated electricity system like Ireland's. Thus, without significantly more electrical interconnection which would essentially increase the size of Ireland's electricity system, Ireland can pursue either nuclear or renewable sources of energy, but probably not both.

Fracking

The exploitation of shale gas using hydraulic fracturing or 'fracking' has increased dramatically in the USA over the past 20 years and by 2013 dry shale gas production had risen to 39 per cent of total dry gas production. Fracking is the process of drilling into the earth to allow a high-pressure water, sand and chemical mixture to be injected into the rock to release the gas inside. The process is carried out vertically or, more commonly, by drilling horizontally into the rock layer. The process can create new pathways to release gas or can be used to extend existing channels.[10]

While the USA and Canada have led the way in fracking, there is increasing interest in the technique in other areas of the world, with potential sites for shale gas extraction through fracking occurring across Europe. However, the extensive use of fracking in the USA, and the consideration of the process by EU governments, has prompted heated environmental debate.

Environmental concerns associated with the fracking process include the vast amount of water that is consumed in the process, which must be transported to the fracking site, at potentially significant environmental cost. The second is the worry that the potentially carcinogenic chemicals used may escape and contaminate groundwater around the fracking site. There are also worries that the fracking process can cause small earth tremors; in fact fracking is currently suspended in the UK following two small earthquakes relating to a fracking event near Blackpool in 2011.

Commentators in Europe have also cautioned against overstating the potential benefits of fracking, saying that while the USA can produce shale gas at low cost, this is due to advantageous geological conditions and 20–30 years of experience. In essence, the shale gas revolution took place 30 years ago in the USA and it is unlikely that the EU will be able to replicate the economies of scale, with anticipated production costs 150–250 per cent higher than those in the USA.

Also, while the USA has seen a reduction in greenhouse gas emissions through the use of shale gas, this has largely come as a result of the low-cost shale gas replacing coal-fired electricity generation. It is unlikely that the EU will be able to produce shale gas at a low enough cost to push out European coal-fired generation, particularly when the USA can export its unused coal and sell it at low cost on the European markets. There are also concerns that potential methane leaks from fracking activities could counteract any CO_2 benefits.

While there may be some longer-term benefits of shale gas extraction in Europe it is unlikely to make more than a few percentage points difference in the energy mix and should not be considered as the panacea for Europe's energy concerns. It is likely that renewable technologies and energy efficiency measures will have a much greater impact than pursuing shale gas extraction.

4 END-USER ENERGY PRICES AND COMPETITION

The second pillar of energy policy is the sustainability of end-user energy prices. As a key input in almost every production process, energy costs have a direct impact on Ireland's international competitiveness and indeed on living standards in Ireland, as the cheaper the energy the better off are consumers. The provision of electricity and heating is also considered to be a basic necessity and thus it is important to protect the financially disadvantaged from excessively high prices. However, prices must also be high enough to attract investment in the energy infrastructure in Ireland into the future. Thus, energy prices are generally discussed as being sustainable; low enough so as not to adversely impact on competitiveness, living standards and vulnerable users, but also high enough to ensure continued investment in supply. Table 10.2 illustrates Ireland's end-user energy prices compared to the EU-15 countries listed.

Table 10.2 End-User Energy Prices (including taxes) in EU-15 countries

	Electricity prices €2012 per 100kWh		Gas prices €2012 per GJ[1]		Transport prices March 2014 € per litre	
	Industrial	Domestic	Industrial	Domestic	Unleaded	Diesel
Austria	11.09	20.24	3.86	7.63	1.35	1.33
Belgium	11.07	22.23	3.47	7.34	1.61	1.45
Denmark	9.93	29.72	7.00	10.83	1.60	1.45
Finland	7.44	15.59	4.76	–	1.61	1.52
France	7.88	14.50	4.03	6.82	1.51	1.41
Germany	12.97	26.76	4.87	6.48	1.49	1.38
Greece	12.22	14.18	5.79	10.17	1.71	1.40
Ireland	*13.96*	*22.89*	*4.24*	*6.72*	*1.53*	*1.46*
Italy	19.88	22.97	3.96	9.68	1.77	1.68
Luxembourg	10.13	17.06	5.12	5.94	1.30	1.20
Netherlands	9.66	18.96	3.65	8.44	1.78	1.51
Portugal	11.48	20.63	4.20	8.53	1.54	1.35
Spain	11.96	22.75	3.75	9.11	1.40	1.34
Sweden	7.76	20.83	5.50	12.68	1.62	1.63
UK	12.05	17.85	3.25	5.78	1.58	1.67

Sources: electricity and gas prices: SEAI, 'Electricity and Gas Prices in Ireland, 2nd Semester 2012', June 2013; unleaded and diesel prices: AA website, www.aaireland.ie, accessed March 2014.
[1] Domestic gas prices unavailable for Finland.

It can be seen that end-user *electricity* prices in Ireland are among the highest in the EU. Electricity prices in Ireland are made up of four components: generation, networks, retail and the PSO levy. Looking at each of these components in turn can help explain Ireland's high electricity prices.

Generation Costs and the Single Electricity Market
The largest component of the electricity bill for a company is accounted for by generation costs, i.e. the cost of generating electricity. The energy industry has traditionally been dominated by statutory monopolies which control the network

and the supply of energy products, e.g. ESB in the electricity sector and Bord Gáis in the gas sector. However, EU directives aimed at increasing competition (in order to reduce end-user prices) in the electricity and gas sectors have increased competition in both of these sectors in recent years.

In order to promote investment, the EU directed each member state to create an open and transparent market for wholesale electricity generation. In Ireland this prompted the development of the single electricity market (SEM), a single market across the Republic and Northern Ireland, which went 'live' in November 2007. It is a supply side auction where power stations bid on the basis of how much electricity they can provide in any hour and their marginal cost. The system operator then selects the cheapest units to meet the demand in any hour. The marginal cost of the last unit selected is the market price for the hour, also known as the pool price. There are also two other payment mechanisms – the uplift and the capacity payment mechanism – designed to allow generators recover their longer-term costs.

The SEM mechanism is generally considered to be operating efficiently and in March 2014 Ireland had over 200 registered units generating electricity through the market. While Ireland has some relatively inefficient generating stations with higher costs, international fuel prices are the key driver of the cost of generation.

Since the second half of 2009 the wholesale price of gas has been increasing steadily and on average the price in the first half of 2013 was 195 per cent higher than at the end of 2009. Ireland has close to the highest reliance on imported fossil fuels for electricity of all EU countries (at 80 per cent in 2010). In fact, of the countries listed in Table 10.2, only the Netherlands has a higher reliance on imported fossil fuels for electricity generation. It is this exposure to international fuel prices, in particular gas, that is the main driver of Ireland's high electricity prices. Exchange rates also play a role for Ireland with a fall in value of the euro against sterling in recent years impacting on the cost of Ireland's gas imports.

Network, Retail and Levy Costs

The second largest component of end-user prices is network costs. These are charges which are used to maintain and upgrade the electricity network. This is essential in order to encourage foreign direct investment into areas with relatively weak network connection. Also, without investment in the electricity network the achievement of Ireland's renewable targets will not be possible. However, as mentioned previously, Ireland's spatial planning legacy has resulted in Ireland having four times the EU average length of power line, thus network costs are higher than those experienced elsewhere in the EU.

The retail component of the end-user bill covers the administrative, accounting and services costs of the electricity supplier. In Ireland, the electricity supply companies buy electricity from the SEM at the pool price, which varies on an hourly basis, and then sell this electricity to end-use customers, usually at a fixed-rate tariff. The retail component accounts for the mark-up between the pool price at which suppliers buy electricity and the fixed tariff at which it is sold. The CER has been successful in promoting competition in the electricity supply business and Ireland now has seven electricity supply companies serving the residential sector.

The final component of electricity bills is the PSO levy. This levy is designed to support the use of indigenous peat and renewable energy sources in electricity generation. In 2013 the PSO levy was €3.57 per month for residential customers and €10.82 per month for business customers. The PSO is justified on security of supply grounds but it is one of the most contradictory policies of the Irish government in the energy area. Peat is the most inefficient fuel for electricity generation and is the highest emitter of CO_2 of all fuels used in electricity generation in Ireland. Thus, while on the one hand the government has developed ambitious targets for renewable sources of energy to reduce emissions, on the other hand it is financially supporting the use of peat, the highest emitter of CO_2.

Heating and Transport Costs

The CER has also been actively promoting competition in the heating sector through deregulation of the gas market. In 2014, residential customers can purchase their gas from one of five suppliers (Airtricity, Bord Gáis Energy, Energia, Electric Ireland and Flogas) and business customers from six suppliers. Competition in this market has ensured that, since 2008, gas prices in Ireland for business customers have been below the EU average (Table 10.2).

In the transport sector, the main driver of end-user prices are international fuel price fluctuations, with other factors such as exchange rates, production, and refining costs also playing a role. In March 2014 the average price of unleaded petrol in the EU countries in Table 10.2 was €1.56 per litre, marginally above the average price in Ireland of €1.53. The price of petrol is determined by transportation costs and the excise rates charged by governments. The excise rates (including the carbon charge) in Ireland on motor fuels in 2014 are 58.7 cent of the price of a litre of petrol and 47.9 cent of the price of a litre of diesel.

5 ENVIRONMENTAL ISSUES

So far two of the pillars of energy policy have been discussed: security of supply and sustainable end-user prices. The third energy policy pillar is environmental sustainability. Energy provision impacts on almost all facets of the environment, from emissions and air pollution, to water consumption and quality, to waste generation and the natural environment. Thus, energy policy should always be considered in parallel with environmental issues; however, environmental policy is also much broader than just energy-related concerns. This section elaborates on some of the environmental issues relating to energy provision but more importantly discusses some of the broader environmental policy issues facing Ireland. Environmental policy is discussed under four headings in this section: emissions; air and water issues; waste; and biodiversity.[11]

Emissions

Due to international concern about climate change, policymakers worldwide have introduced numerous instruments to help curb global emissions. Obviously a goal of zero pollution is unrealistic and undesirable since pollution is a by-product of day-to-day living. Thus, the key for policymakers is to decide upon an optimal level of operation where the costs do not exceed the benefits of pollution (material standard of living).

Kyoto Protocol and EU Trading Scheme

The most wide-reaching agreement is the Kyoto Protocol, which set binding targets for 37 industrialised countries and the EU to reduce greenhouse gas (GHG) emissions. The EU committed to reducing emissions by 8 per cent below 1990 levels in the 2008 to 2012 period, a target which was achieved. Following the Kyoto Protocol target, the EU has set a target for the subsequent period from 2013 to 2020, to reduce emissions to 20 per cent below 1990 levels.

Ireland met its Kyoto Protocol emissions targets for the period 2008 to 2012 and has now been set a target of limiting annual GHG emissions to 20 per cent below 2005 levels by 2020 in line with EU 2020 targets. In order to assist in meeting the Kyoto emissions targets and subsequent targets, the European Union Greenhouse Gas Emission Trading Scheme (EU ETS) commenced operation in January 2005. The EU ETS is now the largest multi-country, multi-sector GHG emission trading scheme in the world.

In accordance with the EU ETS, each member state was required to develop a national allocation plan which stated the total quantity of allowances that it intended to allocate to polluters in the member state and how it proposed to allocate them. Over 100 major industrial and institutional sites in Ireland are covered by the ETS. These include power generation, other combustion, cement, lime, glass and ceramic plants, and oil refining. Also included are large companies in areas such as food and drink, pharmaceuticals and semi-conductors.

While established to meet the Kyoto targets, the EU ETS scheme is now fully operational and will play a significant role in meeting EU targets for 2020. Since 2012 the mechanism has been opened up further to include emissions from airlines and since 2013 to allow trading of other emission types.

In 2012, combustion of fossil fuels was the largest source (over 60 per cent) of GHG emissions in Ireland, with 29 per cent of these regulated under the EU ETS. The *agriculture sector (due to emissions from livestock)* remains the single largest contributor to overall emissions, at 32 per cent of the total, followed by the *energy sector* (primarily power generation) with a 21 per cent share and the *transport sector* with an 18 per cent share. The remainder is made up by the *industrial and commercial, residential and waste* sectors.

While only 29 per cent of Ireland's emissions are currently covered by the EU ETS, Ireland must meet a second target under the EU Commission's Energy and Climate Package to cover emissions not included in the EU ETS, such as emissions from agriculture, transport, residential and waste sectors. Under this package Ireland must deliver a 20 per cent reduction in emissions from these sectors, relative to 2005 levels, by 2020. These are considered to be onerous targets and the Environmental Protection Agency (EPA) predicts that Ireland will not achieve this target. In fact the EPA predicts that without dramatic interventions, Ireland is likely to achieve only a 3 to 10 per cent reduction compared to the 20 per cent target, the consequences of which would be onerous financial penalties.[12]

Renewable energy has been discussed previously and our ambitious national targets form part of Ireland's measures aimed at reducing GHG emissions. Improvements are also planned on the demand side with the 2007 government White Paper, *Delivering a Sustainable Energy Future for Ireland*, setting a target of a 20 per cent improvement in energy efficiency across the whole economy by 2020.

Nuclear Energy

Omitted from Ireland's emissions reduction plans is the potential for nuclear generation. In 2009, Ireland had the second highest CO_2 emissions per capita in the EU, whereas France, with the largest nuclear programme, had one of the lowest. However, it should be noted that nuclear energy is not 100 per cent emission free as CO_2 is released during uranium mining, transportation, decommissioning and waste treatment. Also, nuclear energy can contribute to emissions reduction in the electricity sector but alone does not assist in meeting targets in the heating and transport sectors. Nevertheless, the fact that nuclear energy allows for the generation of large amounts of electricity with minimal levels of CO_2 is the most compelling argument for nuclear power generation.

Nuclear waste and environmental and safety issues surrounding waste storage and disposal are among the most concerning aspects of nuclear power generation. Final disposal methods currently exist for low- and intermediate-level waste; however, there are presently no operating facilities in the world for the final disposal of high-level nuclear waste products. Current practice is to store all high-level waste in intermediate storage facilities based on site at the nuclear power stations.

Coupled with the environmental concerns regarding nuclear waste storage are the potential safety concerns. New nuclear power stations have far superior safety precautions than old stations, with much of the operation now automated. However, the potential for accidents should be considered when examining nuclear energy. The environmental impact of an accident in Ireland is likely to be catastrophic. The prevailing winds are south-westerly so an explosive accident would almost certainly see radioactive clouds spread over land rather than towards the Atlantic. If the power station was located on Ireland's west coast, it is likely that the majority of the island would be affected by the spread of radioactivity, with the radioactive clouds then spreading across Britain and into mainland Europe.

While a fully informed scientific debate about nuclear energy is warranted in Ireland, it is unlikely, as mentioned earlier, that any Irish government would be elected with such a mandate in the foreseeable future. However, despite Ireland's legislative ban on nuclear energy, electricity generated by nuclear power is used in Ireland through the use of electrical imports from Britain. This use of nuclear power is likely to increase into the future as further interconnection to Britain is planned.

Air and Water Issues
Air Quality
Related to the discussion above, which focused on CO_2 emissions, general air quality depends also on other pollutants such as sulphur dioxide, nitrous oxide, particulate matter and volatile organic compounds. Ireland fares very well in terms of air quality, which is among the best in Europe, due largely to prevailing clean Atlantic air and a lack of large cities and heavy industry.

Ireland met all EU air quality standards in 2010, except for the ceiling on oxides of nitrogen (NO_x). The main sources of NO_x in Ireland are from the transport sector, power generation sector and the cement sector. While significant advances have been made to reduce NO_x emissions in the latter two sectors, the transport sector remains the primary reason why Ireland exceeded its NO_x emissions ceiling in 2010. Ireland was not alone: 11 other EU countries also exceeded their national ceilings, France and Germany being the worst offenders.

In order to maintain its good record on air quality, Ireland must continue to be vigilant in meeting its international commitments and ensure that industrial emissions of pollutants continue to be rigorously controlled. Government also needs to remain committed to reducing emissions in the transport sector through measures aimed at reducing travel demand, increasing alternatives to the private car, and improving the efficiency of motorised transport.

Water Quality
One of the primary environmental challenges facing Ireland over the next decade is water quality and preservation. Ireland is fortunate in having a relatively abundant supply of fresh water, with approximately 50 per cent of the land area of the state drained by just nine river systems. In 2000 the EU developed the Water Framework Directive (WFD) in response to the increasing threat of pollution and demand from the public for cleaner rivers, lakes and beaches. This directive is unique as it establishes a framework for the protection of all waters including rivers, lakes, estuaries, coastal waters and groundwater, and their dependent wildlife/habitats under one piece of environmental legislation.

Under the EU WFD, Ireland must achieve at least 'good water status' for all waters by 2015. Currently, much of Ireland's water does not meet this quality status and it is envisaged that substantial measures will be needed for Ireland to comply with this directive by 2015. For example, in 2012 just 46 per cent of Ireland's lakes met the ecological status required in this directive.

One of the reasons for Ireland's poor performance was the proliferation of construction during the housing boom. Construction was permitted without due regard for discharge into surrounding rivers and lakes and as a result Ireland is potentially facing significant fines for non-compliance with EU legislation. Other sources of water pollution are nutrient inputs from agriculture and municipal sources. Table 10.3 illustrates Ireland's poor performance against the requirements set down by the WFD, which states that all waters must achieve at least a 'good water rating' by 2015. The columns in Table 10.3 illustrate the percentage of Irish waters which are of sufficient quality to meet the directive (satisfactory status) and the percentage of insufficient quality (unsatisfactory status).

Table 10.3 Percentage of Ireland's Water Meeting the Requirements of the EU WFD in 2012

Waters	Satisfactory status	Unsatisfactory status
Ground water	85	15
Rivers	71	29
Lakes	46	54
Estuarine and coastal water	46	54
Seawater bathing	97	3

Source: EPA, *Ireland's Environment, An Assessment 2012*, available at www.epa.ie.

In Ireland the majority of drinking water originates from surface water (82 per cent) and the remainder from groundwater (10 per cent) and springs (8 per cent). The most important health indicator of drinking water quality in Ireland is the presence of microbiological particles, in particular *E. coli*. The presence of *E. coli* in drinking water indicates that the treatment process at the water treatment plant is not operating adequately or that contamination has entered the water distribution system after treatment. In Ireland in 2012, a total of 181 supplies (5.6 per cent) failed to meet the standard for *E. coli* at one time or more during the year. The majority of supplies where *E. coli* was detected were private group water schemes, e.g. from local wells. Publicly supplied water continues to be of a very high quality with just 0.04 per cent of supplies failing to meet the standard at one time or more in 2012.

Once water is extracted, it requires treatment in order to make it suitable for consumption. As mentioned previously, given Ireland's legacy of ribbon development the water networks are radial in nature and experience high losses. It is estimated that over 34 per cent of Ireland's water supply is lost in transmission, one of the highest levels in Europe.[13]

Water Charges
Water charges are currently in place for all commercial premises across Ireland and in an effort to ease pressure on water supplies it was announced in Budget 2009 that domestic water charges are to be rolled out across the country. Given

the high cost to the exchequer of maintaining quality water supplies, estimated at €1.2 billion per annum, the introduction of water charges was also a condition of Ireland's assistance programme from the EU, European Central Bank and International Monetary Fund.

Irish Water was established in March 2013 as a semi-state company which will manage the water and wastewater services that were previously under the auspices of the 34 local authorities (see also Chapter 5). Irish Water began the process of installing water meters in August 2013 and it is anticipated that the majority of Irish households will have water meters installed by 2016. Domestic water charges are due to commence at the end of 2014 with customers receiving their first bills in the first quarter of 2015. The rates and pricing structure for domestic customers are currently being considered by the CER.

Water Infrastructure and Flooding
Ireland has undergone significant investment in improving the water services infrastructure (for drinking water and urban wastewater), with over €4.6 billion invested over the last decade. This has resulted in a dramatic improvement in the level of treatment of urban wastewater. However, from Table 10.3, it is apparent that Ireland has a long way to go before it can meet its required water standards.

A related issue which has grown in the public consciousness in recent years is flooding. Floods are a natural and inevitable part of life in Ireland and are usually caused by a combination of events including overflowing river banks, coastal storms, or blocked and overloaded ditches. Numerous severe floods have occurred throughout the country in the last decade and it is widely anticipated that changes in rainfall patterns and rises in sea levels resulting from climate change may make such flooding incidents more frequent and severe in the future. In 2008, the government announced new flooding guidelines and all new developments must adhere to these procedures. However, this initiative is unfortunately a classic example of 'closing the stable door after the horse has bolted' as the proliferation of development before 2008 did not adhere to these guidelines, with much construction taking place on natural flood plains.

Waste
Since 2008, there have been sharp decreases in Ireland in commercial and household waste volumes, in line with the downturn in consumption and economic growth. For example, construction sector waste volumes have collapsed by 81 per cent since 2007. Waste collection also changed significantly in the period 2008 to 2012 with the majority of local authorities exiting the domestic collection market (see also Chapter 5). Ireland has made progress in meeting many EU waste recycling/recovery targets, but challenges remain in relation to reducing the level of waste generated and waste management (see Table 10.4).

The bulk of Ireland's waste is municipal waste which is defined as household waste, commercial waste, and cleaning waste. Packaging waste includes materials such as cardboard, paper, glass, plastic, steel, aluminium, and wood. Since 2001

Ireland has been compliant with all statutory packaging recovery targets and is expected to well exceed the EU target of 60 per cent recovery rate of packaging for 2011. The waste electrical and electronic (WEEE) initiative has been highly successful in Ireland with an average collection of 9kg per capita in 2009, well in excess of the EU target of 4kg.

Table 10.4 Ireland's Compliance with EU Waste Legislation

	Indicator
EU Packaging Directive, target date 2011	Achieved
WEEE Directive, target date 2008	Achieved
End of Life Vehicles Directive, initial target date 2006 (subsequent target 2015)	Not achieved (at risk)
Batteries Directive, initial target date 2011 (subsequent target 2016)	Achieved (at risk)
Landfill Directive, target date 2016	At risk
New waste framework directive, target date 2020	On track

Source: EPA, *Progress towards EU Waste Targets March 2014.*

Currently 40 per cent of Ireland's municipal waste is recycled, with the majority exported to Britain. There has been a significant improvement in Ireland's attitude towards recycling and a two-bin service (general waste and mixed dry recyclables bins) is provided to virtually all households, with a three-bin service (including organics bin) provided to 34 per cent of serviced households in 2012. According to the EPA, in 2009 there were almost 2,000 bring banks in operation for the collection of dry recyclables such as glass, clothes and beverage cans.

While Ireland has outperformed its waste targets in many areas, the main threat to the sustainability of waste management is infrastructural capacity. Ireland's waste infrastructure relies heavily on landfill. There are currently 28 active landfill sites for municipal waste disposal and, at current fill rates, 15 of these sites will have reached their full capacity by 2015. In addition, landfill capacity is not distributed evenly throughout the state and some regions are already reaching a critical capacity shortage.

There is currently only one municipal waste incineration in Ireland, which is in Carranstown in Co. Meath. In 2005 the EPA granted a licence for an incinerator in Ringaskiddy in Co. Cork and in 2008 a licence was issued for an incinerator at Poolbeg in Dublin. All of these developments have undergone lengthy planning delays, with An Bord Pleanála refusing planning permission for the facility in Cork in 2011 and Dublin City Council voting to abandon plans for the Poolbeg facility in light of local opposition in 2014.

Ireland is at an important juncture in waste management with impending EU targets and penalties on the horizon. With this in mind, one of the significant developments in the waste sector in recent years has been the introduction of refuse charges in an effort to manage and reduce waste. Domestic waste charges are now levied on almost all households that use an organised refuse collection service. These charges were brought in at different times by different local authorities and are not uniform across the state. However, without a concerted and significant effort towards a reduction in total waste production, a reduced reliance on landfill and the development of further waste management infrastructure, Ireland is likely to face significant EU non-compliance fines in relation to waste in the coming years.

Nature and Biodiversity

The protection of the natural environment and biodiversity is of ethical and economic concern. While progress has been made in the designation of EU-protected areas in Ireland, several areas of national importance remain undesignated and significant aspects of biodiversity in Ireland are under considerable threat from unsustainable activities. Ireland has international and legal obligations to protect biodiversity, including a commitment to halt biodiversity loss by 2020.

On a global scale, species are currently being lost at a rate of up to 1,000 times faster than the natural rate, primarily as a result of human activities. In the EU it is estimated that only 17 per cent of habitats and protected species are in a favourable state. In terms of Ireland's performance, only 7 per cent of listed habitats are considered to be in a favourable state as defined in the EU Habitats Directive (92/43/EEC).

In relation to species, Ireland's record is also poor, with only 39 per cent of species listed under the Habitats Directive being reported as in a favourable state. These species include bats, seals and certain plants. Other species, such as a number of species of fish (e.g. Atlantic salmon), molluscs and toads, are reported as being in poor to bad status. An assessment by BirdWatch Ireland suggests that of the 199 bird species assessed, up to 29 species are threatened with extinction in Ireland.

The key pressures on Ireland's habitats and species are direct habitat damage through activities such as peat cutting, wetland drainage/reclamation and infrastructural development; overgrazing and undergrazing; water pollution, particularly from nutrients and silt; unsustainable exploitation such as over-fishing and peat extraction; invasive alien species; and recreational pressure. Indirect pressures such as population growth and poor spatial development are also threats to biodiversity. Climate change is also likely to bring additional pressures on a number of species and habitats in Ireland.

Maintaining habitats and biodiversity has economic as well as ethical value, with benefits to the agricultural sector (both in terms of crops and livestock), the tourism sector, in pest control, in the resulting health benefits from pest control, in the fisheries sector, water quality, recreation, and in reducing waste assimilation. Biodiversity is estimated to be worth at least €2.6 billion per annum to Ireland.

6 CONCLUSION

This chapter has examined the development of Ireland's energy provision and environmental measures over the past decade and has highlighted some of the challenges facing each of these sectors. A key message arising from this chapter is the important link between energy and environmental policy. In particular, it has been highlighted how almost every facet of the energy sector (from electricity generation to transport provision to fossil fuel extraction and to domestic consumption) has significant environmental consequences and it would thus be naive and impractical to consider energy policy in an environmental vacuum.

The chapter also emphasised the role of the state in energy provision through direct ownership of assets, in the regulation of strategic behaviour by electricity providers, in the control of emissions and in securing diversity in energy supplies. In particular, the chapter highlights the importance of energy resources on a global scale and the political conflict that has resulted from the control of fossil fuel resources worldwide. Given its island nature and its relative few indigenous fossil fuel resources, Ireland has one of the highest levels of imported fossil fuels in Europe and represents an interesting case study system when it comes to the challenges of energy diversity. This chapter expanded on this issue and highlighted some potential solutions such as renewable energy and, more controversially, nuclear energy and fracking.

One of the real success stories of the economic boom was the huge improvement in transport infrastructure in Ireland, with major upgrades seen in both road networks and public transport infrastructure. However, this improvement is, unfortunately, twinned with missed opportunities in spatial planning. The housing boom did little to address the dispersed nature of the population and the poor quality of housing stock relative to our EU neighbours. The rapid construction period also left a negative legacy in terms of our environmental goals in the areas of water quality and waste management. In fact, planning issues were a recurring theme throughout this chapter, from the high average length of our electricity lines to the security of future gas supplies at the Corrib field, the high level of water losses, and the sustainability of waste management with delays in incinerator construction.

While Ireland continues to make progress towards its environmental targets, issues surrounding air and water quality, waste infrastructure and biodiversity protection are key areas of concern in the coming years. Ireland is also facing significant challenges in keeping up with competitors in terms of the quality of energy infrastructure, end-user energy prices and in securing a more diverse energy supply. Unfortunately these challenges are likely to be heightened by public opposition to necessary energy and environmental infrastructure projects such as network expansion, wind farm development and waste management infrastructure.

Notes

1   This section draws heavily on the Sustainable Energy Authority of Ireland (SEAI), *Residential Energy Roadmap*, available at www.seai.ie.

2   A good evaluation of Ireland's energy policy in each of these areas can be found in J. FitzGerald, *A Review of Irish Energy Policy*, ESRI Research Series No. 21, April 2011.

3   See *Report of the Review Group on State Assets and Liabilities*, April 2011, available at www.per.gov.ie.

4   Housing statistics are from Eurostat, the European Commission statistical database.

5   J. Shine, 'A road map for smart networks', *Engineers Journal,* Vol. 63, No. 5, June 2009.

6   This section draws on M. Klare, *Blood and Oil: The Dangers and Consequences of America's Growing Petroleum Dependency*, Metropolitan Books/Henry Holt, New York 2004.

7   UK oil reserves and estimated ultimate recovery for 2013, available at www.gov.uk.

8   See Department of Communications, Energy and Natural Resources, *Oil Stock Policy*, available at www.dcenr.gov.ie.

9   This section draws on data from the Commission for Energy Regulation (CER), *Joint Gas Capacity Statement* 2010, Report No. 10121, available at www.cer.ie.

10 This section draws on D. Healy, 'Hydraulic fracturing or "fracking": a short summary of current knowledge and potential environmental impacts', Environmental Protection Agency (EPA) (Ireland)/Science, Technology, Research and Innovation for the Environment (STRIVE) Programme 2007–2013, 2012, available at www.epa.ie.

11 This section draws significantly on the EPA, *Ireland's Environment, An Assessment 2012*, available at www.epa.ie.

12 EPA, *Ireland's Greenhouse Gas Emissions Projections, 2012–2030*, April 2013, available at www.epa.ie.

13 European Environment Agency, *Losses from Urban Water Networks*, available at www.eea.europa.eu.

CHAPTER 11

The Agri-Food Sector

Alan Matthews

1 INTRODUCTION

This chapter discusses the role of the agri-food sector in the Irish economy. The agri-food sector is a complex value chain which links the procurement of agricultural raw materials produced on farms, through processing and distribution for final consumption. The industry consists of multiple players, such as farmers, input suppliers, manufacturers, importers, packagers, transporters, wholesalers, retailers, and final customers. The agri-food sector of the Irish economy has traditionally been treated as a distinct sector for economic and policy analysis, in part because of its importance as one of the key indigenous sectors in the economy and in part because of the extent of policy intervention which sets it apart from other traded sectors.

Agriculture no longer has the dominant role in economic activity it once had, but when the contribution of the food industry is factored in, the agri-food sector remains a significant player. In 2011, it accounted for 8 per cent of Irish GNP and 8 per cent of employment. The agricultural sector remains important in other ways. Together with forestry, it occupies over 70 per cent of the land area of the country; it thus has a significant impact on the physical environment and the protection of biodiversity. It is the largest single contributor to Ireland's greenhouse gas emissions, accounting for 30 per cent of the total over the 2008 to 2012 period, well ahead of transport, the next most important emitter, which was responsible for 20 per cent. It remains the single most substantial contributor to the economic and social viability of rural areas.

At the industry level, the food and drink industry is Ireland's most important indigenous sector. Agri-food exports contributed 10 per cent of total merchandise exports in 2012, but this understates their importance relative to the rest of manufacturing; once imported inputs and profit repatriation are taken into account, the agri-food sector accounts for up to 40 per cent of net foreign exchange earnings from merchandise exports. Buoyed by rising global food prices since 2008, the sector is seen to have the ability to drive the Irish economic recovery from the post-2008 recession. Food and drink expenditures are also important to consumers, accounting for 18 per cent of household expenditure (not including meals out). Thus agricultural and food policy is intimately linked to debates on economic competitiveness, rural development, the environment and consumer well-being.

Another reason for the interest in agricultural and food policy is the decisive influence of government interventions on the fortunes of the industry. This dependence can be highlighted in a single statistic: the income accruing to farmers from agricultural activity arises almost entirely from public policy transfers from both EU and Irish consumers and taxpayers. Agricultural production within the EU is highly protected from world market competition. EU tariff levels on agricultural and food imports average around 18 per cent, compared to 4 per cent for non-agricultural goods, and for some agricultural products exceed 100 per cent.

This substantial government intervention in favour of a particular industry raises a series of questions. What objectives are it designed to achieve? Are these objectives justified? Is the support provided achieving these objectives? Is the support being provided efficiently? These are questions which economists are well placed to answer.

These questions are particularly pertinent at present because agricultural and food policy faces challenges on a number of fronts. Agricultural commodity prices, having fallen steadily in real terms for several decades, have increased dramatically; the UN Food and Agricultural Organisation's global food price index reached its highest point in decades in February 2011 and prices have remained high since then in historical perspective. Higher prices, of course, encourage farmers to increase production, but ensuring that this increased production is sustainable in environmental terms will be a major challenge.

High prices have also raised again the spectre of food insecurity and focused attention on the appropriate balance between producing food at home and relying on imports from third countries. This debate is central to the ongoing negotiations on agricultural trade liberalisation under the auspices of the World Trade Organisation (WTO). High food prices reflect in part ambitious government mandates to promote the production of renewable energies and, in particular, biofuels. Whether it makes sense to use agricultural land resources to produce food or fuel is a hotly contested issue. Higher food prices also throw into relief the increasing levels of concentration in the food marketing chain and the possible abuse by supermarkets in particular of their growing market power. At the same time, there is evidence of growing concern among consumers about the safety and quality of food being produced.

The purpose of this chapter is to describe these challenges in more detail and to discuss the appropriate policy responses. Section 2 provides a brief overview of some salient characteristics of the Irish agricultural sector. Section 3 discusses the changing policy context for agriculture at EU and international levels. Section 4 describes the food processing and distribution sectors. Section 5 explores the growing emphasis given to food safety regulation, the promotion of food quality, and the control of market power throughout the food chain. Section 6 concludes the chapter by summarising some of the conflicting tendencies at work as the agri-food sector faces into a more market-oriented and uncertain environment.

2 THE AGRICULTURAL SECTOR

Economic Characteristics

Agriculture has some relevant economic characteristics which help to explain why it has attracted a disproportionate share of government intervention. One is the inherent volatility of farm prices, due to the characteristics of both agricultural supply and demand. On the supply side, agricultural production is subject to natural forces such as weather conditions, pest infestations and disease risk, which means production can be very volatile from one year to another. For example, the drought that hit the US maize belt in 2012, the most serious and extensive in the previous 25 years, lowered its maize production by a quarter and had significant knock-on effects on world maize prices.

On the demand side, demand for food is inelastic with respect to price; indeed, as economies around the world become more affluent, food demand becomes even less responsive to price. The share of raw material costs in the overall consumer food bill is now so low in richer societies that even a doubling in the farm-gate price of food has a relatively small impact on the prices consumers pay in shops. This means that the price changes required to ensure equilibrium between supply and demand in the face of supply shocks are further amplified. For some commodities, such as cereals, storage from one year to the next provides a possible mechanism to help smooth out the volatility in prices, but many agricultural commodities (such as beef) are perishable or can only be stored at great cost, so this option is often not feasible.

The impact of price volatility is exacerbated by the particular structure of agricultural production, which is dominated by family farms. Unlike industry, where artisan and craft production has been gradually replaced by increasingly large enterprises which can exploit economies of scale and scope, agricultural production in nearly all countries around the world remains in the hands of family farms. One way in which family farms try to insure themselves against price and supply risk is through diversification (growing a range of crops and supplementing farm income with off-farm sources of income).

Although highly diversified (but low-productivity) family farms still dominate agriculture in many developing countries, in Europe price-cost pressures have encouraged greater and greater specialisation, leaving farmers more exposed to price and thus income risk. True, income variability will usually be less than price variability in response to supply shocks because output and price move in opposite directions – recall the line in Shakespeare's *Macbeth* about the farmer who hanged himself in the expectation of plenty! Nonetheless, the prevalence of price volatility means that governments are often under pressure to intervene to help farmers during market crises and periods of depressed farm prices.

Farm prices are not only volatile but, at least in the post-war period, they have tended to fall in real terms. This fall in relative food prices also reflects the interplay of the supply of and demand for farm products. On the one hand, the supply potential of the farm sector increased as farmers gained access to a range of productive new inputs such as improved seed varieties, better fertilisers, more powerful machinery, and more effective chemicals and pesticides. However, the market for this increased output did not grow to the same extent. Growth in demand is dependent on growth in population and in per capita incomes. But the rate of population growth in industrialised countries has slowed down and in some cases has virtually ceased. While per capita incomes continue to grow, a smaller and smaller proportion of this increase is spent on food. The consequence has been a downward pressure on the aggregate price level for agricultural products relative to other commodities.

This in turn puts a downward pressure on farm incomes and has encouraged farm family members to take up non-farm job opportunities. In all industrialised countries, the share of the farm workforce in total employment has fallen significantly. In Ireland, the number of people whose principal occupation is farming fell from 330,000 in 1960 to 87,100 in 2012. If this adjustment process proceeds smoothly, the reduction in the numbers engaged in agriculture should ensure that farm incomes, on average, stay in line with average non-farm incomes. For various reasons, however, some farmers may find it difficult to leave farming in the face of this downward pressure on farm incomes. Unemployment may be high in the non-farm sector, or their age and skill profile can make it difficult for them to find off-farm jobs. Suitable off-farm opportunities may anyway be rather scarce in rural Ireland. Many farmers appear trapped in agriculture with low incomes. Fifty-one per cent of farmers are now over 55 years of age, compared to just 40 per cent ten years ago. Government transfers to agriculture have been justified in the past as a response to this perceived problem of low average farm incomes relative to the rest of society.

Nonetheless, a puzzle remains. Why is it that farmers, among all self-employed groups, have received such preferential treatment? Arguably, small shopkeepers or pub owners also experience fluctuating incomes and have difficulty in maintaining their living standards in the face of competitive pressures, yet government support for these sectors has been much more limited. Farmers are able to tap into deep social values by appealing to the need to maintain domestic food production as a guarantee of national food security, and the desire to support rural areas and the rural way of life. The unmatched ability of farmer organisations to defend and lobby for their interests should not be underestimated, and there are few rural constituencies where a TD would feel safe in opposing farmer demands for more support. Thus, the reasons for the extensive government intervention in agricultural markets are found both in the particular economic characteristics of the sector but also in political economy explanations for agricultural policy.

The persistence of the long-term decline in real food prices makes the sudden increase in food prices since 2008 even more striking. The key question is whether this is just a temporary phenomenon, the outcome of a series of chance events such as drought in major producing countries, or whether it represents the start of a new era in which farmers will receive more for their production.

There is much evidence to support the latter view. We can use the same supply and demand framework to understand why this might be the case. On the demand side, rapidly rising per capita incomes in emerging economies are leading to shifts in diet preferences with greater demand for meat and dairy products. Food and energy markets have become increasingly inter-linked, not only on the cost side (where modern agriculture is a heavy energy consumer) but also on the output side (as agricultural land is diverted to the production of energy crops for biomass and biofuels). On the supply side, the increasing scarcity of water and land, and in the longer term, the likely impact of climate change, are putting increasing pressure on supply capacity.

Public and private investment in agricultural research, which has been behind the productivity growth that has driven the decline in food prices in the past, has been cut back or diverted to non-production areas such as the environment, animal welfare or the development of more sophisticated foods. Some of the new technologies available to increase food supply, such as aspects of biotechnology, have met substantial consumer resistance. It is thus very likely that the market environment for the Irish agri-food sector will be very different in the next ten years from what it has been in the past. As a net food exporter, not only farmers but the national economy stands to gain.

Production Structure
The agricultural industry produced food products and raw materials valued at €6.7 billion at producer prices in 2012. Its GNP share was an estimated 2.7 per cent in that year (down from 6.3 per cent in 1996). Climatically, Ireland is more suited to grassland than crop production. Of the total agricultural area, over 90 per cent is devoted to grass and rough grazing. Livestock and livestock products accounted for 72 per cent of total output at producers' prices in 2012 (see Table 11.1). The table also highlights the growing share of material and service inputs as a proportion of gross agricultural output. While this is due partly to the fall in the value of output arising from reform of the EU's Common Agricultural Policy (CAP) (see Section 3), it also reflects the increasing intensification of agricultural production, a phenomenon that has given rise to concern about agriculture's impact on the environment.

An important characteristic of Irish agriculture is its export orientation. The export market absorbs more than 80 per cent of dairy and beef output. Around 40 per cent of Irish agri-food exports go to the UK, around 30 per cent to the rest of the EU and 30 per cent are exported outside the EU. Sales to third country markets outside the EU were heavily dependent on export subsidies, but with the rise in global food prices these now play a much less important role.

Table 11.1 Composition of Agricultural Output and Input, Selected Years (% of gross agricultural output by value)

	1996	2006	2012
Total Output			
Cattle	28.7	28.6	31.6
Milk	29.8	25.3	24.3
Crops	24.6	27.9	28.2
Pigs	6.9	6.1	6.6
Sheep	4.7	3.6	3.0
Other	5.3	8.4	6.3
Gross agricultural output at producer prices	100.0	100.0	100.0
Total Input	60.0	74.4	78.8
Feed, fertiliser and seed	24.4	27.5	29.8
Other current inputs	35.6	46.8	49.0

Source: CSO, *Agricultural Output, Input and Income* (www.statcentral.ie), accessed 20 February 2014.

Farm Structure and Incomes

In 2010, there were around 140,000 farms in Ireland compared to 142,000 ten years previously. Their average size in terms of land area is 33 hectares, although there is considerable diversity around this average. This average area farmed is large in EU terms, but because of the relatively low intensity of land use the average size of farm business in Ireland is at the smaller end of the EU spectrum. There is an important regional dimension to differences in farm size, with a predominance of smaller farms in the west and the northwest, and a greater proportion of larger farms in the south and east. Small farm size is frequently associated with a low-margin farming system (mainly drystock) and a predominance of older farmers, many of whom are unmarried.

The process of structural adjustment in agriculture is slow in Ireland not only because those working in farming, as mentioned earlier, tend to be relatively immobile but also because of the very limited role played by the land market in Ireland. Most agricultural land is transferred within the family. Very little land is sold on the open market, which would enable structural adjustment to take place, allowing younger, more dynamic farmers to acquire additional land from retiring farmers. While renting land provides an alternative mechanism for structural adjustment to take place, land leasing in Ireland is invariably very short term with limited guarantees of security of tenure. As a result of this dysfunctional land market, prices for agricultural land are bid to ridiculously high levels which are very hard to justify by the returns from agricultural production alone.

Income from farming compares unfavourably with average industrial earnings, although comparisons are difficult for statistical and conceptual reasons.

For example, the average family farm income for 2011 was €24,461 compared to 2011 average earnings of €35,600 for workers in the construction industry. However, this comparison is not comparing like with like. The average family farm income on the 30 per cent of farms which were full-time was €56,378 in 2011 (bear in mind that this figure must remunerate the capital invested in the farm and that there may be more than one person engaged on full-time farms, so it is not directly comparable to the construction industry earnings figure). Conversely, the average income from farming on the remaining 70 per cent of part-time farms was only €10,408 (the definition of full-time and part-time here refers to whether the farm has sufficient size and activity to require the time of a full-time person or not, not whether the farmer has off-farm employment). Clearly, this level of income is inadequate on its own to support a farm family.

However, on around 51 per cent of these part-time farms, either the holder and/or the spouse had an off-farm job. The increasing importance of off-farm income means that average farm *household* incomes are much closer to average incomes in the non-farm economy than the figures on farm income alone would suggest. On average, farm household incomes were around 10 per cent lower than for the state as a whole in 2008, the last year for which such comparative figures were available at the time of writing. However, poverty levels among farm households are not that different to non-farm households. Household survey data show that consistent poverty is generally lower among farm households than in other household groups, indicating a low rate of enforced deprivation among farm families.

A closer look at the sources of agricultural factor income shows the high dependence of farming income on transfers from the non-farm sector. Even in 2011, which was considered a very good year for farm incomes, income from commercial farming activity accounted for only one-third of the income accruing to the sector, with the remaining two-thirds coming in the form of subsidies and transfers from the exchequer. In fact, the value of public expenditure on agriculture by the Department of Agriculture, Food and the Marine in 2012 amounted to €2.6 billion in 2012, which just happened to be the same as what the sector received as income from both production activity and public support. When it is recalled that the value of farm output is also inflated by high tariffs on lower-cost imports from outside the EU (see Section 3), the vulnerability of farm incomes to policy changes which might lead to lower support and protection is underlined.

3 AGRICULTURAL POLICY

Common Agricultural Policy (CAP)

Most countries intervene in their agricultural markets in pursuit of the objectives of price stabilisation and income support. This is also true for EU agricultural policy, the objectives of which are spelled out in the Treaty of European Union as follows:

- To increase agricultural productivity by promoting technical progress and by ensuring the rational development of agricultural production and the optimum utilisation of all factors of production, in particular labour;
- Thus, to ensure a fair standard of living for the agricultural community, in particular by increasing the individual earnings of persons engaged in agriculture;
- To stabilise markets;
- To provide certainty of supplies;
- To ensure that supplies reach consumers at reasonable prices.

These objectives of efficient agricultural production – fair incomes for farmers, stable markets, food security and reasonable consumer prices – would be broadly acceptable to most people, though the sharp-eyed will note the ambiguity of the wording (What is a fair standard of living for farmers? What is a reasonable price for consumers?) and that there is potential for conflict between these objectives. However, the mechanisms put in place to achieve these policy goals have prioritised the farm income objective at considerable cost to the EU budget and consumers.

The mechanisms used have changed over time. The original CAP was strongly interventionist. Farm prices within the EU were supported by a combination of policy instruments, including import tariffs, market intervention and export subsidies. *Import tariffs* ensure a high domestic price as long as there is a net deficit on the EU market. Originally, the EU's import tariffs took the form of variable levies designed to help stabilise internal EU prices, but these were transformed into fixed tariffs in 1995 (see below). Price support to producers was further strengthened in the event of excess EU supplies by a guarantee that government agencies would buy farm products at a minimum support price (called the *intervention price*). Intervention was intended to deal with temporary surpluses of supply. Once the market had recovered and prices had risen, intervention stocks could be sold.

As the EU became more than self-sufficient in many temperate-zone foods, greater reliance was placed on *export subsidies* or *refunds*. These export refunds bridge the gap between the high internal market prices and the lower world prices in most years and make possible the export of higher-priced foodstuffs from the EU. High import tariffs, intervention purchases and export refunds were the principal means of supporting prices to farmers under the classical CAP.

The operation of the CAP price support policy ensured a greater degree of internal price stability than in other countries and meant higher per capita incomes for a greater number of farmers than would otherwise have been the case. However, these achievements were bought at a price. The resulting increase in output could not be absorbed by the natural growth in demand, leading to the accumulation of intervention stocks and to dumping on international markets. Thus the EU, which was initially a deficit producer of many agricultural products, became a major net exporter. An obvious consequence of this was the escalating budget cost of purchasing surplus production for intervention storage and of financing export refunds, and growing calls for reform.

Reform of CAP 1992–2012

The first successful attempt to tackle the malfunctioning CAP was pushed through in 1993 by EU Agriculture Commissioner Ray MacSharry. The MacSharry reform initiated a significant reduction in support prices for the first time. Farmers were compensated by direct payments which were tied (coupled) to the level of output on each farm. These payments were accompanied by measures designed to control supply. The market regime reforms were complemented by new agri-environment, forestry and early retirement schemes for farmers, part of an expanded rural development emphasis in the CAP.

A further round of CAP reform was agreed in March 1999 as part of the negotiations on the Agenda 2000 agreement to prepare the EU for eastern enlargement. This pursued the same model of reductions in support prices while compensating farmers by further increasing direct payments. These measures to support farm incomes – market intervention and direct payments – were referred to as Pillar 1 of the CAP. The Agenda 2000 reform also consolidated various socio-structural measures to encourage farm modernisation as well as agri-environment payments into a single Rural Development Regulation, which became known as Pillar 2 of the CAP.

The MacSharry and Agenda 2000 direct payments required that a farmer must plant arable land (in the case of cereals, oilseeds and protein crops) or keep animals in order to draw down these payments. Such payments are called *coupled payments* because they are linked to the amount each farmer produces. A major criticism, as demonstrated by the fact that on many farms the value of income from farming was less than the direct payments received, was that many farmers were keeping livestock or growing crops simply to collect the subsidies, rather than responding to market demand.

Under Franz Fischler, the EU Commissioner for Agriculture in the period 1999–2004, the EU embarked on a further CAP reform in 2003. The most important change in the Fischler reform was to replace the coupled payments by *decoupled payments* (called the single farm payment) to each farmer. This single farm payment was based on the level of assistance received by each farm in the reference period 2000 to 2002. Farmers were entitled to receive this payment regardless of changes in the area planted to crops or the number of livestock on their farm, or indeed regardless of whether they produce on their farm at all. This *decoupling* of the payment from production means that farmers now make their production decisions based on the relative market returns from each enterprise rather than the size of the subsidy available.

The single farm payment, though, is linked to respect for standards in the areas of the environment, food safety, plant health and animal welfare, as well as a requirement to keep all farmland in good agricultural and environmental condition: this is the so-called 'cross-compliance' condition.

The Fischler reform also continued the *reform of the market regimes* by lowering support prices and increasing direct payments in compensation. Subsequently, a rolling programme of reform was implemented (including the so-called 'Health Check' in 2008) which extended the Fischler reforms to a variety of other market regimes (cotton, tobacco, olive oil, bananas, sugar). By 2012, only some limited coupled payments linked to beef and sheep production continued in some member states. A consequence of the sugar market reform, in which support prices for sugar were reduced and incentives provided to encourage the closure of refining capacity, was that Ireland's only sugar processor, Greencore, ceased production at the end of the 2006 season.

As a consequence of these successive reforms, the CAP has changed very significantly. Pillar 1 continues to take the lion's share of the CAP budget, accounting for over 75 per cent of CAP expenditure. However, most of Pillar 1 expenditure is now decoupled and does not provide the same incentive to over-production as before. Nonetheless, farmers continue to benefit from high levels of external protection which in normal years keep food prices on the internal EU market higher than world market levels. These high protection levels have come under sustained criticism from the EU's trading partners in negotiations on trade liberalisation under the auspices of the World Trade Organisation (WTO).

WTO Disciplines on Agricultural Support

The WTO Agreement on Agriculture, to which the EU is a party and which came into force in 1995, establishes rules on the manner and amount of government support to agriculture. These rules discipline agricultural policy in three main areas: the level and type of border protection for farm products; the use of export subsidies; and the amount of domestic support to farmers. Under the new rules, only tariffs can be used to protect domestic producers from low-cost imports; the EU had to replace its former 'variable levy' system of border protection with fixed tariffs. Its use of export subsidies is also capped, both in volume and value terms (although both the CAP reforms described in the previous section and the high world market prices since 2008 mean that the EU no longer needs to use export subsidies in order to export agri-food products to the world market).

With regard to domestic support to agriculture, the Agreement distinguishes between permitted and disciplined forms of support. Support that does not influence, or influences only minimally, farmers' incentives to produce is permitted and there are no limits applied (support of this kind is considered not to cause distortions to trade). Trade-distorting support, such as market price support, on the other hand, is capped. The purpose of these rules is not to prevent governments from providing support to their farmers, but to get them to do so in ways that do not stimulate production and thus lead to unfair trade competition with other countries.

The WTO Agreement on Agriculture was important in clarifying the rules which apply to different forms of farm support, but it did little to reduce its overall level. A new round of negotiations to liberalise agricultural trade began in

March 2000 and subsequently became part of the Doha Round of multilateral trade negotiations under WTO auspices. These negotiations have proved difficult, not least because of disagreements between developed and developing countries over agricultural subsidies. Developing countries sought large cuts in developed country agricultural support in return for giving greater market access to developed country exports of manufactures and services. A small 'mini-package' of measures under negotiation was agreed at a WTO meeting in Bali in December 2013, but it is still unclear if this was simply a one-off success or if it signals a renewed willingness by WTO members to seriously engage in concluding the Doha Round negotiations. Irish farmers view a possible agreement with some trepidation, as the significant tariff reductions for beef and dairy products under discussion would likely lead to lower prices.

Multilateral trade liberalisation under WTO auspices is not the only threat to the continued high tariff protection of EU, and Irish, agriculture. The EU and other countries increasingly pursue trade liberalisation through bilateral or regional free trade agreements. The EU recently concluded a free trade agreement with Canada, and negotiations are under way with the USA (the Transatlantic Trade and Investment Partnership) and with Mercosur, the common market of South America, in which Brazil is the leading player. All these countries seek additional access for their agricultural exports, including beef, which would compete directly with Irish farmers.

The CAP after 2013

Despite the last 20 years of CAP reform (initiated by Commissioner MacSharry in 1993), agricultural support policies remain contentious. True, the worst excesses of the old system of price supports have been removed. Price support was intended to assist low-income farmers, yet by its very nature the bulk of the benefits went to the larger and better-off farmers simply because they had much more to sell. Where support prices were set at levels high enough to provide a minimum income to small farmers, they provided supernormal profits to larger farms with lower unit costs of production, encouraging them to increase production and leading to the build-up of surpluses which could only be disposed of at enormous cost. Following the series of CAP reforms, although price supports are maintained for a limited number of agricultural products, these are now set at much lower, safety net, levels and in a normal year they do not influence the production decisions of farmers.

However, the reduction in support prices was 'purchased' through granting direct payments to farmers, first as coupled payments and currently as largely decoupled payments. It made sense to cushion the shock of lower support prices through a temporary system of direct payments, but these have now become a permanent part of the EU, and Irish, agricultural landscape. What is their rationale? How can payments which only require farmers to observe minimum environmental standards on their farms be justified in the longer term? Are these payments intended as income support, to pay farmers for the provision of environmental public goods, or to compensate them for higher production standards than their competitors?

Because the payments substituted for the price support each individual farmer had received, the distribution of direct payments replicated the uneven distribution of price support. Larger farmers get much higher payments than do smaller farmers, even though it is the latter who are more likely to have low incomes, particularly if they are not also employed off the farm. In any case, most economists would argue that it is more efficient to address problems of low income and poverty directly through the social welfare system than to use agricultural policy indirectly to achieve this end.

The Commission published a new set of CAP reform proposals in 2011 which were eventually agreed in 2013 through the co-decision process between the Council and the European Parliament. This reform linked direct payments more closely to the provision of environmental services by requiring that 30 per cent of the decoupled payment that farmers receive should take the form of a 'green payment'. In return for this payment, farmers are required to undertake specific practices beneficial to the environment and to combat climate change. However, the environmental benefits from the measures proposed by the Commission were seen as very limited, and were further watered down in the legislative process between the Council and the Parliament.

Other contentious issues addressed in the 2013 CAP reform were 'external convergence' – levelling out the distribution of direct payments between member states (where the new member states argued they had got a raw deal on accession) – as well as 'internal convergence'. The latter refers to the flattening of the distribution of payments among farmers within member states. For example, in Ireland the single farm payment for some farmers was as low as €100 per hectare annually, while others received as much as €700 per hectare or more, yet the obligations required of each farmer were exactly the same. Under the new reform, member states are required to move towards a more uniform distribution of payments among farmers. The price of agreeing the 2013 reform was to grant much greater flexibility to individual member states on how they wanted to implement the reform. In many ways, this makes sense because agricultural conditions in a greatly enlarged EU are now much more diverse. It is hardly plausible that the same agricultural measures will be appropriate both in Longford and Latvia.

Of course, this raises the question, why not simply hand agricultural policy back to the member states entirely, leaving only the maintenance of a single market in agricultural and food products as the responsibility of the Commission? The debate over subsidiarity, which functions are best carried out at the EU level and which at the level of the member state, or even regional levels, is an increasingly lively one within the EU. It is generally accepted that social policy should remain a function of member states. If agricultural policy is now largely about the provision of income support through decoupled direct payments not linked to production, the argument can be made that the level and design of these payments should also be left to the member states. The more 'uncommon' the

CAP becomes as member states make use of the greater flexibility they are granted under the latest reform of the CAP, the more insistent this argument will become.

4 FOOD PROCESSING AND DISTRIBUTION

The Food Industry

Few agricultural products are sold directly to the consumer – vegetables, fruit and eggs sold in farmers' markets being the main examples. Most agricultural products are purchased by food processors which prepare food for final consumption for either the domestic or export markets. The importance of the different sub-sectors is shown in Table 11.2. Gross value added (which subtracts the value of raw materials purchased by the industry and gives a better idea of its contribution to the overall economy) amounted to €7.3 billion, equivalent to 6 per cent of GNP at market prices. The industry provides direct employment for around 43,000 people, or one-fifth of the total industrial workforce (other estimates put the total employment at around 55,000 as the census excludes enterprises with one or two employees).

Table 11.2 Key Indicators for the Irish Food Processing and Drink Industry, 2011 (€m)

Industrial Sector	Turnover	Gross value added	Persons engaged
Food products	22,800	5,978	35,217
Meat and meat products	4,839	673	12,464
Fish, crustaceans and molluscs	459	98	1,821
Fruit and vegetables	257	72	1,385
Vegetable, animal oils and fats	59	23	171
Dairy products	4,130	558	5,163
Grain mill products, starches and starch products	110	29	244
Bakery and farinaceous products	763	281	5,151
Other food products	10,852	4,015	6,446
Prepared animal feeds	1,331	230	2,372
Beverages	3,128	1,353	3,605

Source: CSO, *Census of Industrial Production* (www.statcentral.ie), accessed 20 February 2014. Results are presented for industrial enterprises with three or more persons engaged, so total employment in the food and drink industry is underestimated in this table.

Globally, the food industry comprises a limited number of well-known multinational food companies (Nestlé, Unilever, Kraft, Kellogg, etc.) as well as a myriad of much less well-known small and medium-sized enterprises which supply a wide variety of food products. This is reflected in the food industry structure in Ireland, which consists of subsidiaries of multinational firms (for example, there is an impressive cluster of international firms, such as Abbotts, Danone and Pfizer, which together produce 15 per cent of the world's supply of infant milk formula in Ireland), some larger Irish-owned firms which have themselves become multinationals (Kerry Foods, Glanbia, Greencore, etc.) and then a large number of small and medium-sized firms which are a crucial source of employment and potentially innovation for the sector as a whole.

While there are over 670 individual enterprises in the industry, the 40 largest firms, each with over 250 employees, account for around 40 per cent of employment and almost 60 per cent of output. The existence of the multinational sector creates the same need for caution in interpreting statistics on value added and productivity levels as for manufacturing as a whole. There is a pronounced dualism in the sector, to which the phenomenon of transfer pricing may contribute (see Chapter 9).

Food and drink exports in 2012 amounted to around two-thirds of the total from indigenous manufacturing industry. The government set ambitious targets to increase this level in its *Food Harvest 2020* report published in 2010. Because of the importance of the UK market, sales are heavily influenced by the euro–sterling exchange rate. Any sharp appreciation in the value of the euro makes it difficult for the industry to maintain let alone increase its market share in the UK. Shifting sales to the euro zone would limit this exchange rate risk and is a policy objective. Beyond this, the food industry faces significant challenges to improve its competitiveness, including reducing key input costs such as energy and waste, as well as improving its innovation capacity to benefit fully from emerging consumer trends.

The market for food is changing rapidly due to changing consumer demands and market structures. Changing consumer lifestyles are having a decisive influence on food demand. Increased numbers of working women, reduced leisure time and the decline in the traditional family unit are changing eating habits and increasing the demand for convenience foods. Thus important growth areas for the food industry are the food ingredients business (such as dairy ingredients, meat, and by-products such as pizza toppings and meat flavourings, and other ingredients such as colourings, flavourings and malt) for pre-prepared foods, as well as the food service sector (embracing all forms of catering and eating out). Other important changes in consumer preferences are the growing concern over food safety, interest in nutrition/health/obesity management issues as well as the growing importance of ethical and food quality concerns, e.g. organic, fair trade, shop local, food miles and animal welfare (see Section 5).

Distribution

The final element of the food chain is distribution, comprising wholesalers, retailers and food service firms, which provide the link between the food industry and consumers. Wholesaling involves the purchase of goods from suppliers and importers for resale to retailers and food service customers. Wholesalers provide a range of services, such as storage, distribution and other services in connection with the sale of goods. The principal innovation of modern wholesaling is the emergence and growth of wholesaler-franchisers: wholesalers that sell predominantly to retailers which are affiliated to them (symbol groups such as SuperValu, Londis, etc.). Retailers decide whether to operate as an independent retailer or under the brand of a wholesaler-franchiser. Thus, modern wholesaling is very much involved with developments at the retail level.

The wholesale level of the grocery supply chain is highly concentrated. The Competition Authority estimates that over 95 per cent of the wholesale turnover in the Irish grocery sector is attributable to seven groups of operators. Just two firms, Musgrave and BWG Foods, together account for almost 80 per cent of grocery wholesale turnover. Six of the seven groups are wholesaler-franchisers which buy goods from suppliers for resale to retailers and which license one or more retail brands to retailers that are part of their symbol groups. The remaining group combines cash and carry wholesalers, which are engaged in the traditional function of buying goods from suppliers for resale to independent retailers.

The grocery retail sector in Ireland is made up of the major multiples, symbol groups, independent retailers and speciality independents, e.g. greengrocers, butchers, etc. The number of multiples has grown steadily, as well as their size, facilitated by the emergence of out-of-town shopping centres. The main multiples operating in the Irish market have been Tesco, Dunnes Stores, Superquinn (now taken over by SuperValu) and Marks & Spencer. Recent years have also seen the arrival of the German discount own-brand chains Aldi and Lidl into the Irish market. The discount stores have achieved significant market share in some geographic and product markets. The market share of the symbol groups has also grown while the market share of the independents is on a continuing downward trend.

Grocery retailing is also highly concentrated. The Competition Authority estimates that the major multiples together account for 46 per cent of retail turnover in grocery goods in the state. The retailers affiliated to the four largest wholesaler-franchisers account for a further 40 per cent of retail grocery turnover while the other retailers, independent retailers and retailers affiliated to smaller wholesaler-franchisors account for the remaining 14 per cent of grocery sales. From a suppliers' perspective, buying power is even more concentrated. Just three grocery purchasers, Dunnes Stores, Tesco and Musgraves/SuperValu, account for 70 per cent of all retail sales. This higher figure is explained by the fact that Musgraves/SuperValu is a centralised buying group that owns the symbol group franchise for a large number of retailers that individually have a very small market share.

The other main channel for food distribution is the food service sector, defined as 'food consumed away from home', the importance of which has also been growing over time. It now accounts for over one-fifth of all expenditure on food. The channel is made up of fast food restaurants, full service restaurants, pubs and coffee shops, hotels and institutional catering. Food is now more important than drink in sales terms for pubs, and the collapse of the lunchtime trade during the recession hit many pubs hard. The food service market in Ireland is less developed than in other European countries, where the sector accounts for around one-third of consumer expenditure on food, or in the USA, where the share is 50 per cent.

5 FOOD POLICY

Growing Concern over Food Safety

From earliest times food has been particularly susceptible to exploitation, and there is a long history of food legislation passed with the purpose of preventing consumers being either cheated or poisoned. Measures for the protection of the consumer against the adulteration of food and drink are among the earliest examples of social legislation. Since then the scope of food law has been greatly widened. Examples of some of the matters now covered by legislation include the produce of diseased animals posing a threat to human health; sanitary conditions in food preparation, packaging and handling; pesticide and hormone residues in food; packaging materials which may pose a threat to health; food additives; the labelling requirements for food products; and weights and measures legislation.

Despite the undoubted improvement in food purity and in merchandising practices brought about by this legislation, consumers are increasingly uneasy about the safety and quality of the modern food supply. Issues of recent concern include agrochemical residues in food, the increasing number and diversity of food additives, the use of illegal substances in livestock production, the presence of nitrates in drinking water and genetically engineered foods. There have been sharp falls in the consumption of particular foods, caused by publicity given, for example, to bovine spongiform encephalopathy (BSE) in cattle ('mad cow' disease), listeria in soft cheeses, or salmonella in eggs. Consumer concerns also extend beyond the safety of food products to their production methods, including genetic modification, animal welfare, and environmental and ethical concerns.

The risk of food-borne diseases has increased for a number of reasons. Best hygiene practices are not always followed in commercial and domestic kitchens. Fewer people preparing their own food and more eating outside the home means a higher proportion of people at risk in outbreaks. The increasing demand for ready-to-go foods has resulted in food being served in a growing number of non-traditional outlets such as garage forecourts. The global distribution of food has lengthened the food chain.

The increased competition and price constraints on food producers has led the sector to seek cost reductions through ever more complex food processing and may sometimes encourage suppliers to adopt practices which have adverse health effects (the dioxin contamination of Irish pig meat in 2008, which cost the taxpayer over €100 million, resulted from an animal feed compounder using contaminated fuel oil sold as food-grade oil by a Northern Ireland supplier). The news in 2013 was that horsemeat was being passed off as beef, although an issue of fraudulent labelling rather than health underlined the complex nature of an increasingly globalised food chain.

Fortunately, in Ireland, food problems have not emerged to the dramatic extent reached elsewhere. However, the increase in food poisoning notifications (*E. coli*, for instance) suggests that vigilance is essential. An *E. coli* outbreak in Germany in May–June 2011 caused by infected fresh vegetables from an organic farm caused the deaths of 53 people. Food production and tourism are major elements in the economy, and both depend crucially on a favourable international perception of the safety of Irish food. So along with the issue of the health and lives of its own citizens, Ireland has a vital economic interest in becoming a centre of excellence in food safety. Indeed, it was Irish inspectors who in January 2013 first identified the presence of horsemeat in frozen hamburgers, thus revealing the major breakdown in the traceability of the food supply chain.

Economic Considerations

In economic terms, the need for governments to regulate for food safety is the result of a market failure (see Chapter 3). This arises because consumers are not necessarily in a position to determine the safety characteristics of food they consume on the basis of visual inspection alone. There is thus an asymmetry of information between the producer and consumer of food. In this, the market for food safety is like the market for used cars. Sellers have more information about the quality of the car than buyers. Because buyers often cannot tell the difference between a good and a bad used car, both good and bad cars must sell at the same price and the seller of a good car is unable to extract a premium for quality. In the same way, there is a tendency for food safety to be undersupplied by the market because consumers are not always able to distinguish between high and low food standards.

Of course, if we go to a restaurant and subsequently experience illness due to food poisoning, we are unlikely to patronise that restaurant again. Where there is the likelihood of repeat purchases, food businesses have an incentive to maintain high standards in order to maximise the likelihood of retaining our custom. The development of brand names, or supermarkets that monitor quality on our behalf, are other ways in which market institutions can respond to the asymmetry of information. However, sometimes firms themselves may be unaware of, say, the carcinogenic risk associated with a particular additive or production process.

There may also be strong externalities that justify government intervention, either on the production side (one rogue producer who fails to meet adequate food standards can put the reputation of an entire national food industry at risk) or on the consumption side (an infectious food-borne illness imposes wider costs on society that transcend those incurred by the individual consumer). This is the economic case for governments to step in to ensure that minimum food standards are maintained.

While the failure to observe adequate food standards can impose economic costs both on individuals and on society at large, maintaining and enforcing these standards is also a costly exercise. For economists, this raises the question whether the benefits from a particular food regulation (in terms of the avoided cost of food illnesses or, for an exporting country, the loss of market reputation in export markets) exceed its costs. The idea that we should try to balance benefits and costs in setting food regulations suggests that trying to achieve zero risk is not the optimal strategy. Removing all risk from eating food is likely to be hugely expensive, and the economic benefit from lowering risk from a minimal to a zero risk of contracting an illness may not justify taking this extra step.

There may also be an alternative and more efficient instrument available to achieve the same degree of risk reduction, for example by introducing more stringent product liability legislation which allows consumers to claim damages if they have been harmed by consuming unsafe food. Governments, of course, should not take such decisions on the basis of cost benefit studies alone; moral and ethical criteria must also be taken into account. However, the economist's framework of balancing the expected benefits from risk reduction against the costs of achieving such reductions should be an important adjunct to the decision-making process in food safety regulation.

EU Food Safety Framework

These growing concerns prompted the incoming European Commission in October 1999 to make food safety a top priority. In January 2000, the Irish Commissioner for Health and Consumer Protection, David Byrne, produced a White Paper on Food Safety which outlined a comprehensive strategy to restore consumers' confidence in their food supply. There were three elements to the strategy: new legislation on the safety of food and animal feed; a new agency to offer scientific advice on food-borne threats; and more stringent control and enforcement.

A new General Food Law, which brought together the general principles of food and animal feed safety, was agreed in 2002. The new law made food safety and consumer protection the cornerstone of the regulatory regime. Including animal feed in its provisions was a major advance as animal feed has been the source of many food scares in the past decade. This was supplemented by new food hygiene legislation passed in 2004 and which has come into effect since 2006. This modernises, consolidates and simplifies the previous EU food hygiene legislation and introduces a 'farm to fork' approach to food safety, by including primary production (farmers and growers) in food hygiene legislation, for the first time in the majority of cases.

The general principles which now underlie food safety policy emphasise a whole food chain approach (food safety must be ensured at all stages of the food chain, from the producer through to the consumer), risk analysis (meaning that the policy is based on a scientific understanding of risk with due account for the need for precaution when scientific opinion is not yet clear), operator liability (all food sector operators are now responsible for ensuring the safety of the products they import, produce, process or sell), traceability (from 1 January 2005 all foodstuffs, animal feeds and feed ingredients must be traceable right through the food chain) and openness (citizens have the right to clear and accurate information on food and health risks from public authorities).

The General Food Law is supplemented by a large number of targeted regulations addressing specific food safety issues, such as the use of pesticides, food supplements, colouring, antibiotics and hormones in food production; rules on hygiene; food labelling; and legislation setting down procedures for the release, marketing, labelling and traceability of crops and foodstuffs containing genetically modified organisms.

The second Commission initiative was the creation of the European Food Safety Authority (EFSA) in 2002 to provide a source of independent, objective scientific advice on food-related risks. The new authority has responsibility for the EU Rapid Alert System, which links EU countries in cases of food-borne threats. Its role is limited to giving its opinion, and it is up to the Commission (in conjunction with the Council and the Parliament) to initiate the required action. The EFSA works through a series of Scientific Panels of independent experts who are responsible for providing scientific opinions to the authority. Of course, scientists may disagree, and member states in the legislation establishing EFSA were reluctant to grant it the power to act as the ultimate source of food safety information. In the event of a disagreement between the EFSA and a national food safety agency, for example, it would be up to the courts to resolve the conflict.

The third initiative was to improve the EU framework for the control and enforcement of food safety legislation. Enforcement of food regulations is the responsibility of national governments, albeit under the oversight of the EU. An EU framework directive lays down norms and procedures relating to inspection and enforcement, and the Food and Veterinary Office of the European Commission, which is based in Grange, County Meath, controls the performance of national authorities and makes recommendations aimed at improving national control and inspection systems.

Irish Responses

In Ireland, the Food Safety Authority (FSA) was set up in 1999 to ensure that food produced, distributed or marketed in the state meets the highest standards of food safety and hygiene and to co-ordinate food safety activities 'from farm to fork'. The FSA has functions in relation to research, advice, co-ordinating services, and food certification. It operates the national food safety compliance programme by means of service contracts with the agencies involved in the enforcement of food legislation (including government departments, health boards, local authorities and the Radiological Protection Institute). In addition, the authority works with industry and training bodies to improve, harmonise and co-ordinate food safety and hygiene training through the country.

Initiatives such as the National Beef Assurance Scheme and the National Sheep Identification System have been launched to ensure the identification and traceability of animals/meat. Controls on BSE remain in place to ensure that meat from confirmed cases and from herds in which cases have been located does not enter the food or feed chains. Another priority area concerns residue testing, which is particularly focused on detecting illegal growth promoters in cattle and antibiotic residues in pigs. A new cross-border food safety promotion board known as Safefood has been established under the Good Friday Agreement to contribute to the improved co-ordination of food safety activities on the island as a whole. Its functions include food safety promotion; research into food safety; communication of food alerts; surveillance of food-borne diseases; and the promotion of scientific co-operation and linkages between laboratories.

Food Quality

Alongside food safety, consumers are showing a greater interest in food quality. What constitutes quality is very much a subjective matter, especially where food is concerned. Food quality was traditionally associated with properties that could be assessed by the senses (taste, smell, sight and touch). These attributes, such as freshness, colour, degree of blemish or shape, are readily identified by consumers.

However, consumers increasingly seek to make purchases based on lifestyle or ethical considerations. They demand information on specific product or process characteristics, including the place of origin, carbon footprint, whether or not the farming practices are organic, whether the product has been modified by biotechnology, whether it meets 'fair trade' standards, and whether high animal welfare standards were adopted. Because the consumer cannot make an informed decision on these issues just by looking at a food product, he or she relies on accurate labelling. But because of the potential for fraud (e.g. passing off a product as organic in order to obtain the premium price when in fact it is not organic), labelling claims are either regulated by the state or may be substantiated by a credible third party.

Both public authorities and the food industry have an interest in communicating food quality characteristics to consumers. Ireland is a high-cost food producer and cannot compete on cost alone with major agricultural exporters. However, by targeting food quality characteristics for which consumers have a demonstrated willingness to pay, the Irish food industry can hope to attract a premium price and thereby improve its competitiveness. Similarly, food retailers seek to use quality attributes as a means of product differentiation, both to attract more customers to their stores and to persuade them to part with more money when they are there. As a result, there has been an explosion of quality assurance schemes, both private and public, aiming to provide information to consumers. Indeed, one of the problems in this area is information overload such that consumers are confused rather than informed by the plethora of labels and logos that have emerged.

An Bord Bia, as the state body charged with the marketing of Irish food abroad, operates a number of quality assurance schemes, for beef, lamb, chicken, pig meat, eggs and horticulture, which are associated with particular production standards. A Bord Bia survey conducted in early 2009 found that more than four in five consumers in Ireland recognised its Quality Mark and almost half of respondents said that they would be much more likely to buy a product bearing the mark. It also sees an opportunity for the Irish industry to emphasise its environmental sustainability credentials as markets increasingly factor climate change considerations into their businesses.

The growing demand for food safety and improved animal welfare will increasingly impact on farmers. Even in the absence of government regulation, the private sector and particularly the large retail chains are demanding that their suppliers meet stringent hygiene and safety standards. These demands will require farmers to undertake additional investments and will accelerate the process of structural change in the industry. However, they also open up additional marketing opportunities.

Instead of selling beef as a commodity product, for example, it becomes possible to produce beef for particular niche markets and to guarantee consumers that their particular requirements have been met. One fast-growing market is for organic produce. Organic production in Ireland is relatively limited, with 1,400 registered producers and 55,000 hectares (1.2 per cent of the agricultural land area) in organic production or in conversion in 2012. The government objective was to have 5 per cent of agricultural land under organic farming by 2012. Farmers who wish to convert to organic production are eligible for aid under the Organic Farming Scheme.

Market Power in the Food Chain
A major issue in the food chain, not only in Ireland but across Europe, is whether the concentration of buying power in the hands of retailers gives them excessive market power to set prices and trading conditions at the expense of suppliers and farmers. Concern about the abuse of market power in the food chain is not a new issue. Since the beginning of the last century farmers have attempted to increase their collective bargaining power in negotiating prices with creameries, meat factories and grain millers. One outcome of these attempts was the co-operative movement, which still plays an important role in the Irish dairy industry.

With the rise of supermarkets these concerns have now moved further down the food chain. In a situation where it is not unusual that the top three retailers control 50 per cent or more of a country's grocery trade, there is a noticeable asymmetry in bargaining power between retailers and their suppliers. The largest food companies account for only 1 to 2 per cent of a retailer's business at national level, but conversely a retailer may represent 20 to 30 per cent of those companies' business.

There are frequent allegations that retailers have taken advantage of this situation of unequal dependence to increase their profit margins at the expense of consumers and of suppliers and farmers further back the food chain through anti-competitive practices.

There are in fact two separate issues here – buyer power vis-à-vis suppliers and seller power vis-à-vis consumers. These are separate markets and the degree of competition is not necessarily the same in each. Suppliers often complain about unfair practices such as the practice of seeking 'hello money'. This is the name given to the practice where supermarkets seek payments from suppliers to have their goods stocked. Processors and suppliers may be compelled to carry the cost of product discounting campaigns by retailers. Retailers may seek to use exclusive supply agreements with suppliers to withhold supplies from price-cutting rivals. Growth in the sales of own-label brands is also highlighted as another possible factor leading to an increase in buyer power.

Other evidence that the food chain may not be fully competitive comes from the behaviour of food prices. Farmers are often angry when they see prices falling at farm level but increasing to the consumer at retail level, and blame the food chain intermediaries, particularly supermarkets, for pocketing the difference. Indeed, the farmers' share of the retail price of food has steadily decreased over time even for relatively simple products such as a litre of milk or a standard loaf of bread. Between 1995 and 2009 the farmers' share of the retail price for liquid milk fell from 42 to 33 per cent. For cheese, the share fell from 34 to 20 per cent, for pig meat from 51 to 27 per cent, and for beef from 60 to 50 per cent.[1]

The retail price, of course, includes the cost of the marketing services added to the raw material provided by the farmer (processing, transport, assembly, packaging, storage and distribution). There may be good reasons why the cost of these marketing services increases at a different pace from the cost of the raw material. But the generally high price of food in Ireland relative to other EU countries reinforces the suspicion that competition in the retail food market is less aggressive than it should be.

Eurostat produces regular surveys of the cost of a similar basket of food products in different EU member states. The countries with the most expensive food in 2012 were the Scandinavian countries, followed by Austria, Luxembourg and then Ireland. This was an improvement in Ireland's relative position, as over the period 2007 to 2010 we had the second highest food prices after Denmark. The Eurostat figures may even underestimate the high cost of food in Ireland relative to other EU countries because the prices collected include any VAT and other taxes. As food is mostly zero-rated for tax purposes in Ireland (in Denmark, for example, it is subject to a VAT rate of 25 per cent), one would expect this to be reflected in much lower retail prices than abroad. Occasional periods of cross-border shopping (often in response to exchange rate fluctuations between the euro and sterling) also underline that food prices here are often higher than in the neighbouring territory.

Various explanations have been offered for this finding. One argument is that the cost of doing business in Ireland is, in general, higher than in other countries. Indeed, it is not just the price of food, but prices in general that tend to be higher than the EU average. Food prices are not more out of line than other prices. The Competition Authority has highlighted the possible role of retail planning caps on the size of stores laid down by retail planning guidelines introduced in 1982 under pressure from the independent retailers. These guidelines mean that there are no large-scale low-cost grocery retailers such as exist in Northern Ireland (the guidelines were revised in 2012 to reduce barriers to entry to the retail market, but caps on the size of individual stores have been maintained).

Another argument is that supermarkets find it easier to exploit their market power and to gouge the consumer because of more limited competition in the Irish market. When the Competition Authority investigated whether there was excessive profit-taking by supermarkets at the expense of consumers some years ago, it could find no evidence that this was the case. More recently, consumers have become more price-conscious and more willing to shop around and we have already noted the growing market share of the German discount chains. This change in behaviour has, no doubt, contributed to the improvement in Ireland's ranking since 2010.

Despite the Competition Authority's failure to find evidence that anti-competitive behaviour by supermarkets had damaged consumers, in 2009 the then government announced its intention to introduce a Code of Practice, on either a voluntary or statutory basis, that would achieve a balance in the relationships between actors in the food supply chain. The proposed Code of Practice for Grocery Good Undertakings is modelled on a similar code of conduct which was first introduced in the UK in 2002. The Fine Gael–Labour government included in its programme for government in 2011 a similar commitment to enact a Fair Trade Act, which would ban a number of unfair trading practices, such as 'hello money', in the retail sector and would put the proposed Code of Practice on a statutory basis.

The Competition Authority is sceptical that such initiatives would lead to better prices for consumers. It notes that there is inevitably a degree of tension between supermarkets and their suppliers because one party seeks the highest possible price and the other the lowest price, and that regulation could lead to higher prices to consumers. It points out that the unfair practices complained of were already outlawed in the 2006 Competition Act, but only where their objective or effect is the prevention, restriction or distortion of competition. If this 'competition test' is not included, it argues, conduct which could be pro-competitive and ultimately pro-consumer could be prohibited.

The major problem with implementing the existing competition provisions (which also applies to the UK Code of Practice) is the reluctance of suppliers to make a complaint for fear that it would lead to their de-listing by the multiple. The Authority proposes to strengthen the existing provisions in the Competition Act to make it easier for suppliers to make complaints, as well as prohibiting retaliatory delisting for not paying 'hello money'. It would also seem desirable, given their role in the economy, that the large vertically integrated retailers should be obliged to report details of their profitability and turnover in Ireland, which is not the case at present.

6 CONCLUSIONS

The agri-food sector is one of the key sectors of the Irish economy, accounting for around 8 per cent of GNP and 8 per cent of employment. This chapter has emphasised the way in which the sector is heavily influenced by government policies promoting specific objectives. The substantial protection provided to EU agriculture means that almost all the income generated by agricultural production arises because of transfers either from consumers or taxpayers resulting from the operation of the CAP. The share of budget transfers from taxpayers, which now accounts for 70 per cent of Irish farm income, is particularly striking.

Farming faces both challenges and opportunities in the future. The system of transfers is threatened by further WTO trade commitments, by changing EU budget priorities and by an increasingly powerful environmental lobby concerned about the negative impact on the environment of intensive agricultural production. The future justification for the single farm payment, so important for incomes on many farms, is unclear, with many inequities between farmers themselves.

On the other hand, food prices are hardening, driven upwards by growing demand for meat and dairy products in the rapidly growing emerging economies, by the competition between food and fuel for agricultural resources, and by constraints on increasing global supply capacity. There has rarely been a more propitious time to wean farming off protectionism and to encourage a greater market orientation. Over the next decade, more emphasis must be put on strengthening the competitiveness of farm production while ensuring that it lives up to ever-higher consumer demands for safety and environmental sustainability.

The government's *Food Harvest 2020* report, published in 2010, set ambitious targets for the contribution of the agri-food sector to economic recovery. It proposed a 33 per cent increase in the value of agricultural output (including fisheries and forestry) compared to the period 2007–2009, a 40 per cent increase in food industry value added and a 42 per cent increase in export earnings. Higher food prices (see Section 2) will make some contribution towards meeting these targets, but their achievement will also require a step-change in trend growth rates for the sector.

The abolition of milk quotas from 2015 should help to release the competitive dynamism of that sector, but the almost total reliance of the important beef and lamb sectors on subsidies for their viability is a source of concern. There is undoubtedly the technical potential to increase output significantly from current resources – there is an enormous gap in efficiency between the most productive and less productive farms. But unless ways can be found to transfer the use of land more quickly into the hands of younger and more skilled operators it is unlikely that this technical potential will be fully realised.

The paradox should be noted that, at a time when government intervention in agricultural markets is being reduced, the demand for greater regulation of food markets has never been stronger. While the rationale for continued agricultural support becomes less and less persuasive as food prices increase and farm incomes approach equality with incomes in the non-farm sector, the growing complexity of the food chain and fear of the consequences of new technological advances are fuelling consumer demands for greater food regulation. While a perfectly sound case for regulation can be made, it is important to bear in mind that all regulation imposes costs as well as benefits and that the task of the regulator is to find the appropriate balance (see Chapter 5). Economists are particularly well trained to assist in finding this balance through assessing the costs and benefits of alternative regulatory policies.

Notes
1   Irish Farmers' Association, *Equity for Farmers in the Food Supply Chain*, Dublin 2010.

Suggestions for Further Reading
Department of Agriculture, Food and the Marine, *Annual Review and Outlook*, latest issue (available at www.agriculture.gov.ie).

Department of Agriculture, Food and the Marine, 2010, *Food Harvest 2020 – A Vision for Irish Agri-food and Fisheries*, available at http://www.agriculture.gov.ie/agri-foodindustry/foodharvest2020/.

European Commission, Directorate-General for Agriculture and Rural Development, 2013, *Overview of CAP Reform 2014–2020*, available at ec.europa.eu/agriculture/policy-perspectives/policy-briefs/05_en.pdf.

Houses of the Oireachtas, Joint Committee on Agriculture, Food and the Marine, 2013, *Report on the Grocery Goods Sector 'Increasing Equity and Transparency in Producer–Processor–Retailer Relationships'*, available at http://www.oireachtas.ie/parliament/media/Final-Report-on-Groceries-Goods-for-publishing-on-website.pdf.

Phelan, J. and J. O'Connell, 2011, *The Importance of Agriculture and the Food Industry to the Irish Economy*, available at http://www.ucd.ie/t4cms/UCD%20Project%20JP-JOC.pdf.

POLICY ISSUES IN THE NON-MARKET SECTOR

CHAPTER 12

Health: Funding, Access and Efficiency

*Anne Nolan**

1 INTRODUCTION[1]

This chapter examines the health sector, a key component of Irish economic activity and the subject of much recent policy discussion. In terms of its economic impact, expenditure on the health services accounted for 10.7 per cent of gross national income (GNI) and 13.5 per cent of total employment in 2013. The public sector accounts for approximately 70 per cent of total health expenditure in Ireland. After years of expenditure growth barely in line with inflation during the 1980s and early 1990s, public health expenditure increased sharply from the mid-1990s (see Figure 12.1). Indeed, over the period 2000 to 2009, public health expenditure more than doubled in real terms. However, the effect of the sharp deterioration in the public finances since then is reflected in public health expenditure, which declined from €15.5 billion in 2009 to just over €14 billion in 2013.

In terms of per capita health expenditure in Organisation of Economic Co-operation and Development (OECD) countries over the period 2009 to 2011, only Greece has experienced a greater decline than Ireland. The scale of the reduction in public health expenditure over a relatively short period of time has created unprecedented challenges for the Irish health system. The immediate challenge is to ensure that existing service levels and quality are maintained in a period of declining public health expenditure. The oversight of the EU-IMF 'Troika' has focused attention on the efficiency of the Irish public health service, with large components of public health expenditure such as pharmaceuticals receiving particular policy focus. In addition, the current debate over universal health insurance highlights ongoing concerns with access to health services in Ireland. Recent debates have also focused on the impact of the financial and economic crisis on health outcomes, reflecting the wider international discussion about the impact of the economic cycle on population health.

The remainder of this chapter focuses on the themes of access and efficiency in the context of discussions on key issues with regard to the health services in Ireland. Section 2 discusses the rationale for government intervention in the financing and delivery of health services (see also Chapter 3), outlining the various efficiency and equity justifications for government intervention in the sector. Section 3 outlines the key features of the Irish health service, its governance and organisational structure, entitlement, financing and delivery. This section also discusses proposed changes to the structure and financing of the health service. Section 4 looks at the Irish health sector in comparative context, discussing how the Irish experience in terms of expenditure, outcomes, financing and delivery structures compares with other OECD countries. Sections 5 and 6 focus on the two key issues facing the Irish health services at present: access and efficiency. Section 5 focuses on the financing of primary care services in Ireland, as well as the current role of private health insurance in the Irish healthcare system. In the context of declining levels of public health expenditure, Section 6 discusses the issue of cost containment in the health sector. Section 7 concludes the chapter.

Figure 12.1 Public Health Expenditure in Ireland: 1994–2013 (deflated by CPI)

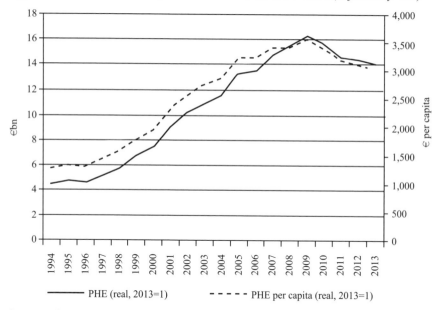

Sources: for expenditure data see Department of Public Expenditure and Reform, *Databank*; for consumer price index data see CSO, *Consumer Price Index*, various issues, Stationery Office, Dublin.

2 WHY GOVERNMENT INTERVENTION?

Despite the fact that the private sector accounts for approximately 30 per cent of healthcare finance (see Section 3), and is heavily involved in the provision of health services in Ireland, the public sector remains the main agent responsible for the finance and delivery of health services in Ireland. Chapter 3 discusses the rationale for government intervention in the economy in general. In terms of the health services, efficiency concerns relating to asymmetric information, uncertainty and the existence of externalities, as well as equity or distributional concerns, motivate government involvement in healthcare. Where the government does not directly involve itself in the provision of healthcare services, it may have a role in financing, regulation, pricing (taxation and subsidies) and information provision.

While asymmetric information, uncertainty and externalities are the most readily identifiable indicators of market failure in the health sector, healthcare markets also suffer from imperfect competition in the sense that many of the conditions for perfectly competitive markets are absent or deficient. Many services, for example hospital services, are subject to economies of scale, producers can often influence the level of demand and/or price, and price signals are often absent, particularly where third-party reimbursement systems (e.g. insurance) are in operation. Most important, however, the assumptions of perfectly informed consumers, the absence of uncertainty and the absence of externalities are violated in healthcare markets.

Asymmetric Information
The nature of the relationship between producers and consumers in healthcare is distorted by asymmetric information. Patients are essentially buying the provider's knowledge and/or information when they consume healthcare. In comparison with other goods and services, information acquisition on the part of the consumer in healthcare markets is made more difficult by the nature of the product. Learning by experience is complicated by the fact that every illness episode is different and the consumer cannot sample the service before purchase and is unlikely to have had prior experience of the same service. In addition, the information is often technically complex, involving many years of study.

The relationship has often been characterised as a principal agent one; due to the high costs of acquiring such technical information, the patient relies on the healthcare provider to act in their best interests in terms of diagnosis and treatment decisions. The presence of asymmetric information justifies a role for government in improving consumers' information and regulating the behaviour of doctors and other healthcare professionals. For example, governments intervene in the licensing and accreditation of providers, the authorisation of pharmaceuticals that can be prescribed to patients and the provision of information to consumers.

Uncertainty
Healthcare markets are also characterised by uncertainty, i.e. lack of information about the future. Ill-health is inherently unpredictable, both in terms of financial costs and physical and emotional suffering. This necessitates a role for insurance in offering the consumer protection against uncertainty. However, the problems

of adverse selection, moral hazard and cream-skimming may arise in a private health insurance market.

Adverse selection arises when the insurer cannot distinguish between low and high risks, because individuals purchasing health insurance have better information about their risk status than the insurer. Insurers must therefore base the premium on the risk pool that includes both low and high risks. Low-risk individuals will not purchase health insurance because the premium does not reflect their risk status, leaving only high-risk individuals in the risk pool. This can make the fund unsustainable. The solution is to have compulsory insurance or differential (i.e. risk-related) premiums. However, due to concerns that high-risk individuals would be denied access to healthcare under a private health insurance system with differential premiums on the basis of age and health status, most governments intervene to provide free or heavily subsidised health insurance for the population for most basic health services.

Moral hazard behaviour, where an individual's behaviour is affected by their insurance status, may arise in the form of excessive utilisation of services on the part of the patient. It may also arise in the form of less preventive activities. User fees, which aim to make patients more aware of the resource implications of their decisions, are often used to temper the moral hazard effects of free or heavily subsidised healthcare. However, the degree to which user fees are effective in changing behaviour has been questioned, and there are well-documented adverse impacts on access (see also Section 5).

A final problem associated with a private insurance market is that of cream-skimming. Insurers seek to encourage low-risk persons to insure with their company. In the market for car insurance for example, premia are substantially higher for high-risk groups such as the young, those with penalty points, etc. Once again, due to equity concerns about certain groups being denied medical treatment, governments intervene to either offer health insurance or to regulate the sector.

In Ireland, the government strictly regulates the behaviour of the major private health insurers in an attempt to prevent cream-skimming through the principles of open enrolment (no one can be refused cover), community rating (all individuals face the same premium) and lifetime cover (once insured, an individual's policy cannot be terminated). The stability of the community rating system means that a risk-equalisation scheme (which aims to remove differences in insurers' costs that result from differing risk profiles among members) is necessary. Section 5 discusses in greater detail risk equalisation and the role of private health insurance in the Irish healthcare system.

Externalities
The healthcare sector may also be characterised by the presence of externalities when private costs or benefits are out of line with social costs or benefits. For a positive/negative externality, private benefits/costs are less than social benefits/costs, meaning that output is below/above the socially optimal level. The standard

317

solution to an externality is to levy a Pigouvian tax, in the case of goods or services that produce negative externalities; or to offer a subsidy, in the case of goods or services that produce positive externalities.

Free childhood vaccinations against infectious diseases and excise taxes on cigarettes are the most obvious examples of government intervention in the health sector due to the presence of externalities. A vaccinated population confers a positive externality on society, while second-hand cigarette smoke confers a negative externality on society; in the absence of government intervention vaccination levels would be less than the socially optimal level due to higher social benefits than private benefits, while smoking levels would be greater than the socially optimal level due to higher social costs than private costs. Of course, the efficacy of taxes in changing behaviour to reflect the socially optimal level depends on the price elasticity of demand for the good/service, the availability of substitutes, budget share, etc. (see also Chapter 4).

Equity

Apart from efficiency concerns, the desire to ensure that healthcare is distributed equitably across the population motivates government intervention in the sector. However, there is much discussion over what is meant by equity in the context of the health services. Is the objective equality of opportunity (i.e. access to health-care) or equality of outcome (i.e. health status)? Many governments intervene to smooth out differences in health outcomes that are not related to need factors such as age, gender or health status, but rather to socioeconomic characteristics such as income, area of residence, level of education, etc. For example, a recent study found that perinatal mortality rates in Ireland among the unskilled manual/ unemployed group were 1.85 times higher than those among the professional group.[2]

However, most governments also subscribe to the notion of equality of opportunity in the sense that access to healthcare should be distributed on the basis of need for care, not on the basis of non-health-related attributes, such as ability to pay (which is the case for many other commodities). But how do we define access? Most studies proxy access by utilisation, arguing that access to health services is equitable if utilisation rates are similar, even after controlling for need factors such as age, gender and health status. However, it is obvious that even if everyone enjoys the same access to healthcare, persons in equal need may end up consuming different amounts of care (and types of care) due to differing tastes and preferences, differing ability to navigate the system, etc. Nonetheless, the principle of access according to need rather than ability to pay is an accepted principle in most countries, and the recent policy changes in the USA that have extended insurance cover to the significant proportion of the population who are uninsured highlights the widespread concern regarding individuals being denied medical treatment simply due to financial circumstances.

An additional issue concerns the progressivity of funding sources, i.e. most governments subscribe to the view that health services should be financed in relation to ability to pay (those on higher incomes should pay a higher proportion of their incomes in taxation, social insurance contributions, etc.). Such thinking motivates government involvement in the financing of healthcare services, offering free or subsidised services to those on low incomes or in particularly vulnerable situations.

Government Intervention in Practice

In practice, the public sector uses a variety of instruments to intervene in the healthcare sector. While the government intervenes heavily in regulation, information provision and financing in Ireland, it mainly leaves the provision of health services to private operators, who consequently receive much of their funding from public sources (e.g. GP services and voluntary hospital services). Due to concerns over the ability of the private market to deliver insurance efficiently and equitably (in particular, adverse selection, moral hazard and cream-skimming behaviours must be absent), governments in Europe have tended to intervene by providing free or heavily subsidised insurance for most basic health services (e.g. in France and Germany all individuals are compulsorily insured for most health services and the system is funded through the social insurance scheme with the contributions of those on low incomes or who are economically inactive paid by the state).

In Ireland, the state intervenes by providing insurance for certain services (mainly hospital services) to the full population, providing insurance for all services to certain vulnerable sections of the population (e.g. those on low incomes) and strictly regulating conduct in the private insurance market (the Health Insurance Authority was established in 2001 to act as regulator of the private health insurance market in Ireland).

While government intervention to correct market failures is an accepted feature of modern economies, government failure may itself lead to efficiency or equity failings. In particular, government intervention in provision may lead to inefficiency, as government-owned and operated facilities face a loose budget constraint. In addition, regulatory capture by vested interests may result in regulations that lead to an inefficient level of output, e.g. the restrictions on pharmacy locations that existed prior to the revocation of the 1996 Health Regulations Act in 2001. Ensuring that public funding sources are progressive in their impact is also an important concern.

3 KEY FEATURES OF THE IRISH HEALTH SERVICE

Governance and Organisational Structure

The Irish healthcare system underwent substantial organisational reform in 2005, partly in response to the recommendations of a number of key reports on the Irish healthcare system in the early 2000s. The key bodies in the current system are the Department of Health (a separate Department of Children and Youth Affairs was established in 2011), the Health Service Executive (HSE) and the Health Information and Quality Authority (HIQA).

The main role of the Department of Health is to advise the minister and government on the strategic development of the health system. The preparation of legislation in accordance with health policy is a key responsibility of the department. HIQA, which was fully established in 2007, is an independent agency responsible for developing standards, monitoring compliance and carrying out investigations in residential services for children, older persons and persons with disabilities. It is also responsible for carrying out health technology assessments (HTAs) in Ireland.

The HSE, which was established in January 2005, is responsible for the delivery of health and social care services in Ireland. Currently, four regional directors of operations (Dublin Mid-East, Dublin North-East, West and South) are responsible for the provision of health and social services in their areas. Many services are provided directly (e.g. district nurses and public nursing homes), while others are provided under contract with the HSE by self-employed health professionals, private health service providers, voluntary hospitals and voluntary/community organisations. Many other advisory agencies and voluntary organisations under the authority of the HSE play a role in service delivery, regulation and development in the health system, for example An Bord Altranais (the Nursing Board) is responsible for the regulation of the nursing profession in Ireland.

The HSE is the largest employer in the state, employing nearly 100,000 staff in 2013, and its budget of €14 billion in 2013 is the largest of any public sector organisation in Ireland. The HSE has undergone numerous organisational changes since its establishment in 2005; for example, the recent Health Service Executive (Governance) Act 2013 established new directorates closely aligned to specific areas of service such as primary care, mental health, hospitals, health and wellbeing and social care. It allows for a reorganisation of services to prepare the way for the health reforms contained in the current Programme for Government (discussed in greater detail below).

Eligibility for Free Public Health Services
All individuals who are ordinarily resident in Ireland are granted either full or limited eligibility for public healthcare services. Individuals with full eligibility, termed 'medical card holders' or 'public patients', are entitled to receive all health services free of charge under the General Medical Services (GMS) Scheme. This includes GP services, prescribed medicines, all dental, ophthalmic and aural services, maternity services, in-patient services in public hospitals and specialist treatment in outpatient clinics of public hospitals. However, from 1 October 2010, medical card holders are required to pay a fixed charge per prescription item (currently €2.50 per item, up to a maximum of €25 per family per month). At the end of December 2013 approximately 40 per cent of the population had a medical card (see Table 12.1).

The remainder of the population, those with limited eligibility ('non-medical cardholders' or 'private patients'), are entitled to free maternity services, in-patient services in public hospitals (subject to a €80 charge per day up to an annual maximum of €800), specialist services in outpatient clinics (again, subject to a €80 charge per day up to an annual maximum of €800), assistance towards the cost of prescribed medicines over a monthly limit of €144 per family (under the Drugs Payment Scheme) and assistance towards the cost of prescribed medicines for certain chronic conditions (under the Long Term Illness Scheme) or high-cost treatments (under the High Tech Drugs Scheme). In most cases, they must pay in full for GP consultations and all dental, ophthalmic and aural treatments. However, those who satisfy an income means test are eligible for a GP visit card (introduced in 2005), which grants the recipient access to free GP services only (other entitlements are the same as for those with limited eligibility).

Eligibility for a medical card is dependent upon income and is decided on the basis of a means test, with the income thresholds set nationally and updated annually. The intention is that the decision to seek medical care should not be dependent on ability to pay. The income thresholds for the GP visit card are 50 per cent higher than those for the standard medical card. In special circumstances, such as a cancer diagnosis, an individual who is otherwise ineligible on the basis of income may be granted a medical card or GP visit card.

As of December 2013, approximately 3 per cent of medical cards, and 20 per cent of GP visit cards, were issued on a 'discretionary' basis.[3] From 1 July 2001 to 31 December 2008, all individuals aged 70 years and over were also entitled to a medical card, regardless of income. Concerns over the cost of the entitlement motivated the policy change, and signalled a return to a policy favouring means testing of eligibility for public health benefits (rather than an extension of automatic entitlement to particular population groups). Current proposals in relation to public health cover will be discussed in greater detail below .

Table 12.1 shows the change in coverage since 1990. Medical card cover fell throughout the 1990s as income guidelines failed to increase in line with increases in average incomes. Due to rising unemployment, medical card coverage has risen sharply in the last five years. Take-up of the GP visit card is increasing.

Private health insurance in Ireland is primarily taken out by non-medical card holders to cover the costs of private or semi-private hospital care in public and private hospitals (although many plans are now offering limited cover for primary care). At present, just under 45 per cent of the population are covered (see also Section 4). Medical and GP visit cardholders may also take out private health insurance. Section 5 discusses the equity issues associated with medical card and private health insurance cover in Ireland in greater detail.

Table 12.1 Public Health Cover (percentage of the population), 1990–2013

Year	Full eligibility (medical card)	Limited eligibility (GP visit card)	Limited eligibility (no medical or GP visit card)
1990	34.8	–	65.2
1995	35.5	–	64.5
2000	30.3	–	69.7
2005	28.0	0.1	71.9
2006	28.9	1.2	69.9
2007	29.2	1.7	69.1
2008	30.1	1.9	67.9
2009	32.6	2.2	65.2
2010	35.5	2.6	61.9
2011	37.0	2.7	60.2
2012	40.4	2.9	56.7
2013	40.6	2.7	56.7

Sources: Calculated from General Medical Services Payments Board, *Annual Report*, GMSPB, Dublin, various issues; Primary Care Reimbursement Service, *Statistical Analysis of Claims and Payments*, PCRS, Dublin, various issues; Department of Health and Children, *Health Statistics,* Stationery Office, Dublin, various issues; HSE, *Health Service Management Data Report December 2013*, HSE, Dublin 2013; CSO, *Database Direct* (www.cso.ie/en/databases/index.html), accessed 18 March 2014.

Financing of Health Services

There are three main sources of finance in the Irish healthcare system: public resources; out-of-pocket payments by individuals; and private health insurance. Table 12.2 presents the breakdown of financing sources in Ireland over the period 1990 to 2011. General government resources (primarily taxation) account for around two-thirds of total Irish health expenditure. Out-of-pocket payments by individuals (e.g. GP fees by non-medical card holders) account for a further 18 per cent. Despite the fact that around 45 per cent of the population hold private health insurance, it accounts for only 12 per cent of total financing in Irish healthcare.

Since the onset of the recession in 2008, the proportion of total health expenditure accounted for by public resources has decreased, while that contributed by direct out-of-pocket payments by individuals and private health insurance has increased. This reflects the increasing reliance on out-of-pocket charges as a financing mechanism in the Irish health service as a response to the financial and economic crisis. However, this trend is contrary to that observed in other OECD countries, where the share of public funding has tended to increase in order to safeguard access to public health services.

Table 12.2 Sources of Finance for Total Health Expenditure (percentage of total health expenditure), 1990–2011

	General government[1]	Out-of-pocket payments	Private insurance	Other private sources
1990	71.7	16.5	9.1	2.7
1995	72.5	15.3	9.2	3.0
2000	75.1	16.0	7.0	2.0
2005	76.0	16.1	7.3	0.7
2006	75.4	16.1	8.3	0.3
2007	75.7	14.8	8.1	1.4
2008	75.4	15.3	8.1	1.2
2009	72.6	16.1	10.1	1.2
2010	69.6	18.2	11.5	0.8
2011	67.0	18.1	11.9	3.0

Source: OECD, *Health Data 2013*, OECD, Paris 2013.
[1] Includes social insurance contributions, which contributed less than 1 per cent to total health resources over this period (see also Table 12.4).

Delivery of Health Services

While the state is heavily involved in the financing of health services in Ireland, it mainly leaves the delivery of health services to the private sector, with the hospital and primary care sectors providing particularly good examples of the intermix between the public and private sectors in the financing and delivery of health services in Ireland.

There are three different types of hospital in Ireland: voluntary hospitals, which are run on a not-for-profit basis by private organisations (usually religious institutions) but which receive most of their funding from the state; HSE hospitals, which are owned and operated by the HSE; and privately owned, operated and funded hospitals. Public hospital services are provided in voluntary and HSE hospitals and most of these hospitals also provide private healthcare. Consultants employed in public hospitals may treat private patients in the same public hospital (depending on their contract). While there are controls on the proportion of beds that may be used by private patients (nationally, 20 per cent for in-patients and 30 per cent for day patients) and consultant activity is monitored to ensure that they do not exceed their private activity cap, there are concerns that acute public hospitals and consultants are sidestepping restrictions on their private practice, resulting in public hospital resources potentially being diverted away from public patients towards their private counterparts, although recent statistics suggest that the proportion of in-patient and day cases treated on a public basis has been increasing.

Primary care services are mainly provided by independent professionals (GPs, pharmacists, dentists, etc.) who may be contracted to provide services in the public sector, in addition to services provided to private patients (approximately 75 per cent of GPs also have contracts to provide services to medical card holders). The Primary Care Reimbursement Service (PCRS) undertakes the reimbursement of providers of GP, dental, optical and pharmaceutical services supplied to medical card holders as well as the reimbursement of pharmacists for services provided to non-medical card holders under the various community drugs schemes.

The Irish healthcare system therefore has a mixture of a universal public health service and a fee-based private system. Some services are publicly funded and delivered (e.g. treatment as a public patient in a public hospital), some are publicly funded but privately delivered (e.g. GP consultations by medical card holders), some are privately funded and delivered (e.g. GP consultations by non-medical card holders), while some are privately funded but publicly delivered (e.g. non-medical card holders must pay a modest charge for treatment in public hospitals). This complex mixture has implications for the allocation of resources both between the public and the private sector and between different types of care (see Section 5 for further discussion).

Proposals for Reform

The 2011 Programme for Government provides for a major reform of the Irish health service. The most significant commitments relate to the introduction of free GP care for the entire population, the introduction of a system of universal health insurance, the abolition of the HSE, the establishment of independent hospital trusts and reform of the financing mechanism for public hospitals (from block budgets to activity-based funding, or 'money follows the patient').

By far the most significant recent proposal concerns the commitment to move towards a system of universal health insurance (UHI) for Ireland. A White Paper, setting out the details of the UHI model in addition to the estimated costs and financing mechanisms associated with the introduction of UHI, is due to be published in 2014. Initially, while the two current coalition parties both proposed UHI as their preferred method of healthcare financing during the election campaign in early 2011, they differed on how the system would be organised (Fine Gael favoured the Dutch system of competing private insurers, while Labour favoured a single public insurer). The proposed solution is a combination of the two positions in offering individuals a choice between competing insurers, one of which would be public.

Despite the lack of detail on the proposal, the core features of the proposed UHI system, namely a system in which the purchase of health insurance is compulsory (although subsidised by the state for those on low incomes), and in which private practice in public hospitals is no longer a feature, would represent a major change in Irish healthcare financing. In other countries with UHI, the purchase of supplementary private health insurance is not prohibited, but the provision of private healthcare is completely separate under such a system and individuals are generally not eligible to opt out of the public system.

In addition, the proposal to move towards the provision of free GP care services for the entire population represents a major departure in the financing of primary care services in Ireland. In the initial proposal, free GP care for all was to be introduced on a phased basis, with free care extended to those on the Long Term Illness Scheme in year one and to those on the High Tech Drugs Scheme in year two, with subsidised care extended to all in the next phase, followed by access to free care to all in the final phase (i.e. by 2016). Initial targets were not met and in October 2013, the government announced that in the first phase free GP care would be extended to all children aged six and under.

This marks a significant departure from the principle of extending free GP care to all on a phased basis, beginning with those most in need of free GP care, and it is not clear what principles will guide the next phases. However, the importance of removing access barriers to primary care services has been highlighted repeatedly in previous research on the Irish healthcare system. As the first point of contact with the health service in most cases, and as an important source of preventive healthcare, it is important that individuals are incentivised to register with a primary care provider, to seek care with a primary care provider in the first instance wherever possible, and to seek care at the earliest possible stage of illness.

In the current system, such incentives only exist for people who have a medical card or GP visit card. A new GP contract will be necessary if free primary care is extended to the full population. The 2011 Programme for Government makes a number of commitments in relation to a new GP contract, including that remuneration will be reduced, that incentives for the provision of services to chronically ill patients will be introduced, and that GPs will be paid on a predominantly capitation basis. A draft contract for GPs for the provision of care to the under-six age group is currently in preparation.

Major changes in the financing of Irish healthcare would also have significant implications for how healthcare in Ireland is delivered. One of the most important changes proposed is the eventual abolition of the HSE. HSE ownership and management of public hospitals would end, and the purchasing role of the HSE would transfer to a new purchasing agency (the Healthcare Commissioning Agency).

In 2013, six hospital groups were established, each with its own governance and management structure. The eventual aim is the establishment of a system of independent, competing hospital trusts. If this change is implemented the current system whereby the HSE owns and operates the majority of public hospitals will end. Under the current proposals, hospitals would no longer receive fixed budgets but would be paid instead for the services they provide and the number of patients they treat ('money follows the patient'), thereby incentivising them to treat more patients and to be reimbursed according to the complexity of treatment.

4 THE IRISH HEALTHCARE SYSTEM IN COMPARATIVE CONTEXT

Health Expenditure

Table 12.3 illustrates that Ireland, along with most other OECD countries, experienced an increase in the share of national income devoted to health over the period 2000 to 2011. The share has increased at a faster pace in Ireland than in many other OECD countries; of the 13 countries presented in Table 12.3, Ireland moved from having the second lowest share of national income devoted to health in 2000 to the seventh highest in 2011. This is despite the fact that Ireland has a relatively young population by international standards, although there is much debate in the literature about the extent to which an ageing population is a significant driver of health expenditure (see also Section 5).

Table 12.3 Health Expenditure as a Percentage of GNI[1] in Selected OECD Countries,[2] 2000 and 2011

	2000	2011	% aged over 65 (2011)
Australia[2]	8.3	9.3[2]	13.7
Austria	10.1	10.9	17.7
Canada[2]	9.1	11.6[2]	14.7
Denmark	8.4	10.6	17.1
Finland	7.3	9.0	17.8
France	9.9	11.4	17.1
Germany	10.4	11.0	20.7
Ireland	*7.1*	*10.7*	*12.2*
Netherlands	7.8	12.0	15.9
New Zealand[2]	8.2	10.4[2]	13.3
Sweden	8.2	9.3	19.3
UK	7.1	9.2	16.2
USA	13.2	16.7	13.2

Sources: OECD, *Health Data Statistics 2013,* OECD, Paris 2013; European Commission, *AMECO Macro-Economic Database*, available at: http://ec.europa.eu/economy_finance/db_indicators/ameco/index_en.htm), accessed 18 March 2014.
[1] While health expenditure is usually expressed as a proportion of GDP, the large divergence between Irish GDP and GNP/GNI figures means that, for comparative purposes, it is more appropriate to express health expenditure as a proportion of GNP/GNI.
[2] 2011 data for Australia and Canada relate to 2010, while 2011 data for New Zealand relate to 2009.

Healthcare Financing

Table 12.4 presents the sources of finance for selected OECD countries for 2011. In terms of public sources of finance, countries such as France and Germany rely much more heavily on social insurance contributions than general government sources, such as taxation, for their revenue. Social insurance contributions, which are compulsory and generally shared between the employer and employee, tend to be earmarked for specific purposes; in Ireland the 'health levy' (which has since been replaced by the universal social charge) contributed less than 1 per cent of total healthcare finance prior to its abolition in 2011. As in other countries, revenue from general taxation in Ireland is not earmarked specifically for the health services, which means that it must compete with other areas for public funds.

Due to universal eligibility for free public health services in many countries, the share of total expenditure funded through private sources (out-of-pocket payments by individuals, private insurance payments and other sources of finance, e.g. voluntary donations) is much smaller than that accounted for by public sources. The exception is the USA, which in 2011 provided free healthcare only for the old and those on low incomes (through the Medicare and Medicaid schemes respectively), and consequently relied more heavily on private sources of finance, particularly insurance.

The Affordable Care Act, finally enacted in 2012, will over time ensure near-universal health insurance in the USA through a substantial expansion of Medicaid, tax credits that will cap premium contributions as a share of income for people purchasing private health plans through new state insurance exchanges, and new insurance market rules that will prevent health insurers from denying coverage or charging higher premiums to people with pre-existing health conditions.

The prevalence of universal entitlement to free public health services across Europe results in monetary costs for healthcare consultations that are effectively zero, meaning that there is little incentive to control utilisation. User fees, in the form of co-payments, co-insurance or deductibles, can help to control utilisation, although there are concerns that such initiatives may reduce necessary as well as unnecessary utilisation. Nonetheless, most countries levy minimal user fees on consumers in an attempt to make them more aware of the resource implications of their behaviour.

For example, in Ireland a fee of €80 per day applies to individuals without medical cards for treatment as an in-patient in the public hospital sector. As Table 12.4 illustrates, out-of-pocket payments are now more important than private insurance as a source of finance for all countries examined except France and the USA. However, there are concerns that as governments come under increasing pressure to fund public health programmes, and out-of-pocket payments become more important as a source of revenue, a greater share of the funding burden will fall on those in ill health (see Section 5 for a discussion of equity issues surrounding user fees in healthcare).

Table 12.4 Sources of Finance for Total Health Expenditure for Selected OECD countries[1] (percentage of total health expenditure), 2011

Country	General government	Social insurance	Out-of-pocket payments	Private insurance	Other private sources
Australia[2]	68	0	19	8	5
Canada	69	1	15	12	3
Denmark[3]	85	–	13	2	0
Finland	61	14	19	2	4
France	4	73	8	14	1
Germany	9	68	13	9	1
Ireland	*67*	*0*	*18*	*12*	*3*
New Zealand	75	8	11	5	1
Sweden	82	0	16	0	2
UK	83	0	11	3	3
USA	6	41	12	34	7

Source: OECD, *Health Data 2013,* OECD, Paris 2013.
[1] Data for Austria and the Netherlands are not available.
[2] Data for Australia relate to 2010.
[3] Figures for Denmark do not distinguish between general taxation and social insurance contributions.

Health Outcomes
Levels of expenditure provide no guidance as to whether this expenditure is efficiently and effectively spent or distributed equitably across different sectors of the population. As the ultimate objective of health policy is to improve population health, it is useful to examine where countries rank in terms of health outcomes and whether there is any correlation between such measures and health expenditure.

Table 12.5 confirms the weak association between health expenditure and health outcome indicators such as life expectancy and infant mortality. Most striking is the case of the USA, which spends by far the most per capita on health, yet performs poorly in terms of life expectancy and infant mortality.

In an attempt to quantify the contribution of the health sector more accurately, the concept of amenable or avoidable mortality has been developed to assess the quality and performance of health systems. Amenable mortality refers to deaths from conditions considered amenable to healthcare, such as treatable cancers, diabetes, and cardiovascular disease. A recent study across 16 high-income countries found that 24 per cent of deaths under the age of 75 could be classified as 'avoidable'. Deaths from causes amenable to medical intervention were found to have fallen substantially over the period 1997 to 2007, with the largest decline observed for Ireland, although the USA continues to lag behind other high-income countries.

Table 12.5 Total Health Expenditure Per Capita and Health Outcome Rankings, Selected OECD countries,[1] 2011

Country	Expenditure	Life expectancy		Infant mortality
		Male	Female	
Australia[1]	8	2	2	10
Austria	3	8	3	6
Denmark	5	10	11	9
Finland	11	11	5	2
France	6	6	1	4
Germany	4	7	6	7
Ireland	*9*	*9*	*10*	*5*
Netherlands	2	3	7	8
New Zealand	12	4	9	3
Sweden	7	1	4	1
UK	10	5	8	11
USA	1	12	12	12

Sources: for data on expenditure (total health expenditure per capita expressed in USA $ PPP), male and female life expectancy (at birth) and infant mortality (per 1,000 live births) see OECD, *Health Statistics 2013*, OECD, Paris 2013.
[1] Australian expenditure data refers to 2009. Canada is excluded due to incomplete data.

In the debate about the role of health expenditure in improving population health, the literature highlights the fact that social, environmental and cultural factors such as diet, exercise, genetic inheritance, lifestyle, education, social status, income distribution, social support and housing, and their complex interactions, may be more important in determining the level and distribution of health outcomes than simple health expenditure. The recent increases in resources devoted to health promotion and prevention (e.g. through the smoking in the workplace ban, breast cancer screening, promotion of healthy eating, etc.) reflects this realisation that lifestyle factors are also crucial in influencing population health outcomes.

In an attempt to evaluate the impact of health policy on health systems performance and outcomes, a recent study examined health policies across 43 European countries. The results showed that Ireland was ranked 11th out of 43 European countries in terms of health policy performance, with Ireland scoring well in terms of policy in relation to tobacco control, but poorly in relation to policy on child safety (e.g. measles immunisation).

More recently, research has focused on the impact of the financial and economic crisis on health systems performance and health outcomes. In general, there is no simple answer to the question of how financial and economic crises impact on health outcomes, behaviours and inequalities. An important study in the USA in the early 2000s found that total mortality and most causes of mortality exhibited a procyclical fluctuation over the period 1972 to 1991, with suicides representing an important exception, although more recent evidence finds little relationship between the economic cycle and mortality.

Recently, the impact of the economic crisis on health outcomes in Ireland has been debated in a series of responses to an editorial in the *British Medical Journal* on health and the economic crisis in Europe, although some commentators note that it is probably too early to make definitive conclusions about the impact of the crisis on population health, due to time lags in effects, absence of timely data, etc.

5 HEALTH SECTOR FINANCE AND ACCESS

While the proportion of private financing in Irish healthcare is not unusual internationally, what sets Ireland apart from other OECD countries is the large proportion of the population who must pay out of pocket for primary care, particularly GP care. In addition, despite its relatively small contribution to overall health sector financing in Ireland, private health insurance has important implications for equity in the Irish system, particularly in relation to the interaction of public and private care in public hospitals.

User Fees and Access to Primary Care

While the proportion of the population eligible for free GP services has increased recently with rising unemployment, and currently stands at approximately 43 per cent of the population, the fact remains that nearly 60 per cent of the Irish population must pay out of pocket for GP (and other primary care) services. The effect of user fees on healthcare utilisation has been extensively studied. User fees are payments at the point of use and can take a number of different forms, including co-payment (a fixed fee per service), co-insurance (a fixed percentage of the cost of the service) and deductible (full cost of the service up to a certain threshold).

The primary motivation for user fees is to reduce moral hazard behaviour among consumers of healthcare services (i.e. the unnecessary use of healthcare services by patients). A secondary motivation is to generate revenue. However, there is extensive empirical evidence that user fees discourage both necessary as well as unnecessary healthcare utilisation. This research highlights also the negative equity implications of user fees. While demand for healthcare is relatively price inelastic, those on lower incomes have a higher price elasticity than those on higher incomes. Therefore, any increase in the cost of healthcare will have a greater deterrent effect on the poorer sections of society.

In the Irish system of primary care, non-medical card holders pay a co-payment for each GP visit, while they pay for all prescriptions up to a monthly deductible of €144 per family. Medical card holders receive free GP visits, and pay a €2.50 charge per prescription, up to a monthly limit of €25 per family.

Notwithstanding the current proposals in relation to free GP care for all (see Section 3), the current system has been criticised on a number of grounds, principally in relation to those just above the income threshold for a GP visit card. The sharp distinction between those with and without eligibility for free GP care means that a relatively small increase in weekly income can render an individual ineligible for a GP visit card and thus liable for the full cost of GP care. Previous research (prior to the introduction of the GP visit card) found that GP visiting rates were lowest among those just above the income threshold for a medical card (even controlling for differences in health need), although the deterrent effect of user fees for GP services among non-medical card holders was found to persist throughout the income distribution.

Role of Private Health Insurance

Private health insurance in Ireland is primarily taken out by non-medical card holders to cover the costs of private or semi-private hospital care in public and private hospitals. However, increasingly, the major insurers have started to offer (limited) cover for primary care expenses, usually in the form of a fixed amount per visit (subject to an annual maximum number of visits). It is difficult to gather data on the proportion of private health insurance plans that cover primary care expenses, but data from the recently released *Growing Up in Ireland* survey show that approximately 25 per cent of nine-year-old children live in households with private health insurance that provides some cover for primary care expenses. Notwithstanding the recent proposals in relation to a system of UHI for Ireland, there is still considerable uncertainty about the operation of the private health insurance market in Ireland.

Apart from a small number of restricted membership private health insurance schemes, there are four main private health insurance companies in Ireland: VHI, Laya Healthcare, Aviva Health and Glo Health. At the end of 2012, VHI Healthcare accounted for 56 per cent of the private health insurance market, while Laya Healthcare had a 22 per cent share, Aviva 17 per cent, Glo Health 1 per cent and the restricted membership schemes accounted for the remaining 4 per cent.

The government strictly regulates the behaviour of the major private insurers in the Irish market via the principles of open enrolment (no one can be refused cover), community rating (all individuals face the same premium) and lifetime cover (once insured, an individual's policy cannot be terminated). A stable community rating system means that a risk-equalisation scheme (which aims to remove differences in insurers' costs that result from differing risk profiles among members) must be implemented.

After years of legal challenges, the government finally introduced a risk-equalisation scheme in January 2013. The scheme provides for a system of age-related health credits in respect of those over the age of 60 that help to meet their higher claims costs. The health credits vary by age, sex and by level of cover. The credits are funded by a community rating health insurance levy paid by health insurers.

The proportion of the population with private health insurance cover has been falling steadily since the peak in 2006, when 51.6 per cent of the population had private health insurance. Currently, 44.7 per cent of the population are covered.[4] The age structure of membership is also changing, with the ratio of younger to older members falling over time (in 2008 there were 2.2 members aged 18–39 for every one member aged over 60, while the corresponding figure for 2012 was 1.5).

An important driver of falling membership is price inflation in private health insurance premia; in the year to July 2013, the price of private health insurance premia increased by 12.1 per cent, in comparison with overall health prices, which increased by just 1.0 per cent. Recent policy changes are likely to put further pressure on consumers. In Budget 2014 the government announced that the amount of the private health insurance premium that qualifies for tax relief will be limited to €1,000 for adults and €500 for children, while legislation was enacted in mid 2013 to allow for increased charges for private patients treated in public hospitals.

Private health insurance in Ireland essentially provides cover for services already available free of charge (or heavily subsidised) in the public sector. It therefore fulfils elements of a duplicate role, in contrast to other countries where its role is strictly supplementary to that of the public system (e.g. Canada). The UHI scheme is in part a response to the frequent criticisms of the two-tier system of care in public hospitals that is supported by the current role of private health insurance in Ireland. As noted, the precise details of the proposed UHI scheme have yet to be determined and therefore the potential role of the current insurers in the proposed UHI system is unclear.

6 CONTROL OF HEALTHCARE EXPENDITURE

Over the period 2009 to 2013, public health expenditure fell by over €1.5 billion, or nearly 10 per cent. Maintaining quality and existing levels of service in such an environment is a serious challenge. Many of the determinants of health expenditure are outside of the control of government, such as demographic change and increasing consumer expectations. However, there are measures that can be taken to limit the growth of healthcare expenditure, and there is much debate on the merits of the different approaches. Before outlining the various measures, it is worth discussing the determinants of healthcare expenditure in greater detail.

Determinants of Healthcare Expenditure

Cross-country comparisons of the determinants of health expenditure typically focus on three main factors: national income, population age structure and institutional features of the healthcare system. National income is consistently found to be one of the most important drivers of health expenditure increases; a recent study of cross-country differences in health expenditure found that 90 per cent of the variation in health expenditure across the 30 OECD countries examined was due to differences in gross domestic product (GDP) per capita. Related to the role of national income is the influence of rising consumer expectations (see also the discussion on Wagner's Law in Chapter 3).

While the potential impact of demographic change (both the size and age structure of the population) on health expenditure has been widely discussed, cross-country comparisons of health expenditure growth typically find that demographic change explains only a small proportion of health expenditure growth over time. A more important driver of healthcare expenditure is the 'end of life' cost and to the extent that population ageing simply delays such costs, the overall impact on health expenditure is unclear. In addition, there is evidence to suggest that the end of life cost is lower for those who die at older ages, although the costs of long-term care do increase.

There is also some evidence that as life expectancy increases, the number of disability-free life years gained may increase at a greater rate. The net impact of population ageing on future health expenditure is therefore complex and difficult to predict. Similarly, the impact of the increasing prevalence of chronic disease on future healthcare expenditure is hard to estimate. Approximately 80 per cent of total health expenditure relates to the treatment of chronic disease, and this proportion is likely to increase with population ageing and adverse trends in diet, exercise and obesity. While increasing rates of chronic disease may increase the demand for healthcare, changing models of care (i.e. a movement away from acute, episodic care to more preventive care in the community) may mean that the overall impact on healthcare expenditure is more modest.

On the supply side, factors such as rising healthcare prices, technological change, the regulatory regime governing behaviour in the healthcare sector and the incentives facing healthcare providers are all important drivers of healthcare expenditure. Empirical evidence suggests that the contribution of technological change to health expenditure growth is large and significant (and often greater than that of population ageing), but it must be remembered that many technological advances are hugely beneficial for human health and well-being. The role of health technology assessment in adjudicating on the costs and benefits of new technologies is therefore crucially important in this regard.

Given the labour intensity of the sector, the impact of labour costs on health expenditures cannot be underestimated. In Ireland, labour costs account for approximately 50 per cent of health expenditure (in the acute hospitals sector, the proportion is closer to 70 per cent); therefore changes in the level and type of employees have implications for spending on health services. Related to this is the concept of Baumol's disease (see also Chapter 3) whereby public sector employees demand wage increases in line with those of their private sector counterparts. While in the private sector (the 'progressive' sector), wage increases are accompanied by improvements in productivity, in labour-intensive sectors such as health, education and public administration (the 'non-progressive' sectors), productivity improvements are harder to implement. Resistance to technological change on the part of providers may also hinder productivity gains; for example, in 2008 only 56 per cent of Irish GPs made active use of a computer during consultations with patients (ranked 19th out of 29 European countries).

The financial incentives facing healthcare providers, which are largely determined by how they are paid for the services they provide, have important implications for healthcare expenditure. Taking the example of GPs, in a fee-for-service system, GPs receive a fee for each consultation, while in a capitation system, they receive a payment that is risk-adjusted for the health needs of the patient (e.g. by age and sex). No one system is preferred as there are trade-offs involved in choosing one method over another. Fee-for-service payments promote activity, although there are concerns that doctors can engage in demand-inducement behaviour under such a system.

While capitation payments incentivise the provision of preventive care, unless the capitation payment is appropriately risk-adjusted, such payments can give doctors an incentive to engage in 'cream-skimming' behaviour. However, cross-country comparisons have found that healthcare expenditure is higher in countries with fee-for-service systems than in those with capitation systems, controlling for other determinants of expenditure such as national income, population age structure, etc. In that context, shifting the financial risk of healthcare costs from insurers/government to providers via capitation can be effective in controlling costs.

Expenditure Control Measures
Essentially, there are three broad approaches to achieving sustainable levels of public health expenditure: increasing revenue; lessening the obligations of the public system via changes to public health cover; and increasing efficiency. In the current economic environment, the degree to which public revenue can be increased (via taxation or social insurance contributions) is limited, although a recent report examined the case for the introduction of a tax on sugar-sweetened drinks in Ireland.

Shifting the responsibility for financing healthcare to individuals via new or increased user fees, while attractive for a government trying to limit public health expenditure, does not necessarily lead to lower total health expenditure. As discussed in the previous section, user fees discourage both necessary and unnecessary healthcare utilisation and are disproportionately borne by the poorer, sicker members of society. Even with exemptions for vulnerable population groups, the level of user fees needs to be sufficiently high, and the administrative costs of collection sufficiently low, to generate significant revenues. However, where the objective is to discourage the consumption of low-value care (e.g. branded pharmaceuticals where a generic equivalent is available), user fees can be an appropriate strategy and this is the logic behind the recently introduced system of reference pricing and generic substitution (discussed in greater detail below).

Measures that seek to enhance the efficiency of the health sector offer a more appropriate mechanism for ensuring long-term sustainability of healthcare expenditure. Reforming the way providers are paid for the services they provide is becoming increasingly common, with many countries moving away from pure fee-for-service remuneration of healthcare professionals. In some cases, contracts are increasingly including pay-for-performance elements in an attempt to encourage behaviour on the part of providers that is aligned with health policy objectives.

In the UK, approximately 25 per cent of GPs' income is derived from payments for performance on a range of indicators, including cost-effective prescribing behaviour, increased use of IT and on-going monitoring of patients with chronic disease, although there is limited evidence on the effectiveness of such payments in terms of health outcomes, cost control and quality. Additional microeconomic measures such as promoting the use of the GP as a gatekeeper to hospital services; funding hospitals on a case mix (i.e. adjusting for the nature and intensity of treatments undertaken) or prospective budget basis rather than on a simple retrospective budget basis; encouraging day surgery over in-patient stays; and encouraging the prescribing of generic pharmaceuticals are all seen as increasingly important in containing costs.

With the increasing incidence of chronic disease, the provision of healthcare is increasingly focusing on health promotion and prevention rather than on the traditional roles of diagnosis and treatment, in particular through an expanded role for GP and other primary care services. The degree to which the health sector is oriented towards primary care has been found to influence health expenditure; international comparisons show higher health expenditure in countries with weaker primary care. The supply of primary care doctors and better primary healthcare is associated with lower total expenditure on healthcare, in part due to better preventive care and consequent lower rates of hospitalisation.

Greater use of electronic health records and associated technologies has been suggested as an important mechanism to improve quality and efficiency in healthcare. In 2013, the government published an eHealth Strategy, outlining priority projects relating to a national health identifier, ePrescribing, online referrals and scheduling, telehealthcare, etc. Increased investment in information and communications technology (ICT) may be required, however; Ireland's current expenditure on ICT of 0.85 per cent of the public health budget is substantially below the EU average of 2 to 3 per cent.

In Ireland, the HSE has pursued a number of avenues in seeking to reduce public health expenditure in recent years. The pharmaceuticals budget has been the subject of particular policy attention, with a number of recent policy changes targeting the ex-factory price of pharmaceuticals and the fees and mark-ups paid to wholesalers and community pharmacists. In 2013, legislation for a system of reference pricing and generic substitution was enacted; currently reference prices have been set for six major pharmaceuticals, with substantial price reductions achieved in comparison with the pre-reference price level.

On the pay side, salaries of HSE staff were reduced in January 2010, in line with the general public service pay cuts, and again in 2013. In 2013, following extensive negotiations, agreement was reached with a number of unions representing public service workers on a range of reform and productivity measures, including an increase in the working week, deferral of increments and reduction in overtime payments (these agreements are collectively known as the Haddington Road Agreement).

7 CONCLUDING COMMENTS

This chapter provided an overview of the financing and delivery of health services in Ireland, as well as key policy issues. The challenges facing the Irish health service today are very different from those of just a few years ago. In the latter part of the last decade, the sustainability of ever-increasing levels of health expenditure was a major concern, but now the continuing financial and economic crisis and its impact on the resources available for the public health sector is the most immediate challenge. In particular, the focus is now on ensuring that existing service levels and quality are maintained in a period of declining public health expenditure.

This will require increased efficiencies across the health sector, with recent initiatives focusing on some of the largest components of public expenditure, such as labour and pharmaceutical costs. In addition, there are on-going concerns about access to health services in Ireland, and the governance and organisational structure of the health service. The Programme for Government proposes the introduction of an alternative financing mechanism, UHI, the extension of eligibility for free GP care to all, as well as the abolition of the HSE and the establishment of all hospitals as not-for-profit, independent entities. While the proposals have the potential to radically change the manner in which Irish health services are financed and delivered, with important implications for equity and efficiency in the system, there have been considerable delays in implementation.

Notes

* The author would like to thank Carol Newman and John O'Hagan for comments on an earlier version of the chapter. All views expressed are those of the author and are not necessarily shared by Trinity College Dublin or the Economic and Social Research Institute (ESRI).

1   This section draws in particular on: OECD, *Health at a Glance 2013*, OECD, Paris
     2013; European Commission annual macroeconomic database (AMECO) (http://
     ec.europa.eu/economy_finance/db_indicators/ameco/index_en.htm); Central Statistics
     Office (CSO) database (www.cso.ie/en/databases/index.html); Department of Public
     Expenditure and Reform databank (www.per.gov.ie/databank/), last accessed 18 March
     2014.
2   R. Layte and B. Clyne, 'Perinatal mortality in Ireland', *Economic and Social Review*,
     Vol. 41, No. 2, 2010.
3   Calculated from HSE, *Health Service Management Data Report December 2013*,
     HSE, Dublin 2013.
4   Calculated from Health Insurance Authority *Newsletter*, February 2014; CSO
     Databank (www.cso.ie/en/databases/index.htm), last accessed 18 March 2014.

CHAPTER 13

Education: Market Failure and Government Interventions

*Carol Newman**

1 INTRODUCTION

Education equips individuals with the knowledge and skills necessary to participate in society both economically and socially. It is a fundamental input to the functioning of society, even at a most basic level. The public good characteristics of education underpin the argument for government support in its provision. In most developed countries, government plays a role in ensuring education provision occurs in an efficient and equitable way. This is achieved either through the direct provision of the service or the regulation of some aspects of its provision.

This chapter focuses on the broad policy issues associated with government provision of education services but also considers in detail Irish education policy and the effectiveness of delivery of education services. In Ireland, education is largely publicly provided with a small private component. There are three core layers to the Irish education system: primary, second level, and third level or the tertiary sector. In recent times, the pre-primary and fourth-level sectors have also become increasingly important. Unlike many other countries, pre-primary education is predominantly privately funded with the exception of one year of free early childhood care and education provided by the state. Approximately one million students are enrolled in full-time education in Ireland. Publicly supported services are delivered by over 3,000 primary schools, over 700 second-level schools, seven universities, 14 Institutes of Technology (ITs) and five teacher training colleges.[1]

The delivery of education services is increasingly set in a global context and so a core aim of this chapter is to examine Ireland's performance relative to its main competitors. The availability of internationally comparable data through, for example, the Organisation for Economic Co-operation and Development's (OECD) Programme for International Student Assessment (PISA) rankings for primary and second level and the various published rankings of higher education institutions, allows the quality of education to be compared across countries. This places the education system under scrutiny at a national level, particularly given the significant media attention that these rankings receive every year. Policy makers are placed under increasing pressure to deliver on quality, not only to provide value for money for taxpayers but also to send the right signal to foreign investors attracted to Ireland because of its well-educated workforce.

At higher levels, where education is an internationally traded service, the rankings also play an important part in attracting international students, an increasingly important source of funding. Improving quality, however, is made all the more difficult in a constrained funding environment, not only for Ireland but for most countries.

The way in which education is delivered is also changing, and at a rapid pace. Technological advances allow for new adaptive learning approaches that combine software with traditional teaching methods. These provide students with more interactive lessons that are better tailored to their needs while reducing the number of actual teachers required. It will take some time, though, before these new approaches are introduced into mainstream education systems. Nevertheless, when evaluating the current system of education service delivery in this chapter the potential improvements in efficiency and quality that these developments offer should be given some consideration.

The chapter begins by providing the economic justifications for government intervention in the provision of education in Section 2. Section 3 examines government education policy in an Irish context, focusing on recent policies aimed at promoting growth through various education initiatives, and equity both within the system and as an end goal in the wider distributional context. Section 4 examines the effectiveness of government in delivering an efficient and equitable education service, focusing in particular on how Ireland compares to other countries. Section 5 concludes the chapter.

2 ECONOMIC PERSPECTIVES ON EDUCATION

In the absence of an education system, citizens will lack the basic social skills necessary to participate in the economy and, more important perhaps, society in general: for example, an illiterate individual may be unable to follow basic rules and regulations imposed by government such as reading road signs or informing themselves on key personal items like medicine dosages or the terms and conditions of a loan application. A properly functioning education system performs an important social engineering function by facilitating the transfer of common values and morals. Government policy on education can cover a wide range of issues. In most developed economies, government regulation requires that all individuals remain in education up to some minimum age: in Ireland education is compulsory up to the age of 16.

A large part of education policy is concerned with easing the financial constraints associated with purchasing education services by providing free schooling, for example. The government also has a say in the quality of service provision (e.g. curriculum design, training of teachers, monitoring the performance of teachers and schools). It is also common that governments have in place education policies for individuals with special needs to ensure that the most vulnerable in society are given the opportunity to fully participate in the labour force and integrate into society more generally.

In most developed economies the state plays a very direct role in the provision and funding of compulsory education. There is no dispute in Ireland, or other developed nations, about state funding of education up to compulsory level. There is a vast body of research which highlights the efficiency improvements that could be achieved in public spending by diverting human capital investment towards the young, including both pre-school and primary levels. However, that said, in Ireland at least, the state increasingly takes a very proactive role in higher education up to and including the funding of postgraduate students and postdoctoral researchers. In this section, the extent to which the government has a necessary role in the provision of education is explored. Government intervention in any market can be justified where the market fails to optimally provide the good or service. Intervention may also be justified on equity grounds to promote distributional objectives. The arguments for intervention differ depending on the level of education, a factor also considered in this section.

Education as an Investment: Private and Social Returns

Education is an investment in human capital yielding both private and social returns. The decision to invest in human capital accumulation, like any other investment, will depend on the investor's evaluation of the expected present value of the stream of costs and benefits flowing from that investment. A parent deciding whether or not to send their child to school will compare the expected costs, such as tuition fees, books, cost of travel to school, etc. with the expected benefits for the child, for example the ability to function in society, and better job and earnings prospects. They may also consider the benefits that accrue to themselves, such as reduced childcare costs or the possibility that their children, if successful, might be able to look after them financially when they are older.

At higher levels of education, these decisions are taken by individuals or firms. An individual's decision to invest in personal human capital, such as a third-level degree for example, will also involve a comparison of the costs with the benefits. As well as the cost of tuition fees and books, etc., the cost of foregone earnings will also be considered. At this level individuals may also place more or less weight than their parents on the personal benefits, such as greater employability and higher earnings. A firm making a decision to invest in training courses to improve the human capital of its workers will undertake the investment if the present value of the expected future returns to that investment, in the form of higher productivity and reduced costs, is greater than the cost of the investment.

Investment in education, however, may also confer *positive externalities* on the rest of society that will not be taken into account by parents, individuals or firms. At a fundamental level, the most significant social return to education, as mentioned earlier, is having a population who can function at a basic level in society and understand basic rules and regulations. For higher levels of education, social returns can take the form of productivity improvements which will contribute to economic growth above and beyond those for which an individual/firm is remunerated through higher wages/profits; improvements in the quality of services, for example in the health or legal professions; or other social benefits such as increased political participation and a healthy democratic system.

These arguments also apply to early years education and care, which is linked with immediate benefits such as better school readiness and cognitive outcomes but also long-term effects such as lower rates of lone parenthood and lower crime rates. By ignoring these social returns, parents, individuals and firms will under-invest in education and training (i.e. education will be provided below the socially optimal level), thus providing justification for government involvement in its provision.

Returning to the investment decision-making process, and with this in mind, it is clear that the government, when making a decision on whether and how much to invest in the education system, will weigh up the cost of the investment (including the actual cash outlay, the opportunity cost of people not contributing to production while in full-time education and any efficiency losses associated with the financing of education through the tax system) with the aggregate economic returns to the economy of having a well-educated workforce (such as the extent to which it will contribute to the more productive use of resources, higher levels of output and faster economic growth) but also the other social returns mentioned here, such as greater equality in terms of opportunities, social inclusion, improved cultural and political participation, etc.

Placing an economic value on intangible social returns is difficult. Nevertheless, even though the social returns to primary and second-level education are difficult to quantify, it is well established that they will far exceed the private returns, thus justifying government provision. At higher levels of education, however, it is more difficult to reach this conclusion given that the private returns are known to be significantly higher than those at first and second level, raising questions about the justification for government provision of third-level education, at least on these grounds. In what follows, the empirical evidence on the private and social returns to education is evaluated.

Empirical Evidence on Private Returns
An extensive literature exists on quantifying the private returns to individuals from investing in education. Studies typically show that the returns to education are around 6 to 8 per cent per school year for men and 9 to 11 per cent for women. These so-called Mincer returns (after the pioneering labour economist Jacob Mincer who first established an empirical framework for estimating human capital structural models) apply to all levels of education but are generally larger for higher education. The earnings return to education has been well documented in the Irish context, with evidence suggesting not only a positive relationship

between earnings and educational attainment but also that this earnings advantage increases with the length of time spent in the labour market.

Higher levels of education are also found to be associated with higher levels of labour force participation and lower unemployment risk. For example, the unemployment rate for early school leavers in the 25 to 34 age group was 37 per cent in 2011 compared with an unemployment rate of 15 per cent for all persons in the same age group.[2] The evidence shows that in the Irish case, as for many other OECD countries, the individual returns to education are significant in terms of earnings, labour market participation and employment.

While findings suggest that education leads to higher private returns, the link between educational attainment and productivity has been more difficult to quantify. An alternative to the human capital view is the screening theory of education, which suggests that there is no link between individual educational attainment and productivity improvements, and that the only purpose of education is to serve as a signalling device to employers as to who the most productive employees are likely to be. This argument is based on the observation that those with the greatest ability, which is determined by unobservable factors such as family background, opportunities, access to quality schools, etc., are more likely to be educated but are also more likely to be productive. Employers will choose to recruit and pay higher salaries to well-educated individuals who through attaining an education have signalled their productive ability.

From an empirical point of view, no consensus has been reached on which theory holds: does education lead to more productive individuals or are more productive individuals likely to stay in education for longer? One reason for this is that it is statistically very difficult to disentangle the two theories as the end result is the same – more educated people earn more. In any case, where there are private returns to education, be they a reward for productivity improvements or otherwise (for example, personal fulfilment or satisfaction), the investment should be undertaken by the individual themselves with no justification for government intervention on these grounds.

Empirical Evidence on Social Returns
The social returns to primary and second-level education are undeniably important for any functioning economy. For this reason, most of the attention in the literature focuses on the social returns to third-level education in an attempt to justify public provision. However, any attempts to quantify the social returns to education investment (at any level) are faced with serious difficulties in establishing causal relationships between education attainment and socially desirable outcomes.

For example, political scientists have highlighted correlations between voter participation and education for many years and have used this to argue that education leads to more informed voters, and hence a more democratic society. Some of the most rigorous evidence suggests that *entrance* into higher education increases the probability of voter participation by 21 to 30 per cent. However, correlation does not imply causation. There may be unobservable characteristics of people who value schooling that make them more likely to value civic duties and responsibilities. If this is the case, estimates of the correlation between education and civic participation, such as voting behaviour, may overstate the true civic returns to education and mislead policy makers into thinking that policies that improve access to higher education will necessarily increase the probability of active civic participation.

The literature on the impact of education on health status again suffers from problems of establishing causation. For example, ability clearly affects an individual's success in schooling, but healthier people will generally be more productive and more able. Similarly, initial assets or family wealth may affect an individual's access to both education and health care.

Much less documented but equally significant is establishing the extent to which investment in ongoing training and education by firms or individuals yields benefits to society in excess of those for which firms are rewarded in terms of productivity improvements, lower costs and higher profits, or for which individuals are rewarded in terms of higher earnings or better employment prospects. For example, continuous education and training will prevent skills shortages, create a more adaptable labour force with greater innovative ability, and make the economy more attractive to outside investors, all of which will facilitate economic growth. In addition, lifelong learning may create a happier, more personally fulfilled society.

The OECD has long acknowledged that improving the skills of the workforce on an on-going basis (an area where the Nordic countries perform particularly well) will be important for economic growth by facilitating the development of an adaptable and flexible labour force (see Chapter 6). There are, however, wide divergences across countries in the extent to which adults engage in on-going training and education, and a declining trend across European countries in the complexity of jobs and the scope they offer for learning.[3] This is perhaps worrying given emerging empirical evidence that finds causal links between lifelong learning and earnings, but also social returns in the form of social position.[4]

Despite the dearth of empirical evidence, the existence of social returns is the key argument made for government intervention in education provision. The social capital developed at primary and second level (for example respect for social norms and rule of law) are fundamental to the functioning of any economy. There is also no doubt that higher levels of education lead to a more skilled and productive labour force, capable of producing greater levels of output, facilitating technological advancement and attracting investment. In relation to lifelong learning, it is clear that investment can help to create an adaptable and flexible workforce, an important advantage for any economy undergoing major structural change.

Market Failures

In addition to justifying state involvement in the provision of education on the grounds that the social rate of return exceeds the private rate of return, other market failures may prevent education from being optimally provided in the absence of government intervention.

Credit Market Failure

Education would be unaffordable for large segments of the population if privately provided. While at first and second level the burden of tuition fees would be borne by parents, at higher levels of education individuals would rely on credit markets to finance schooling. Credit markets will fail to operate efficiently in this environment, for two reasons. First, most students applying for loans to pay for their studies will lack collateral of any kind to guarantee the loan, and second, the benefits of education will vary substantially between individuals, with no guarantee of success and hence no guarantee that the student will be able to repay the loan in the future. In the absence of collateral and a means of repayment, banks will be unwilling to finance individuals to pay for private education.

This failure of credit markets to finance private education may warrant government intervention in the provision of education services, especially at third level, where government involvement usually comes in the form of direct financial assistance to students (for example free tuition fees, government-guaranteed loan schemes, etc.). At primary and second level, education would become a luxury service for the wealthy or for those to whom banks are willing to lend money. While this does not constitute a credit market failure it would be undesirable on equity grounds (see later).

Imperfect Information

Aside from credit market failure, the provision of education itself is characterised by imperfect information resulting in sub-optimal outcomes in the absence of government intervention.

First, it can be argued that parents and individuals do not have full information on the benefits of schooling and will under-invest in education. Furthermore, the extent of this knowledge gap may be unevenly distributed across the population, depending on factors like social class and family background. To overcome this failure, the government can introduce regulations to ensure that children reach a certain minimum level of education (i.e. compulsory schooling age) and at higher levels of education can provide incentives to encourage participation through, for example, free fees or maintenance grants for those living below a certain income threshold.

Second, individuals lack information regarding the quality of the education service being provided. In the case of primary and second-level education, if all parents could afford to pay fees for their children to attend private schools, market forces would operate in the standard way with higher fees potentially signalling better quality institutions. However, in most cases parents cannot afford to pay for their children to receive a private education and so the choice of school becomes limited. In the absence of government intervention to ensure that certain standards are met, there will be no incentive for schools to deliver a high-quality service.

An alternative to the regulation of quality standards is to allow schools to be privately run and for the government to regulate the credit markets used to finance education. For example, the government could grant vouchers to all individuals that can be spent at their own discretion, allowing them to choose freely the schools that suit their preferences and meet their standards. A possibility at third level is for the government to guarantee loans to students to pay for their tuition fees which they must repay once their studies have been completed. Of course, this can lead to similar problems to those outlined at the start of this section as there is no guarantee that students will be in a position to repay these loans at a later stage.

Many OECD countries operate publicly secured student loans to finance tuition fees or living costs associated with third-level education. For example, in the UK all students are eligible for government-funded loans for tuition and maintenance at a nominal interest rate that do not have to be repaid until after graduation. High tuition fees combined with well-developed student support systems in the form of graduate loans, grants or scholarships have also been introduced in Australia, Canada, the Netherlands and New Zealand.[5]

Equity

Government intervention in the provision of education is also justified on equity grounds. As argued earlier, education is a key determinant of earnings and employment prospects and so plays an important role in determining not only the level of income in society but also the distribution of that income. A key role for government is therefore to promote *equality of opportunity* by attempting to ensure equal access to education for all of its citizens (see also Chapters 2 and 8).

Governments attempt to achieve this through various initiatives such as free compulsory education up to a certain age or financial support for third-level education. Many governments also ensure that discrimination on gender, race, ethnic, disability, or any other grounds does not take place within the education system by ensuring equal access to all groups in society. However, since individuals' educational prospects and information on the benefits of education are unevenly distributed across the population, it is more likely that specific socioeconomic groups, usually those at the lower end of the income distribution, will underachieve in relation to educational attainment.

Therefore, on *horizontal equity* grounds it is justified for the government to target education expenditure and programmes at potentially educationally disadvantaged socioeconomic groups. In fact, this is also justifiable on efficiency grounds if the extent of the information problems outlined above is more pronounced among these groups, justifying targeted higher levels of expenditure. Intervention on these grounds will also satisfy the principle of *vertical equity*. Since education determines future earnings, by redistributing tax revenues to poorer socioeconomic groups in the form of education investments, a more equal outcome will result once the returns to these investments have been realised.

3 EDUCATION POLICY IN IRELAND

Irish education policy developed later than many other OECD countries. The most significant development took place in 1967 with the introduction of free second-level education for all. Since the 1960s, education expenditure as a percentage of national income has doubled and since the early 1990s, the Irish government has demonstrated an increased level of commitment to investment in education and training, recognising its importance for economic, social and cultural development.

Education policy in Ireland can be divided into two strands, each of which attempts to achieve different objectives for the economy. First, education policy aims to facilitate the accumulation of human capital in the economy for the purpose of fuelling economic growth. Second, education policy aims to contribute to the government's policy objective of equity by ensuring equal access to and opportunities within the system for all. Much co-operation also happens at an EU level in the development of education and training policies. For example, most EU countries, including Ireland, signed up to the Bologna Declaration in 1999, agreeing to co-operate on achieving a range of objectives for higher education within the EU, including comparable degree programmes, a system of credit transfers to aid student mobility and the promotion of inter-institutional co-operation in research. In this section the focus is on specific Irish policy initiatives, but bearing in mind the fact that many are motivated by recommendations made at higher levels of governance.

Policies Aimed at Promoting Economic Growth

A key rationale for government intervention in education provision is the importance of education for the creation of a skilled labour force. Thus, a key role of education is to produce a well-educated workforce that can meet the demands of an expanding economy. A more skilled and productive labour force will produce more output, facilitate the development and diffusion of new technologies, further fuelling growth, and will make the economy a more attractive place to invest, particularly if the skills of the labour force match labour demand. This is the assumption underlying the notion that modern-day economies are both 'knowledge based' and 'knowledge driven', where the ability to innovate is the key to successful economic development.

Much of the current education policy in Ireland in this regard is targeted at achieving outcomes that will contribute to Ireland's smart economy and so focuses on innovation-driven, high-technology sectors (see Chapter 9).

The idea that education initiatives should be industry-led is not new. Acknowledging the fact that a well-educated and skilled labour force is a key determinant of competitiveness, in 1997 the Irish government established an Expert Group on Future Skills Needs to assist in the development of national strategies to ensure a flexible and adaptable labour force. Since its establishment, the expert group has produced a range of reports monitoring trends in Ireland's skills supply and making recommendations as to how education and training should best be oriented towards improving labour productivity, minimising unemployment, and developing a labour force that can support high-value knowledge-based industries. These have ranged from sector-specific reports (for example *ICT Skills Action Plan* in 2014 and *Future Skills Needs Requirements of the Manufacturing Sector to 2012*) to more general reports focusing on the skills needs of the labour market in a broader context.

Research of this kind is particularly important where there is a mismatch of skills between those who are unemployed and the types of highly skilled jobs that are increasingly in demand, particularly in the internationally traded services sector (see Chapters 6, 7 and 9). The extent to which policy initiatives deliver on these objectives is discussed in Section 4. It is clear, though, that future education policy aimed at achieving economic growth objectives will be strongly guided by the needs of industry.

Initiatives at Primary and Second Level

The responsibility for the government's role in the provision of education at primary and second level rests with the Department of Education and Skills. One of the key functions of primary and second-level education is to set the foundations for the development of a labour force equipped with the necessary social capital to contribute to the economy and the society more generally. The quality of primary and second-level education will also play a huge part in determining standards at third level given that it is still the case that most students at third-level universities and institutes in Ireland have come through the Irish education system.

Therefore any policies aimed at improving the level of preparedness of school leavers for the challenges of third-level education will fall under this umbrella. For example, in recent years the Irish government has introduced initiatives such as better career guidance at second level, particularly in the junior cycle when students begin making career choices, and initiatives aimed at promoting the application of new technology in teaching methods.

There are also an increasing number of initiatives being introduced at primary and second level that are specifically focused on preparing the future labour force to meet the needs of Ireland's smart economy. Particular attention has been given to increasing the number of graduates in finance, science and engineering. A focus of the Department of Education and Skills in recent years has been to improve on the downward trajectory in the mathematics scores of Irish students in international comparisons such as PISA (see later). Initiatives have included giving students extra points for grades achieved in Higher Level Mathematics, the key determinant of entry into third level, and Project Maths, an alternative approach to teaching mathematics at second level rolled out in schools nationally in 2010.

The impact of initiatives and reforms at first and second level aimed at improving economic growth can take quite some time to realise. For example, the first cohort of primary school children to engage fully in the 1999 reform of the primary school curriculum is only now reaching third-level education. Similarly, the benefits, or otherwise, of initiatives like Project Maths will take a number of additional years before any impact will be seen in the job market. The long lag between the introduction of initiatives of this kind and when their benefits are realised means that attention is often focused on initiatives at third level where more immediate benefits can potentially be realised.

Initiatives at Third Level
The higher education sector in most developed economies plays an important role in achieving economic growth objectives, both by producing well-qualified graduates with the skills demanded in the labour force, but also in contributing to high-level research and innovation. In Ireland, the Higher Education Authority (HEA), an independent statutory body, largely manages the provision of education at third and fourth level while remaining answerable to the Minister for Education and Skills. In January 2011, the Department of Education and Skills in Ireland published the *National Strategy for Higher Education to 2030*, which emphasises the importance of higher education for economic recovery. The proposals are wide ranging, covering teaching and learning, research, the engagement of the higher education sector with the wider society and the internationalisation of education at third level.

While a number of detailed proposals relating to the quality of the teaching and learning experience at third-level institutions are included, a notable emphasis is placed on the internationalisation of the third-level sector. The rationale for internationalisation is twofold: first, it is expected that increased exposure internationally will improve the quality of learning, teaching and research by introducing the third-level sector in Ireland to new ideas and practices; and second, education should be viewed as an internationally traded service that can make a significant contribution to the output of the economy. Ensuring that the third-level sector delivers a high-quality and internationally competitive learning experience for students will be an important component of any successful internationalisation strategy and this in turn will depend to a large extent on the level of resources available to achieve this.

Another key feature of the strategy is the emphasis placed on research, both in relation to its importance for teaching but also more generally for the generation of ideas and innovation. Linkages between higher education institutions and industry are also highlighted as potentially playing an important role in facilitating economic recovery. A notable example of this is the Innovation Alliance, a partnership between two of the main universities in Ireland, Trinity College Dublin and University College Dublin, the state and business communities, that aims to develop a culture and framework for innovation in Ireland that, it is hoped, will help to deliver on the goals set out under Ireland's *Smart Economy Framework*.

These, of course, are not new ideas. Government support for research through third-level institutions began in a real way with the establishment of Science

Foundation Ireland (SFI) in 2000. The role of SFI is to support research in science and engineering. In 1998 the Programme for Research in Third-level Institutions also provided a new general source of research funding and in 1999 and 2001 respectively, the Irish Research Council for Humanities and Social Sciences and the Irish Research Council for Science, Engineering and Technology were established, providing new and significant sources of funding for individual researchers and research projects in these fields. In 2012 these were merged into the Irish Research Council to form one national body for the delivery of research programmes funded by the government under the National Development Plan. Much of this funding is targeted at doctoral students and post-doctoral researchers, commonly referred to as 'fourth-level' education.

The shift in focus of expenditure on research from providing direct financial supports to industry to diverting resources through third-level institutions provides a clear indication of the government's view that higher education is important for economic growth. A causal relationship, however, between the different elements of higher education (formation and production of graduates, and research and development) and economic growth have yet to be established in a formal and convincing way.

Policies Aimed at Promoting Equity
An important rationale for government intervention in the provision of education is to promote equality of opportunity by ensuring equal access to the education system for all. While participation rates in education have increased significantly in Ireland over the last number of decades, up to the 1990s education policy in Ireland focused on increasing the overall level of participation in education with few attempts to promote equity in access to the system. Inequalities in education can manifest themselves in two ways, either through inequalities in educational achievement or in the level of education attainment of different groups. These inequities are not confined to educational divides on the basis of social class but could manifest themselves as inequities across ethnic divides, among people with disabilities, or in relation to gender or race.

With the introduction of free second-level schooling in the 1960s and compulsory education up to the age of 16, participation in schooling is almost universal across all groups in society. In 2010 this was extended to early years education: under the Early Childcare and Education Scheme, all children in Ireland are now entitled to one year of free pre-schooling in the year before they begin primary school. However, the provision of compulsory and free schooling does not necessarily mean that all individuals will realise their true potential within the schooling system and this often is a function of circumstances or social background. Increased levels of funding can go some way to alleviating these inequalities in the education system; however, targeting expenditure at the most vulnerable groups will be more effective.

Initiatives at Primary and Second Level
Specific policy initiatives aimed at promoting equity within the education system have largely targeted compulsory education, since the main determinants of post-compulsory education achievement are educational background and the foundations laid at an early stage of educational development. Over the years a range of different schemes have been put in place to target educational disadvantage at first and second level. The current initiative, Delivering Equality of Opportunity in Schools, specifically targets disadvantaged schools and through the Schools Support Programme delivers a range of interventions aimed at eliminating educational disadvantage. Many of these initiatives and programmes, such as the School Completion Programme, Home School Community Liaison Scheme and School Meals Programme, have been in place for a long time.[6]

Initiatives at Third Level
By far the most significant development in higher education policy aimed at promoting equality of access to third-level education was the introduction of free tuition fees for full-time third-level undergraduate EU students in 1996. Over the last number of years the increase in the number of places at third-level institutions has aimed to further improve access to third-level education. The government also provides specific financial incentives to individuals participating in third-level education through the Student Grants Scheme (which provides maintenance grants, fee grants and postgraduate contributions on a means-tested basis). In addition, third-level institutions themselves operate programmes to encourage participation by all groups in society (e.g. the Trinity Access Programme).

The promotion of equal opportunities in third level falls under the remit of the HEA's National Access Office, which recognises the promotion of social inclusion as a key national policy objective. *The National Plan for Equity of Access to Higher Education 2008–2013* set out a range of targets for improving access to third-level education including targets for increased representation at third level of lower socioeconomic groups, mature students, and students with disabilities. It also highlighted the importance of access programmes, lifelong learning and the introduction of non-traditional entry routes as a means to achieving these targets. Improvements in access have been observed (see below). Following on from its success, the National Access Office has committed to preparing the next Access Plan during the 2014 to 2016 period.

4 DELIVERY AND EFFECTIVENESS OF EDUCATION SERVICES

Evaluating the performance of government in the provision of a service like education is complicated by the fact that many of the returns to education are intangible, as discussed in Section 2. This makes traditional cost-benefit analysis very difficult as often the benefits are impossible to quantify. This also creates problems in attempting to compare outcomes across countries.

In this section, the level of provision of education services is examined by looking at public expenditure on education in Ireland and how this relates to other countries. How funds are allocated at different levels of the education system is also analysed both relative to other countries and in the specific Irish context. Notwithstanding the difficulties in measuring outcomes in the education sector, how education outcomes in Ireland relate to those in other countries is analysed. From an efficiency point of view it is important that the government achieves value for money in its spending decisions and so the trade-off between achieving quality outcomes and productivity improvements is discussed. The section concludes with some discussion on the extent to which the system offers equal opportunities or improves the distribution of income by leading to more equal outcomes.

Public Expenditure on Education

In 2013, total government expenditure by the Department of Education and Skills was approximately €8.5 billion, 15.6 per cent of total government expenditure. This is up from only 12.2 per cent in 1995, highlighting the increased importance of education relative to other public expenditure items.

Table 13.1 Expenditure on Educational Institutions as a Percentage of GDP/GNI

| | 1995 | 2000 | 2010 | Of which (%): | |
	Total	Total	Total	Public	Private
Austria	6.1	5.5	5.8	91.0	9.0
Denmark	6.2	6.6	8.0	94.5	5.5
Finland	6.3	5.6	6.5	97.6	2.4
France	6.6	6.4	6.3	89.8	10.2
Ireland[1]	*5.8*	*5.3*	*7.6*	*92.5*	*7.5*
Netherlands	5.4	5.1	6.3	83.3	16.7
UK	5.2	4.9	6.5	68.6	31.4
USA	6.2	6.2	7.3	69.4	30.6
EU-21[2] Average	5.3	5.2	5.9	89.3	10.7
OECD Average	5.4	5.4	6.3	83.6	16.4

Source: OECD, *Education at a Glance, OECD Indicators 2013*, OECD, Paris 2013.
[1] Expenditure on educational institutions expressed as a percentage of GNI.
[2] These are the 21 OECD countries for which data are available that are members of the EU. They are Austria, Belgium, the Czech Republic, Denmark, Estonia, Finland, France, Germany, Greece, Hungary, Ireland, Italy, Luxembourg, the Netherlands, Poland, Portugal, Slovenia, the Slovak Republic, Spain, Sweden and the UK.

Table 13.1 presents statistics on the proportion of education expenditure in gross domestic product (GDP) (gross national income (GNI) for Ireland) in a selection of countries. With a declining birth rate and a reduction in the proportion of the population of school-going age, the demand for education expenditure will fall over time. As a result, across most OECD countries a stabilisation or even a fall in spending on education is expected. This was the case for most countries between 1995 and 2000 but since then some increases have been observed. This may in part be explained by slow growth in GDP in many European countries since 2000, particularly in the latter part of the last decade, but also may be due to increasing expenditure levels in response to new EU targets as set out in the Lisbon Agenda. Also illustrated in Table 13.1 is the small proportion of private expenditure on educational institutions, with the exception of the UK and the USA.

Table 13.2 Annual Expenditure by Educational Institutions per Student for all Services by Level of Education in 2010 (expressed in equivalent US dollars converted using PPPs)

	Pre-primary	Primary	Secondary	Third level	Third level (excl. research)
Austria	8,893	10,244	12,551	15,007	10,488
Denmark[1]	9,454	10,935	11,747	18,977	–
Finland	5,372	7,624	9,162	16,714	9,802
France	6,362	6,622	10,877	15,067	10,309
Ireland[2]	–	*8,384*	*11,380*	*16,008*	*11,512*
Netherlands	7,664	7,954	11,838	17,161	10,818
UK	7,047	9,369	10,452	15,862	10,546
USA	10,020	11,193	12,464	25,576	22,744
EU-21 average	7,085	8,277	9,471	12,856	8,334
OECD average	6,762	7,974	9,014	13,528	9,274

Source: OECD, *Education at a Glance, OECD Indicators 2013*, OECD, Paris 2013.
Note: figures include expenditure on both public and private institutions, with the exception of Ireland, where data relate to public institutions only.
[1] Spend per student at third level exclusive of research expenditure not available for Denmark.
[2] Spend per student at pre-primary school level not available for Ireland.

Table 13.2 shows the level of expenditure on educational institutions by student in 2010. In all countries spend per student increases across education level with the highest spend per student at third level, although once research expenditure is excluded from these figures the levels of expenditure at third level are for the most part similar to those at second level. European countries lag behind the USA in terms of investment in education at all levels but particularly at third level. It should be noted, however, that while these figures are adjusted for differences in purchasing power across countries they are not adjusted for differences in costs of education.

Ireland spends above the EU and OECD average at all levels but lags behind some of the countries represented in the table. Even this gap is narrowing, though, particularly at primary and second level: in 2000 spend per student in Ireland was 24 per cent lower for primary and 15 per cent lower for secondary than the OECD average. In contrast, expenditure at third level was at the OECD average in 2000. This suggests a faster pace of growth in primary and second-level expenditure in Ireland relative to third level. Of course the level of expenditure tells us nothing about the quality of service provision (dealt with later in this section). It is also difficult to ascertain whether it is more efficient for the government to allocate funds to one level of education over another without understanding the full returns to each type of investment; the difficulties in doing this are highlighted in Section 2. In what follows, the allocation of funds at different levels in Ireland is discussed.

Allocation of Funds at Primary and Second Level
The government adopts a centralised approach to allocating resources to primary and second-level schools with some variation across different types of school, such as vocational, community and comprehensive schools. Private fee-paying schools are allocated resources to cover teachers' salaries. The allocation of teachers to schools is also important and is based on the government's targeted student to teacher ratio. Currently, teachers are allocated on the basis of student enrolment, but there may also be a number of ex-quota posts, such as language support or resource teachers allocated on the basis of school size or need. In some cases there may also be lower student–teacher ratios linked to certain programmes aimed at tackling disadvantage.

Overall, student–teacher ratios were reduced at both primary and second level during the 1990s. In 2011, the average student–teacher ratio in primary schools in Ireland was 15.7 compared with an OECD average of 15.4. For secondary schools the average student–teacher ratio was 14.4 in 2010 (latest year of comparable data available), also slightly above the OECD average of 13.6.[7] Recent budget cuts, however, have eroded some of the gains achieved in reducing class sizes in Ireland in an attempt to reduce the number of teachers on the payroll. Coupled with cuts in other ex-quota posts and special needs assistants, many teachers find themselves in front of classes of well in excess of 30 students.

The main motivation for cuts in the number of teachers is that a significant proportion of government expenditure on education is made up of wages and salaries (see later). Capital expenditure accounted for less than 5 per cent of total expenditure on education in 2013. While some resources (book grants, free school meals, back to school clothing allowances, etc.) are allocated directly to students, these types of individual transfers play a much more significant role in the third-level sector in the form of maintenance grants to third-level students.

Allocation of Funds at Third Level
The higher education system in Ireland is predominantly publicly funded. The HEA is responsible for the allocation of funding to universities, institutes of technology and some other higher education and research institutions. As already

mentioned, in 1996 free tuition fees were introduced for eligible full-time undergraduate EU students. These fees are paid to higher education institutions by the state and the HEA manages the allocation of grants in respect of the 'Free Fees' scheme along with the core recurrent grants to the various institutions.

The HEA is also responsible for general capital funding for the university sector and for research and other capital funding under specific programmes.[8] While external research funding for higher education institutions has, in general, increased, they continue to rely to a very large extent on the recurrent grants. The vast majority of funding for higher education comes from the exchequer.

By far the most contentious issue in relation to the allocation of third-level funding, and an issue that is currently very much up for debate, is government expenditure on student transfers, both in the form of tuition fees and maintenance grants, which form a significant component of expenditure on third level. As discussed in Section 2, the private returns to third-level education are significant in terms of higher earnings, higher labour force participation rates, and lower unemployment risk. In addition, statistics show a high correlation between third-level participation and social class of parents. It is therefore difficult to justify the use of taxation income, collected from the general public, to finance individual participation in the accumulation of human capital which may yield significant private returns to those individuals in the future. Given the current public finance crisis and very large predicted increases in student numbers in the future, it appears that the introduction of student contributions is inevitable.

There are many possible models for introducing student contributions for tuition fees.[9] It is clear from the discussion presented in Section 2 that both the individual and the wider economy will benefit from an individual engaging in third-level education. It would therefore seem appropriate for the state to continue to supplement the cost of tuition. On the principle of equity, however, it is also important that the system is designed to ensure that all potential students have access to the education system and that no students are excluded because they are unable to pay. The introduction of means-tested grants for tuition fees or free fees for those on low incomes, a reform of the maintenance grant system and offering state-guaranteed loans to students are all potential policy options in the event that fees for third level are reintroduced.

The final issue for consideration is the level at which the fees should be set. The introduction of fees could create an opportunity to foster more competition between third-level institutions if they were allowed a say in the level of fees. For example, if one university offers a better quality of service than another, this can be reflected in the price of the courses on offer. The price of similar 'student experiences' in other countries would also have to be considered in setting the level of the fees, given that education is now an internationally traded service.

Benchmarking Education Performance
While Ireland was late to make any substantial investments in the education sector, with free second-level education only introduced in the 1960s, the

previous analysis highlights the fact that the level of investment in education in Ireland is now comparable to many other EU and OECD countries. Overall, in terms of access to education, there is some evidence that education outcomes are also improving in Ireland.

Table 13.3 presents the percentage of 25–34-year-olds with upper secondary or post-secondary (non-tertiary) education and, of those, the percentage with tertiary education. The improvement in education attainment levels in Ireland is notable. The proportion of the 25–34-year-old population with at least upper second level or post-secondary (non-tertiary) increased from only 73 per cent in 2000 (below the EU-21 average) to 85 per cent in 2011, above the EU-21 average. Ireland also performs remarkably well on the proportion of the 25–34-year-old population with a tertiary-level qualification at 47 per cent in 2011, above the EU-21 average of 36 per cent and up from only 30 per cent in 2000.

Table 13.3 Proportion of Population Aged 25–34 by Level of Education Attainment

	Upper second level or post-secondary (non-tertiary)			Tertiary level		
	2000	2005	2011	2000	2005	2011
Austria	83	88	88	14	20	21
Denmark	86	88	81	28	40	39
Finland	87	90	90	39	38	39
France	76	82	83	31	40	43
Germany	85	85	87	22	23	28
Ireland	*73*	*81*	*85*	*30*	*41*	*47*
UK	67	73	83	29	35	46
USA	88	86	89	38	39	43
EU-21 average	77	81	84	24	29	36
OECD average	75	80	83	26	33	39

Source: OECD, *Education at a Glance, OECD Indicators 2013*, OECD, Paris 2013.

On the basis of these numbers it is clear that public investment in education is leading to an improvement in graduation rates and these gains are, to some extent, borne out in measures of literacy and numeracy among Irish students. The recent results of the OECD's PISA reveals an improvement in the performance of Irish students (15-year-olds) on a number of different measures. The rankings for reading, mathematics and science are presented in Table 13.4. In 2009, Ireland ranked 17th in reading scores, a dramatic decline on its ranking of fifth place in 2000 (not shown in the table). It has recovered over the last three years to resume its position as fifth in the OECD in 2012. A similar improvement is evident in the mathematics scores. Ireland ranked 26th in mathematics in 2009 (down from

15th in 2000), but rose to 13th in 2012. Ireland also improved in sciences, moving up from 14th in 2009 to ninth in 2012.

When the entire labour force is considered, however, Ireland continues to perform poorly. The OECD Programme for the International Assessment of Adult Competencies also ranks countries on the basis of performance in relation to literacy, numeracy and other problem-solving skills but for the entire working age population.[10] Ireland ranks significantly below the EU and OECD average on all of these measures. This suggests perhaps that initiatives aimed at up-skilling the adult population in older age cohorts should be given more policy focus.

Table 13.4 Ranking of OECD Countries on Student Performance 2009 and 2012

	Mathematics		Reading		Science	
Ranking	2012	2009	2012	2009	2012	2009
1	Korea	1	Japan	5	Japan	2
2	Japan	4	Korea	1	Finland	1
3	Switzerland	3	Finland	2	Estonia	6
4	Netherlands	6	Canada	3	Korea	3
5	Estonia	11	*Ireland*	*17*	Poland	13
6	Finland	2	Poland	12	Canada	5
7	Canada	5	Estonia	10	Germany	9
8	Poland	19	Australia	6	Netherlands	8
9	Belgium	8	New Zealand	4	*Ireland*	*14*
10	Germany	10	Netherlands	7	Australia	7
11	Austria	18	Switzerland	11	New Zealand	4
12	Australia	9	Belgium	8	Switzerland	10
13	*Ireland*	*26**	Germany	16	Slovenia	12
14	Slovenia	14	France	18	UK	11
15	Denmark	13	Norway	9	Czech Rep.	18

Source: rankings for 2012 extracted from OECD, *Pisa 2012 Results in Focus*, OECD, Paris 2013; rankings for 2009 extracted from OECD, *Pisa 2009 at a Glance*, OECD, Paris 2010.
* indicates statistically significantly below the OECD average.

When set in a global context it is clear from Table 13.4 that Japan and Korea are the top performers in the OECD. When non-OECD countries are also considered the performance of other South Asian economies is even more remarkable. China and Singapore outperform Japan and Korea on all measures. Also of note is the fact that Vietnam, a lower–middle-income country, outperformed many OECD countries in 2012, the first year it was included in the analysis, ranking higher than Ireland in mathematics and science.

While in Ireland's case there appears to be some correlation between increased levels of expenditure and student performance, this is not the case for all countries. In fact, if the countries represented in Table 13.2 are ranked in terms of expenditure levels on education there appears to be very little correlation between investment and outcomes. For example, Finland spends below the EU-21 average on second-level education and ranks first of all EU countries in terms of performance. In contrast, Austria, Denmark and France, which rank highly in terms of spend per student (Table 13.2), are consistently among the poorly performing countries.

Efficiency of Education Expenditure
It is difficult to draw conclusions on the performance of the sector on the basis of the level of government expenditure, as is clear from the previous analysis. Higher levels of government expenditure do not automatically imply a higher-quality service. In general, the empirical evidence is mixed on whether increased expenditure per pupil positively impacts student achievement and the evidence presented here suggests that it may not.

In contrast to other sectors of the economy where productivity improvements are often associated with using fewer labour inputs to achieve the same level of output, in the education sector, where the objective is achieving a higher-quality service, increasing the number of labour inputs (i.e. reducing student–teacher ratios) is inevitable as over time the public demand higher-quality education services (Wagner's law, see Chapter 3). There is much debate, however, on whether reduced student–teacher ratios result in improved academic achievement; some empirical studies support the notion that class sizes matter, but many others provide little evidence for such a relationship. Achieving productivity improvements (or value for money) is further impeded by the phenomenon known as Baumol's Disease (see Chapters 3 and 12), where inflationary cost increases lead to high wages in the non-productive sectors (primarily public services) of the economy. This is particularly the case for education as it is a labour-intensive service where the majority of the budget is absorbed by salaries and wages.

At first and second level, salaries, wages and pensions account for over 75 per cent of current education expenditure in Ireland. As is revealed in Table 13.5, salaries of Irish teachers are out of line with the average for the EU-21 at all levels of education. They are, however, similar in magnitude to Denmark, Germany and the Netherlands.

Of particular note is the difference in salaries between Ireland and England, perhaps our closest comparator; in 2010, the annual average salary for teachers in Ireland with 15 years of experience was $53,677, while in England it was considerably lower at $44,145. Public sector pay cuts and a cap on the starting salaries of new teachers will have partially closed this gap, although further cuts are becoming increasingly difficult to negotiate, as demonstrated during the 2011 Croke Park Agreement and 2013 Haddington Road Agreement negotiations (see Chapter 3). These negotiations have promised changes in work practices and improvements in productivity, but it is difficult to see what improvements can be made to justify such a significant difference in salaries as is evident from Table 13.5. Finland, for example, is the top performing country in Europe in terms of comparable educational outcomes (Table 13.4) but the annual salaries of teachers in Finland are over $10,000 lower than in Ireland at all levels.

Academic salaries in Ireland have also come under scrutiny in recent years. In particular, a number of high-profile media stories have tracked the evolution of 'superstar' academics in the Irish university sector. In general, Irish academics in higher grades, such as professor, are comparatively highly paid, but this is mainly due to the relativity maintained between professorial grades and higher civil service grades at assistant secretary level. It is, however, commonplace in other countries to top up salaries of top academics, particularly in market-sensitive disciplines such as economics, law, medical sciences and business.

For example, in the USA the contractual arrangements for salaries are on a one-to-one basis, while in the UK scales go up to professor level, and thereafter personal contracts and agreed salaries reflecting market norms and competitive pressures take effect. So while in terms of salary scales it appears that Irish academics fare well internationally, it is difficult to make comparisons due to differences in hiring practices. It is unlikely that any change to the current system of remuneration of academics in Ireland will happen in the short to medium term, given the current constraints on academic hiring rules and the proposals for future controls on the way in which higher education institutions recruit academic staff.

Table 13.5 Annual Statutory Teachers' Salaries after 15 Years of Experience, 2010 (expressed in equivalent US dollars converted using PPPs)

	Primary	Lower secondary	Upper secondary
Austria	40,818	44,179	45,425
Denmark	50,253	50,253	58,256
England[1]	44,145	44,145	44,145
Finland	37,455	40,451	42,809
France	32,733	35,583	35,819
Germany	55,771	61,784	66,895
Ireland	*53,677*	*53,677*	*53,677*
Netherlands	50,621	61,704	61,704
USA	45,226	45,049	48,446
EU-21 average	38,280	40,211	42,470
OECD average	37,603	39,401	41,182

Source: OECD, *Education at a Glance, OECD Indicators 2013*, OECD, Paris 2013.
[1] Figures for the UK as a whole not available.

In an increasingly constrained funding environment, the extent to which taxpayers achieve value for money is under scrutiny in most countries. This is particularly the case in Ireland due to the disproportionately high wages and salaries bill. Recently, attention has been placed on innovation in education service delivery which achieves productivity improvements that reduce costs while maintaining or even improving quality.

As discussed in the introduction to this chapter, adaptive learning technologies allow students to combine traditional classroom-based teaching with interactive software that is tailored to their needs and abilities. Recent evidence from the USA suggests that such approaches may be very effective in improving outcomes while at the same time reducing the human input required.[11] Similarly, advances in communications technology reduce the need for students to be physically present at the point of delivery of education services. Most of the service, particularly at third level, can be delivered online, for example, via a live online classroom where teachers speak to hundreds or thousands of students across the world at one time. There are very successful examples of this already, such as the Open University and Hibernia, an online teacher training college in Ireland. There is, however, extensive on-going debate on the extent to which this may affect the quality of education services provided, although part of this opposition may be fuelled by a resistance to change and technological improvements, as emphasised in other parts of this book (see Chapters 3 and 12).

At third level, other productivity improvements are possible. For example, higher education institutions could benefit from economies of scale by merging together. In some ways this is already happening, for example with the TCD–UCD Innovation Alliance mentioned above, and the creation of the Innovation Academy, a collaborative joint venture in PhD education. Of course, merging all universities and other higher education institutions may not be desirable as it would stifle competition within the sector.

Equity in Education Access

Since earnings are a key determinant of well-being, a lower probability of participating in the labour force, a higher probability of unemployment and lower average earnings of those with lower levels of education attainment together imply that inequalities in educational opportunities will have serious implications for the distribution of income in the economy. This does not take into account the other negative welfare effects associated with early school leavers such as social exclusion or crime for example which exacerbate the need for government education policies which target such inequities.

Across countries, evidence suggests that those who fail to complete upper second-level education are more likely to come from disadvantaged backgrounds. In an Irish context research has shown that those from working-class and unemployed families are more likely to underperform in Junior and Leaving Certificate examinations relative to their initial ability compared with other social groups. In addition, participation in tertiary education is highly correlated with the educational attainment and social background of parents.[12]

At primary and second level, government policy has focused on the retention and achievement of students, particularly students from disadvantaged backgrounds. Some of these were discussed in Section 3. At second level, there have been substantial increases in the provision of, and numbers taking, the special Junior Certificate School Programme and the Leaving Certificate Applied Programme, which were introduced to target equality in second-level education for all. The benefits of interventions of this kind are evidenced by the increasing rates of second-level completion: as revealed in Table 13.3, 85 per cent of 25–34-year-olds had completed at least upper second-level education in Ireland in 2011.

Of more significance, however, is the extent to which this follows through to equality of access and achievement at third level. The evidence suggests that equality of access to third level has improved in Ireland over the last number of years, but there are still inequities in the system.[13] For example, the socio-economic groups least likely to enter higher education are those from non-manual and semi-skilled and unskilled manual households and these groups are particularly under-represented at the universities. There has been some improvements in access for other targeted groups, though. For example, the number of adult learners in higher education increased from less than 2 per cent of new entrants in 1986 to over 13 per cent of new entrants in 2010, while the proportion of students with disabilities in higher-level education increased from 0.6 per cent in 1994 to 5 per cent in 2010. Overall, however, there is a clear need for continued government efforts to promote equity at all levels of the education system.

5 CONCLUSION

Education plays a very important role in the economic, social and cultural development of all economies. Not only is education a key to economic development in the contribution it makes to the enhancement of the skill level, productivity and competitiveness of the economy, it also plays a vital role in determining the income level and social status of individuals and will directly impact on the distribution of income. Private markets will fail to optimally provide education, and so the government has a crucial role to play in ensuring that education services are delivered.

In an Irish context, education policy attempts to ensure the delivery of an efficient and equitable service. While funding levels are high by international standards, evidence suggests that the Irish education system falls short. The statistics presented in this chapter are worrying, particularly given the emphasis on education and skills in the government's National Reform Programme.

The Irish government has continually emphasised that a key component of Ireland's economic growth will be the creation of jobs in new and emerging high value-added sectors that require a skilled and flexible labour force. The education sector will play an important role in this process both in re-skilling those who have lost their jobs and in conducting research with commercial potential through links between academia and industry. However, the resources available to government to even maintain the current level of service delivery are significantly constrained. Careful consideration needs to be given to the way the activities of the education sector are funded to ensure value for money. Recent evidence on the potential for technological advances to improve the efficiency and quality of education delivery should also be taken seriously. Perhaps they hold the key to achieving a world-class education system at a substantially lower cost.

Notes

*   This chapter builds on Chapter 12 from the 10th edition of this book, which was co-authored with Colm Harmon, and Chapter 13 from the 11th edition. I would like to thank John O'Hagan for his comments and suggestions.

1   See Department of Education and Skills, *Key Statistics 2012–2013*, available at www. education.ie; and Higher Education Authority statistics, available at www.hea.ie.

2   OECD, *Education at a Glance 2013, Country Note: Ireland*, OECD, Paris 2013; and Central Statistics Office, *Quarterly National Household Survey: Educational Attainment Thematic Report 2011,* CSO, Dublin 2011.

3   See, for example, OECD, 'Lifelong learning and adults', *Education Today 2013: The OECD Perspective,* OECD, Paris 2013.

4   J. Blanden, F. Buscha, P. Sturgis and P. Urwin, 'Measuring the returns to lifelong learning in the UK', *Economics of Education Review*, Vol. 31, No. 4, 2012.

5   OECD, *Education at a Glance,* OECD, Paris 2011.

6   For details of these schemes and programmes see www.education.ie.

7   OECD, *Education at a Glance 2013, OECD Indicators: A Country Profile for Ireland*, OECD, Paris 2013.

8   Current programmes managed by the HEA include the Programme for Strategic Cooperation between Irish Aid and Higher Education and Research Institutions. The HEA also serves as the National Contact Point under FP7 and Horizon 2020. For details of these programmes see www.hea.ie.

9   The discussion here draws on Department of Education and Skills, *Policy Options for New Student Contributions in Higher Education: Report to the Minister for Education and Science*, Dublin 2009.

10   OECD, *OECD Skills Outlook 2013: First Results from the Survey of Adult Skills*, OECD, Paris 2013.

11   'Education technology: catching on at last', *The Economist*, 29 June 2013.

12   Higher Education Authority (HEA), *National Plan for Equity of Access to Higher Education 2008–2013: Mid-Term Review*, HEA, Dublin 2010.

13   Statistics presented are taken from HEA, *op. cit.*

Index